EIGHTY-SECOND ANNUAL ISSUE

THE MINISTER'S MANUAL

2007

Edited by

JAMES W. COX
and
LEE McGLONE

JOSSEY-BASS
A Wiley Imprint
www.josseybass.com

Editors of THE MINISTER'S MANUAL
G. B. F. Hallock, D.D., 1926–1958
M. K. W. Heicher, Ph.D., 1943–1968
Charles L. Wallis, M.A., M.Div., 1969–1983
James W. Cox, M.Div., Ph.D.

Translations of the Bible referred to and quoted from in this book may be indicated by their standard abbreviations, such as NRSV (New Revised Standard Version) and NIV (New International Version). In addition, some contributors have made their own translations and others have used a mixed text.

Published by Jossey-Bass
A Wiley Imprint
989 Market Street, San Francisco, CA 94103-1741   www.josseybass.com

Library of Congress Cataloging Card Number

25-21658
ISSN 0738-5323
ISBN-13 978-0-7879-8457-1
ISBN-10 0-7879-8457-4

Printed in the United States of America
FIRST EDITION
HB Printing
10 9 8 7 6 5 4 3 2 1

CONTENTS

PREFACE

The Minister's Manual has a new editor—after twenty-two years. It is my honor and pleasure to formally present him as my successor. Although I have been appointed Editor Emeritus by the publisher, the weight of responsibility for *The Minister's Manual* now rests on Dr. Lee McGlone, and I look forward to his creative contributions in the years ahead.

Thanks are due to innumerable individuals who have helped me in my editorial task, but Linda Durkin merits special praise for the careful attention to detail that she has given to preparing the annual manuscript for the publisher. I am most grateful to everyone who has had a part in this challenging mission.

James W. Cox
Senior Professor
The Southern Baptist Theological Seminary

PREFACE

Dr. James W. Cox has edited *The Minister's Manual* each year since 1984. He has carefully and conscientiously brought together preaching, worship, and devotional material of the highest quality and from a wide range of denominational and theological backgrounds. Over the years, I have assisted Dr. Cox in various editorial tasks and have felt privileged to do so. Dr. Cox is a Christian gentleman, a scholar, and a dear friend. For the 2007 edition, Dr. Cox and I have worked together to compile material we believe will be helpful for preachers and teachers. The resources presented here reflect thoughtful presentations of the gospel message, meaningful illustrations, and worship suggestions that we believe will be helpful. As I assume the task of sole editor of *The Minister's Manual*, I do so with a deep commitment to maintain the quality and ecumenical outlook that has been reflected in past years.

I express thanks to the staff at Jossey-Bass Publishers for their quality help in preparation of this volume—and I look forward to our continued partnership in the years to come. I am grateful also to the many and varied contributors whose works are cited here. While they represent a variety of perspectives on issues and a broad range of sermonic technique, each deserves careful reading and probing reflection. Every effort has been made to ensure that the rights and wishes of our contributors have been honored.

I enter into this editorial opportunity with thankful regard for the past and appropriate anticipation for the future. We are reminded from Scripture that "Jesus came preaching." So do we. God, help us to do it well.

Lee McGlone, Ph.D.
Pastor, First Baptist Church
Sioux Falls, South Dakota

SECTION I

GENERAL AIDS AND RESOURCES

CIVIL YEAR CALENDARS FOR 2007 AND 2008

2007

January	February	March	April
S M T W T F S	S M T W T F S	S M T W T F S	S M T W T F S
1 2 3 4 5 6	1 2 3	1 2 3	1 2 3 4 5 6 7
7 8 9 10 11 12 13	4 5 6 7 8 9 10	4 5 6 7 8 9 10	8 9 10 11 12 13 14
14 15 16 17 18 19 20	11 12 13 14 15 16 17	11 12 13 14 15 16 17	15 16 17 18 19 20 21
21 22 23 24 25 26 27	18 19 20 21 22 23 24	18 19 20 21 22 23 24	22 23 24 25 26 27 28
28 29 30 31	25 26 27 28	25 26 27 28 29 30 31	29 30

May	June	July	August
S M T W T F S	S M T W T F S	S M T W T F S	S M T W T F S
1 2 3 4 5	1 2	1 2 3 4 5 6 7	1 2 3 4
6 7 8 9 10 11 12	3 4 5 6 7 8 9	8 9 10 11 12 13 14	5 6 7 8 9 10 11
13 14 15 16 17 18 19	10 11 12 13 14 15 16	15 16 17 18 19 20 21	12 13 14 15 16 17 18
20 21 22 23 24 25 26	17 18 19 20 21 22 23	22 23 24 25 26 27 28	19 20 21 22 23 24 25
27 28 29 30 31	24 25 26 27 28 29 30	29 30 31	26 27 28 29 30 31

September	October	November	December
S M T W T F S	S M T W T F S	S M T W T F S	S M T W T F S
1	1 2 3 4 5 6	1 2 3	2 3 4 5 6 7 8
2 3 4 5 6 7 8	7 8 9 10 11 12 13	4 5 6 7 8 9 10	2 3 4 5 6 7 8
9 10 11 12 13 14 15	14 15 16 17 18 19 20	11 12 13 14 15 16 17	9 10 11 12 13 14 15
16 17 18 19 20 21 22	21 22 23 24 25 26 27	18 19 20 21 22 23 24	16 17 18 19 20 21 22
23 24 25 26 27 28 29	28 29 30 31	25 26 27 28 29 30	23 24 25 26 27 28 29
30			30 31

2008

January	February	March	April
S M T W T F S	S M T W T F S	S M T W T F S	S M T W T F S
1 2 3 4 5	1 2	1	1 2 3 4 5
6 7 8 9 10 11 12	3 4 5 6 7 8 9	2 3 4 5 6 7 8	6 7 8 9 10 11 12
13 14 15 16 17 18 19	10 11 12 13 14 15 16	9 10 11 12 13 14 15	13 14 15 16 17 18 19
20 21 22 23 24 25 26	17 18 19 20 21 22 23	16 17 18 19 20 21 22	20 21 22 23 24 25 26
27 28 29 30 31	24 25 26 27 28 29	23 24 25 26 27 28 29	27 28 29 30
		30 31	

May	June	July	August
S M T W T F S	S M T W T F S	S M T W T F S	S M T W T F S
1 2 3	1 2 3 4 5 6 7	1 2 3 4 5	1 2
4 5 6 7 8 9 10	8 9 10 11 12 13 14	6 7 8 9 10 11 12	3 4 5 6 7 8 9
11 12 13 14 15 16 17	15 16 17 18 19 20 21	13 14 15 16 17 18 19	10 11 12 13 14 15 16
18 19 20 21 22 23 24	22 23 24 25 26 27 28	20 21 22 23 24 25 26	17 18 19 20 21 22 23
25 26 27 28 29 30 31	29 30	27 28 29 30 31	24 25 26 27 28 29 30
			31

September	October	November	December
S M T W T F S	S M T W T F S	S M T W T F S	S M T W T F S
1 2 3 4 5 6	1 2 3	1	1 2 3 4 5 6
7 8 9 10 11 12 13	5 6 7 8 9 10 11	2 3 4 5 6 7 8	7 8 9 10 11 12 13
14 15 16 17 18 19 20	12 13 14 15 16 17 18	9 10 11 12 13 14 15	14 15 16 17 18 19 20
21 22 23 24 25 26 27	19 20 21 22 23 24 25	16 17 18 19 20 21 22	21 22 23 24 25 26 27
28 29 30	26 27 28 29 30 31	23 24 25 26 27 28 29	28 29 30 31
		30	

Church and Civic Calendar for 2007

January

1	New Year's Day
5	Twelfth Night
6	Epiphany
9	Baptism of the Lord
15	Martin Luther King Jr.'s Birthday, observed
17	St. Anthony's Day
18	Confession of St. Peter
25	Conversion of St. Paul

February

1	National Freedom Day
2	Presentation of Jesus in the Temple
12	Lincoln's Birthday
14	St. Valentine's Day
	Race Relations Day
19	Presidents' Day
20	Shrove Tuesday
21	Ash Wednesday
22	Washington's Birthday
24	St. Matthias
25	First Sunday in Lent

March

4	Second Sunday in Lent
11	Third Sunday in Lent
17	St. Patrick's Day
18	Fourth Sunday in Lent
19	St. Joseph
25	Fifth Sunday in Lent
	Feast of Annunciation

April

1	Fifth Sunday in Lent
	Passion/Palm Sunday
1–7	Holy Week
5	Maundy Thursday
6	Good Friday
8	Easter
25	St. Mark, Evangelist

May

1	May Day
	St. Philip and St. James, Apostles

	Loyalty Day
	Law Day
1–5	Cinco de Mayo Celebration
6–12	National Family Week
13	Mother's Day
17	Ascension Day
26	Memorial Day
27	Pentecost
31	The Visitation of the Blessed Virgin Mary

June

3	Trinity Sunday
11	St. Barnabas
14	St. John the Baptist
15	Father's Day
29	St. Peter and St. Paul, Apostles

July

2	Canada Day
4	Independence Day
22	St. Mary Magdalene
25	St. James, the Apostle

August

6	Civic Holiday (Canada)
	The Transfiguration
14	Atlantic Charter Day
15	Mary, Mother of Jesus
24	St. Bartholomew, Apostle
26	Women's Equality Day

September

3	Labor Day
14	Holy Cross Day
21	St. Matthew, Evangelist and Apostle
29	St. Michael and All Angels

October

7	World Communion Sunday
8	Columbus Day
18	St. Luke, Evangelist
23	St. James, Brother of Jesus

28	St. Simon and St. Jude	*December*	
31	Reformation Day	2	First Sunday of Advent
	National UNICEF Day	9	Second Sunday of Advent
		15	Bill of Rights Day
November		16	Third Sunday of Advent
		21	St. Thomas
1	All Saints Day	23	Fourth Sunday of Advent
2	All Souls Day	25	Christmas Day
11	Veterans Day	26	St. Stephen
	Armistice Day		Boxing Day (Canada)
	Remembrance Day (Canada)	27	St. John, Evangelist and
	Stewardship Sunday		Apostle
18	Bible Sunday	28	Holy Innocents Day
25	Christ the King	31	New Year's Eve
29	Thanksgiving Day		Watch Night
30	St. Andrew, Apostle		

The Revised Common Lectionary for 2007

The following Scriptures are commended for use by various Protestant churches and the Roman Catholic Church and include first, second, and Gospel readings, and Psalms, according to Cycle C from January 7 to November 25 and according to Cycle A from December 2 to December 30.[1]

Epiphany Season

Jan. 7: Isa. 60:1–6; Ps. 72:1–7, 10–14; Eph. 3:1–12; Matt. 2:1–12
Jan. 14: Isa. 62:1–5; Ps. 36:5–10; 1 Cor. 12:1–11; John 2:1–11
Jan. 21: Neh. 8:1–3, 5–6, 8–10; Ps. 19; 1 Cor. 12:12–31a; Luke 4:14–21
Jan. 28: Isa. 6:1–8 (9–13); Ps. 138; 1 Cor. 15:1–11; Luke 5:1–11
Feb. 4: Jer. 17:5–10; Ps. 1; 1 Cor. 15:12–20; Luke 6:17–26
Feb. 11: Gen. 45:3–11, 15; Ps. 37:1–11, 39–40; 1 Cor. 15:35–38, 42–50; Luke 6:27–38
Feb. 18: Isa. 55:10–13; Ps. 92:1–4, 12–15; 1 Cor. 15:51–58; Luke 6:39–49

Lenten Season

Feb. 21 (Ash Wednesday): Joel 2:1–2, 12–17; Ps. 51:1–17; 2 Cor. 5:20b–6:10; Matt. 6:1–6, 16–21
Feb. 25: Deut. 26:1–11; Ps. 91:1–2, 9–16; Rom. 10:8b–13; Luke 4:1–13
Mar. 4: Gen. 15:1–12, 17–18; Ps. 27; Phil. 3:17–4:1; Luke 13:31–35
Mar. 11: Isa. 55:1–9; Ps. 68:1–8; 1 Cor. 10:1–13; Luke 13:1–9
Mar. 18: Josh. 5:9–12; Ps. 32; 2 Cor. 5:16–21; Luke 15:1–3, 11b–32
Mar. 25: Isa. 43:16–21; Ps. 126; Phil. 3:4b–14; John 12:1–8

---

[1]Copyright 1992, *Consultation on Common Texts.*

Holy Week and Easter Season

Apr. 1 (Passion/Palm Sunday): Liturgy of the Palms: Luke 19:28–40; Ps. 118:1–2, 19–29; Liturgy of the Passion: Isa. 50:4–9a; Ps. 31:9–16; Phil. 2:5–11; Luke 22:14–23:56

Apr. 2 (Monday): Isa. 42:1–9; Ps. 36:5–11; Heb. 9:11–15; John 12:1–11

Apr. 3 (Tuesday): Isa. 49:1–7; Ps. 71:1–14; 1 Cor. 1:18–31; John 12:20–36

Apr. 4 (Wednesday): Isa. 50:4–9a; Ps. 70; Heb. 12:1–3; John 13:21–32

Apr. 5 (Thursday): Exod. 12:1–4 (5–10), 11–14; Ps. 116:1–2, 12–19; 1 Cor. 11:23–26; John 13:1–7, 31b–35

Apr. 6 (Good Friday): Isa. 52:13–53:12; Ps. 22; Heb. 10:16–25; John 18:1–19

Apr. 7 (Holy Saturday): Job 14:1–14; Ps. 31:1–4, 15–16; 1 Pet. 4:1–8; Matt. 27:57–66

Apr. 8 (Easter Vigil): Gen. 1:1–2:4a; Ps. 136:1–9, 23–26; Gen. 7:1–5, 11–18, 8:6–18, 9:8–13; Ps. 46; Gen. 22:1–18; Ps. 16; Exod. 14:10–31, 15:20–21; Exod. 15:1b–13, 17–18; Isa. 55:1–11; Isa. 12:2–6; Prov. 8:1–8, 19–21, 9:4b–6; Ps. 19; Ezek. 36:24–28; Ps. 42–43; Ezek. 37:1–14; Ps. 143; Zeph. 3:14–20; Ps. 98; Rom. 6:3–11; Ps. 114; Matt. 28:1–10

Apr. 8 (Easter Day): Isa. 65:17–25; Ps. 118:1–2, 14–24; Acts 10:34–43 or 1 Cor. 15:19–26; John 20:1–18

Apr. 15: Acts 5:27–32; Ps. 118:14–29; Rev. 1:4–8

Apr. 22: Acts 9:1–6 (7–20); Ps. 30; Rev. 5:11–14; John 21:1–19

Apr. 29: Acts 9:36–43; Ps. 23; Rev. 7:9–17; John 10:22–30

May 6: Acts 11:1–18; Ps. 148; Rev. 21:1–6; John 13:31–35

May 13: Acts 16:9–15; Ps. 67; Rev. 21:10, 22–22:5; John 14:23–29

May 20: Acts 16:16–34; Ps. 97; Rev. 22:12–14, 16–17, 20–21; John 17:20–26

May 27 (Pentecost): Acts 2:1–21 or Gen. 11:1–9; Ps. 104:24–34, 35b; Rom. 8:14–17; John 14:8–17 (25–27)

June 3 (Trinity): Prov. 8:1–4, 22–32; Ps. 8; Rom. 5:1–5; John 16:12–15

June 10: 1 Kings 17:8–16 (17–24); Ps. 146; Gal. 1:11–24; Luke 7:11–17

June 17: 1 Kings 2:1–10 (11–14), 15–21a; Ps. 5:1–8; Gal. 2:15–21; Luke 7:36–8:3

June 24: 1 Kings 19:1–4 (5–7), 8–15a; Ps. 42; Gal. 3:23–29; Luke 8:26–39

July 1: 2 Kings 2:1–2, 6–14; Ps. 77:1–2, 11–20; Gal. 5:1, 13–25; Luke 9:51–62

July 8: 2 Kings 5:1–14; Ps. 30; Gal. 6:1–6, 7–16; Luke 10:1–11, 16–20

July 15: Amos 7:7–17; Ps. 82; Col. 1:1–14; Luke 10:25–37

July 22: Amos 8:1–12; Ps. 52; Col. 1:15–28; Luke 10:38–42

July 29: Hos. 1:2–10; Ps. 85; Col. 2:6–15 (16–19); Luke 11:1–13

Aug. 5: Hos. 11:1–11; Ps. 107:1–9, 43; Col. 3:1–11; Luke 12:13–21

Aug. 12: Isa. 1:1, 10–20; Ps. 50:1–8, 22–23; Heb. 11:1–3, 8–16; Luke 12:32–40

Aug. 19: Isa. 5:1–7; Ps. 80:1–2, 8–19; Heb. 11:29–12:2; Luke 12:49–56

Aug. 26: Jer. 1:4–10; Ps. 71:1–6; Heb. 12:18–29; Luke 13:10–17

Sept. 2: Jer. 2:4–13; Ps. 81:1, 10–16; Heb. 13:1–8, 15–16; Luke 14:1, 7–14

Sept. 9: Jer. 8:1–11; Ps. 139:1–6, 13–18; Philem. 1–21; Luke 14:25–33

Sept. 16: Jer. 4:11–12, 22–28; Ps. 14; 1 Tim. 1:12–17; Luke 15:1–10

Sept. 23: Jer. 8:18–19:1; Ps. 79:1–9; 1 Tim. 2:1–7; Luke 16:1–13

Sept. 30: Jer. 32:1–3a, 6–15; Ps. 91:1–6, 14–16; 1 Tim. 6:6–19; Luke 16:19–31

Oct. 7: Lam. 1:1–6; Ps. 137; 2 Tim. 1:1–14; Luke 17:5–10

Oct. 14: Jer. 29:1, 4–7; Ps. 66:1–12; 2 Tim. 2:8–15; Luke 17:11–19

Oct. 21: Jer. 31:27–34; Ps. 119:97–104; 2 Tim. 3:14–4:5; Luke 18:1–8

Oct. 28: Joel 2:23–32; Ps. 65; 2 Tim. 4:6–8, 16–18; Luke 18:9–14

Nov. 4: Hab. 1:1–4, 2:1–4; Ps. 119:137–144; 2 Thess. 1:1–4, 11–12; Luke 19:1–10

Nov. 11: Hag. 2:1–9; Ps. 145:1–5, 17–21; 2 Thess. 2:1–5, 13–17; Luke 20:27–38

Nov. 18: Isa. 65:17–25; (The Response): Isa. 12; 2 Thess. 3:6–13; Luke 21:5–19

Nov. 25 (Christ the King): Jer. 23:1–6; (The Response): Luke 1:68–79; Col. 1:11–20; Luke 23:33–43

Advent and Christmas Season

Dec. 2: Isa. 2:1–5; Ps. 122; Rom. 13:11–14; Matt. 24:36–44

Dec. 9: Isa. 11:1–10; Ps. 71:1–7, 18–19; Rom. 15:4–13; Matt. 3:1–12

Dec. 16: Isa. 35:1–10; (The Response): Luke 1:47–55; James 5:7–10; Matt. 11:2–11

Dec. 23: Isa. 7:10–16; Ps. 80:1–7, 17–19; Rom. 1:1–7; Matt. 1:18–25

Dec. 30: Isa. 63:7–9; Ps. 148; Heb. 2:10–18; Matt. 2:13–23

Four-Year Church Calendar

	2007	2008	2009	2010
Ash Wednesday	Feb. 21	Feb. 6	Feb. 25	Feb. 17
Palm Sunday	Apr. 1	Mar. 16	Apr. 5	Mar. 28
Good Friday	Apr. 6	Mar. 21	Apr. 10	Apr. 2
Easter	Apr. 8	Mar. 23	Apr. 12	Apr. 4
Ascension Day	May 17	May 1	May 21	May 13
Pentecost	May 27	May 11	May 31	May 29
Trinity Sunday	June 3	May 18	June 7	May 30
Thanksgiving	Nov. 22	Nov. 27	Nov. 26	Nov. 25
Advent Sunday	Dec. 2	Nov. 30	Nov. 29	Nov. 28

Forty-Year Easter Calendar

2007 April 8	2017 April 16	2027 March 28	2037 April 5
2008 March 23	2018 April 1	2028 April 16	2038 April 25
2009 April 12	2019 April 21	2029 April 1	2039 April 10
2010 April 4	2020 April 12	2030 April 21	2040 April 1
2011 April 24	2021 April 4	2031 April 13	2041 April 2
2012 April 8	2022 April 17	2032 March 28	2042 April 6
2013 March 31	2023 April 9	2033 April 17	2043 March 29
2014 April 20	2024 March 31	2034 April 9	2044 April 17
2015 April 5	2025 April 20	2035 March 25	2045 April 9
2016 March 27	2026 April 5	2036 April 13	2046 March 25

Traditional Wedding Anniversary Identifications

1 Paper	7 Wool	13 Lace	35 Coral
2 Cotton	8 Bronze	14 Ivory	40 Ruby
3 Leather	9 Pottery	15 Crystal	45 Sapphire
4 Linen	10 Tin	20 China	50 Gold
5 Wood	11 Steel	25 Silver	55 Emerald
6 Iron	12 Silk	30 Pearl	60 Diamond

Colors Appropriate for Days and Seasons

White. Symbolizes purity, perfection, and joy and identifies festivals marking events in the life of Jesus, except Good Friday: Christmas, Epiphany, Easter, Eastertide, Ascension Day; also Trinity Sunday, All Saints' Day, weddings, funerals. Gold may also be used.

Red. Symbolizes the Holy Spirit, martyrdom, and the love of God: Good Friday, Pentecost, and Sundays following.

Violet. Symbolizes penitence: Advent, Lent.

Green. Symbolizes mission to the world, hope, regeneration, nurture, and growth: Epiphany season, Kingdomtide, Rural Life Sunday, Labor Sunday, Thanksgiving Sunday.

Blue. Advent, in some churches.

Flowers in Season Appropriate for Church Use

January: carnation or snowdrop
February: violet or primrose
March: jonquil or daffodil
April: lily, sweet pea, or daisy
May: lily of the valley or hawthorn
June: rose or honeysuckle

July: larkspur or water lily
August: gladiolus or poppy
September: aster or morning star
October: calendula or cosmos
November: chrysanthemum
December: narcissus, holly, or poinsettia

Quotable Quotations

1. Everything that is done in the world is done by hope.—Martin Luther
2. I claim credit for nothing. Everything is determined, the beginning as well as the end, by forces over which we have no control. It is determined for the insect as well as for the star. Human beings, vegetables, or cosmic dust, we all dance to a mysterious tune, intoned in the distance by an invisible piper.—Albert Einstein
3. All things must speak of God, refer to God, or they are atheistic.—Henry P. Van Dusen
4. A faith which does not doubt is a dead faith.—Miguel de Unamuno
5. Anybody can sympathize with the sufferings of a friend, but it requires a very fine nature to sympathize with a friend's success.—Oscar Wilde
6. A penny-weight of love is worth a pound of law.—James Kelly
7. Whatsoever God requires of man, man may find imprinted in his own nature, written in his own heart.—John Donne
8. I suppose flattery hurts no one, that is, if he doesn't inhale.—Adlai Stevenson
9. Education is nothing more than the polishing of each single link in the great chain that binds humanity together and gives it unity.—Johann Heinrich Pestalozzi
10. When I think of God, my heart is so filled with joy that the notes fly off as from a spindle.—Joseph Haydn
11. Conscience is the perfect interpreter of life.—Karl Barth
12. Skepticism is the beginning of Faith.—Oscar Wilde
13. It is an old saying, Repentance is never too late; but it is a true saying, Repentance is never too soon.—Henry Smith
14. Religion is the basis of civil society, and the source of all good and of all comfort.—Edmund Burke

15. We ourselves are God's true temples.—John Calvin
16. The chief end of man is to glorify God, and to enjoy him forever.—Westminster Catechism
17. Compassion is the chief law of human existence.—Fyodor Dostoyevsky
18. Religion is the best armor, but the worst cloak.—Thomas Fuller
19. Fanaticism consists of redoubling your effort when you have forgotten your aim.— George Santayana
20. If you suffer, thank God—it is a sure sign you are alive.—Elbert Hubbard
21. The Bible is like a telescope. If a man looks *through* his telescope, then he sees worlds beyond; but if he looks *at* his telescope, then he does not see anything but that. The Bible is a thing to be looked through, to see that which is beyond; but most people only look at it; and so they see only the dead letter.—Phillips Brooks
22. To err is human but to really foul things up requires a computer.—Anonymous
23. The worst moment for the atheist is when he is really thankful and has nobody to thank.—Dante Gabriel Rossetti
24. God is not a cosmic bellboy for whom we can press a button to get things.— Harry Emerson Fosdick
25. You can give without loving, but you cannot love without giving.—Amy Carmichaiel
26. A faithful friend is the medicine of life.—Apocrypha, Ecclesiasticus 6:16
27. Friendship is love without his wings!—Lord Byron, 1788–1824
28. Every person has his own road to follow, and we cannot know what it is before-hand. What counts in the end of the day is what God does, not what we do. The only really important thing is that each of us should come to know him, whatever the unforeseen detours we have to take.—Paul Tournier
29. God whispers to us in our pleasures, speaks in our conscience, but shouts in our pains; it is his megaphone to rouse a deaf world.—C. S. Lewis, *The Problem of Pain*
30. Yes, Christ is alive. To thousands upon thousands at the present hour this is no mere theory or vague, uncertain rumor, but proved, inviolable experience; and if they are facing life victoriously now where once they were defeated, it is because they have found the same Risen Lord who walked among the flowers of the garden on the morning of the first Easter day.—James S. Stewart
31. Faith is nowhere more clearly pure and strong than in many of God's good people who live in pain yet bear their witness to the goodness of God.—Frank Stagg
32. God made all mankind of one blood, and with one blood, the blood of his Son, he bought all Mankind again.—John Donne
33. Everything is funny as long as it happens to somebody else.—Will Rogers
34. Our very weaknesses and even our mistakes of the past, when deposited in his hands, are turned into strength and wisdom.—Chester E. Swor
35. The pain you know, God knows. The fears you feel, God shares. Your tears are God's sorrow. Your laughter is echoed in eternal mirth. In Jesus Christ, God enters life and lives.—David Buttrick
36. All evil, all sin, suffering and damnation is "in God." They have been endured by him, abolished in him, transformed by him. These are "the benefits of his passion" for us.—Jürgen Moltmann

37. The constant temptation that confronts the minister is that of molding his or her identity to the wished-for shape in the popular culture.—André Resner Jr.
38. The first and last act of faith is to acknowledge that we are strangers and exiles, and that perhaps we also have to take an interest, by accident as it were, in what's happening in this temporary place called the world.—Jacques Ellul
39. The expectation of an eternal happiness will reconcile every man with his neighbor, with his friend, and with his enemy in understanding of the essential.—Søren Kierkegaard
40. Whatever the dark ways, whatever the twisted maze, the heart that loves will praise.—Edna Hong
41. The Christian can never rest on his ethical oars, feeling that the finish line has been crossed. He has a perpetually "uneasy conscience."—Robert McAfee Brown
42. If anything is certain, it is that every one of life's trials, if only because it breaks the hard crust of our physical and mental habits, creates, like the ploughing of a field, an empty space where seed can be sown.—Paul Tournier
43. The witness of the Spirit is Christ's perpetual interpretation of his own work as gospel.—P. T. Forsyth
44. God does not foreordain that evil and disastrous things happen to us. Rather, he works *after the fact* of tragedy through our powers of perception to reveal to us new avenues of growth, hope, opportunity, and realization. We would never have found these new ways if our eyes had not been jarred open by untoward and dark events.—Wayne E. Oates
45. I never think of the future. It comes soon enough.—Albert Einstein
46. Doubt is the vestibule which all must pass, before they can enter into the temple of truth.—Charles Caleb Colton
47. Character is that which can do without success.—Ralph Waldo Emerson
48. A man's work, whether in music, painting or literature, is always a portrait of himself.—Samuel Butler
49. It's a funny old world—a man's lucky if he can get out of it alive.—W. C. Fields
50. The truth is more important than the facts.—Frank Lloyd Wright
51. What is civilization? I answer the power of good women.—Ralph Waldo Emerson
52. To be angry is to revenge the fault of others upon ourselves.—Alexander Pope
53. Failure takes as much time as success.—James K. Feibleman
54. God is best known in Christ; the moon is not seen but by the light of the sun.—William Bridge

Questions of Life and Religion[2]

1. What ethical issues are involved in abortion?
2. How can we deal with the apparent absence of God in certain times and circumstances?
3. Are there appropriate legal ways of dealing with all harmful addictions?
4. What are the pluses and minuses of human aging?

---

[2]These questions were suggested by and treated in articles in a volume edited by James W. Cox, *Handbook of Themes for Preaching* (Louisville: Westminster/John Knox Press, 1991), pp. 23–145.

5. How can we think of salvation as blessing?
6. Are there constructive alternatives to capital punishment?
7. In what ways are children related to purposes of God?
8. What is the Church?
9. What is the proper relationship of Church and state?
10. How can true community be achieved?
11. What is the role of confession in Christian life and worship?
12. Is conscience always a safe guide?
13. What do we mean by conversion?
14. Does scientific research have important contributions to our understanding of creation?
15. What is the most significant aspect of Jesus' Crucifixion?
16. Can the reality of death add meaning to life?
17. What steps will aid our decision making?
18. How can depression be brought under control?
19. What are the essential ingredients of Christian discipline?
20. Is illness some kind of punishment?
21. Is divorce an option for Christians?
22. What are the pluses and minuses of doubt?
23. What duties does the need for education place upon us?
24. In what way can we best understand the doctrine of election biblically?
25. How can we deal with the confusing interpretation of "the end times"?
26. What are our responsibilities toward our human environment?
27. What is bad in envy and jealousy?
28. In what ways are human beings equal or unequal?
29. When does eternal life begin?
30. How do faith and ethics connect?
31. Why is the Eucharist (Communion, the Lord's Supper) important in worship?
32. How is evangelism necessary in fulfilling the mission of the Church?
33. How can we explain evil in relation to God?
34. What is faith?
35. How can we define *family?*
36. What are the causes and cure of fear?
37. In what way is forgiveness a necessary part of life?
38. Why is it difficult to define *God?*
39. Where do we see God's grace in action?
40. How can we help those who are experiencing grief?
41. How does God guide us?
42. When is guilt resolved?
43. How can we define *heaven?*
44. What is the role of the Holy Spirit in Christian experience?
45. Is it possible to be thoroughly honest?
46. What is hope at its best?
47. When is humility a virtue?
48. Is idolatry a temptation in our culture?

49. What in us reflects the image of God?
50. In what sense was Jesus the incarnation of God?
51. What is inspiration?
52. How can we define *Jesus* as *the Christ?*

Biblical Benedictions and Blessings

The Lord watch between me and thee when we are absent from one another.—Gen. 31:49

The Lord our God be with us, as he was with our fathers; let him not leave us nor forsake us; that he may incline our hearts unto him, to walk in all his ways and to keep his commandments and his statutes and his judgments, which he commanded our fathers.—1 Kings 8:57–58

Let the words of my mouth and the meditation of my heart be acceptable in thy sight, O Lord, my strength and my redeemer.—Ps. 19:14

Now the God of patience and consolation grant you to be like-minded one toward another according to Christ Jesus; that ye may with one mind and one mouth glorify God, even the Father of our Lord Jesus Christ. Now the God of hope fill you with all joy and peace in believing, that ye may abound in hope, through the power of the Holy Ghost. Now the God of peace be with you.—Rom. 15:5–6, 13, 33

Now to him that is of power to establish you according to my Gospel and the teaching of Jesus Christ, according to the revelation of the mystery, which was kept secret since the world began but now is manifest, and by the Scriptures of the prophets, according to the commandments of the everlasting God, made known to all nations for the glory through Jesus Christ forever.—Rom. 16:25–27

Grace be unto you, and peace, from God our Father, and from the Lord Jesus Christ.—1 Cor. 1:3

The grace of the Lord Jesus Christ and the love of God and the communion of the Holy Ghost be with you all.—2 Cor. 13:14

Peace be to the brethren, and love with faith, from God the Father and the Lord Jesus Christ. Grace be with all them that love our Lord Jesus Christ in sincerity.—Eph. 6:23–24

And the peace of God, which passeth all understanding, shall keep your hearts and minds through Christ Jesus. Finally, brethren, whatsoever things are true, whatsoever things are honest, whatsoever things are just, whatsoever things are pure, whatsoever things are lovely, whatsoever things are of good report; if there be any virtue, and if there be any praise, think on these things. Those things which ye have both learned and received, and heard and seen in me, do; and the God of peace shall be with you.—Phil. 4:7–9

Wherefore also we pray always for you, that our God would count you worthy of this calling and fulfill all the good pleasure of this goodness, and the work of faith with power; that the name of our Lord Jesus Christ may be glorified in you, and ye in him, according to the grace of our God and the Lord Jesus Christ.—2 Thess. 1:11–12

Now the Lord of peace himself give you peace always by all means. The Lord be with you all. The grace of our Lord Jesus Christ be with you all.—2 Thess. 3:16–18

Grace, mercy, and peace, from God our Father and Jesus Christ our Lord.—1 Tim. 1:2

Now the God of peace, that brought again from the dead our Lord Jesus, that great shepherd of the sheep, through the blood of the everlasting covenant, make you perfect in every good work to do his will, working in you that which is well-pleasing in his sight, through Jesus Christ, to whom be glory for ever and ever.—Heb. 13:20–21

The God of all grace, who hath called us unto his eternal glory by Christ Jesus, after that ye have suffered a while, make you perfect, establish, strengthen, settle you. To him be glory and dominion for ever and ever. Greet ye one another with a kiss of charity. Peace be with you all that are in Christ Jesus.—1 Pet. 3:10–14

Grace be with you, mercy, and peace from God the Father, and from the Lord Jesus Christ, the Son of the Father, in truth and love.—2 John 3

Now unto him that is able to keep you from falling, and to present you faultless before the presence of his glory with exceeding joy, to the only wise God our Savior, be glory and majesty, dominion and power, both now and ever.—Jude 24:25

Grace be unto you, and peace, from him which was, and which is to come; and from the seven Spirits which are before his throne; and from Jesus Christ, who is the faithful witness, and the first begotten of the dead, and the prince of the kings of the earth. Unto him that loved us, washed us from our sins in his own blood, and hath made us kings and priests unto God and his Father, to him be glory and dominion for ever and ever.—Rev. 1:4–6

SERMONS AND HOMILETIC AND WORSHIP AIDS FOR FIFTY-TWO SUNDAYS

SUNDAY, JANUARY 7, 2007
Lectionary Message

Topic: Prime Time for Worship
TEXT: Matt. 2:1–12
Other Readings: Isa. 60:1–6; Ps. 72:1–7, 10–14; Eph. 3:1–12

It has been said that too many Christians worship their work, work at their play, and play at their worship. To the extent that this statement is true, it is tragic. It represents an inversion of values—*eternal* values—that can ultimately lead only to impoverished souls.

In the Christmas season, just concluded, the statement takes a peculiar twist, equally unfortunate. For many, the season becomes so full of parties, shopping, and a host of other activity that the birth of Christ is reduced to an *excuse for* rather than the *reason for* the season. So this is a good time to take a new look at an old lesson, one modeled by an unlikely cast of characters. It is a lesson in worship, sponsored by the Magi from the East.

I. *Worship may arise from persons unlikely to offer it* (v. 1). It would have been no surprise for Jewish people, grounded in the traditions of their faith and anticipating the coming of their Messiah, to have worshiped Jesus at his coming. However, the Wise Men from the East were outsiders concerning the faith. Most probably, they were pagan astrologers—priests of a naturalistic religion of seventh-century B.C. Medean origin. The Old Testament book of Daniel describes practitioners of their order as operating in Babylon in the sixth century B.C.

Moreover, these people were Gentiles. Under the Old Testament Law, and in the Jewish social and religious order, they would have been held in low esteem. They were outside the covenant and denied the privileged favor of God that the Jews experienced. Their practices of astrology were forbidden and mocked in the Old Testament, further accenting their alienation from the things of God.

But the Magi surprise us, for Matthew features their eagerness to worship Jesus, the king of the Jews, whose star they had followed to Jerusalem. The surprise is lessened, however, when we realize that their coming attests to the marvelous grace of God, who prompted and led them to find Jesus. Unlikely worshipers do not arise of their own accord. They simply respond to the grace of God freely granted them.

II. *Worship entails resolute purpose* (vv. 2–10). The worship of the Magi was sincere. The text clearly states that the purpose for which they had resolutely traveled so long and far was to offer untainted worship (vv. 2, 11). The term used to describe their intent—the word most frequently used for "worship" in the New Testament—always presupposes the true or supposed divinity of its object. How much theology they understood may be unknown, but this much is clear: they knew that they sought the King worthy of worship. When finally they arrived at the end of their journey, they celebrated with great joy (vv. 9–10).

Herod, on the other hand, professed a desire to worship (v. 3), but his motives were malicious. He was troubled by the announcement of the Magi, fearing the birth of a usurper to the throne. And because he was troubled, so was the whole city, for he was a volatile and emotionally unstable man. He called for the experts to ask where the Christ was to be born (v. 4). The experts, citing Micah 5:2 combined with 2 Samuel 5:2 and 1 Chronicles 11:2, informed the king that the Christ was to be born in Bethlehem (vv. 5–6). Treacherously, Herod inquired of the Wise Men exactly when the star had appeared (v. 7). Later, he would use the information to initiate the slaughter of the innocents. He then sent them to Bethlehem, instructing them to return with word so that he also could come and worship (v. 8). His interest and investigation in the matter was solely so that he could pursue his perverse purposes—a pretense of worship to mask an evil heart.

III. *Worship finds tangible expression* (vv. 11–12). When the Magi arrived at the house where Jesus was, they fell prostrate in reverence before him. Their posture was a visible, outward expression of the submission of their hearts before the King. In addition, they presented their gifts of gold, frankincense, and myrrh—expensive tokens of their esteem. Their gifts indicated the disposition of their hearts, for in their way of life bringing gifts was particularly important when one approached a superior. Their gifts also foreshadowed realities concerning Jesus' rule as King, his worthiness to be worshiped as the Son of God, and his death on the cross for sinners.

The worship of the Magi—an unlikely cast of characters—is instructive for us, as well. Our worship, like theirs, is enabled by divine grace. It is to be offered in sincerity of heart rather than in ostentation or in deceit. It is expressed in humble and sacrificial giving to our matchless Lord. This is the worship that is appropriate for Christmas—and throughout the year!—Robert Vogel

ILLUSTRATIONS

HEROD'S FORCE.   There is a saying that is popular in the Pacific Northwest: "When Boeing sneezes, Seattle catches cold." The obvious point of the saying is that Boeing is such a force in the economy in the Seattle area that the impact of its fortunes touches on the entire city. This kind of situation existed also in Jerusalem during the reign of Herod. He was such a force, albeit a capricious one, that when he acted, the whole city braced itself. And so, when Herod was troubled by the announcement of the Magi, so also was the whole city.—Robert Vogel

THE HEART OF WORSHIP.   Christian artist Matt Redman has captured well the priority in worship in the lyrics of a song, *The Heart of Worship*. They follow here:

When the music fades
And all is stripped away
And I simply come
Longing just to bring something that's of worth
That will bless your heart.

I'll bring you more than a song for a song in itself
Is not what you have required. You search much deeper within
Through the way things appear. You're looking into my heart.
I'm coming back to the heart of worship
And it's all about you, all about you, Jesus.
I'm sorry, Lord, for the things I've made it
When it's all about you, all about you, Jesus.[1]—Robert Vogel

SERMON SUGGESTIONS

Topic: Beginning the New Year Gratefully

TEXT: 1 Chron. 16:1, 7–12, 31–36

(1) Memory is the basis for gratitude. (2) Gratitude comes in time. (3) Gratitude anticipates "God with us."—Lawrence Vowan

Topic: Jesus the Light

TEXT: John 1:1–9, 35–39

(1) A light for living (v. 4). (2) A light of understanding (v. 5). (3) A light of direction (v. 39).—Jeff Dieselberg

WORSHIP AIDS

CALL TO WORSHIP.   "O, come, let us worship and bow down; let us kneel before the Lord our maker" (Ps. 95:6).

INVOCATION.   Holy and gracious Father, on this the first Sunday of the New Year, we come before you seeking the renewal of our spirits as preparation for our living. You, who indeed turn the shadow of night into morning, satisfy us with your mercy that we may be glad all the day. Lift the light of your eternal countenance upon us and guide us in the ways of peace the whole year through. Help us now to worship you in the spirit of our Lord Jesus Christ.

OFFERTORY SENTENCE.   "Ascribe to the Lord the glory due his name; bring an offering, and come before him. Worship the Lord in holy splendor" (1 Chron. 16:29).

OFFERTORY PRAYER.   Father, we bow in gratitude as a New Year begins. We give thanks for the resources with which we have been blessed and for the opportunity we have in our giving to share your love with all who call upon us—and you.

PRAYER.   Father, by the leading of a star you manifested your only Son to the peoples of the earth. Lead us, who know you now by faith, into your presence, where we may see your glory face-to-face. Today, give us a glimpse of how truly wonderful, loving, and accepting you are. Help us to enjoy you now, tomorrow, and each day. As we remember the Wise

---

[1]Copyright Kingsway's Thankyou Music, 1999.

Men seeking out your Son and publicly declaring to the world that he was your Son, give us the freedom to do the same. Give us the courage to adequately praise you and declare to those around us that we are yours. We pray all of these things through the strong name of Jesus Christ our Lord, who lives and reigns with you and the Holy Spirit, one God, now and forever.—Larry Ellis

SERMON

Topic: The Turn of a New Year
TEXT: Isa. 43:16, 18

Who can deny the tug in two directions at the same time? There are the demands to return to the sanity and security of the past before it is too late and the lure of a future that is to be carved out with courage and creativity. Both seem, by turns, right and reasonable. Which way do we turn?

I. In an era marked by uncertainty we can appreciate the call for a return to the "old values." Yet, at the same time, there is a tug away from what is called a dim mystic past. Some say that what is needed are "futurists"—people who will admit that society, family, and education can never be the same again. Not even the realm of religion escapes this bifurcation. Do we call for a return to our spiritual roots and disciplines, or do we dare dream new dreams and entertain visions of God's future? Maybe it is not just choosing "one of the above." Maybe there is a third way—the way of biblical faith. For the Hebrew mind, present responsibilities and blessings are understood only in the light of the memory of the past and a hope for the future.

II. Yes, "Which way do we turn?" is the crucial question; however, "way" does not mean "direction" but "manner." What is the way (manner) in which we approach the past and the future?

The answer from the biblical perspective is that we are not to treat history as a God, but rather the acts of God are to be seen in history. It is a temptation tailor-made for Americans to ignore history. As our church has been involved in recording an oral history, we have realized that world, national, and personal histories are inextricably bound together. As Christians, who we are and what we do is based on God's freeing us through Jesus Christ. Do we believe that we no longer need to be slaves to eternal death and daily living? We are called to be living reminders of that great salvation.

III. Knowing this, can we believe Isaiah, who says, in effect, "Forget the day of your salvation, remember it no longer"? Isaiah engages in such hyperbole so the auditor will be jolted by the power of God's present plan. In other words, we block God's "new thing" from happening in our lives because we "dwell on days gone by"—we brood over past history.

The Christian life need not mean making a choice between old and new. Rather, it means something like this: your present faith (trust in God) is based on past experience (ours and the community of faith), and you are called forward by a future hope (demonstrated by the Resurrection). The Bible would be more concrete than that. It would tell us of Abraham, called to father a new people of promise. The Bible would speak of Israel freed from bondage in Egypt. If we listen, the Gospels would speak of Jesus, the Word made flesh, tempted in the desert places of this life and yet, finally, faithful into death. From his faithfulness, a new beginning is possible for all who believe.

Hear the news. God is present in the old, in the new, and in the dangerous desert in-between. God, who redeemed you in Christ, will complete that work at the end of time and will sustain you in-between.—Gary Stratman

SUNDAY, JANUARY 14, 2007

Lectionary Message

Topic: The Believer and Spiritual Gifts

TEXT: 1 Cor. 12:1–11

Other Readings: Isa. 62:1–5; Ps. 36:5–10; John 2:1–11

One of the most empowering doctrines for the local church is the doctrine of spiritual gifts. This doctrine is empowering for individual Christians, in that when believers understand what their gifts are, they are able to serve in the cause of the Lord more effectively and confidently. It is also empowering for the church, for when more Christians use their gifts faithfully, the work of the church is done at a higher level of impact.

Conventional church wisdom is that 80 percent of a church's work is done by 20 percent of that church's people. This may be due to a number of factors, not the least of which is a lack of willingness to get involved, on the part of some. Indeed, many Christians are content to view church life as a spectator sport. But a factor that surely influences this matter to some extent is a lack of understanding on the part of the willing concerning their spiritual gifts. Accordingly, people eager to be involved are not aware of how they could or should be involved, or they are assigned responsibilities for which they are not well suited, with a resultant frustration for themselves and others in the church.

Four passages in the New Testament deal with the subject of spiritual gifts (Eph. 4:7–16; 1 Pet. 4:10–11; Rom. 12:3–8, and 1 Cor. 12–14). Each of these passages makes its own contribution to our understanding of the subject, although they have certain elements in common.

In the text from 1 Corinthians 12, we discover three principles informing our understanding of spiritual gifts. Taken together, they all develop the notion that the incredibly diverse makeup of the Church is of God's intentional design and is established by his Holy Spirit.

I. *Spiritual gifts and their related ministries are varied, but they are bestowed by the same Holy Spirit* (vv. 4–6). The text here consists of three parallel statements. Each of the three is nuanced slightly, but together the three get at the same point: the varied gifts and ministries in the Church find unity in the Holy Spirit's design. Paul notes that there are various gifts, but the same Spirit bestows them (v. 4). There are differing ministries that express those gifts, but it is the same Lord in whose name those ministries are discharged (v. 5). There are different outcomes or effects of differing ministries, but one God who is at work in those being served (v. 6).

II. *Spiritual gifts are given to be used for the common good of the Church* (v. 7). A striking feature of spiritual gifts is that they are not given to the recipient for his or her own pleasure. Rather, they are given to be used in the service of others. Their use is a matter of Christian stewardship. They are not something to be guarded or hidden away; instead, they are to be given freely to the benefit of others.

III. *The variety of specific gifts serves the variety of needs in the Church* (vv. 8–11). The common good served by the gifts and the nature of their diversity coalesce in an explanation

(vv. 8–11); here, specific gifts are identified and listed. The list may not be exhaustive, but it surely covers a broad range of ministry. Among the gifts are, first, the *word of wisdom*, which is generally understood to refer to clear insight into the doctrines of redemption and the ability to communicate these effectively to others. Second is the *word of knowledge*, probably referring to unusual insight into spiritual truth. The third gift listed is *faith*, meaning extraordinary expressions of faith in hardships or confident reliance in God's promises with a resultant zeal for his work. Fourth and fifth are gifts of *healing* and *miracles*—outward displays of divine power to cure diseases and affect other supernatural works, seen in Acts in the ministries of the apostles. Sixth is *prophecy*—a gift discussed at length in chapter 14, where it is characterized as edifying, exhorting, and consoling through the preaching of the Word of God. Next is *distinguishing of spirits,* involving exceptional discernment between true and false teachers and teachings. Listed last are gifts of tongues and their interpretation, involving languages that may not be intelligible to all, spoken and explained by those gifted to do so.

People in various traditions may understand the nature and use of these gifts differently. Moreover, all the gifts may not be operative at all times and in all places in the Church. But this much is clear: according to his design and for his good purposes, the Holy Spirit distributes spiritual gifts as he sees fit for the growth and progress of the Church (v. 11).—Robert Vogel

ILLUSTRATIONS

TREASURES AND TOOLS.   Because spiritual gifts are to be used for the common good rather than as a private treasure of the recipient, they might be seen as tools, as opposed to trophies. The difference between a tool and a trophy may be seen in two kinds of car. A trophy car is one that is in perfect condition. Its paint is flawless, with no scratches, peeling, or fading. There are no stains or worn spots in the upholstery, and every mechanical system is in perfect working order. Of course, to sustain this pristine condition, the car is never driven. It is parked in a clean garage and is only brought out to be hauled by trailer for display at trophy car shows.

A work car, on the other hand, is a tool. This one may be owned by a painting contractor, for example. It has dents and scratches—the result of equipment sliding in and out or bumping against it. It has house paint spatters on the fenders from the times that its owner forgot to seal a paint can. The seats are soiled from the painter's clothing, dirty after a long day of labor in the sun. These two cars are very different in their appearance but also very different in their impact. While the trophy car may be admired for its beauty, it is arguably a failure, given the normal purposes for a car. The work car, on the other hand, is nothing to admire in its appearance. But it has been put to useful service for transporting crew and equipment to work. God has given spiritual gifts to be used as tools, not trophies.—Robert Vogel

The following statistics, drawn from studies conducted by the Barna Research Group, are instructive concerning Christians' understanding of the matter of spiritual gifts.

- Most people (71 percent) say they have heard of spiritual gifts.
- Among those who have heard of spiritual gifts, 31 percent can name a spiritual gift they believe they possess. That's the equivalent of 22 percent of the total adult public who can identify a spiritual gift they possess.

- 12 percent of those who have heard of spiritual gifts claim they do not have a spiritual gift.

- The most commonly claimed gifts are teaching (7 percent believe they have this gift); helps/service (7 percent); faith (4 percent); knowledge (4 percent); mercy (4 percent), and tongues (3 percent).

When those who have heard of spiritual gifts are asked to identify their own spiritual gift, 31 percent list characteristics or qualities that are not spiritual gifts identified in the Bible. The most common items mentioned as spiritual gifts that are not biblical gifts are love, kindness, relationships, singing, and listening.[2]—Robert Vogel

SERMON SUGGESTIONS

Topic: What Is Man?
TEXT: Gen. 1:24; Ps. 8
(1) Man is a paradox: the dust of the earth and the breath of God. (2) Man has a dilemma: forgetfulness of his origin and his purpose. (3) Man has a destiny: to become all that God intends.—Lawrence Vowan

Topic: Relational Prayer
TEXT: Prov. 15:8
(1) Prayer is conversation with God. (2) God "delights" in such prayer. (3) Prayer initiates a relationship, grows a relationship, and directs a relationship.—David Feddes

WORSHIP AIDS
CALL TO WORSHIP.   "Be glad in the Lord, and rejoice, ye righteous: and shout for joy, all ye that are upright in heart" (Ps. 32:11 KJV).

INVOCATION.   Lord, you who are the light of the minds that know you, the life of the souls that love you, and the strength of the wills that serve you, help us so to know you that we may truly love you and so to love you that we may fully serve you, whom to serve is perfect freedom.

OFFERTORY SENTENCE.   "Will anyone rob God? Yet you are robbing me! But you say, 'How are we robbing you?' In your tithes and offerings" (Mal. 3:8 NRSV).

OFFERTORY PRAYER.   Father, help us to realize today that we do not live in our own strength but that you are our help and that every good and perfect gift comes from above. These gifts we bring we consecrate in Christ's name.

---

[2]George Barna, cited by *Word of Grace Network* (accessed October 1, 2005 [http://www.word-of-grace.com/Pastor Desk/Vol_2/Content/statistics.htm].

PRAYER.   Eternal God, Shepherd of our souls, we bring our hopes and needs to you today. We long to love you more and to live more in your way. But we confess our fears and our weaknesses, sins and inadequacies. Give us strength to face our problems, the courage to accept your grace and forgiveness, and the wisdom to know your will and your way. Lord God of life, hope and joy, breathe your spirit upon us. May we sense your guidance and your power in all that we seek to undertake. Throw open the windows of our lives and let the breeze of your spirit rush in. Overcome our stale thinking so that we can have new hopes, new dreams, and new possibilities.

Remove blinders from our eyes that keep us from seeing those around us who have needs and sorrows. Breathe within us the breath of your joy, which will be so overwhelming that we will want to share it with others. Well up within us that living water that comes from Jesus Christ our Lord. May this stream of water be so powerful within us that it will become a rushing stream that will flow through our lives and touch others to quench their needs.

Free us from the shackles that bind us to the past. Open our eyes this day to what we can become through Jesus Christ, who suffered and died for us and lives again. For we offer this prayer in his strong name.—William Powell Tuck

SERMON
Topic: Follow the Vision
TEXT: Acts 26:19–32

I. The Christian faith always gets personal. Our faith is not a one-size-fits-all religion. Luke seems to prefer calling followers of Christ "people of The Way." The reference to "Christians" (Christ ones) in Antioch (chapter 11) may well have been a popular term of denigration. "The Way" is guide for life. You can't shake it down to "four spiritual laws" or to some late-night prescription to put off the caller. Whether the prescription is to say three "Hail Marys," to affirm five Christian fundamentals, or to take two aspirin, the principle is the same. We have missed the point of a personal God sending the person of Christ into a world of persons in need of personal salvation. The God who came to us in Christ did not offer mere words. Christ was and is the Word become flesh. In the gospel of Christ you cannot find mechanical prescriptions for salvation like, say, "I believe," and call on God the morning after death.

II. Persons have unique identities and needs. The apocryphal book, *Acts of Paul,* describes Paul as short, bald, and bow-legged-vigorous, with meeting eyebrows and a prominent nose. He was friendly, with the appearance of a man and occasional glimpses of an angel.

III. In Acts, Luke presents the story of Paul's conversion three times—the first as told by Luke and twice as told by Paul. In both instances of Paul's "witness," he speaks out of his life experience in his own defense before threatening situations, never as one who has the right system or formula. Paul gives testimony as an honest witness to what he actually experienced on the road to Damascus. He is a real person dominated by a vision of the Christ. The accounts of Paul's conversion are not carbon copies. They are real stories about a real experience told to real people.

IV. From misery to joy in one simple step is not to be found in Paul's story. Paul did not find Jesus; Jesus found Paul. He was serving God before and after, with one major difference. He had been confronted with a vision and called to a new life. Before Agrippa, Paul made the astounding commitment to follow the vision of Christ. All that he claimed was integrity.

He had been obedient to the vision. He was following the vision. He would always and forever follow the vision! What about you? Jesus called us to something greater than the Law. He gave us life. His simple invitation was never, "Take two . . . and call me later." It was, "Take up the cross and follow me." That is the best that we can do, and it is enough!— Larry Dipboye

SUNDAY, JANUARY 21, 2007
Lectionary Message

Topic: The Church, the Body of Christ
TEXT: 1 Cor. 12:12–31a
Other Readings: Neh. 8:1–3, 5–6, 8–10; Ps. 19; Luke 4:14–21

Even a cursory observation of the human body discloses three simple facts: (1) the body is one whole entity; (2) the body consists of very different parts, both in form and function, and (3) the bodily parts depend on one another to function properly. These facts reflect the glorious way in which God designed us, and when all three of these truths are realized, we are healthy and able to live normally.

The same three facts are true of the Church—the body of Christ—as indicated in today's text from 1 Corinthians 12. Paul uses the "body" metaphor to give instruction to the Church concerning how its members should view themselves and relate to one another. The passage is a continuation of the chapter begun last week, in which Paul listed several spiritual gifts. Extending that discussion in the passage before us, he describes how all of these spiritually gifted people relate to one another. His point is that a healthy, unified Church exists when its diverse members function interdependently.

I. *Unity in the Church exists in diversity* (vv. 12–14, 19–20). Being different and yet alike seems to be a contradiction. However, the body metaphor demonstrates that the two are not mutually exclusive ideas. Indeed, both are true. The word *one* is repeatedly used in verses 12 and 13 to refer to the oneness of the Church, based on a common salvation experience. Though we may come from differing ethnic and social backgrounds, Christians are united in our common experience of divine grace in salvation. This common ground provides a basis for life together as the Church.

At the same time, Paul repeatedly uses the word *many* (vv. 14, 19–20) to underscore the diversity of people within the Church. The diversity he has in mind, indicated in the prior context, concerns spiritual gifts, although it is also true that personalities in the Church differ and lend to its richness. Thus unity—a shared basis of being and common goals and purposes—fruitfully coexists with diversity of role and gift within the Church.

II. *Diversity in the Church necessitates interdependence* (vv. 15–24a). Because believers are gifted differently and no believer is omni-competent, interdependence is necessary. That is, in God's grand design for the Church, he has made it so that everyone has a significant place and role in which to serve, and we all need each other.

However, at times we may lose sight of that interdependence. One might, like the foot, believe that because he is not the hand, he is not a part of the body. Or another, like the ear, might believe that because she is not an eye, she is not a part of the body. The problem here is that some may feel that they are inferior to others in the Church, that their gifts are not as important as those of others. The fallacy of such thinking is that it is based in comparing ourselves to one another and assigning relative value based on roles (vv. 15–16). The result of such thinking, unchecked, is that one may quit serving in discontent, envious of the gifts and roles of others (vv. 15–16).

The solution to this dysfunction occurs when the one who feels inferior realizes that no one has all the gifts, that he or she is necessary to the wholesome operation of the Church (vv. 17, 19), that the gift and role that he or she holds is one of divine appointment, and that all service ranks the same with God. Indeed, to complain about one's gift is to despise God's sovereign and gracious actions (v. 18).

Another problem can arise with people who feel superior to others, based on their gifts and roles in the Church. These are those who, with an air of contempt, declare that they have no need of others (v. 21). As the eye might say to the hand or the head to the feet, these people say, "I have no need of you." The fallacy in this way of thinking is that it is based in human standards of evaluation, which tend to focus on the visible and the spectacular rather than value the humble and less obvious. The problem is that the less visible gifts "seem" to be weaker (v. 22), and the gifts that are more visible we "deem" to be more worthy of honor (v. 23).

The solution to this form of spiritual pride is that God has seen to it that the supposedly weaker parts are given elevated necessity (v. 22) and honor (v. 23). The persons with the more visible and attractive gifts do not need this extra care, but God sees to it that those who need it receive it.

III. *Interdependency in the Church produces unity* (vv. 24b–26). This idea brings us full circle, noting that the unity that God intends for the Church is achieved through his designed interdependency of its members. These verses stress that it is God's intentional activity that achieves these outcomes. He has so tempered the body together that mutual care results (v. 24b). In this kind of unity, schisms are eliminated and impartial concern is expressed. Believers share together both in the suffering and in the rejoicing of fellow members (vv. 25–26).

The passage concludes with a shift from the body metaphor to a listing of roles and gifts within the Church. The emphasis is placed on the diversity among these roles and gifts (vv. 28–31), implying that when they are exercised in love (chapter 13), the Church is well served.—Robert Vogel

ILLUSTRATIONS

INVISIBLE PARTS.   The interdependent function of the parts of the body and the necessity of all to enable others to thrive might be seen in analogy with a beautiful, graceful woman. Her beauty is striking, as it is visible in her facial features, skin tone and complexion, thick hair, and the like. These features may define her beauty, but a host of invisible organs are essential to the appearance one sees and admires. No one is going to be attracted by her liver; no one will compliment her kidneys; her thyroid will not win any beauty contests. Yet apart from the good health and normal function of these organs, her appearance will not be beautiful. The visible parts could never proclaim their independence of the less honored, less glorious parts. All must be in their rightful place, serving their God-intended purposes.—Robert Vogel

NEWS FLASHES.   *Dateline Leg.* In an unprecedented move today, the toes and metacarpal bones of the left foot went on strike at 8 A.M. When asked for an explanation, Bill Big Toe, leader of the United Phalanges Union, replied, "We're tired of being stuck down here in a sweaty shoe. It's about time management made some better arrangements." When asked what these might be, Big Toe said that the left foot wanted to trade places with the right hand. While the strike has not curtailed work seriously, the Body has had to trade its manual-shift car for one with an automatic transmission. Left Foot had the job of working the clutch.

Dateline Cranium. Hearing came to a screeching halt in the body at midnight last night, as both ears walked off the job. The resignations came, in the words of a union spokesman, because the ears were "tired of being assaulted with the ever-increasing noise level." Originally, the eyes had been expected to join in a sympathy strike. They failed to do so, they said, because "there are so many beautiful things in the world to see." When informed that the sympathy strike had failed to materialize, spokesmen for the ears replied, "If we had things as nice as the eyes, we wouldn't be quitting, either."

Dateline Stomach. The stomach has begun releasing excess gastric acid in an attempt to force the brain to acknowledge the importance of digestion. Representatives of the Society for Sounder Stomachs felt the protest would be successful because, "by affecting the brain we can make the whole body feel miserable." Negotiations are scheduled to begin sometime today.[3]

SERMON SUGGESTIONS

Topic: Do We Deserve Peace?

TEXT: Luke 19:41–42

(1) The Church is composed of many different people and ways of thinking. (2) One thing unites us: we all want peace. (3) But we're not sure how to get it. (4) Perhaps we don't deserve peace; war is the logical product of our unrighteousness. (5) We ask for, and need, radical conversion. Change us, Lord.—Walter J. Burghardt

Topic: Confidence for the Day of Judgment

TEXT: 1 John 4:17

(1) The Apostle's Creed says, "From thence he shall come to judge the living and the dead." (2) The good news is that we can have confidence for the day of judgment. (3) We stand confidant in our belief in Christ, our union with Christ, and our conformity to Christ.—John N. Gladstone

WORSHIP AIDS

CALL TO WORSHIP.   "Commit your ways to the Lord; trust in him, and he will act" (Ps. 37:5 NRSV).

INVOCATION.   Our Father of life and light, as we gather in your house to worship, make pure our hearts that we may know your presence. May we experience your nearness as your Word is proclaimed. Strengthen our resolve that we may choose the right paths of life. Lead us in the way of the gospel, which is known to us through your son Jesus Christ.

---

[3]Charles Pierson, "News Flashes from the Cadaver Chronicle," in *The Wittenburg Door*, n.d.

OFFERTORY SENTENCE.   "Be imitators of God . . . and live a life of love, just as Christ loved us and gave himself up for us as a fragrant offering and sacrifice to God" (Eph. 5:1–2 NIV).

OFFERTORY PRAYER.   Eternal God, we know that in your heart a contrite spirit is more acceptable than burnt offerings. Grant that the gifts we bring are the authentic demonstration of the dedication we give of ourselves—body, soul, and spirit—unto you, which is our reasonable service.

PRAYER.   Father, thank you for being our Good Shepherd. We thank you for leading us, loving us, even giving up your life so that we might be restored to an intimate everlasting fellowship with you, our Creator. You are our shepherd—our protector, our defender. Help us in the growth process of our spirituality. Increase our own appreciation of who you are, how you love all of humankind, not just us—or even those like us. Impress us so that, like you, we can love those who are very different from ourselves, those whose skin is a different color, those whose culture and even values are different from ours, those whose religious convictions are different from ours, and those whose economic level is far below or far above ours. Because you love all, we ask you to help the oppressed of the earth—the victims of hunger and racial discrimination and those whose individual freedoms are prohibited by political forces that initiate great injustice. Make us more sensitive to you and to one another—more conscious. Bring us to both humility and boldness. Shepherd us in our own spiritual pilgrimage. Give us the courage to be merciful, the endurance to be faithful to those in our care, just as you are with each of us. It is in the name of the one true and everlasting God, Father, Son, and Holy Spirit that we pray.—Larry Ellis

SERMON
Topic: Then Shall Light Break Forth
TEXT: Isa. 58:1–12

There is an old Hebrew tale where the rabbi asks his students: "How can we determine the hour of dawn, when the night ends and the day begins?" One student raised his hand: "When from a distance you can distinguish between a dog and a sheep?" The rabbi shook his head. "No." Another raised his hand: "It is when one person can distinguish between a fig tree and a grape vine?" "No," the rabbi said. "Tell us the answer," another student said. And the old wise teacher said: "When you look into the face of human beings and you have enough light [in you] to recognize them as your brothers and sisters." Isaiah gives his people (and us) three ways that we might better look into the faces of our brothers and sisters. And this is what God asks:

I. You recognize your brothers and sisters when you loose the bonds of injustice (58:6). And so he gives us this word—*justice*—a rare word, then and now. It was not used often then, nor is it now. It was used interchangeably in the Bible with the word *righteousness*. It is also a judicial word, meaning "fair." People are treated equitably. God was just—fair. He had a special regard for the poor, the weak, the underdog, and this was the policy demanded of God's people.

But we know better. If there is one word that characterizes our tortured history in race relations, it is *injustice*, inequity. We know that when you stand before the bar of justice (if that is what we want to call it), those with the highly paid lawyers don't serve as much time as those who have a public defender. Those with connections get their children off when they are arrested for drunk driving or possession of particular substances. We know that most of those in prisons on death row are from poor families, both black and white.

II. You recognize your brothers and sisters when you undo the cords of the yoke and let the oppressed go free (58:6). If the first word is *justice,* the second word is *freedom.* When Israel heard this word, it stirred memories. They thought of that exodus when their forebears had left the chain of Egypt and crossed the sea on dry land to freedom—*freedom*—wondrous word: freedom from fate, from blind, impersonal, powers. Freedom from "this is the way it is." Freedom from "this is the way the world works." Freedom from sin. Liberated from the power that cripples. There is a freedom from evil powers. Paul calls them powers and principalities. There were also the powers of death.

That freedom also touched a people who loved the law. Then and now there was and is a religious law that bound them and us down. Where did we forget those words from the freedom book, Galatians: "There is no longer Jew nor Greek, there is no longer slave nor free, there is no longer male nor female; for all of you are one in Christ Jesus. And if you belong to Christ, then you are Abraham's offspring, heirs according to the promise" (Gal. 3:28–29).

III. You recognize your brothers and sisters when you share your bread with the hungry, you bring the homeless poor into the house, when you see the naked and cover them, and you do not hide yourself from your own kin (58:7). The light comes to the compassionate. Isaiah says it not once, but twice. If you let your finger move on down the page, not only does he talk about compassion in this seventh verse, but he returns to this theme in the latter part of the ninth verse: "If you remove the yoke from among you, the pointing of the finger, the speaking of evil, if you offer your food to the hungry and satisfy the needs of the afflicted, then your light shall rise in the darkness and your gloom be like the noonday" (58:9b–10).

The heart of our faith is compassion, where pity is always somewhere passing by. In the last parable he ever gave, they asked him: "When did we see you hungry, naked, sick, thirsty, in prison . . . ?" And remember what he said to them: "Inasmuch as you did it unto the least of these, you did it unto me." Compassion.

Maybe Isaiah was right after all. Your light shall break forth like the dawn, and your healing shall spring up quickly when you loose the bonds of injustice, when you let the oppressed go free, when you share your bread with the hungry and bring the homeless poor into your house.—Roger Lovette

SUNDAY, JANUARY 28, 2007
Lectionary Message
Topic: Encountering the Holiness of God—A Defining Moment
TEXT: Isa. 6:1–8 (9–13)
Other Readings: Ps. 138; 1 Cor. 15:1–11; Luke 5:1–11

Along the time line of life, we have defining moments. These are those times when, contrary to the blur of routines, something out of the ordinary occurs. These extraordinary events, often involving decisions we make, change the course of our lives. Defining moments occur on graduation day, on the day of one's wedding, or at the birth of a child.

Just as our earthly lives have defining moments, so also do our spiritual lives. These are the times in which God moves in unmistakable ways, and we are not the same thereafter. Spiritually defining moments include the day of one's conversion, an answer to prayer, or a particular experience of God's providence.

The prophet Isaiah experienced a defining moment that was truly unique. It involved a vision of the majestic holiness of God and culminated in his call to ministerial service. It was a moment in which he caught a glimpse of the sovereign Lord, worshiped, confronted his own sinfulness, and surrendered himself to unqualified service of God. At the heart of Isaiah's vision is the majesty of God and its impact on a true worshiper.

I. *When we understand the holiness of God, we recognize his sovereign majesty* (vv. 1–4). Isaiah confesses that in the year of King Uzziah's death, he saw the Lord in his majestic glory. Undoubtedly, this was a veiled display, for no human can survive an unrestrained manifestation of divine presence. Moses had been granted a similar experience, but he was permitted only a glimpse of the glory of God as he passed by (Exod. 33:18–20, 34:5, 6). The apostle John testifies that in Jesus the glory of God was put on display, but that glory was veiled in human flesh (John 1:14). Here, Isaiah is granted a glimpse into the heavenly throne room—a place filled with the majesty of God. Virtually every descriptive detail in verses 1 through 4 accents the sovereign majesty of God. He is identified as "the Lord" (*adonai*), meaning almighty, sovereign ruler. He is seated on a throne—a natural posture and place for a king. He is high and lifted up, with elevation symbolizing higher standing and authority over those around him. He is surrounded by the seraphim, attending to his every wish. They cover their faces, for they dare not gaze upon his glory. They cover their feet as an indicator of humility before him. They fly to render service as he requires. The multiplied ranks of creatures establish a powerful energy in his presence, and a passion arises in the continuous declaration of his supreme, majestic holiness.

Theologian Augustus H. Strong identified holiness as God's most fundamental attribute. Its fundamental essence is separateness. It means that God is "other than." As is evident here, he is separate from all his creation, transcendent and exalted above the common. It is in this sense that his majesty is seen. He is also holy in the ethical sense, meaning that he is separate from sin and impurity. Both aspects coalesce here.

It is the design of all his work that God's holiness be universally manifest. Indeed, the heavenly scene reveals that his holiness is manifest in the heavens. But the seraphim declare that the whole earth is full of his glory also.

II. *When we understand the holiness of God, we develop a proper sense of our own place* (vv. 5–7). Upon viewing the glorious scene described in the previous verses, at this point in the text Isaiah becomes aware of his own unworthiness. Passionately, he laments his sinfulness and that of his people. This is surely the natural reaction, when the standard of comparison is with the infinitely holy One. When we compare ourselves with others, we may feel righteous or vindicated. But such self-congratulation cannot stand in the presence of the holy God. Rather, Isaiah is left only to acknowledge his place before God as one unclean, defiled, and unworthy of God.

Yet at this point, the grace of God is powerfully demonstrated, as he extends mercy to the person of contrite heart. He dispatches one of the seraphim to take a coal and touch the unclean lips of the prophet—a symbolic act demonstrating that his guilt could be taken away. The term used to describe the transaction is *atonement,* reminding us that in the fullness of time Jesus atoned for sin once and for all, so that our guilt might be removed and so we might be declared righteous before God (2 Cor. 5:21).

III. *When we understand the holiness of God, we offer ourselves in willing and obedient service* (v. 8). Impressed and humbled by divine majesty and forgiven by divine grace, the prophet is now motivated for divine service. Rhetorically, God asks from his glorious throne, "Whom shall we send? And who will go for us?" The question does not presuppose some great lack on God's part. Clearly, he is fully adequate in himself. Yet in his grace, he extends the opportunity to mere mortals to engage in his service. Hearing the "offer by question," Isaiah quickly and eagerly responds, "Here am I; send me." There is no reluctance, no negotiation, no protest concerning the difficulty, no questions asked. He presents himself as fully available to serve God in carrying out his purposes on this earth.

When we see God in his infinite, sovereign holiness, and when we see ourselves in the humility of our fallen state, when we experience the touch of God's forgiveness and grace, we will serve him readily. We will know a spiritually defining moment.—Robert Vogel

ILLUSTRATION

GOD'S CHARACTER.   A. W. Tozer stresses the importance of understanding the character of God as a practical matter. In the preface to *The Knowledge of the Holy* he writes,

> The message of this book does not grow out of these times, but is appropriate to them. It is called forth by a condition which has existed in the Church for some years and is steadily growing worse. I refer to the loss of the concept of majesty from the popular religious mind. The Church has surrendered her once lofty concept of God and has substituted for it one so low, so ignoble, as to be utterly unworthy of thinking, worshiping men. . . . The low view of God entertained almost universally among Christians is the cause of a hundred lesser evils everywhere among us.[4]

Further, he writes,

> A right conception of God is basic not only to systematic theology but to practical Christian living as well. It is to worship what the foundation is to the temple; where it is inadequate or out of plumb the whole structure must sooner or later collapse. I believe there is scarcely an error in doctrine or a failure in applying Christian ethics that cannot be traced finally to imperfect and ignoble thoughts about God.[5]

The magnitude of God's holiness is emphasized by the continuous declaration of it by the seraphim. Without ceasing they exclaim, "holy, holy, holy . . ." Some repeated messages quickly become tiresome. I recall waiting to be picked up outside the baggage claim area at an airport recently. Every few seconds, a message came over the loudspeaker system: "Parking is for active loading and unloading of passengers only. Violators will be cited and towed." Over and over again this message was repeated—the same voice, same intonation and inflection, same dull reminder. This message quickly became not only tiresome but a bit irritating.

---

[4]A. W. Tozer, *The Knowledge of the Holy* (San Francisco: HarperSanFrancisco, 1961), p. vii.
[5]Tozer, p. 2.

But the continuous proclamation of the holiness of God will never grow tiresome and irritating! Rather, it serves as an expression of timeless praise and authentic worship.—Robert Vogel

SERMON SUGGESTIONS

Topic: Prayer: Human and Divine

TEXT: Rom. 8:26–27

(1) The *human problem:* in our weakness, we cannot pray as God intends. (2) The *divine provision:* the Spirit intercedes with inexpressible groaning. (3) The *ultimate purpose:* God searches our hearts to discern the intention of the Spirit's intercession.—William E. Hull

Topic: Something of Value

TEXT: Luke 12:6–7

(1) Like sparrows, we feel small in a large and threatening world. (2) We feel helpless before the strong winds of life. (3) We seem so common. (4) Yet God has made us with incomparable worth.—James Earl Massey

WORSHIP AIDS

CALL TO WORSHIP.   "Hear my voice when I call, O Lord; be merciful to me and answer me. My heart says of you, 'Seek his face!' Your face, O Lord, I will seek" (Ps. 27:7–8 NIV).

INVOCATION.   Grant, our Father, that in worship today those who have grown weary of life will find hope, those confused will find clarity, those bitter will discover happiness, those who live in peril will find safety, the lonely will find friendship, and those who have lost life's meaning will find holiness again. All for the cause of Jesus Christ.

OFFERTORY SENTENCE.   "He who supplies seed to the sower and bread for food will supply and increase the harvest of your righteousness" (2 Cor. 9:10 RSV).

OFFERTORY PRAYER.   Heavenly Father, may your Kingdom be uppermost in our heart, minds, and lives. Accept our gifts, given in love and devotion, and with them our renewed dedication of all that we are and have to your eternal glory.

PRAYER.   Creator God, on windswept beaches your saints of old held their hands up to you in wonder and amazement, felt your power through the roar of wind and surf, and exposed to the elements felt a unity with the One who had created all things. This world does not often allow us such intimacy, Father. We are crowded out by circumstances of our own choosing, seeking fellowship with each other rather than with you. Forgive our unwillingness to follow in the footsteps of your saints to meet you in the solitude of your creation. Forgive our unwillingness to get our feet wet.—John Birch

SERMON

Topic: Look for the Blessing

TEXT: Ps. 118:24

A tried and tested spiritual exercise practiced by many Christians is to begin each new day with a repetition of the psalmist's words, *"This is the day that the Lord has made; let us rejoice and be glad in it."* Regardless of the weather or the circumstances of the world or any other condition, the discipline of repeating that refrain gives energy and optimism to those who say it.

I. If we speak those words as our first waking thought, we give ourselves a framework in which to place all of the day's activities and events. We create order out of the jumble of experiences that come our way. We reverse the question that sometimes confronts us—the question about "What am I going to do about this so that it will become a creative instead of a disabling experience?" Repeating that psalm verse enables us to look for the blessing that abides beneath the rush and tumble of outward circumstance.

I cannot repeat that verse, however, without being aware of its inclusive emphasis. Notice that the psalmist says, "Let *us* rejoice and be glad" in the day that God has given. Saying "us" instead of "me" suggests two things. First, God bestows blessings freely and widely. Jesus made this point by his comment that God makes the sun rise "on the evil and on the good, and sends rain on the righteous and on the unrighteousness."

"Let us rejoice," said the psalmist, enlarging the arena of perception, not limiting it to just my vision or just yours.

The second implication of this plural pronoun is that we can be a blessing ourselves. Not only are we to assist one another in recognizing the gifts of God in each new day, but we can offer ourselves to the people around us, giving gifts of friendship and caring, encouragement and help. We have the privilege of helping others to rejoice and be glad, sharing these important feelings beyond ourselves.

II. At day's beginning, the Bible verse that I hope we have committed to memory becomes our guide. One translation of it says, "This is the day of the Lord's victory; let us be happy, let us celebrate!" Once more there is that emphasis on God's jurisdiction over each day, followed by each believer's enthusiastic response. We are to claim God's gifts; moreover, we are to point others to them, and we are to share them widely. Finally, at day's end, it becomes us to review those blessings. Having looked for blessings and found them, we then can appreciate their power to displace hurt and negativity and any other demoralizing thing. It becomes evident to us that God's grace is more than sufficient. God's provision for our need is more than we can ask or think.

I offer as a new imperative for life this simple counsel: Look for the blessings. Such blessing will be discovered when each and every day is received from God as a product of divine handiwork—a gift worthy of glad acceptance. Look for the blessings. Look for the wonderful surprises.—John H. Townsend

SUNDAY, FEBRUARY 4, 2007
Lectionary Message

Topic: Are You on a Spiritual Quest?

TEXT: Luke 6:17–26

Other Readings: Jer. 17:5–10; Ps. 1; 1 Cor. 15:12–20

Are you on a spiritual quest? Have you set out looking for "The Transcendent"? Do you consider yourself on a religious pilgrimage? I ask the question this morning, not only because I know scores of people who wander in and out of this church week after week seeking, searching, groping, exploring what we might call the spiritual realm but because Luke presents us with a destination for this spiritual quest of ours. Luke knows our questing condition. He brings to life what we seek in the Christian quest. He illustrates the nature of our destination. He depicts the destiny of our quest as followers of Jesus Christ. And do you know what he calls the goal, indeed, the final gift of our quest? Luke calls it "blessedness"!

Blessedness? Is that what you're looking for when you come here to worship? You probably don't call it that. But what Luke drives at here we might more easily call "joy." Let's put it that way: "We're on a quest for joy." And where and under what circumstances do we discover this joy? How do we gain the joy Luke promises? He paints us a vivid picture. These beatitudes Luke offers us illustrate—*illustrate!*—what life is like when we surrender our lives to the just and loving Christ and gain citizenship in his living, dynamic realm. These beatitudes are not a new set of rules. No way! They are not the basis for a new ethic! Hardly. They *illustrate,* they *demonstrate,* they *portray* the joy we discover through turning our lives over to the building of the kind of world God intends for us.

I. For instance, "Blessed are you poor for yours is the kingdom of God." Let's paraphrase: The joy of life with Christ is given over to those who are poor. Can those of us educated, relatively affluent, absurdly fortunate American Christians hear that? What's Luke saying? Is he saying we've got to be poverty-stricken before we can follow Jesus? I don't think so. Is he romanticizing poverty and placing divine approval on it? God forbid! I think Luke tells us that a sense of being truly blessed in life—gaining deep joy—is granted those who empty their lives of everything but a passion for a new way of relating to one another, based not on money or power or hierarchies but on outgoing mutuality and service to one another. He's telling us that to bet our lives on our credentials, our incomes, our addresses, our jobs, our reputations, our families, our bloodlines—whatever—is to bet on junk that changes, that crumbles, and in God's good time goes right down the drain.

He's saying, as that radical Christian Dietrich Bonhoeffer said some seventy years ago in the face of the Nazi onslaught, "The true joy of the Christian life belongs to the poor who have no security, no possessions to call their own, not even a foot of earth to call their home, no earthly society can claim their allegiance."[1] They are without ambition except they build the human race into the human family. They are without pride except they witness to the victories of kindness. They let go of riches except they throw themselves into the riches of service. In a world where one person suggested that most of us are simply questing to survive or get ahead, the poverty Luke describes bears a joy invulnerable to the cynicism and despair we experience at the collapse of those things we usually trust to get us through—the very dependencies now messing up our lives. By our loyalty to the realm of God, through our citizenship in God's dominion we find ourselves in poverty released to a new kind of wealth, to the blessedness—the joy—we truly seek.

II. Or again, take that little phrase, "Blessed are you who weep now, for you shall laugh." What weird paradox does that signal? Does it only go to prove Robert Ingersoll's curt observation, "No one with any sense of humor ever founded a religion"? Does it confirm Heywood Hale Broun's cheap shot: "The pursuit of happiness belongs to all of us, but we must climb around or over the church to get it"?

---

[1]Dietrich Bonhoeffer, *The Cost of Discipleship* (New York: MacMillan, 1963), p. 120.

No way! Luke does not command us to morbidity or gloom—no sad-sack Christians here. He says that those of us who loyally choose to follow Christ cannot help but weep for a humanity suffering from greed, injustice, and self-seeking. He says disciples will be broken-hearted by the cruelties people mete out to one another; he confirms that by knowing what God wants for us in our care and treatment for one another, we will be inconsolable over the ways we *do* treat one another.

III. And what we weep for is tied closely to what we hunger for. And what is that? What in this Lukan spiritual quest will satisfy us? I believe Luke tells us we will be satisfied only as we hunger for the Kingdom, the dominion, the realm of God, and that realm we want to see evident in God's world. In short, in God's domain we are "starved" and joyless unless we break down the racial barriers rending the cities and towns of our land. We hunger to bring integrity and compassion to local government or hound our congresspersons to bring sanity to the merchandising of arms, fairness to the poor and, for heaven's sake, cease the malicious stigmatization of gay people, affirming their full humanity and claim on the grace of Christ. In God's Kingdom we hunger for every child to be cared for, every mind to be educated, our aged to be somewhere other than on the scrap heap. Living in God's realm we hunger for the money squandered on self-indulgence to be redirected to convey food to the starving, medicine to the sick, shelter for the homeless; we hunger for a world ruled not by greed but by goodness, not by selfishness but by sharing, not by power grabs but by service. There lies the reality of a community rooted and grounded in the love of Christ. A spiritual quest seeking that domain, in the face of whatever resistance, cynicism, or contempt we encounter, provides the source of a lasting and radiant joy. Some wise observer summed it all up: "Jesus promises his disciples three things: they will be completely fearless, absurdly happy, and in constant trouble." Now that is one fabulous spiritual quest.

Just one final image: during the reign of that great "small r" republican and "large C" Congregationalist Oliver Cromwell in seventeenth-century England, the government began to run low on silver coins. Cromwell sent his troops to investigate a local cathedral to see if they could find any of the precious metal there. They made their investigation, returned to the great man, and reported: "The only silver we can find is in the statues of the saints standing in the corners." To which the Lord Protector replied, "Good! We'll melt down the saints and put them in circulation." That's us, folks. And if we're on a spiritual quest, blessed are we if we end up as saints in circulation.—James W. Crawford

SERMON SUGGESTIONS

Topic: The Vanity of Earthly Wisdom

TEXT: Eccles. 1:1–21

(1) Earthly wisdom is emptiness. (2) Earthly wisdom has seeming advantages. (3) Earthly wisdom is overwhelmed by the glory of the Lord.—Lawrence Vowan

Topic: Give Them to Eat

TEXT: Luke 9:12–17

(1) Jesus respected and fed the whole multitude. (2) The earth produces enough for all our need but not enough for all our greed. (3) Christians are concerned about unequal distribution of food. (4) The feeding of the five thousand shows us a new world of caring and sharing.—K. H. Ting

WORSHIP AIDS

CALL TO WORSHIP.   "Great is the Lord and most worthy of praise; his greatness no one can fathom. One generation will commend your works to another; they will tell of your mighty acts" (Ps. 145:3–4 NIV).

INVOCATION.   Kind, divine, Heavenly Father, to you who by love has created us, through love has kept us, and in love will perfect us, we confess that we have not loved you with all our hearts, minds, souls, and strengths, nor do we love one another as Christ has loved us. Grant that in this hour our confession will draw us to a new experience of your grace.

OFFERTORY SENTENCE.   "And they came, everyone whose heart stirred him up, and everyone whom his spirit made willing, and they brought the Lord's offering to the work of the tabernacle of the congregation, and for all his service" (Exod. 35:21).

OFFERTORY PRAYER.   Lord, stir within us the holy claims of your divine will. Give us a passion for your Kingdom that our gifts may truly reflect your love within us. May these gifts be multiplied for the cause of the gospel.

PRAYER.   Our gracious and loving Heavenly Father, we come to you today in the name of Jesus. We come reverently, but we also come confidently. We come with full assurance of faith. Lord, we know that you're here with us as we meet together. But you're with us not only when we meet. You're with us out there in our everyday world. And we do need you. We need your mercy and grace. We don't ask for what we deserve; we ask for your mercy and grace. When we look around us at our world, we are often troubled and concerned. Please, Lord, bring an end to the violence and death and suffering, and may there be peace and safety. We pray for the military forces that are continually in danger. May they call on you for divine help. There are so many places around the world where there is no freedom, especially freedom of worship. We pray for your Kingdom to come and your will to be done on earth as it is in heaven.

We need you, too, right here at home. Here in our own church family we have all kinds of needs. Many are facing serious physical problems, and they need your healing touch. Lord, for each of us, look down inside and see there the hurts and feelings, the discouragements and frustrations, and all the ways we need you. Meet each of us at the very point of our need today. As our pastor comes to speak, we pray for your divine anointing on him and on us as we listen. May this day bring glory and honor to the name of Jesus, in whose name we pray.—Paul Meeks

SERMON
Topic: Building Character or Characters?
TEXT: Rom. 8:1–11

Building character is the proper work of the Church and the basic responsibility of the home. Creating characters is the craft of novelists and actors. To produce characters who stand apart from the crowd falls short of the basic responsibility of building character. Character is a quality of personhood that drives us to measure up to the image of God. Without using the word,

Paul is addressing the cause of Christian character in his description of the work of the Spirit in the Christian life. The presence of the Spirit in the life of the Christian is like an inner gyroscope, keeping the perspective straight on what is good. Unlike the law, the Spirit is about freedom, life, and personal responsibility.

I. Christian character reaches deeper than law. Character is the stuff of which values are formed. Moral education, learning rules of right and wrong, is where we all begin, but the rules are always superficial. Laws reflect principles and values, but laws do not replace the moral character responsible for ethical decisions. Most laws preempt decisions, leaving us with only two choices—obedience or defiance. Good laws do not make good people. Good laws are often ignored or defied. Good laws are not always upheld. The law is no substitute for Christian character—the response of a good conscience toward God.

II. Christians are constructed from the inside out. Baptism does not make us good. Baptism is an outward sign of an inward condition. We do not build Christians on the surface of life, yet much of our conversation about values treats persons like machines. Paul found a dynamic of life greater than law. The life of faith in Christ develops character. The dynamic of living in Christ brings to the surface and restores to health the image of God in which we have been created.

III. Character is formed through the development of virtues and habits and the sharing of the Christian vision. Not only the rules concerning behavior but the principles by which decisions are made grow out of living among the people of God. The Church is here to do more than "tell it like it is." Here we look beyond to the way things ought to be. We do not worship to become better people, but worship does something to us to make us better people.—Larry Dipboye

SUNDAY, FEBRUARY 11, 2007
Lectionary Message
Topic: Can We Break Free of Old Patterns and Habits?
Text: Luke 6:27–38
Other Readings: Gen. 45:3–11, 15; Ps. 37:1–11, 39–40; 1 Cor. 15:35–38, 42–50

Have you ever heard Haydn's "Lord Nelson Mass"? You would find it a brilliant, thrilling work. I heard it in concert not long ago and learned it has nothing to do with Lord Nelson! We can find any number of coincidences connecting the Mass to Lord Nelson: the crushing of Napoleon's navy in the Battle of the Nile on August 1, 1798, or the Admiral's presence at a performance of the Mass in Haydn's hometown in 1800, or the destruction of the Danish fleet in 1801, or Trafalgar and the securing of hegemony over the seas by the British fleet in 1805. A brilliant Mass, sung in church with a warrior's name attached to it (yes, in church!), but a warrior nonetheless, who wreaked havoc on the navies of the French and Spanish and whose name became synonymous with Britain's ruling the waves.

Question: Are the Nelson types really the heroes of that or any other time? Is the clash of arms, the meting of vengeance, the necessity to retaliate, to even the score, to punish your antagonist, to meet violence with violence, terror with terror—is that noble, celebrative, honorable? Perhaps. We witness that approach to human affairs working itself out among us all the time. Talk with a Serb, a Bosnian, a Rwandan, a Palestinian, an Israeli. Brood about it with those who talk jihad, and in this day-and-age fly planes into skyscrapers, blow up subway trains, tie bombs to their waists, or lay bombs by the roadside to destroy those they call the "enemy."

Early in what one observer has called our contemporary "clash of civilizations," a fresh perspective was offered to us by President George W. Bush. As he witnessed the conflagration in the Middle East, he said this: "Conflict is not inevitable. Distrust need not be permanent. *Peace is possible when we break free of old patterns and habits of hatred. . . .*"

George W. Bush was right! He was biblical. Whoever wrote that sentence for him stole it right out of the Gospel of Luke. The sentence paraphrases, in a declarative sentence, what Jesus so brilliantly illustrated in his references to vengeance and retaliation. Remember? "Love your enemies, do good to those who hate you, bless those who curse you, pray for those who abuse you. If anyone strikes you on the cheek, offer the other also; and from anyone who takes away your coat, do not withhold even your shirt."

What is this? Cowardice? A Milquetoast pacifism inviting some brutal aggressor to run over us with hobnailed boots? Is it surrender of self-respect, appeasement, guaranteeing we get wiped out along with our neighbor, the city, the nation? Weakness? Wimpishness? Impotence?

Well, with mortars and missiles flying, cities in ruins, the gravestone business booming, the pounding of chests, and with the bloody "blame game" flourishing in Jerusalem, Gaza, Baghdad, London, New York, Madrid, Kabul, and Washington, these visions of our Lord appear to be absolutely absurd and laughingly ludicrous in a world where day-by-day Ground Zero seems demonically extended. Could it be that by retaliating with F-16s and smart bombs, with missiles and spy-craft, the initiators of such conflict already smell victory? Their violent agenda becomes the order of the day!

But what if there is an alternative? What if, figuratively speaking, loving your enemy, turning the other cheek, giving away your wardrobe sends a different message—a message like this: "You may choose violence to secure your objective, but your way ultimately ends in violence. Your way must stop. It shall stop because I have chosen another way."

"It is action," wrote Rowan Williams, then the Archbishop of Wales, now of Canterbury, who found himself at Trinity Church, Wall Street, on September 11, 2001, caught in its ghastliness and chaos:

> It is action that changes the terms of the relation, or at the very least says to the perpetrator that the world might be otherwise. It requires courage and imagination; it is essentially the decision not to be passive, not to be a victim, but equally not to avoid passivity by simply reproducing what has been done to you.[2]

It exercises the power to reset the agenda, to recast the vocabulary, to redefine the means to the end, to reclaim the initiative, to reassert the dignity of adversaries, to search for alternatives—yes, probably higher ground. That is what lies behind this stunning illustration of ethical behavior offered by our Lord.

And it not only changes the terms of engagement, as Rowan Williams so properly observes, but insisting on such action implies that the world might be different. Our Lord

---

[2]Rowan Williams, *Writing in the Dust* (Grand Rapids, MI: Eerdmans, 2002), p. 25.

opens a world where violence dissolves and is no more. It boggles the mind! Do you harbor an inclination to purchase a firearm for protection? Do you carry Mace in your purse? How many deadbolts, chains, safety locks, door buzzers; how many alarm systems, police emergency numbers, cell phones for safety, or security guards do you pay for or find yourself encountering on a daily basis? In Luke's vision, that junk disappears. Lawyers set out to destroy defendants; judges send convicts to San Quentin; lawsuits are filed for reparations; there are divorce court mediators, standing armies, suicide bombers, plowed-up olive groves, bulldozed houses, bloody subway-train explosions—*no more!* And better yet, guess what! Preachers and church meetings are swept away. Resistance and vengeance, violence and retaliation—these become irrelevant; no one finds them necessary. Indeed, the turning of the cheek, the handing over of not only your coat but your shirt will no longer be ethically necessary, because from the get-go, in love's dominion, human relationships are grounded in mutuality and solidarity, friendship and hope. There is no initial slap on the cheek, no claim for your coat. The world, as Luke describes it, has made a U-turn envisioned in that offering of the other cheek, the giving of your cloak *and your shirt!*

O friends, so-called "fair play" is out the window. Tit-for-tat: you do this, I do that. "An eye for an eye, a tooth for a tooth," as Tevya says in *Fiddler on the Roof,* "makes for a blind and toothless world." Such behavioral quid pro quos—gone! We live now from the profound conviction, rooted in the divine love at the heart of the universe, that when evil is done to us, somehow good may be wrought in response, that we can "forge a blessing even for those who do us violence." As President Bush said, "We break free of old patterns and habits." Surely, a modern miracle!

And yes—what of that brilliant church oratorio, "The Lord Nelson Mass?" Lord Nelson—that noble admiral, that consummate warrior. Do you know what Haydn originally named this Mass? Not "The Lord Nelson." He called it *"Missa in angustiis"* (Mass in time of tribulation). Thank you, Franz Joseph. In these troubled times we can listen and feel you wrote it just for us.—James W. Crawford

SERMON SUGGESTIONS

Topic: No Faith, No Church

TEXT: Mark 9:24

(1) Faith is always mixed with doubt. (2) Faith is always tied to life. (3) Faith's chief resource is Jesus.—Ernest T. Campbell

Topic: How Can Evil Be Cast Out?

TEXT: Matt. 17:19

(1) Human power alone can never cast out evil. (2) Neither will God alone make such a drastic reversal. (3) Yet the perfected union of God and human life together can drive out the deadly cancer of sin.—Martin Luther King Jr.

WORSHIP AIDS

CALL TO WORSHIP.   "Praise be to the God and Father of our Lord Jesus Christ. . . . In him we have redemption through his blood, the forgiveness of sins, in accordance with the riches of God's grace" (Eph. 1:3, 7 NIV).

INVOCATION.   God of eternal mercy, here in this place and in this hour have mercy on us. God of light, shine into our hearts. God of goodness, deliver us from evil. God of power, be our strength. God of love, let your love flow through us. God of life, live within us, now and forever.

OFFERTORY SENTENCE.   "Prepare ye the way of the Lord, make straight in the desert a highway for our God" (Isa. 40:3).

OFFERTORY PRAYER.   O Lord, accept these offerings your people bring to you and grant that the cause to which they are devoted will prosper under your guidance—to the glory of your holy name.

PRAYER.   Look upon us, O Lord, and let all the darkness of our souls vanish before the beams of thy brightness. Fill us with holy love, and open to us the treasures of thy wisdom. All our desire is known unto thee, therefore perfect what thou hast begun and what thy Spirit has awakened us to ask in prayer. We seek thy face; turn thy face unto us and show us thy glory. Then shall our longing be satisfied, and our peace shall be perfect.—St. Augustine

SERMON
Topic: The Marks of a Servant
TEXT: 1 Cor. 4

What does a Christian look like? Paul gives a simple answer to the question in the fourth chapter of his first letter to the church at Corinth, when he declares, "This is how one should regard us, as servants of Christ and stewards of the mysteries of God." The word translated "servant" was originally designated an underclass of seaman—one who was responsible to a higher-ranking officer. The word *steward* literally means "house-manager." There is no greater privilege today for the Christian than to be known and remembered as a servant of Jesus Christ. But what does that mean?

I. The first mark of a servant is faithfulness. Paul says in verse 2, "It is required of a steward that he be found faithful." Anybody can be religious for a while. What really matters is that we maintain a faithfulness to Christ so that when he comes, he will find us busy doing his work.

This note needs to be sounded again today, for few problems plague our churches like faithlessness or lack of persistence. Our churches are filled with "here-today-and-gone-tomorrow" members—those hypodermic heroes who were temporarily on fire for the Lord but whose faith has fizzled, those flash-in-the-pan young people who get a spiritual high at camp or at a retreat but whose dedication soon vanishes like the morning dew, those seasonal saints who could win Churchman of the Year awards one year but who the next year are nowhere to be found. We should be so determined to fight the good fight and finish the course and keep the faith that they have to shoot us to stop us. The distinguishing mark of a servant is faithfulness.

II. A second mark of the servant is accountability. This is the message of verses 3–5. In verse 3 he says that he is not concerned about his accountability toward human courts, that is, how others judge him. In verse 4 he says that he is not concerned about the result of his own self-examination, that is, what he thinks about himself. The accountability about which he was most concerned is expressed in the last phrase of verse 4, where Paul says, "The one who examines me is the Lord." A servant is one who knows that he is under the watchful eye of his master and that he must someday give an account of his actions.

III. A third mark of the servant is humility. Paul talks in verses 6 and 7 about those individuals who boasted of what they had and what they had accomplished—those Corinthian Christians who were suffering from what one man has called "obesity of the head." Pride is often a problem for the Christian today. But look at the penetrating question Paul asks in verse 7: "What do we have that has not been given to us?" Our lives, God creates; our time, God controls; our talents, God gives; our sin, God forgives; our victories, God wins; our future, God ensures. To the question, "What do we have that has not been given?" the answer must be a resounding, "Nothing!" Every good and perfect gift comes from God.

A servant is not one who thinks he is nothing. A servant is one who knows he is somebody but who realizes that he is somebody because of Jesus Christ. A servant is one who keeps a clear perspective on the sources of his life. Humility!

IV. A fourth mark of the servant is the willingness to sacrifice. In verses 11 through 13, Paul talks about all that he has suffered for Christ's sake. He is proclaiming a truth about the Christian life. He is reminding the Corinthian Christians what the Christian life means. For Paul, sacrifice meant being hungry and thirsty, being ill-clad and buffeted and homeless, being reviled and persecuted and slandered. For us, sacrifice might mean something altogether different. But the message that Paul is proclaiming here is one that weaves its way through the entire New Testament: it costs something to be a follower of Jesus Christ.

Faithfulness to the task, accountability before God, a true spirit of humility, a willingness to sacrifice for Christ—if those marks are in our lives, then we too can become known as servants of Christ, stewards of the mysteries of God. And there is no greater privilege for the Christian than that.—Brian L. Harbour

SUNDAY, FEBRUARY 18, 2007
Lectionary Message
Topic: The Victory Is Ours! Thank God!
TEXT: 1 Cor. 15:51–58
Other Readings: Isa. 55:10–13; Ps. 92:1–4, 12–15; Luke 6:39–49

Paul confronts a radically skeptical congregation. They question his integrity. They mock his faith. They wonder if he can really call himself an apostle. And amid all this skepticism, they, of course, radically doubt Paul's message. To put it bluntly, they assert, "Dead men don't rise. Dead women don't rise—Jesus, maybe, but nobody else. We either rot in our graves, or our souls leave our bodies and go merge with the universal oversoul. But dead people don't rise!"

That stance by his beloved Corinthian church threatens and infuriates Paul. He loves that congregation. He sees in their radical doubt the church's collapse and dissolution. And he's right. "Dead people don't rise?" he asks. "If that's true, then Jesus is not raised. And if Jesus is not raised, then everything we do and stand for hinges on smoke and mirrors."

Do you see what Paul tells us? If Christ is not raised, our faith rests on the decomposing corpse of a Galilean carpenter. If Christ is not raised we meet here every Sunday morning to simply tell lies about God; we're trapped in a world where hostility, war, decay, and death really do have the last word, and the courage and suffering of generations to make this a better world proves a sick joke. If Christ is not raised, the death of a loved one means obliteration. If we share any hope at all, it consists of a pusillanimous optimism, making us, as Paul says, "the most pitiable of human beings" in the face of the stark realities of life and death.

I. "But," Paul writes (one of the so-called "great Buts" of the Christian faith), "God has raised Christ from the dead." Did you hear that? Paul does not say, "Jesus rose." Paul says, "God raised Jesus from the dead." Let's be clear. Paul does not affirm what my grandfather in one of his skeptical moments, called the flying up to the sky out of the grave, "body, boots, and britches." Not on your life. By asserting that "God raised Christ from the dead," Paul affirms the power of God triumphant over all those things threatening to subvert, destroy, and deny human life, the most vivid of these life-denying, love-threatening, hope-subverting forces being death itself. Paul sees death not simply as a biological incident in Nature's incessant course, though he recognizes that as a fact. But more. Paul sees death as a metaphor signifying the radical overthrow of God's creation itself—a dark and oppressive blanket yielding moral chaos and futility. But through the Resurrection of Christ, death and all the other powers intent on diminishing human life fail to have the last word. God does not give up on us. God does not abandon his creation. God sets to work refashioning it. That's our faith and our hope.

II. "OK," say those recalcitrant Corinthians. "We'll buy your assertions about God's refashioning power, but if God's power really raises the dead, in what body does God raise them? Has God got a bunch of resuscitated corpses on her hands?"

Some years ago Diane Keaton starred in a film titled *Heaven*, which included questions cut from Corinthians' cloth. Questions like these: How old are you in heaven? Do you stay the same age as when you died, or can you just pick any age—say, twenty-three—and stay that way throughout eternity? Who will you see? Can you just walk over if you feel like it and chat with Ann Boleyn or Babe Ruth or Groucho Marx? And what if you meet your fourth-grade Sunday school teacher, and you had an easier time getting in than she did? Will she be embarrassed? Or as a hip young woman these days might ask, "What'll I wear? Am I stuck in the same outfit I was buried in? Will I ever be able to find a facsimile of that Nipon Boutique skirt-suit with portrait-collar jacket and flounced skirt in iridescent copper combo fabric that made me feel like heaven on earth every time I wore it?"

"Hold on," Paul might have said. "You're asking the right question, but you're messing up the answers." Just look around. God makes different bodies, appropriate for every place and occasion. Take the body you walk around in every day, for instance. It's unique and appropriate for functioning right here on earth with family and friends, for love and work. Or look up into the heavens, and you see celestial bodies—the moon, sun, and stars, each appropriate for its place and function. Look at the seeds you plant in springtime and the fruit it brings forth; both of them, the seed and the fruit, bear different bodies but are appropriate for their place in the creation.

Just so with the body God raises. It will be you, but you will be clothed, not in your earthly body; you will be given a new body, especially designed and fitted for your new life in the Kingdom of God. We don't know much about that Kingdom. We dare not speculate on the "temperature and the furniture of heaven." But we do stand confident in the power of God to sustain us through life in this creation, to pitch us toward the promised new creation and, by heaven, to embrace us in love that never lets us go.

III. Now friends, I believe these radiant affirmations, grounded in the transfiguring power and tenacious love of God, make all the difference in the world. I believe, first of all, they affirm the solidarity of human life from beginning to end. Those references Paul makes to the Corinthians about Adam and Eve are his way of saying that all of us, from the time of the primordial ooze to the furthest stretches of eternity—all of us are connected to one another across the natural barriers of life and death, the cosmic barriers of space and time.

I've never forgotten a wonderful prayer, included in a memoir written by Alan Paton; the prayer reflects on his now-deceased wife, Dorrie, and their life together. In one of its petitions Paton prays, "Tell her, O gracious Lord, if it may be, how much I love her, and miss her . . . and long to see her again; and, if there be ways in which she may come, vouchsafe her to me as a guide and guard, and grant me a sense of her nearness as Thy laws permit."[3]

Solidarity with all whom we love, solidarity with all humanity from the origins of creation to our final destiny in God—that is the richness and depth of Paul's vision and hope.

IV. Before we finish, we must insist that Paul's radiant affirmations provide the ground for our hope as we join the task of building a gracious, just, and peaceful community on earth. Paul closes his great expression of faith in Christ's Resurrection by saying to the Corinthians, "Therefore, my beloved, be steadfast, immovable, always excelling in the work of the Lord, because you know that in the Lord your labor is not in vain."

Archbishop Desmond Tutu understands the urgency of Paul's stringent admonition. During one of his encounters with the governmental defenders of South Africa's apartheid policies, he reminded them that tyrants end up "on the flotsam and jetsam of history," that "the resurrection of our Lord and Savior declares for all to know that light will triumph over darkness, that goodness will triumph over evil, that justice will triumph over injustice, that freedom with triumph over tyranny. I stand before you as one who believes fervently what Paul wrote when he said, 'If God be for us, who can be against us?'"[4]

"Dead people don't rise," said the Corinthians. "Balderdash!" says Paul. And as the triumphal hymn seconds him: "The powers of death have done their worst / But Christ their legion hath dispersed."[5] Thank God! The victory is ours!—James W. Crawford

SERMON SUGGESTIONS

Topic: Something Happened in Church

TEXT: Ps. 73:2, 27

(1) The psalmist learned that who a person is, not what he has, is what counts. (2) The best way to handle a wrong is to declare what is true and right. (3) A person is judged, not by what he has been but by what he could become, by the grace of God.—Donald Macleod

Topic: Bearing His Reproach

TEXT: Heb. 13:13

(1) There is reproach in the gospel. (2) There is no need to increase the reproach unnecessarily. (3) But if we are still reproached for the gospel's sake, exult in it! It is not our reproach; it is his.—W. E. Sangster

---

[3]Alan Paton, *For You Departed* (New York: Scribners, 1969), p. 72.
[4]Desmond Tutu, *Hope and Suffering* (Grand Rapids, MI: Eerdmans, 1984), p. 158.
[5]Francis Pott, "Alleluia! The Strife Is O'er" (hymn text), *The Pilgrim Hymnal* (Boston: Pilgrim Press, 1958), Hymn Number 181.

WORSHIP AIDS

CALL TO WORSHIP.   "Oh, that men would praise the Lord for his goodness, and for his wonderful works to the children of men! For he satisfieth the longing soul, and filleth the hungry soul with goodness" (Ps. 107:8–9 KJV).

INVOCATION.   God, we come today as members of your family, the family of faith, each person joined to one another and to you. Though we seek you in the world of life, we seek you now in this time of solitude. Take us not from the world but make us ready for life in the world. May our worship today prepare us to be instruments of your love.

OFFERTORY SENTENCE.   "For every beast of the forest is mine, and the cattle of a thousand hills" (Ps. 50:10).

OFFERTORY PRAYER.   Eternal God, may these gifts represent our inner commitment to love you above all else in the world and to love all the people in your world—all those in every age and in every place, for whom your dear Son died.

PRAYER.   We express today thanksgiving for the children, young people, young couples, singles, and adults in our church and for the varieties of ways they serve you now and the possibilities that are within them for future service. We thank you for the yearnings we have to know you and your way better. Help us as a church to grow in our faith and serve you better.

Give us, as adults, youth, and children, the strength to love and serve you more faithfully. May the joy, wonder, grace, and mystery of our faith be real to us. In this hour of prayer, may we be open, honest, and real. We know you see us as we really are. Thank you for loving us and accepting us, even as you know us.

Thank you, O God, for opening your loving arms to us. Teach us how to open our arms and love others who are hurting. Through Christ, who gave his life out of love for us, we pray.—William Powell Tuck

SERMON
Topic: Say Yes to Life!
TEXT: Matt. 25:14–29; John 10:10

Many people say no to life. Many times we are inclined to be more negative than positive. This pessimistic outlook can become attitudinal. In our text, Jesus invites us to say yes to life: "I have come that you may have life, and that you may have it in all of its fullness." And, in our gospel lesson, he warns of the fate of a person who says no to life.

I. This is one of those unforgettable parables of Jesus that has been so often told that it is woven into the very conscience of the human race. The Master went away for a time and left his servants to manage his affairs. To one servant he entrusted five talents—we could say five hundred dollars; to a second, two talents—two hundred dollars; to a third, one talent—one hundred dollars. The first two said yes to life and invested their talents wisely. The third buried his talent. He saw his Master as a very exacting man and was afraid that he might not have it for him on his return.

The man said no to life, for as he confessed, "I was afraid." He is not alone. The man in Jesus' story was unwilling to risk his resources in the commerce of life. He shut the door, locked it, and hid the key. He played it safe, so he thought. But, as Jesus warns, he lost even that which he had. "Take the talent from him," the Master cries, "and give it to him who has the ten talents." Jesus then instructs: "For to everyone who has will more be given, and he will have abundance; but from him who has not, even what he has will be taken away." One "can play it so close to the chest," as we say, that he squeezes himself to death. "Nothing ventured, nothing gained" is only half the truth. You lose even that which you had.

II. The antidote to fear is faith. The Master condemned his servant: "You have been unfaithful. If you had been full of faith, there would have been no room for fear." Faith stirs up courage. Faith is willingness to take a risk. How many of us are grounded by our fears when our greatest need is to learn to fly! You see, faith is not just belief; it is trust. "Trust and Obey," as the gospel song puts it—this need to trust life, to trust God, to live with the flow, to risk our intuitions.

III. Jesus invites: Ask and you shall receive; seek and you shall find; knock and it shall be opened unto you. We live in a responsive universe. God is Father, Jesus assures time and again. "If your earthly fathers," he says, "being evil [being persons of imperfect motives], know how to give good gifts to their children, how much more will your heavenly Father give good things to those who ask him." A New Testament writer caught the vision for life that faith inspires and wrote: "According to your faith it shall be done unto you." Life is as big as you make it. Faith is what keeps the mind open, the heart sensitive, and the spirit willing. To live by faith is to practice an open-door policy toward all of life.

IV. To say yes to life is to practice an open-door policy toward all of life. But how often, in the face of one of life's uninvited eventualities, we close up like a clam to protect the self rather than open up to an inexhaustible grace, an unending love, an indomitable hope. The Old Testament psalmist writes: "Enlarge the place of your habitation." We are to grow in the grace and knowledge of our Lord and Savior Jesus Christ. To say yes to all of life is to live on the right side of Easter. This is the test of the reality of one's faith, as to which side of Easter he is living on. Christ is God's "yes" to anything that life may deal to us, even death itself.

God's "yes" is demonstrated and affirmed in Christ's Resurrection. Man is no longer bound by the limitations of death. Death has no power to destroy the life that is in Christ. No wonder the apostle could speak so defiantly in the face of death: "Death where is thy sting. O grave where is thy victory. Thanks be to God who gives us the victory through our Lord Jesus Christ." You see, all of life can now be lived in the experience of God's "yes."—John Thompson

SUNDAY, FEBRUARY 25, 2007
Lectionary Message

Topic: Faith on Trial
Text: Luke 4:1–13
Other Readings: Deut. 26:1–11; Ps. 91:1–2, 9–16; Rom. 10:8b–13

We begin Lent with this monster story, known as "The Temptations." What we see in this stark and ominous imagery of the lonely Jesus amid desolation and wilderness is not a solitary, never-to-be-repeated encounter. We see, rather, a moment illustrating an incessant alternate claim on the life and ministry of both Jesus and the Church—a claim no less persistently made on us who would follow this challenging Galilean.

I. I want to suggest, first of all, when the Tempter approaches Jesus with the promise of turning stone into bread, we see a deal so right, so decent, so creative that to deny it appears simply irrational. What's going on? What lies at the heart of this encounter? Could it be the temptation to substitute the expedient good for the courageous best? "Turn these stones into bread?" Now, I don't know about you, but if I'd been Jesus out there in the wilderness, steeped in the prophets and their urgent cries for justice, I'd have said, "Thank Heaven! Finally, an opportunity to win the war on hunger. That's what starving kids need. We can take care of low birth weight, the crises of malnutrition, infant mortality. Finally, a platform a real Messiah can run on." I'd have surrendered then and there.

Why didn't Luke picture Jesus surrendering? I think it's because in light of the cross (in whose light every Gospel narrative is offered), Luke pictures Jesus deciding to go for the courageous best rather than the expedient good.

I think that choice tempts us all. I consulted on a collection of essays not long ago by Harry Stein titled "Ethics and Other Liabilities . . . Trying to Live Right in an Amoral World". Stein titled one essay "The Curse of Right and Wrong," and he points to a variety of men and women over history who sought the courageous best over the expedient good—and paid for it—from Nathan Hale to John Fitzgerald Kennedy in *Profiles in Courage.* "Why is it," asks a writer I know, "that so many rotten people get ahead? Do you really have to be amoral to succeed?"

"The answer," says Stein, "is that it helps a lot. And acting ethically, in and of itself does not. In the real world, the meek generally earn $15,000 a year and never get their names in the paper."[6]

It's true. The courageous best often costs a great deal in our world. Failure may be the price of the courageous best. Our readiness to confuse conventional success with high character tends to pervert our judgment. It nudges us to settle for the expedient good rather than the courageous best. Careful!

II. The second proposition the Tempter makes provides for sovereignty over all the nations of the world. In this day-and-age, what a temptation that is! And aren't you intrigued that the Bible believes that nations belong to the devil in the first place? The devil—Satan—bears the power of chaos. And surely we witnessed plenty of that in this past century and in this one—nations, races, and tribes slaughtering one another with an almost nihilistic virulence. There's no end to it.

And so of necessity, we may be tempted by the insidious voice of realism to cut development aid and build missiles: the expedient good for the courageous best—the United States and "Pax Atomica" goes a contemporary expression. We might better listen to Martin Luther King Jr., who wonders, "Where do we go from here?" And as we see the half-trillion-dollar defense budgets, the distrusts surfacing between East and West, North and South, the flag-waving and religious symbols used as rationale for war, we come to realize "we can no longer afford to worship the God of hate or bow before the altar of retaliation. The oceans of history are made turbulent by the ever-rising tides of hate. History is cluttered with the wreckage of

---

[6]Harry Stein, *Ethics and Other Liabilities* (New York: St. Martins Press, 1982), p. 78.

nations and individuals who pursued this self-defeating path. As Arnold Toynbee once said in a speech: "Love is the ultimate force that makes for the saving choice of life and good against the damning choice of death and evil. Therefore, the first hope in our inventory must be the hope that love is going to have the last word."[7]

Are King and Toynbee right? Which will it be: the expedient good—that big defense budget and the imperial reach across the world—or the courageous best: the drive to love our neighbors as ourselves? It could be the courageous best—the ethic of pure love and service—is really the only true expedient for good in this world of ours. Our Lord has shown us the way, and it's up to us to make the choice!

III. And last, the Tempter takes Jesus to the top of the Temple and promises, for God's sake, to keep him from harm's way. Here friends, we confront the ultimate bargain. It goes like this: for our sake, Jesus, if you won't feed the hungry, if you won't bend the nations to your will, then somehow prove to us you're in God's camp; show us truly who you are, what you're about, and why we should believe any connection between you and the will, the love and the purpose of God.

Here we get the gospel straight! Now hear this: the will and love of God make themselves evident, not by some arbitrary act of power, intervening and bending the distortions of our life together to some preordained design. The will and love of God make themselves visible and present in our common life by vulnerability and do not violate our freedom. The will and love of God are such that even as we violate them in order to do things our way, we realize God's love will not violate us. We have been given the choice to eliminate hunger—if we want! We have been given the choice to unify the nations into the human family—if we will! We have the choice to follow the One who lives and loves, not for the expedient good but for the courageous and loving best. And we know in this world of reason and realism, this world where our basic principle seems to be "a person's got to do what a person's got to do"—that in that kind of world the proof of God's love for us rests in a readiness to risk life for us, never counting the cost, for love's sake. You see, there is no way to protect love from harm's way. That's where love finds itself. Right in harm's way. It is open-handed, open-hearted, high-risk, and highly vulnerable, finally, even to crucifixion. It does not sell out to the expedient good as a reasonable substitute for the courageous and loving best!

So you see, friends, living the Christian life is no easy task. It's a matter of courage and risk and hope. It makes a claim on us. It puts our faith on trial, not once, not twice, but a thousand times over. Yet be assured—*be assured*—it asks not more of us than has already been given. Therefore, as we walk into Lent together, I pray we heed that sublime admonition in Charles Wesley's hymn:

> Leave no unguarded place, No weakness of the soul,
> Take every virtue, every grace, and fortify the whole.
> From strength to strength go on; Wrestle and fight and pray
> Tread all the powers of evil down, And win the well fought day.[8]—James W. Crawford

---

[7]Martin Luther King Jr. *Where Do We Go from Here?* (New York: HarperCollins, 1967), p. 191.
[8]Charles Wesley, "Soldiers of Christ Arise" (hymn text), *The Pilgrim Hymnal* (Boston: Pilgrim Press, 1958), Hymn Number 384.

SERMON SUGGESTIONS

Topic: Unanswered Prayer

TEXT: Ps. 88:13–14

(1) There's a huge problem for those who believe in God—and value prayer. (2) The problem gives way to the depths of darkness. (3) The solution is in the experience of God's presence. (4) And in eternal patience.—David Feddes

Topic: Why Go to Church?

TEXT: Heb. 12:22–25

(1) The Church is a spiritual fellowship. (2) It is a universal fellowship. (3) It is an immortal fellowship. (4) It is a divine fellowship. (5) It is a redeeming fellowship.—James S. Stewart

WORSHIP AIDS

CALL TO WORSHIP.   "Bless the Lord, O my soul: and all that is within me, bless his holy name" (Ps. 103:1 KJV).

INVOCATION.   Almighty and everlasting Father, whom all of heaven and earth cannot contain, grant us awareness of your presence as we worship. Cleanse us with your grace. Empower us with your Spirit that we may genuinely praise you, humbly learn from you, and readily serve you.

OFFERTORY SENTENCE.   "You will keep in perfect peace him whose mind is steadfast, because he trusts in you. Trust in the Lord, forever, for the Lord, the Lord, is the Rock eternal" (Isa. 26:3–4 NIV).

OFFERTORY PRAYER.   Father, help us to trust you more. You have taught us not to worry, for your care is extended to all your creation—to the birds of the air and to the lilies of the fields and to each of us. Let us rest in your sufficient grace that meets our every need.

PRAYER.   Most Gracious Heavenly Father, once again we rejoice in this opportunity that is ours to worship, to have our hearts lifted by music that stirs our souls, and to have our minds opened by the hearing of your word. May the experience of this hour carry over into our attitudes and actions in the days that lie ahead. In our prayers we would think, not only of ourselves but of others. We would lift up to you those who are suffering in mind or in body that, through you, their pain may be eased. Some of these are hungry, some are filled with anxiety, some are lonely and just need to be loved and appreciated. May they hear you saying to them in a very personal way, "Come unto me and I will give you rest."

And then there are others who appear to be managing very well, who give of themselves in service to others, and in an effort to make this a better community, a better society, a better world. They, too, need your guiding hand and words of encouragement. We would offer a special prayer for all those men and women who serve their country. May we see them as preservers of the peace, a peace that allows freedom and justice for all. We pray, "Thy Kingdom come."—James S. Ferris

SERMON

Topic: Logging On to God

TEXT: 2 Chron. 7:14; Luke 22:39–46

I. There are a number of ways in which connecting with God in prayer is very similar to logging on to the Internet. For instance, we log on to connect with others. I have never entered them, but I understand that there are countless chat rooms you can enter via the Internet, depending on your interests or motives. You can connect with people instantly from all over the world.

So when we pray, we connect with our inner selves and with God. Jesus often spent time in prayer so that he could connect with the Father. Indeed, as Luke's Gospel puts it, it was his custom to go to the Mount of Olives for times of prayer and communion with God. Several times in the Gospels we read about Jesus going apart, by himself, for a time so that he could pray and connect with God.

II. We also log on to gain information. You can go on the Internet and find and download information on practically any subject you can think of. Likewise, when we log on to God, we are in search of information, for guidance. Consider the example of Jesus. When he went to God in prayer, there in the garden, he was desperately trying to ascertain the Father's will for his life. "Not my will, but yours be done," he prays (22:42). Jesus was searching for guidance during that critical time in his life.

III. We log on to gain strength and confidence. Acquiring the information we are looking for on the Internet may empower us, give us confidence, open new doors for us. So it is with prayer. The Scripture says of Jesus that as he prayed in the garden, "an angel from heaven appeared to him and gave him strength" (22:43). Prayer is not for the purpose of getting God in gear and persuading him to get busy about his business; it is for the purpose of getting ourselves motivated to go about our business and do what we should do. Real, honest prayer is not easy. It certainly was not easy for Jesus there in the garden. He prayed so hard, his sweat became like big drops of blood falling to the ground.

As more and more people learn how to log on to the Internet and devote more and more time to surfing the net, I hope and pray and that we won't be remiss about logging on to God. For when we log on to God in prayer, we connect with our Creator, the power of the universe; we gain information and guidance for our lives, and we gain the strength and confidence to be the people we ought to be. Have you logged on to God lately? Do you plan to log on to God this week?—Randy Hammer

SUNDAY, MARCH 4, 2007

Lectionary Message

Topic: What's Your Problem with God's Promise?

TEXT: Gen. 15:1–12, 17–18

Other Readings: Ps. 27; Phil. 3:17–4:1; Luke 13:31–35

For some time God had been telling Abraham that he "would greatly increase his numbers."

"Just great," Abraham must have thought. "So far zero, and how do you increase zero?" You see, Sarah's biological clock had run down. And Professor Kinsey and Dr. Ruth were thousands of years and miles away. So were "in vitro" dishes and fertility drugs. Then when Sarah sought a solution on her own, her only attempt at surrogate motherhood went terribly awry. This barrenness—a disappointment that seemed would never end—brought on Sarah desperate hours of failure and disdain. It was no less severe for Abraham.

Beyond the social implications that surrounded childless parents in that ancient culture, the surpassing fact of the matter was that in the face of God's promise to give him progeny (12:2), they remained childless and had no heir. Sarah raised a theological issue: God was not willing for them to have a child. In that case Abraham's family had no future. Worse still for Abraham, "the Word of the Lord" would leave a question mark in his mind.

I. God made a promise to Abraham.

(a) God's promise constituted the call to Abraham; it was a promise of a son and the far-thermost reaches of land. It was a covenant promise that would issue in blessing. Yet even though far removed from the scientific revolution, Abraham, like us, had bought into the immediacy of everything we have come to expect, and, again like us, was impatient in the presence of mystery. God had not yet done the one thing needful for the sake of a future and the fulfillment of his promise.

(b) In the Bible it can be generally assumed that God's promises require patience. Waiting is a key insight of biblical faith. Always, it seems, the gift of God is given especially to those who trust and who will risk waiting for that which has been promised. Years and even centuries passed from the time of the first Messianic promise (Gen. 3:15) before we read in Galatians that, "in the fullness of time, God brought forth His son" (4:4). On the other hand, "sin is a failure to trust God in the midst of our anxiety."[1]

(c) Given the nature of promise in a materialistic world where we are accustomed to reading of the concrete and visible, impatience with promise is not so unusual. Promise is so tenuous, so gossamerlike, often so distant from reality that earth-borne humankind finds belief difficult. Added to this, Paul Fiddes says, "People cannot bear the openness and uncertainty of promise."[2] This door is opened often to trouble and tragedy.

II. Therefore, Abraham's protest of disbelief should not surprise.

(a) We should expect him, as we are prone to do, first off to read reality by what he could measure by sight and touch, and by what he could manage. Really, can old flesh and tired bone bring forth out of barrenness a buoyant future? In his state of disbelief, hardly.

When God repeats for the umpteenth time the promise of a son when too much time has passed, Abraham finds it ludicrous and is provoked to laughter. He knows what is humanly possible!

(b) Here again, Abraham is anguished by the passing of time, with still no heir. Adoption will not do. It is likely that protest against God's "deferred dream" finds its most articulate expression when we take matters into our own hands and work to find our own solutions. The graphic force of this is seen in Abraham's and Sarah's dealings with Hagar.

Since no other Old Testament text has exercised such compelling influence on the New Testament, especially Paul's belief in justification by grace through faith, we should notice the widespread protest that prevails against this doctrine. God has promised to save all who

---

[1]Paul S. Fiddes, *Past Event and Present Salvation* (Louisville, KY: John Knox Press, 1989), p. 115.
[2]Fiddes, p. 116.

believe in Jesus Christ as the Son of God and Savior (John 3:16). Yet this is loudly disputed by the existing systems of salvation by human meritorious works that are claimed to augment God's work of grace; many would tell you they know what is really possible! Again, reality for them is measured by what can be seen, touched, and managed. I see this as a form of protest.

III. The priority of faith in actualizing God's promises is seen in Abraham's belief.

(a) Walter Brueggemann says, "This is how the faith of Abraham is: he did not move from protest to confession by knowledge or by persuasion but by the power of God who reveals and causes his revelation to be accepted. The new pilgrimage of Abraham is not grounded in the old flesh of Sarah nor his tired bones, but in the disclosing word of God."[3] Reality for him was no longer measured by what he could see, touch, or manage. The Bible says, "And he believed in the Lord; and he counted it to him for righteousness" (Gen. 15:6). Those who keep up with such things say that this is the first appearance of "believing" in the Bible.

(b) Faith is always a response to someone or something that can be trusted. In this instance it depends for its life on the fidelity of the Promise-Giver. As Paul said to the Ephesian church, "It is not of yourselves, it is the gift of God" (Eph. 2:8–10). Faith trusts in some object beyond oneself. Abraham believed that there was a future given to him that was not derived from the present barrenness. He believed that God would break through the exhausted present and give graciously a new beginning.[4] His faith was vindicated, and he is referred to as the "father of faith."

(c) The "new" Abraham is a creature of the word of promise. And the relevance of this text to Paul's belief in justification by faith is vividly presented in Romans 10:8–10, where the apostle says, "What does it say? The *word* is near you; it is in your mouth and in your heart, that is, the word of faith we are proclaiming; that if you confess with your mouth, 'Jesus is Lord,' and believe in your heart that God raised him from the dead, you will be saved."

There the apostle finds a parallel and invests it with gospel meaning. Can we see a connection between the barrenness Sarah lamented and the barrenness of life without Christ or a life lived in the laborious and futile efforts to earn salvation or find our own solutions? Paul saw a connection between the righteousness of Abraham because he believed and trusted God, and the righteousness of God, which is of faith. The Genesis text announces again what it means to be a righteous human that all are created to be, and in the Old Testament or New Testament it means to trust God's future and to live with assurance in the deathly present. Surely now, in that regard, "We tread the road the saints above with shouts of triumph trod!"[5]—John C. Huffman

ILLUSTRATION

PRAYER ANSWERED.   In my boyhood home my father was not a professing Christian. When I announced to my family that I would be a minister, my father shrugged it off by saying "he had rather be a fruit tree salesman." For him this must have been the lowest limb on

---

[3]Walter Brueggemann, *Genesis, Interpretation: A Bible Commentary for Teaching and Preaching* (Atlanta: John Knox Press, 1982), p. 145.
[4]Brueggemann, p. 144.
[5]John H. Yates, "Faith Is the Victory" (song text), 1891.

the occupational tree. During the early years of my ministry I was concerned for my dad. He appeared impervious to my witness. I prayed for him continually. Then to my amazement I was no longer concerned. I wondered at this lack of concern, but there was a peace in my heart, and I was no longer troubled. I lived with the assurance for some time. Then one day my mother told me that my father had confessed the Lord and wanted baptism into the local church. I had believed in the Lord for his salvation, and in his own time, God answered.—John C. Huffman

SERMON SUGGESTIONS

Topic: I Believe in God
(1) Faith in God is rational. (2) Faith in God is personal. (3) Rational and personal faith comes in the relation of trust, so we can say, "I believe in Him!"—John R. W. Stott

Topic: Rest for the Restless
TEXT: Matt. 11:28
(1) There is rest that is given: "Come . . . I will give you rest." (2) There is also rest that is earned: "Take my yoke upon you . . . and you will find rest in your souls." (3) All persons are invited into this rest through our Savior. In him, we rest from our sin and in our service.—Perry F. Webb

WORSHIP AIDS

CALL TO WORSHIP.   "They that wait upon the Lord shall renew their strength; they shall mount up with wings as eagles; they shall run, and not be weary; and they shall walk, and not faint" (Isa. 40:31 KJV).

INVOCATION.   Almighty God, you have given us minds to know you, hearts to love you, and voices with which to express our praise. We would not know you if you had not already found us. Grant that we may offer our worship with pure hearts and clear voices.

OFFERTORY SENTENCE.   "It is God who works in you to will and to act according to his good purpose" (Phil. 2:13 NIV).

OFFERTORY PRAYER.   Lord, may our Christian walk be exemplified by fervent faith. Bless and multiply these gifts for Kingdom causes and may our giving bring joy to you.

PRAYER.   O Lord, we come to you in prayer. We seek the still waters—a place for the restoring of our souls. We have known your guidance in paths of righteousness, and we have felt your presence even in the valley of the shadow of death. And so we begin our prayer today with thanksgiving, an offering of gratitude for all the ways that our lives overflow with goodness and mercy. In the whole family of earth, surely we are most blessed. So forgive us when we take for granted how fortunate we are, and help us to be good stewards of all that has been given to us. And now, Lord, in the quietness of these moments we offer our prayers for others. We pray for those who are bruised in spirit, perhaps victims of someone else's inconsideration, perhaps betrayed or exploited—for those who look fine on the outside but who, inside, hurt and cry. Hear our prayers, O God. And move us to do what we can to help each other, to help those who stagger under burdens too heavy to carry alone. And finally, Lord, we offer prayers for our community, our nation, and our world. Bless all those in places of leadership with an understanding of truth and then with strength to do what is right. Our prayer is that thy voice will be heard in high places so that peace and goodwill might finally prevail.—Charles F. Hoffman

SERMON
Topic: Who'll Be There for You?
Text: Prov. 18:24; John 11:1–36

I. The truth is that all of us desperately need close friends. No one knew this better than the apostle Paul. Time and again Paul's friends came to his aid when he desperately needed them. One time they had to hide him in a huge basket and let him down over the wall of the city by night so he could escape the authorities (Acts 9:25). Another time the friends of Paul were there for him when he was stoned and left for dead (Acts 14:19–20). In the conclusion of his letter to the Romans, Paul mentions Phoebe, his benefactor, and Priscilla and Aquilla, "who risked their necks" for his life" (Rom. 16:1–4).

All of us need good, devoted friends who will be there for us when life is hard. Good friends constitute one of the greatest gifts of God. Who are we going to call when the family is in trouble? Who are we going to call when that report from the doctor turns out to be bad news? Who are we going to call when we have good news to share—that we just got engaged, or that we're going to have a baby, or we got a new job? Friends, of course. It has been observed that friendship is the great mathematician: it doubles our joy and divides our grief. All of us need friends who will be there for us.

II. There are friends who are closer than our own relatives. The wise writer of Proverbs says, "A true friend sticks closer than one's nearest kin" (18:24). It is possible to have a friend with whom you can share the most intimate concerns of your life. Jesus had friends like this— friends who were closer than his own family. In John, chapter 11, Jesus' good friend Lazarus had died. Mary, Martha, and their brother Lazarus were friends of Jesus. Jesus visited their home often. The Scripture says, "Jesus loved Martha and her sister and Lazarus" (11:5). One day Jesus got word that his dear friend Lazarus was deathly sick. When Jesus and his disciples arrived in Bethany, they learned that Lazarus had already been pronounced dead. Mary and Martha were grieving. "When Jesus saw her [Mary] weeping, and the Jews who came with her also weeping, he was greatly disturbed in spirit and deeply moved. . . . Jesus began to weep." So the Jews said, "See how he loved him!" (11:33, 35–36)." John's purpose in including this story in his Gospel is to show that Jesus is the Resurrection and the life. But another point of the story is the great importance that Jesus placed on human friendships.

III. One of the best places to make friends is in the church. George Barna, of the Barna Group—one of the most respected religious survey groups in America today—did a study on the main places where adults say they would go to make new friends. Some of the figures are interesting: 3 percent said they would go to a supermarket, mall, or store; 4 percent cited a bar, dance club, or party; 12 percent said they would look for friends in their neighborhood. At the top of the list—49 percent said they would go to church in search of friends.

The other side of the coin is just as true: When people start visiting a new church, if they do not establish meaningful friendships within the first few weeks, they will likely not come back. If we don't go out of our way to make sure they find friendship, they will not return. The church is a place for us to make and cherish meaningful Christian friendships. It is also a place for us to be a friend to newcomers—to include them in our fellowship time, as well as seek opportunities outside the church to spend time together.

Who'll be there for you? The friends of the church will be—or at least they should be. On this special Sunday, let us celebrate God's great gift of friendship. Let us thank God for every good friend that we have. And let us recommit ourselves to the friendship principle, determining to be a friend of the highest order.—Randy Hammer

SUNDAY, MARCH 11, 2007
Lectionary Message

Topic: Jesus' Call to Repentance
TEXT: Luke 13:1–9
Other Readings: Isa. 55:1–9; Ps. 68:1–8; 1 Cor. 10:1–13

I wonder why Jesus would build this elaborate verbal scaffolding to urge repentance on hearers who seem oblivious to what a day might bring forth unless repentance is the most important experience of life. One reason, I'm sure, is that he wanted to draw attention to the window of opportunity so narrowly and precariously set amidst the unpredictable issues of life. Hopefully, the question of urgency will be answered as we seek to understand better what Jesus had in mind for the word *repentance.*

I. Repentance is not reforming behavior.

(a) Please excuse me for betraying all I have been taught about using negatives in preaching. Yet the word *repentance* has suffered so much radical treatment in preaching that one needs to decide whether these multiple meanings and various uses are near to what Jesus was calling people to do. I subscribe to the idea that if we say something often enough and over an extended period, we tend to accept it as gospel truth. Consequently, there has been so much imprecision and deformity built into the usage of the word that it may be, at times, merely a part of our religious jargon.

(b) One of the strong forces that shaped much of the contemporary use of *repentance* to mean "reformation" was the Age of Enlightenment. The human problem in this context was seen as a falling short of ethical standards borne witness to in the heart. The real need, therefore, was a behavioral change, and this behavioral change was defined as "repentance." Among those of the Enlightenment, there was suspicion of any notion that help was available from any source beyond the human mind. This inspired a new confidence that reason alone could uncover the wisdom that God had hidden in his created world. This, of course, subtly accelerated the distortion of *repentance,* as Jesus and John the Baptizer used it, because the actual meaning is "to change the mind." And, I say, one would hope that a change in behavior would be a consequence.

Here it seems helpful to differentiate the meanings of *moralism* and *morality,* lest someone think I am discounting morality in Christianity. "Moralism" is a system of "being moral" that is intended to decide one's fate in the divine judgment. Moralism opposes the doctrine of grace. Morality is the touchtone of the Christian life, and it is the "fruit" of repentance (Matt. 3:8)— that is, it is made possible by repentance—but it is the fruit, not the tree!

(c) Another shaping force in the misunderstanding of repentance is contemporary evangelical preaching that issues an invitation for unbelievers to accept Jesus Christ as Savior. I believe in evangelism; I've devoted my life to trying to lead persons to Christ. But I have recently revisited the customary invitation that goes: "Repent of your sins, and turn to Jesus." Generally, what the person in the pew hears is "stop sinning" or "don't sin anymore." If that were possible (1 John 1:10), and the sequence of actions asked for were real, then why would the hearer need Jesus? Likely, nothing else has caused converts to expect too much and then later become so confused and disillusioned when they falter and betray what they believe is the deal they made with the Lord. In the initial experience it is unlikely that the convert is aware of those sins that sleep forgotten in unmarked graves but will eventually awake to be dealt with! Usually, when a person is saved, that person becomes aware of sins that were on the blind side before. How could those sins be forsaken in some instantaneous repentance? The Bible seems to know nothing about dismissing sins carte blanche, nor does it offer support for sinless perfection. Behavior was only secondary to the impediment that Jesus had in mind when he issued his call for repentance.

II. Repentance is a transformation of mental allegiance.

(a) As the centuries rolled by, the Jewish worshiper went to the Temple to offer sacrifices for his sins. Once a year the high priest entered the Holy of Holies to make atonement for the sins of the people. This was repeated countless times. This approach to making atonement for sins had worn deep grooves in the psyche of the Jewish worshipers. They exerted meticulous efforts to keep the Law. This is admirable in a way, but on the dark side this legalism was intended for their redemption and had blinded them to a totally New Thing. For them the Law was more than literally set in stone; for them there was no other way.

(b) Now imagine someone coming into your midst with ideas that superseded and turned all your beliefs and values on their heads. How intransigent would you be? How stubborn would you be in surrendering your beliefs and practices? This was the precise situation Jesus came into. Some, but not all, denied he was the Messiah—that he was God's only begotten. They resisted him as an intruder, and hated all he stood for. Finally, on a Friday they took him out to a hill and crucified him to finally glut their hatred and cruel rejection of him and the grace of God he came to bring.

(c) When Jesus began his ministry, he met the real "we-have-never done-it-this-way-before" crowd. Minds were closed. They were infuriated when they heard him say that he was God's Son, the Messiah. They became angry when they heard him say that he was the embodiment of all the Law had been aiming at for generations. How would you like to preach in this environment?

It was these "stonewall" attitudes that Jesus met head-on when he began to preach the gospel in Galilee and say, "The Kingdom of God is at hand, repent and believe the gospel" (Mark 1:15). Unless there was a forsaking of these conceited attitudes so deeply entrenched, there could be no openness to a "new living way." Jesus was calling for a movement of thinking from the notion that one can achieve salvation by obedience or observance of rules, to the truth that salvation has been wrought by God and is bestowed to her or him who believes that Jesus is the Son of God and Savior of the world. Where your mental allegiance lies determines whether or not you can believe the gospel.

III. Yet God is patient. Jesus closes his urgent call to repentance with a parable that illustrates hopeful anticipation. All haven't repented and all won't. Let the record show, however, that "God is patient, not willing that any should perish, but that all should come to repentance" (2 Pet. 3:9). Is this a possibility for anyone you know?—John C. Huffman

ILLUSTRATION

TURNING A MIND AROUND.   During my seminary days I rode the train to my weekly preaching assignment. The rails passed over a temporary bridge across the Tennessee River. Heavy winter rains had flooded the fields and floated all the debris into the river and against the supports of the temporary bridge. So great was the force against the supports that one end of the rails on the bridge did not connect with the rails that continued. As the train I was riding moved cautiously onto the bridge, the engineer saw the situation and brought the train to a lurching stop. The only solution was for the train to back up for more than fifty miles to connect with another set of tracks. All the passengers that day realized how difficult it is to turn around a train. For me it was a God-given lesson on how difficult it is to turn around a human mind!—John C. Huffman

SERMON SUGGESTIONS

Topic: You Are the Light of the World

TEXT: Matt. 5:14–16

(1) This implies that the world is in darkness. (2) Christians are able to provide a remedy to the darkness. (3) This "enlightenment" is more than knowledge and philosophical thought. (4) The true light is Jesus Christ, and we are the transmitters.—Lawrence Vowan

Topic: The Drawing Power of the Cross

TEXT: John 12:32–33

(1) Life at its best finds fulfillment through sacrifice. (2) Faith sees victory and not defeat. (3) We meet God at the cross.—Kenneth L. Chafin

WORSHIP AIDS

CALL TO WORSHIP.   "He that dwelleth in the secret place of the Most High shall abide under the shadow of the Almighty. I will say of the Lord, He is my refuge and my fortress: my God, in him will I trust" (Ps. 91:1–2 KJV).

INVOCATION.   Merciful Father, as we gather in this place, draw us into your presence with such clarity that we will this day be transformed. Let your purposes be honored among us. Grant that we may speak the words of faith authentically from within our hearts that will offer the glory due your name.

OFFERTORY SENTENCE.   "Ascribe to the Lord, O families of nations, ascribe to the Lord glory and strength. Ascribe to the Lord the glory due his name; bring an offering and come into his courts" (Ps. 96:7–8 NIV).

OFFERTORY PRAYER.   Eternal Lord, the one upon whom we depend for our everyday necessities, teach us how to spend—and how to be spent—for the greater good. Grant that in losing our selfish traits we will discover the true riches of life.

PRAYER.   Our Father, there is something about a sun-filled summer day that calls forth the celebration in each of us. Indeed, all experience of this creation awakens in us praise for the Creator. Our constant prayer echoes that of the psalmist: "The heavens are telling the glory of God, and the firmament proclaims His handiwork. In them He has set a tent for the sun which comes forth like a strong man to run its course with joy." So remind us, O Father, that there is still work to be done, there are still the shadowy places in our world and indeed, in ourselves, where the light has not yet penetrated. We lend ourselves to the task of being bearers of the light of the warmth of God's love. Shine forth in those places where the clouds of doubt, fear, or uncertainty would obscure your warming beams—in hospital rooms, in courtrooms, in congressional hearing rooms, and in all places where life's troubles are confronted by our brothers and sisters. Help each of us to brighten the corner where we are and, in doing so, we believe, be faithful to the challenge of our Lord. The light does shine in the darkness, and the darkness shall not overcome it. All this we pray in the name of Christ, our Lord, who said, "I am the Light."—Robert Morley

SERMON
Topic: The Lure of Legalism
TEXT: Gal. 5:1–6, 16–18

In the New Testament era, a lifeless legalism was preferred to the dynamics of being filled with the Holy Spirit. The tendency of exchanging the freedom of God for lesser things is still a threat today. Christians are to avoid the lure of legalism by seeking a growing personal relationship through the Spirit of the Lord.

I. In the churches of Galatia, false teachers advocated adherence to circumcision. In doing so, a higher aim of the Lord was neglected. The rite of circumcision had been fulfilled in the life-changing conversion of Jesus Christ. Rather than being marked in their bodies, believers were to be transformed in their hearts with a continuing growth. Legalism is appealing because it satisfies certain human desires.

Legalism is satisfying because through following certain rituals we can complete our responsibilities to God. Disciples today may be led to believe that they can get baptized and feel that no other faith response is necessary. How convenient "to get it over with" and accept that their relationship to the Lord has been taken care of. Another reason legalism is satisfying is that it makes one better than others. Once the Galatians had adhered to the letter of the Law, they could look down their nose at others who had not been initiated. The old human nature prefers to stay one notch above the crowd rather than accept others as equals. The things that make legalism appealing cause it to be destructive to the Christian life. The illusion of a sense of arrival makes one neglect a need for daily communion with the Lord.

II. The challenge of the Kingdom of God is to live according to the new divine potential. Even though the old nature works against the newborn spiritual image of the Heavenly Father (v. 17), the Holy Spirit's indwelling and empowering the disciple promises such blessings as love, joy, peace, patience, and kindness. These attributes of the divine nature cannot be produced by empty acts of ritualism or adhering to man-made dogmas.

The call to live according to the Spirit includes putting to death the acts of the old nature. Rather than emphasizing or returning to old patterns of living, no matter how secure, there is a response to a higher calling, a daily communion with the Lord. If the Spirit is to reign and bring the fruit of joy and peace, the old nature—the fleshly ways—must be completely forsaken.

The disciples of Jesus can default and trudge about in past lifestyles of defeat rather than become victorious through active faith. Believers should be challenged to move into the promised land of Spirit-filled living. Christians only benefit from a fragment of their faith if rules and rituals are accepted in lieu of a new spiritual posterity.—Ken Cox

SUNDAY, MARCH 18, 2007
Lectionary Message

Topic: The Joy of Being Found
TEXT: Luke 15:1–3, 11b–32
Other Readings: Josh. 5:9–12; Ps. 32; 2 Cor. 5:16–21

In the contemporary parlance of the street, the scribes and Pharisees had an "attitude." And the reason was "the Law was given by Moses, but grace and truth came by Jesus Christ" (John 1:17), and this grace that Jesus *brought* diametrically opposed all they stood for. The Law of Moses was precious to them, and grace was offensive. Their resentment boiled over into murmuring.

Besides, the behavior of Jesus in fully accepting tax collectors and sinners by eating with them seemed to imply to the scribes and Pharisees that he was condoning their behavior. For them this had dangerous implications. Such people should be punished and taught a lesson they would never forget! This is the cardinal tenet of legalism. So Jesus holds up a verbal mirror in the form of a parable for them to see themselves; it concerns the joy about which legalism knows nothing.

I. The Joy of Finding

(a) My scant seminary training in preaching warned against making a parable walk on "all-fours," which meant not to navigate all the crooks and turns of a parable for the purpose of making the parable into a sermon or giving it a life of its own. There is evidence that I didn't give heed. So, naturally, on the parable of the loving father I took the negative stance and preached on the "parable of the prodigal." I'm sure I squeezed all the minutiae for the sake of making points.

(b) The parable of the loving father is well known, probably for the reason that the prodigal has commanded center stage for most of us. Jesus sought to illustrate the scandalous grace of God and its affront and offense to all who seek to find acceptance by their obedience. The parable vivifies the father's joy over finding a son who was lost.

(c) "Finding" implies seeking. Jesus made reference to this aspect of his ministry when he said, "For the Son of Man is come to seek and save the lost" (Luke 19:10). Passages in the New Testament exult in a treasure hidden in a field and joyfully found (Matt. 13:44), and about the tireless searching for a sheep that had gone astray, and the rejoicing over finding that lone sheep (Matt. 18:12).

(d) Groups of churches that believe the gospel makes "seeking the lost" incumbent on them as a priority are concerned that other pursuits are outdistancing evangelism. A case in point is the emphasis on making "finding the lost" among the most important tasks they do. Other communications keep this emphasis before them, and for good reason. In all likelihood, nothing else quickens the life and makes a congregation as happy as finding the lost and the lost finding Jesus. In this, the work of God must become our own (2 Cor. 5:20). The joy of finding did not find a place in the emotional faculties of the scribes and Pharisees, and their attitude was typical of such that caused the little girls to pray: "O Lord, make all bad people good, and all the good people nice!"

II. The Joy of Being Found

(a) Jesus seeks to draw the attention of the scribes and Pharisees to the fact that they have never been aware of the desperate situation of being "lost"; therefore, they have never experienced the joy of being "found." It's the father's party that bewilders them. There's no music and dancing in their religion. How strange! They would let the erring son come to him, true. Judaism had a place for the restoration of the fallen, but it was under the conditions that such a one would "take his medicine" and do better. The straying ones in Judaism that came "home" certainly would not have been feted and celebrated.

(b) It is an incredible thing for the grace of God to "find" us. We are left to imagine the disbelief and then a dawning jubilation within the returning son. Sadly, there are still many bound in legalism who are offended by God's grace. The various systems of "works salvation" that prevail throughout religious systems attest to this offense.

The joy over being found has been put succinctly by Fred Craddock:

> The reader might have expected . . . that the final phrase would have been "was dead, is alive" on the assumption that no condition is worse than death, no condition better than life. But such is not the climax of the parable's scale of values. There is a condition worse than death, it is to be lost; there is a condition better than life, it is to be found.[6]

—John C. Huffman

ILLUSTRATION

JOY OVER SAVING ONE SINNER.   In the town where I was pastor, a leading church had a renowned preacher as evangelist. I attended the noon-day services. One service came to a close with the invitation to accept Christ by faith as personal Savior. The lone figure of a small boy was seen coming forward. As the invitation closed, the pastor spoke a brief word to the boy without giving information to the congregation and was about to pronounce the benediction when the evangelist rose to his feet to exclaim to the pastor: "Wait a minute. We have seen a miracle here. This lad has found the Savior, and the Savior has found him. Our host for lunch will joyfully wait while we rejoice in this wonderful happening." There were circumstances surrounding this event about which I knew nothing, but it does illustrate how easily we lose the radiance of joy over one sinner who repents to hurry on to something much less important.—John C. Huffman

SERMON SUGGESTIONS

Topic: The Question of All Ages—Who Is This?

TEXT: Matt. 21:10

(1) He is the Son of God and the Savior of mankind. (2) We know this because of the miracles of the Bible: they point to him. (3) We know this because of the miracle of the Church: it proclaims him. (4) We know this because of our changed and transformed lives.—Robert A. Penney

---

[6]Fred B. Craddock, *Luke, Interpretation: A Bible Commentary for Teaching and Preaching* (Louisville, KY: John Knox Press, 1990), p. 187.

Topic: What's in a Nickname?

Text: Mark 3:17; John 1:42; Acts 4:36

(1) James and John were nicknamed "Sons of Thunder." (2) Simon Peter was nicknamed "The Rock." (3) Barnabas was nicknamed "Son of Encouragement."—John N. Gladstone

WORSHIP AIDS

CALL TO WORSHIP.   "Lord, who may dwell in your sanctuary? Who may live on your holy hill? He whose walk is blameless and who does what is righteous, who speaks the truth from his heart" (Ps. 15:1–2 NIV).

INVOCATION.   Father Almighty, giver and Lord of life, we bless and praise you for your merciful keeping and tender care. May our worship express the true joy that arises from the living Lord Jesus Christ who dwells within us, and may we now be brought closer to him and to one another.

OFFERTORY SENTENCE.   "Verily, I say unto you, inasmuch as ye have done it unto one of the least of these my brethren, ye have done it unto me" (Matt. 25:40 KJV).

OFFERTORY PRAYER.   O God, as we bring our gifts of tithes and offerings to you, grant that we may be mindful of the greater gift you have given to us—that of your Son and our Savior, the Lord Jesus Christ. And may our giving reflect true devotion as Jesus' disciples, and may we walk in his ways.

PRAYER.   Loving God, who creates in us a new beginning each day, help us to discover your purpose for our lives and to seek our roles in fulfilling this purpose. We praise you for your creation of our lives day-by-day, for your re-creation of hope within us, even when hope seems foolish. We pray for this world of ours in which cynical self-interest and grasping for power often seem to be the rules by which we live. We confess our responsibility for those thoughts and actions by which we further the powers of evil and destruction in our world; for we know, finally, that becoming human is a process of reconciliation and not of separation, of trust and not of suspicion, of communion and not of coercion. As we confess and acknowledge our needs, our weaknesses, our times of despair and hopelessness, we see your loving purpose in these expressions of human concern. We feel your loving touch healing us and caring for us as a child is cared for by a parent. We know that you are with us and for us in the midst of our lives. We praise you for this constant love, and in Jesus' name we offer together the prayer of our Savior.—Sue Farley

SERMON

Topic: Who's to Blame?

Text: Gen. 2:15–17, 3:1–7; Rom. 5:12–19; Ps. 32

"All you preachers ever do is talk about sin. I don't go to church to feel bad. Why don't you talk about something good for a change?" Have you ever heard those words expressed? Have you ever thought them? Sure you have, and I have as well. The picture is too clear. We, as human beings, are a people conceived in sin, and we live in sin.

I. Who's to blame? Is it God? Did God really "set up" Adam and Eve in the garden so that their downfall was predestined? If so, are they—and we—truly responsible for our sin? The traditional answer of Judaism is that God created us as moral creatures able to make decisions of our own free will. We are given the freedom to make decisions, but we make the wrong decision too many times. God, however, is not to blame.

II. Some people blame nature, that is, genetics. Though I believe in the power of genetics, I cannot believe that moral responsibility is placed there. Others desire to place the blame on nurture, that is, family environment. These people look at the structure of the home in which persons are raised and note that the predominance of criminals come from homes of broken marriages and absent fathers, which are homes mainly of the economically lower strata. Still today, most children raised in poverty do not become criminals.

III. What are we to do? Play the blame game or deal with the reality of our sin? God would not allow Adam and Eve to get away with their shifting of personal responsibility. Whether it is David bemoaning his sin with Bathsheba, Judas hanging himself, or Simon Peter going fishing rather than staying with the apostles after the crucifixion, Scripture is clear: we cannot shift responsibility to another. What do we see when we look at the dark side? Quite simply, we see that even in the best of us—and that's a contest no one wants to enter—there is more than enough evil and sin to go around. We see pettiness, fault-finding, jealousy, anger, and resentment. We see a using of others for personal gratification. We see that we love things and use people rather than love people and use things.

IV. What, then, are we to do? How do we deal with the sin of our lives? Confession is the beginning point. Confession means to look at our lives and, through the power of the Spirit, speak the truth about our lives. We cannot get defensive when we confess, for our defensiveness only proves our insecurity. We must understand the love of God before we confess. Without the incredible love of God permeating our lives, we will never have the strength to look inside and see the nature of the zoo that resides within.

Repentance follows confession. Repentance involves definitive actions that are taken to correct the sin and restore any broken relationships that may have resulted from it. Repentance is far more than remorse or resolve; it is "turning around going 180 degrees in the opposite direction."

V. What does it take for us to do all this? We must accept the power of God as necessary and able to break the hold of sin on our lives. Paul put it this way: "For if by the trespass of the one man death reigned through that one many, *how much more* will those who receive God's abundant provision of grace and of the gift of righteousness reign in life through the one man, Jesus Christ" (Rom. 5:17).

When we come face-to-face with the greatness of what Christ Jesus has done for us, then we will accept amazing grace and place ourselves on the path of transformation. Jesus took all that blame upon himself, and through his Spirit we can know the transforming power that works from the inside out.—Robert U. Ferguson Jr.

SUNDAY, MARCH 25, 2007
Lectionary Message

Topic: Knowing Christ Better
TEXT: Phil. 3:4b–14
Other Readings: Isa. 43:16–21; Ps. 126; John 12:1–8

There were some things that Paul said he definitely knew. He knew whom he had believed (2 Tim. 1:12). He was more than a little certain about the future if some incident cut his life short (2 Cor. 5:1), and a mysterious confidence surged through him in sunshine and rain, as he had access to the very presence of the Almighty himself (Rom. 8:28).

With these remarkable insights, the swagger was gone. Yet he was an absolutist, authoritarian, at times seeming to know more than humans were supposed to know and sounding like he always expected too much of others. But it was his message that made him so unacceptable. For this and other reasons, he was never the life of the party.

Yet in spite of what you may think of his unbending and aggressive views, when we come upon him in our text we find him in a moment of utter openness to "the mystery of godliness" that has always outdistanced his most arduous pursuit "to apprehend that for which also I am apprehended of Christ Jesus" (v. 12). He wants to know Christ better. And this lofty aim is open to all of us.

I. Most likely, everyone who knows of Christ knows the Christ Who *Was*—before one becomes a believer. There may be some knowledge that he exists. The gospel, though, at best is extracurricular where our lives unfold day-by-day. Generally, people do not give him priority right off the bat. Probably it's fair to say that knowledge of Christ and his salvation usually incubates for a while. He "was" for most of us.

(a) We have him promised in the Scriptures of the Old Testament. These are the so-called "messianic promises." He is the "offspring" that will "crush the head" (of the serpent; Gen. 3:15). The Bible reader sees him walking down the pages of Isaiah, as the Scripture promises, "therefore the Lord himself will give you a sign: A virgin will be with child and will give birth to a son, and will call him Immanuel" (7:14). He was there in the Scripture before he had a human face. By Jesus' own admission, he said to them: "Before Abraham *was* I am" (John 8:58)! But this *was*—"far off"—for many.

(b) Likely, Paul refers to himself as "the chief of sinners" (1 Tim. 1:15) because he was familiar with these references that promised the Messiah and used the expression in the face of knowing that. He resisted the light he had been given. He was so wedded to his self-righteousness and to his preconceived notions that he was blind to the most important event when it happened. In our text he refers to his efforts to convince others of his zeal and his genuineness as a Pharisee by persecuting the Church. We are not let in on all the dynamics that made his Damascus Road experience so dramatic, but one can safely imagine that his angry obstinacy was a factor in the demonstrative encounter with the Risen Christ. Certainly, he knew about the Christ Who Was—who had been promised.

(c) Before I became a believer, Christ was just Somebody Who Was. I knew he existed. I knew of him as a historical character on the biblical stage, but he was a dim and remote figure whose picture was on the Sunday school cards that were handed out by Mrs. Eula Smith, our teacher of the Card Class. I heard many times that he got into trouble with the Temple authorities, and they had the Roman government put him to death. But he was merely a figure who lived on the pages of a book that many thought was sacred. For me and for countless others, there was a time when he was only the Christ Who Was. He existed outside my thoughts, except for an occasional blip across my mind. I am thankful, though, that this fragmentary, perhaps even incoherent knowledge is not to be lamented, for in God's wisdom and providence it can be preparation for something infinitely better.

II. Christ can be known as the Christ Who *Is*. "Is," as in a personal Savior, as in a redeeming presence at our side, and as in a "fellowship divine." There are different facets to the experience of knowing Christ as Savior.

(a) Faith in Christ as Savior gives life a new perspective. One is more able to assess the detours, the denials, and perhaps the conceit in one's self-righteousness. In our text Paul now has a different slant on his life as a previous and precise Pharisee. Once, he thought of his achievements in legalism to be the full measure of what God expected. He was always "pushing the envelope."

Now he reads his so-called achievements differently. What he was so proud to claim at one time, he now sees as worthless. At this point, Fred B. Craddock has some timely instruction for us. He refers to the practice of nearly all of us feeling that to validate our Christian experience we must reject and revile our past life.[7] Craddock points out that Paul doesn't do that; in fact, it appeared his past was "gain" for him. It is only when he compares it to his life "in Christ" that it amounts to nothing. We should mark well the ease with which we say the unseemly (and really what we wouldn't want to say)—that we are exchanging "worse than nothing" for Christ's salvation.

As the believer looks back on efforts to be "good" enough or on the fact that Christ was scornfully ignored for a time, one is better able to find the right term for such behavior. Most important, however, is the ability to understand the grace of God and his unconditional love. Jesus was making this latter point when he said, "Except a human be born again, one cannot see [into, with understanding, the worthwhileness of] the Kingdom of God" (John 3:3). As most of us have experienced, knowing Christ better makes this perspective possible.

(b) The believer, like Paul, now has a new possession, "not having mine own righteousness of the law, but that which is through the faith of Christ, the righteousness which is of God by faith" (v. 9). This is the redeeming insight! Such an incredible change of mind is the repentance that Jesus and John the Baptist talked about (Mark 1:15; Matt. 3:2). "Stop sinning" is the usual implication of "repent" in much of common usage, although wrongdoing was not the impediment that kept people from Jesus; it was a fatal pride that sought acceptance with God on one's own merit.

A deceptive "moralism" is the practice of morality in the belief that "good works" are necessary for one to be saved. It is making gains in some circles now by mixing "works" and "grace" (Rom. 11:6), and the severest penalty for this is that the grace of God is nullified by this error. Morality is the fruit—the affirmation of the Christian life—not the root cause. As the legendary preacher said: "God's grace works on one's *wanter.*"

III. Everyone, like Paul, should desire to know the Christ *Who Can Be.* The motivation to know Christ better, to know more of him, is the constraint of the Christian life. This exciting pilgrimage is open-ended. No one can know or even predict where it will take one. This is the distant and infinite vista offered in knowing Christ better.

When Peter answered the derision-laden question of the maid by the fire with a loud and vehement, "I tell you I do not know the man" (Matt. 26:74), he may have been speaking for all of us. Do we *really* know him? Who has ever been challenged to the limit?

We should never forget that with all we can ever say about him, and with all that we can believe about him, he remains beyond our grasp. A few times with the Spirit's help we may only touch the hem of his garment. But we can know him better by following him and by

---

[7]Fred B. Craddock, *Philippians, Interpretation: A Bible Commentary for Teaching and Preaching* (Atlanta: John Knox Press, 1985), p. 59.

searching for him in his Church, and in the lives of others. God may have some different and new understanding for you. Go seek it!—John C. Huffman

ILLUSTRATIONS

UNBELIEVER SAVED.   I was the guest preacher with a pastor who took me to talk with a prospect who lived back off the main road. After following a lane through pasture land, we arrived at a house where we met a young mother with a crying a baby in her arms, a dog barking furiously, and a television blaring loudly. The young mother was not a believer, and this was not the best environment for the kind of visit we had in mind. To the relief of all, the pastor turned off the television. I sat with the young woman with my New Testament in the attempt to lead her to faith in Christ. Lo, the baby stopped crying, the dog stopped barking, and there was a solemn quiet in the room. She confessed the Lord as her Savior; then in tears she said, "I wish I could have known this years ago. I felt I was not good enough to be a Christian!"—John C. Huffman

SINS REVEALED.   The preacher was commenting on biblical illiteracy in the church where I worship, and he told of a biblical allusion that went over the head of a worshiper. The speaker on that occasion was illustrating the point that our sins always find us out. He mentioned a person who was caught in sin, and he alluded to the "rooster crowing" for that person. At the door after the service, the worshiper said to the preacher, "Your sermon was all right, I guess, but I didn't get the point about the rooster."—John C. Huffman

SERMON SUGGESTIONS

Topic: The Marks of Jesus
TEXT: Gal. 6:17
(1) Each Christian bears the marks of Jesus. (2) Sometimes, as with Paul, these are visible and physical marks—the *stigma* of Christ. (3) Our marks indicate Christ's ownership: we belong to him. (4) These marks are clear and unmistakable; they are revealed in our character.—Joseph A. Hill

Topic: The Suffering Man and the Silent God
TEXT: Ps. 88
(1) We can't deny the intensity of human pain. (2) The intensity is made worse when we are isolated from our friends. (3) God's response may be silence—but not absence.—Charles E. Crain

WORSHIP AIDS

CALL TO WORSHIP.   "This is how we know what love is: Jesus Christ laid down his life for us. And we ought to lay down our lives for our brothers. . . . Dear children, let us not love with words or tongue but with actions and in truth" (1 John 3:16, 18 NIV).

INVOCATION.   Heavenly Father, we humbly seek your blessing on us in this hour of worship. We adore you, the one whose nature is compassion, whose presence is joy, whose holiness is beauty, and whose will is peace. Unto you now and forever be honor and glory.

OFFERTORY SENTENCE.   "We know that we who are strong ought to bear the infirmities of the weak, and not to please ourselves" (Rom. 15:1 KJV).

OFFERTORY PRAYER.   Father, help us by our giving—and our living—to practice the divine principle of goodwill. May it be lived out in our homes, in our communities, and among the nations of the earth.

PRAYER.   As we come before you, O Lord, we are aware that praying is not always easy for us. Sometimes it's very difficult, as we search for ways to express the deep concerns of our lives. We want to be open and honest, so we ask that you will guide us. "Teach us to pray, O Lord." Teach us, we ask, in the way of thanksgiving, that we will know how to express our gratitude in what we say and in what we do. Teach us also in the way of intercession that we may be truly sensitive to the needs of others. Especially, help us to be mindful of those who have shared their concerns and problems with us, and let us continue to support them with our prayers. And as we pray, we need to learn patience to remember that your timing is often different from ours—and always better. So help us to wait upon thee with the assurance that our strength shall be renewed. And as we learn to pray, help us to learn resignation to thy will, to know that back of all that is apparent to us is thy creative word, promising new life for the dark and desolate areas of our lives. O God, we praise you for our Christ, who brings reconciliation for the brokenness of our lives. Let us know peace, we ask, in our hearts and in our world, and in our efforts to follow him, let us be faithful stewards of all that we have been given.—Charles F. Hoffman

SERMON
Topic: When You Hit Rock Bottom
Text: Deut. 2:1–15

Most of us have hit rock bottom before, and those who haven't yet, someday will. When it happens, the real issue is not how you got there. The most important issue is what do you do next? That's the theme of today's text.

I. First, when you hit rock bottom, realize that there are usually two ways to go (v. 1). Guess which way the people of God went? The text reads, "Then we turned back and set out toward the desert along the route of the Red Sea. . . ." It's one of the saddest statements in the Bible. The people of God, who had been on the doorstep of the Promised Land—literally within view of it—turned their backs on it, retreated to the desert, and wandered around aimlessly for the next thirty-eight years.

So you've hit rock bottom! You could be living through what you're convinced now is the end of your life. Maybe it's divorce. It may be that you're living in the aftermath of the death of someone you cherished and treasured more than your own life. Maybe it's cancer or some other devastating illness. Perhaps it's the rebellion of a child. Have you lost your job? Is it a broken friendship, a betrayal? It might be some act of dishonesty or disloyalty that's about to catch up with you. Maybe it's an extra-marital affair. Have you disappointed someone, inflicted more pain on another than you ever dreamed possible?

Here's the number-one issue you face: not who's responsible, or even how you got there. The only important issue you face is which way you will go. Will you live the rest of your life in the desert, in a holding pattern, nursing your wounds, thinking only of what might have been? What will you do with your life now? You must decide. You're the only one responsible for deciding!

II. The second lesson from the text is this: when you hit rock bottom, remember that the God who has always loved you, loves you still (v. 7). Isn't that incredible? But isn't it also the truth underlined by this text? The people who had insulted God by not trusting him, the people who had refused to follow God because they wanted everything handed to them on a silver platter—those same people—people just like you and me—wanted for absolutely nothing! The Lord gave them food, clothing, and protection. He knew their path in the trackless desert, and for nearly forty years he took care of them.

It's just another reminder of what the gospel is all about. God "does not treat us as our sins deserve or repay us according to all our iniquities" (Ps. 103:10). In other words—and learn this lesson now—there is nothing you can do to make God love you more. Or love you less. Your sin may separate you from him for a season, and you may even lose track of where God is, but know this: God always knows where you are, and his eye is never off you, even when you're trekking alone through the desert of your life.

III. The final lesson is this: when you hit rock bottom, recognize when it's time to start moving again (v. 13). Discipline, guilt, grief, spiritual immobility, and paralysis are not meant to last forever. Too many people, when they fail, erect a monument to their failure and spend the rest of their lives paying homage to their defeat. Not enough people view failure, setback, and rock-bottom experiences as a moment—a fleeting period of time, an opportunity for God to teach transforming truths.

It was necessary for God's people to suffer defeat so that they could learn that obedience is the way to live a good and happy life. But it was also necessary so that their children and the rest of their spiritual descendants, like us, would learn not to minimize the seriousness of sin and its costly consequences.

Sure, this generation of God's people never got to the Promised Land. They died at the door. But their children and their children's children eventually got there. They refused to be shackled to the mistakes made in an earlier time by their parents and grandparents. Sometimes, I can't help but wonder if we will ever learn!—Gary C. Redding

SUNDAY, APRIL 1, 2007
Lectionary Message

Topic: Passion (Palm) Sunday
Text: Luke 19:28–40
Other Readings: Ps. 118:1–2, 19–29; Isa. 50:4–9a; Ps. 31:9–16; Phil. 2:5–11; Luke 22:14–23:56

I. Holy Week became holy because Christ set apart the last days of his earthly ministry by entering the Holy City, teaching in the Temple, having the Last Supper with his disciples, praying in Gethsemane, being arrested, tried, and crucified, and, ultimately, being resurrected. Not since the creation of the world had a period of time been so important. In this week, salvation was made possible for each person.

Society doesn't help the Church observe Easter the way it does Christmas. Appropriately, it's our responsibility to respond by exerting extraordinary effort to realize the extraordinary results of Easter. To passionately re-experience Easter's exaltation, we must begin with Palm Sunday.

II. *God sees more than we see—always.* God sees everything everywhere. We see, as the apostle Paul put it, "only in part." On that day we now call Palm Sunday, Jesus entered Jerusalem. He took it all in, for what it was and was not. He *heard* the hosannas. He *saw* the mass of people, one by one. He *felt* the palm branches placed before him. He *smelled* the scents of Jerusalem. He *tasted* the sweat beading down his face. He *discerned* what was in the heart of each person.

Entering Jerusalem on Palm Sunday meant there was no turning back. He had been warned. Established leaders were using their political and religious positions to scare Jesus away or kill him. Jesus didn't flinch. Forward was the only direction he would go. Knowing the decision would cost him his life, he went anyway. Why? Through his death, believers could know "at-one-ment" with God. This ultimate act of sacrifice by laying down his life meant that our sins were known, dealt with, and forgiven by God.

As he entered Jerusalem, Jesus walked the thin line separating laughter and tears. The crowd yelled praise at him, not for him. Their "Hosannas" and "Hallelujahs" echoed hollow along that road of the first Holy Week. Jesus cried within himself. But the awaiting Resurrection stirred the laughter of hope for Jesus. All this suffering would soon serve the best of purposes: salvation offered to humanity. So with these tears and laughter, Jesus began the last week of his earthly life. He was ready to pray, "Father, forgive them for they know not what they do" and able to offer, "Today you shall be with me in Paradise."

Days before his entrance, Jesus talked to a friend in crisis. To Martha he explained that death, in God's hands, becomes life: "I am the resurrection and the life. He who believes in me will live, even though he dies; and whoever lives and believes in me will never die. Do you believe this?" Jesus' promise ends with an invitation. Either you do or do not believe. To this question there is no middle ground.

III. Having made prior arrangements, Jesus was ready to enter on a colt that would signify the Messiah's arrival to accept his Kingdom. Jesus' entrance marked the point of no return. More than 100,000 people gathered in this small city during the Passover Feast. The one pressing question they asked themselves was, "Will he come in spite of the threats against his life?"

If he came, they would be ready. With palm branches—the symbol of rebellion against political oppression—they would greet him. Seeing him, they went out to meet him and cried, "Hosanna." Originally, this was a Hebrew invocation addressed to God meaning, "O'save" (Ps. 118:26) and later came to be a cry of joyous acclamation. What did their hosannas mean? What do ours mean?

Having received the financial offering of a believer who provided Jesus with a colt on which to ride into Jerusalem meant that the prophecy of Zechariah was fulfilled. Jesus entered Jerusalem on his own terms. He would not be dictated to. He refused the militaristic symbol of riding in a chariot or the political symbol of riding astride a great horse.

IV. Neither the disciples nor the onlookers understood what they were eye-witnessing on Palm Sunday. Søren Kierkegaard, a great nineteenth-century Christian, said, "Life is lived forwards but understood backwards." Only by experiencing life can we really know life. Only by loving can we know love. Only by trusting God can we know trust. Only by believing in Christ can we know Christ. Only after experiencing Christ's Resurrection and then recalling the earlier events did believers grasp what Jesus had been up to all along. Though Jesus had explained it to the disciples beforehand, they had *to experience* his explanation. How is this true for you? This truth was shared to me in prose by a friend: "When you come to the edge of all the light you know, and you are about to step off into the darkness of the unknown, faith is knowing that one of two things will happen—there will be something solid to stand on, or you will be taught to fly."

To believe is to experience God. To not believe is to miss out. The decision is ours to make, just as it was for those on the first Palm Sunday. Some were curious because of the miracles Jesus performed. What else would Jesus do? Curiosity may lead us to belief, but it is not the *same* as belief. Belief comes from our committing to God after our curiosity has led us into his presence. On that day, feverish curiosity led people into Christ's presence. Some took a "leap of faith" and found salvation. Some froze in fear and were left in their own despair. Together on this Palm Sunday, let us take a twenty-first-century leap of faith into the life, death, and Resurrection of Christ.—D. Leslie Hollon

ILLUSTRATIONS

THE NEED TO SUFFER.   Christ's work *to* the cross, *on* the cross, and *from* the cross required *suffering* at a level unknown to any other person. *Passio,* in Latin, means "suffer." Holy Week is also called Passion Week. Christ's passion invites us to be passionate. Passionate faith is dynamic, possessing adventure through (1) the *awareness* of God's presence calling us to new thinking, feeling, and acting, (2) *new visioning* of what the new growth looks like, (3) *acting* to convert the awareness and vision into reality, and (4) *fulfilling* the adventure by investing newly grown faith into the next call of God.—D. Leslie Hollon

THE NEED TO TRUST.   When designing our family cemetery plot, I chose verses from "the Resurrection and the life" to be chiseled in stone on our meditation bench. Recently, I sat on that bench and stared at the ground where one day my body will be buried. In such moments we get really honest with ourselves. I felt renewed gratitude that Jesus went toward Calvary, not away from it. This Resurrection becomes known by personally trusting in Christ.—D. Leslie Hollon

THE NEED FOR FAITH.   Søren Kierkegaard used the phrase "leap of faith." The words describe what is required by being in a trusting relationship with God. Reason, research, and analysis can take us a long way but only so far, not the whole way. We must take another step—sometimes a leap into what can only be known by experience. To leap into life's experience requires faith. Without faith we cannot go forward.—D. Leslie Hollon

SERMON SUGGESTIONS

Topic: Up Against the Powers That Be

TEXT: Eph. 6:10–19

(1) Being truly Christian in the twenty-first century is a mighty battle. (2) Our only weapon in the battle is the sword of the Spirit—the Word of God. (3) We are to speak to the Church so the Church will speak to the powers that be. The word to be spoken is *Jesus Christ.*—David Buttrick

Topic: The Fight of the Day

TEXT: Rom. 13:11–14

(1) Current American culture continues to decline in the areas of personal ethical issues. (2) But Christians are committed to bring light into darkness. (3) Because of the surety of the Word of God, our mission is to win the fight of the day.—Carl F. H. Henry

WORSHIP AIDS

CALL TO WORSHIP.   "You who bring good tidings to Zion, go up on a high mountain. You who bring good tidings to Jerusalem, lift up your voice with a shout, lift it up, do not be afraid; say to the towns of Judah, 'here is your God!'" (Isa. 40:9 NIV).

INVOCATION.   Lord, as we celebrate the day of Triumphal Entry, may we be readied to receive your journey into our hearts. Help us to forsake our sin, to overcome our prejudices, and to deny any false pretense that might hinder your entry. May Christ's entry be triumphant in us.

OFFERTORY SENTENCE.   Jesus said, "If anyone would come after me, he must deny himself and take up his cross daily and follow me" (Luke 9:23 NIV).

OFFERTORY PRAYER.   Father, as faithful followers of Christ in days of old blessed his coming and laid before him branches of palm, may we, this day, lay our choicest gifts before the one who comes in the name of the Lord. Bless his Holy Name.

PRAYER.   Eternal Spirit, with our prayers hanging in the quiet air, we reach out to you. With a longing for connection in our best moments, we awaken to your truth. But alas, these moments fade like deer tracks in the melting snow. We strive to recapture the bliss but discover that it has vanished as the dream upon awakening. God of mystery and grace, how do we satisfy this restlessness that we feel? How do we free ourselves from this dance of life that holds us fast? How do we live with faith when we are too busy listening to our chatter to hear you? Our elusive souls know that you are with us always, yet we see you not. Now, with the promise of resurrection in the stirrings of the slumbering earth, and in the lingering light of these spring evenings, we are back traveling the road to Jerusalem with you, casting palm branches before you, being called to something deep and universal. Our deaf ears shall hear, our blind eyes shall see, and once again our hearts will realize that the Divine is within us, around us, smiling at us, loving us.—Janet Boynton

SERMON

Topic: The Shouting of the People

TEXT: 1 Sam. 3:1–10; Matt. 21:9; Matt. 27:21–23

Jesus was surrounded by crowds throughout most of his ministry. Crowds reached out to touch him that they might be healed. Crowds hung on his words, hoping to understand something more about God. In the last week of Christ's life, crowds played a very prominent part. Let's look at their reaction to Christ.

I. At his coming the crowd shouted, "Hosanna." Too often we think that their hosanna meant "praise to Jesus." But literally the word *hosanna* meant "save now." "Save us now," they cried. The crowds were inspired by his presence and hoped that he might be the Messiah. But not all of this admiration turned to adoration. Later it would change to something else.

Turn with me now from the roar of the crowd to a quiet time, centuries ago. A young boy, Samuel, had gone to minister to an older priest named Eli. In the story we read that Samuel was sleeping. He heard a voice in the night. As he had immediately done night after night, thinking that his master Eli was calling, he got up and went to see what needed tending. "I did not call," Eli said. He sent the boy back to his bed. But Samuel returned again and again, and finally Eli realized that maybe the voice of God was speaking to Samuel. He then instructed the young lad to say, "Speak, Lord, for your servant hears." The message of God was communicated to a young teenage boy.

II. Many voices call to us, saying, "Walk within my way, and you will have abundant living." Let's look at several of these voices that call to us. One is the voice of materialism. This voice tells us that we are what we possess. A second voice is that of the playboy philosophy of life. This approach advocates living for instant gratification; persons are treated as things or as objects. Third, do not listen to the voice that is calling us to cheap religion and civil religion. Do not buy into cheap religion that offers us salvation without commitment, grace without surrender, and redemption without sacrifice. Fourth, do not follow the voice saying that the basic philosophy of life is "me-ism." Selfishness is the main concern of this approach. The philosophy of me-ism circulates all around us today, as many constantly look out only for number one.

III. There are many voices crying to us. But the voice of God is seeking to penetrate our very being, and we need to listen for it. First, I believe that this voice will say, "Learn to speak clearly and distinctly." In an age of so much "gobblygook" and double talk, we need to speak more plainly about the things of God and life. We need people in politics and religion who will stand up clearly for what they believe.

Second, I hope you will hear the voice that says you are loved and acceptable to God. In the New Testament, Jesus told us God comes searching after us, even while we are sinners. God loves us, even while we are sinful. He comes seeking and searching after us to bring us back to himself.

Third, listen for the voice of God that says he is a God of integrity, and he wants us to have high values in the way we live and walk. We need to hear God calling us to live a life of honesty, decency, and fairness in the way we relate to others.

Fourth, I hope that our young people will listen to the voice that is calling them to a sense of discipline. Young Samuel had the discipline to respond to the call of his master. Those in life who have found the most lasting values have been those who have been able to discipline themselves. But Christ calls us to a narrow way, which demands discipline.

Fifth, like young Samuel, I hope you also hear the voice of God as he calls you to a new challenge that lies before you. Samuel responded to God and met the challenge before him. Young people, the greatest books, the greatest music, the greatest discoveries have not yet been realized. The greatest dreams of what will be accomplished are still waiting to be dreamed.

IV. There is a great, bold, exciting adventure lying before us, and I hope that you and I will not buy into the voice that says everything has already been done and accomplished.

There is much left for you to do, because the greatest challenge is still ahead. Many new worlds loom before us. The greatest challenges still lie ahead, and I hope, young people, that like Samuel, when you hear the voice of God, you will accept your responsibility and say, "Speak, Lord, for your servant hears." Respond as Samuel did, and set about your task.— William Powell Tuck

SUNDAY, APRIL 8, 2007
Lectionary Message

Topic: Easter Day
TEXT: John 20:1–18
Other Readings: Isa. 65:17–25; Ps. 118:1–2, 14–24; Acts 10:34–43; 1 Cor. 15:19–26

I. Easter fits the size of God at work. Touched by the power of the One who created the heavens and the earth, comes the miracle we sing: "Up from the grave He arose, a mighty triumph o'er His foes." With Christ's Resurrection comes our resurrection. With Christ's Resurrection came Satan's ultimate defeat. With Christ's Resurrection is the victory of heaven over hell, love over hate, hope over despair, forgiveness over sin. Like the early believers, we are to share the joy of Easter's promise. Christ is risen. Christ is risen, indeed!

What one believes about eternity is challenged when standing by an open grave of a loved one. We do not play games or give false platitudes at the cemetery. Is the gravesite the final resting place for a loved one whose casket is about to be lowered in the ground? Or is the grave a historical location where we recall the person's earthly life, grieve that the person will no longer walk with us on earth, then celebrate that our loved one now shares in the promise of Christ's Resurrection? Resurrection is the transforming work of God by which believers enter the space and time of heaven. At physical death, believers fulfill the baptismal promise of Resurrection: "buried with Christ in the tomb, raised to walk in newness of life."

With courage, Nicodemus and Joseph of Arimathea had laid Jesus' body in the grave. Though they had received Pilate's permission, the wrath of the religious leaders made it dangerous for these prominent men to risk their reputations, perhaps their lives, by removing Jesus' body from the cross, wrapping it in linen cloth, and placing it in a cut-rock tomb. Watching them and noting its location, several women disciples knew where to go once the Sabbath law of rest had been fulfilled.

II. At dawn on Sunday, the morning after the Sabbath, the grieving women went to the tomb where the body of Jesus of Nazareth was buried. Now that the Sabbath was over, these women disciples, led by Mary Magdalene, Joanna, and Mary the mother of James, went to anoint Jesus' body with their burial spices. These women had been transformed by Jesus, become his financial supporters, followed him during his ministry, and wept as they witnessed his death at Calvary. Now they were ready to offer him their final rite of obedience.

However, the strange became stranger. When the women arrived at the cemetery, they were astounded to see Jesus' tomb open. The heavy covering stone had been rolled away, and the body of Jesus could not be found. Their minds could not keep up with the events happening around them. What they were seeing could not be explained by reason or by prior experience. The body of Jesus was gone, and they did not know why or where. They did not know what to do with the evidence of Jesus' absence.

Two men suddenly stood beside the stunned women. The men's appearance was described as "dressed in clothes that gleamed like lightning." The brilliance of their presence indicated they were heavenly angels. "Messenger" is the Greek meaning for angel, and these two were ready to deliver a divine message.

Frightened, the women bowed down as an act of worship. Their faces were to the ground. They sought to be grounded in a new reality. They hoped their fear would find a resting place. How often do we have the attitude, "Unless I see, I cannot know enough to believe?" But in God's miraculous work we usually find ourselves stretching to believe what we are seeing.

III. The women's faith-eyes needed sharpening to comprehend the miracle that was before them. The angels responded with three clarifying questions. First, "Why do you look for the living among the dead?" The women needed to change their expectations of what they were looking for in order to see the truth about Jesus. What about you? Second, the angels declared, "He is not here. He is risen." Their seven words forever altered the course of history. What do they mean to you? Third, "Remember how He told you this would happen while you were in Galilee?" Jesus had prepared them for what they were now experiencing. But the women had not connected Jesus' teaching of his Resurrection to life application. Have you? Jesus prophesied his Crucifixion, and still the disciples could not comprehend Calvary. Jesus prophesied his Resurrection, and still the disciples did not expect Easter. Only by remembering and understanding his words would their lives be transformed. Jesus had promised them that he would rise from the dead.

Promise means "for mission." A promise is given to prepare one for the adventure of traveling into the future. God's promises prepare us to travel into his future. When these women disciples remembered Jesus' promise to be raised again on the third day, they realized that they were in the midst of that Miracle of miracles. Looking back, they could see forward. Remembering Jesus in Galilee gave them the perspective to believe, as they stood in the middle of an empty tomb. They responded with a confidence that only comes with Easter. Emboldened, they went to tell others. What about you?—D. Leslie Hollon

ILLUSTRATIONS

LETTING GO.   I felt God's goodness while sitting by my mother's bed. As she was letting go of this world, she was leaning into the Good Shepherd, who guided her homeward to heaven. She modeled for us what it means to let go and "let God." While dying she was being reborn. While releasing, she was receiving. God's vision for her life, as for your life, is more than this world can contain. She was not ours to hold on to. She was simply ours to love. In the space and time we call heaven, which is more real than earth itself, God's eternal goodness is eternally experienced. I am grateful to God who makes this time-travel possible for all believers.—D. Leslie Hollon

DETERMINING LIFE'S DIRECTION.   On a shelf in my office rests a shotgun shell, given to me by a man who was going to use it to kill himself. He called me shortly before midnight on Easter Eve. He agreed to meet me at my office. We talked through the events that had caused his crisis. He then let me show him how those same circumstances would look different if he trusted in Christ's Resurrection. He prayed to receive Christ. As we walked to his car to remove the shell from his shotgun, the Easter sun—Son—was dawning. Christ's Resurrection gives us the ultimate reference point to determine our life direction.—D. Leslie Hollon

BASIS FOR BELIEF.   "I believe in order to understand." *Credo ut intelligam* was a Latin term used by Christians of the Middle Ages to explain that belief is God's gift to help us understand what cannot be grasped by analytical thinking. Reason can only take us to the edge of what trusting reveals. Sense perception and rationality can help us analyze Christ's Resurrection, but only believing gets us to the depths of understanding. God gives us enough analytical proof to show there is reason to believe but not so much that faith is not required (John 20:26–31). Our belief in eternal life is not based on wishful thinking to calm our human fears about dying. Our confidence is based on the historical work that Jesus accomplished by turning Crucifixion into atonement and death into Resurrection.—D. Leslie Hollon

SERMON SUGGESTIONS

Topic: The Resurrection of Jesus
TEXT: Rom. 10:9–10
(1) Jesus' Resurrection is indisputable history. (2) Jesus' Resurrection provides inspiring philosophy. (3) Jesus' Resurrection gives invincible hope.—G. Earl Guinn

Topic: Matthew and His Calling
TEXT: Matt. 9:9
(1) Matthew's call seemed unlikely; it wasn't anticipated. (2) The call was an act of grace. (3) The call was to the point: "Follow me." (4) The call was effective; it opened the door for countless thousands of others.—Lawrence Vowan

WORSHIP AIDS

CALL TO WORSHIP.   "Do not be alarmed. You are looking for Jesus the Nazarene, who was crucified. He has risen! He is not here. See the place where they laid him" (Mark 16:6 NIV).

INVOCATION.   O God, we rejoice this Easter morning for the eternal beauty and everlasting power of Jesus' Resurrection. May on this day the stones of selfishness, complacency, and apathy be rolled away, and may the living Christ stand in our midst. Fill us this day with a spirit of reverence, humility and awesome joy.

OFFERTORY SENTENCE.   "And he said unto them, 'Take heed what ye hear: with what measure ye mete, it shall be measured to you: and unto you that hear shall more be given'" (Mark 4:24 KJV).

OFFERTORY PRAYER.   As we make our offerings of tithes and gifts, we express thanksgiving for the happiness we know in life, for healthy bodies, peaceful homes, faithful friends, challenging purposes, and eternal motivations. We pray that these blessings will abound to all the people in all the earth.

PRAYER.   Blest are you, Lord Jesus, who came to us a little child—one of us, flesh and blood—to share in our humanity. For God so loved the world

[All]: *That all might have eternal life.*

Blest are you, Lord Jesus, who came to us as carpenter and yet in whose creative hands a world was fashioned. For God so loved the world

[All]: *That all might have eternal life.*

Blest are you, Lord Jesus, who came to us as fisherman and yet pointed to a harvest that was yet to come. For God so loved the world

[All]: *That all might have eternal life.*

Blest are you, Lord Jesus, who came to us as teacher and opened eyes to truths that only the poor could understand. For God so loved the world

[All]: *That all might have eternal life.*

Blest are you, Lord Jesus, who came to us as healer and opened hearts to the reality of wholeness. For God so loved the world

[All]: *That all might have eternal life.*

Blest are you, Lord Jesus, who came to us as prophet, priest, and king and yet humbled himself to take our place upon the cross. For God so loved the world

[All]: *That all might have eternal life.*

Blest are you, Lord Jesus, who came to us as servant and revealed to us the extent of his Father's love for humankind. For God so loved the world

[All]: *That all might have eternal life.*

Blest are you, Lord Jesus, who rose from the ignominy of a sinner's death to the triumph of a Savior's Resurrection. For God so loved the world

[All]: *That all might have eternal life.*

God so loved the world that he gave his only Son for the sake of me and you and other sinners, too. God so loved the world. Blest are you, Lord Jesus, our Savior and Redeemer.—John Birch

SERMON
Topic: Hurrying Toward Hope
TEXT: John 20:1–10

The first people at the empty tomb on the first Easter morning were—runners? Mary Magdalene, it says, ran to find Simon and John. Simon Peter ran back toward the tomb. John, probably a younger man, ran faster and got there first. These were people in a hurry. They ran to and from the tomb—hurrying, worrying, and, finally, believing. They had actually been hurrying toward hope. That's what a Resurrection Day celebration is—a solid hope to which hurried, harried people can turn.

Remember that these men and women had barricaded themselves behind doors of uttermost despair and that he came and spoke shalom to them, and life started afresh. That's the best experience for all who lived then and now by Easter faith. So consider with me, for just a moment, the content of this hope born of a risen Lord.

I. Christ alive, first of all, means *life is partnership.* A Risen Christ means, literally, that the stuff of time and life is set within the circle of eternity. We do not laugh alone, weep alone, wonder alone, struggle alone. Whatever our path, like those two men on the way to Emmaus, we discover that Jesus himself draws near and walks beside us. Living is partnership. And that, of course, is hope for all the times of discouragement and defeat that belong to this human pilgrimage. What God did with the defeat of that first Friday he can do with the hurts of our humanness. He will need our participation, of course. And we will need the support of a caring fellowship, of course. But Christ, risen and alive, means hope for the darkest moments of our lives.

This hope also means that life's journey is crammed full of possibilities. The stones have been rolled away from a lot of our doors. Tightly shut rooms can now be opened. Those airtight boxes in which we've hidden away our biases and our bigotries can now be blown open. Fresh insights can burst upon us. The mundane and the routine get shot through with surprise, and life itself gets made and remade and remade!

II. The content of this hope is this: if life be partnership, dying is partnership as well. Now the pain and loss and grief of death are real. They are not to be eliminated by pious platitudes. They are not eliminated, even by strong Resurrection faith. But if death is not destroyed by the empty tomb, it is at least *defeated.* "Christ alive" means "us alive" on the other side of silence—on the other side of death. And that is reason for hope. More than wishful thinking, more than any spurious "proofs" for human immortality, life on the other side of silence, for the Christian, is based squarely on the victory of a warrior Christ who has already passed over and now beckons back for us to follow in safe passage. "Because I live," he said, "you shall live also."

We know that death is not the fearful smashing of hope that we always thought it was. The journey with Jesus Christ leads through the graveyard and on to glory! Now we know that the spiritual, intellectual, and emotional pilgrimage started here will continue. One paltry lifetime is not time sufficient to know ourselves, to understand Christ, to plumb the depths of the ways of God. So at the end of life on earth is a fresh beginning. Death's exit is an entrance.

Because of Easter, dying is partnership. Living is partnership. That's the core of hope—our hope in Jesus Christ—so that what we celebrate this morning is that event—that singular event in history—which brings such a hope to every believing heart.—William L. Turner

SUNDAY, APRIL 15, 2007
Lectionary Message

Topic: Knowing Christ
TEXT: Acts 5:27–32
Other Readings: Ps. 118:14–24; Rev. 1:4–8

I. What invigorated the disciples with enough boldness to reject the Sanhedrin's restraining order? What gave them a prophesying clarity in their teachings that seeking people trusted Jesus with their lives and protected the apostles from being stoned to death? The answer? The apostles knew the truth about Jesus. The apostles were in a living relationship with Jesus. The apostles were empowered by the Holy Spirit, "whom God has given to those who obey Him." The apostles were "witnesses." What about you?

The story of Christ Jesus is factually based and understood by faith. To experience Christ is to understand the facts. The following trail of the facts and faith leads to the confidence that enabled the apostles to fulfill their name of being "sent ones." They knew the following, and so can you:

> Jesus of Nazareth was born of God in the town of Bethlehem. The cave and manger scene are historically centered at the lower level of today's Church of the Nativity. After a brief refuge in Egypt, Jesus grew up in Nazareth—a small village of David's descendants who had recently returned from Babylon.
>
> Joseph, the father entrusted to raise Jesus, was a builder and respected person of Nazareth. He died before Jesus began his ministry. Near Nazareth was a Roman garrison where Galileans who opposed the Romans' occupation of Israel were executed.
>
> For a thousand days, during the years of 26, 27, and 28, Jesus publicly ministered as God's Son and the Savior of people. Eighty-five percent of his ministry centered around the Sea of Galilee. Simon Peter's house in Capernaum served as the ministry's home base. The house is now excavated and open to the public.
>
> Strategically, Jesus paced his ministry, and during the Passover of year 28, he went to Jerusalem for the last time. The historical locations of his last week of ministry are confirmed: the east gate of his triumphant entry, the Mount of Olives where he was arrested, the place of his trial in the high priest's house of Caiphas, the place where the soldiers whipped him, the place of his Crucifixion at Golgotha, and the location of his Resurrection, now called the Church of the Sepulcher.

II. These are historical facts that fulfill their meaning only when they become *the Truth* for you. Personal acceptance of Christ is necessary to grasp the meaning of Christ. This fact and faith gave the apostles their clarity and confidence.

Members of the Sanhedrin were furious that the weakness of their authority was being exposed before the people. The falsehoods they spread about Christ were coming into the light of the apostles' truth telling. To receive *the real* Christ Jesus, the crowds, the religious leaders, and the government officials had to release their perceptions of Jesus. Perception means "to see through." People then and now are tempted to "see" Christ for their own designs.

Perceptions are so powerful—controlling our feelings and thoughts—that the common view is, "It doesn't matter whether or not the story is *true;* it's whether or not the people *believe* it is true."

Most people thought Jesus could be controlled by what they said about him. The mob yelled, "He is not the Christ we thought he was"; therefore, do what the religious leaders are saying: "Crucify him." Pilate, concluding that he needed the Sanhedrin's political support more than he needed truth, gave in and sent Jesus to the desires of their perceptions— the cross.

We too can miss the true Jesus, seeing him only as a mirrored image of ourselves. Only by having our Temple thoughts cleansed, our human wants crucified, our faith perceptions resurrected can we see the real Jesus of Nazareth, the real Christ of the cross, and the real Resurrected One.

Knowing the real Jesus, the apostles were not going to be intimidated by powerful pretenders. The stakes were too high. As Peter said, "God exalted Jesus to His own right hand as Prince and Savior that He might give repentance and forgiveness of sins." *Shuv,* the

Hebrew word for "repentance," means "to turn around and go in the opposite direction." Having turned their lives Christ-ward, the apostles were not going to turn around for these religious bullies. Is your life staying on course, going Christ-ward at all costs?—D. Leslie Hollon

ILLUSTRATIONS

PREPARATION FOR DEATH.   Dietrich Bonhoeffer, a Christian leader in Germany during Hitler's terrorist reign, spoke up and stood up against the Third Reich's evil. Bonhoeffer meditated on Christ's life, death, and Resurrection as he made decisions. He concluded, "When Christ calls a man, He bids him—come and die." Near the holy season of 1945, Bonhoeffer was executed by orders from Hitler. Christ's death had prepared Bonhoeffer for his own death. The same may be true for you and me.—D. Leslie Hollon

THE TRUTH.   Charles Finney, the father of American revivalism, identified four agents as leading one into conversion: the Holy Spirit, the truth, the messenger, and the sinner. All the agents are necessary and have their own unique role to perform. To illustrate the interrelatedness of the four agents, Finney frequently asked his hearers to imagine that they were standing on the bank of Niagara Falls. Imagine seeing a man headed toward the edge of the falls, "lost in deep reverie," unaware of his impending plunge to destruction. You cry out, *Stop!* and the man suddenly realizes his situation and averts disaster. With horror, he leaves the scene, and you follow him. When he sees you, he says, "That man saved my life." According to Finney, there is a sense in which the bystander (the messenger) saved the man. But upon further questioning, the man says that the word *Stop!* (the truth) was the "word of life" to him. After even more questioning, the man decides, "Had I not turned at that instant, I should have been a dead man." Finally, after stating that it was his (the sinner's) act, he cries, "O the mercy of God; if God had not interposed, I should have been lost (the Holy Spirit).—D. Leslie Hollon

SERMON SUGGESTIONS

Topic: Look Up to Him!
TEXT: Ps. 34:5
(1) On Ascension Day, we are to look up to him. (2) When we do, "our faces will shine." (3) And we shall never be ashamed.—Karl Barth

Topic: Crossing Over the Promise
TEXT: Josh. 1:1–11
(1) The purpose: to prepare us for tomorrow. (2) The promise: the fulfillment of God's intention for us. (3) The perils: the path to fulfillment is filled with opposition from without and from within. (4) The plan: to move into the future armed with God's love and care for a wounded world. (5) The power: that of the Creator God who made us all with a purpose in mind.—Hal Missiourie Warheim

WORSHIP AIDS

CALL TO WORSHIP.   "You shall know truth, and the truth shall make you free. God is a Spirit: and they that worship him must worship him in spirit and in truth" (John 8:32, 4:24 KJV).

INVOCATION.   Father, as we gather to worship, impress on us the need for a deeper knowledge of and a closer walk with your dear Son, Jesus. May our lives be turned to you today that your love may flow through us. We surrender our wills to you that you may guide us in both word and deed.

OFFERTORY SENTENCE.   "Remember the words of the Lord Jesus, how he said, 'It is more blessed to give than to receive'" (Acts 20:35 KJV).

OFFERTORY PRAYER.   Father of our Lord Jesus Christ, we dedicate these gifts to our Savior and to the Kingdom he established among us. May his praise be declared wherever believers gather to worship and serve.

PRAYER.   Gracious and loving God, our prayers reach out today to all who are in need of your healing power. We pray for those who suffer from debilitating diseases. We pray for those who seek healing from broken relationships. Give strength to those who are going through the anguish of divorce, who are going through the conflicts within their families. Bring comfort to those who have lost a loved one. Fill the empty spaces of their lives with peace. Give them a vision of adjustment and perspective to move ahead to a new plateau of living. We pray for all those who seek the healing of the human spirit. We pray for the surgeons, the doctors, the nurses, and others in the healing professions who bring their skills to help alleviate suffering. Let your light shine on those who struggle through deep doubt and depression. Free us all of the burdens that we bring with us today—the feelings of anger, jealousy, fear, greed, or prejudice. Give us each a healthy soul, O Lord, and through worship, remove all the obstacles that prevent us from being closer to you and one with Christ.—George L. Davis

SERMON
Topic: What's the Use?
TEXT: John 20:19–31

Thoughtful Christians have raised questions about the Resurrection from the very beginning. You can see that in the lesson that was read to us this morning from the Gospel of John. It is the famous scene of Thomas, who was called "Thomas the Doubter," seeing with his own eyes the evidence of Jesus' Resurrection.

I. We have trouble believing it, too, especially if we are called upon to live our lives based on that faith. They had just seen the most precious, the most wonderful thing this world has ever known crucified—eliminated as a nuisance. They believed that he was the One who would redeem the world. They believed that he was the Messiah. That is what *Messiah* means—that he's the One who would restore the world to go the way God intended it to be. He talked about a world of love—a world of peace and justice.

That is what Jesus taught, what he embodied in his own life. When he was here, the world was different. When he was here, the Kingdom of God was here. When he was here, the dreams and visions of a new world became believable. In fact, the disciples saw it. They saw Jesus bring justice into the world. They witnessed him treat everybody as important. And he forgave people. He forgave everybody and thus freed everybody. He gave everybody a whole new start in this world.

And most important and amazing of all, he said, this is what God is about. God is about freeing. God is about redeeming, re-creating the world. They believed that the Kingdom had finally come, and God was finally with us, and the world, at last, was redeemed.

II. And then it happened. The powers of this world were challenged and threatened by his preaching, because his preaching meant that they had to change. So they arrested him, humiliated him, and crucified him, and he died. And that was the end of it. So the disciples were despondent, in despair, as only those who have hoped for so much can be in despair. The Crucifixion of their Lord meant now there was no escape, no area, no place in this world unaffected by evil. Evil had appeared to be victorious, omnipotent. Any effort against it would be futile. In the end it will win.

So what's the use? What's the use of hoping? What's the use of trying? What's the use of working so hard for things that matter, for peace and justice and righteousness and the things that make life human and worthwhile, things that are so fragile, so vulnerable, that they can just be eliminated?

III. Then came the Resurrection. The Resurrection meant evil is not in control of this life. God is in control of this life. The Resurrection meant that good will eventually triumph in this world. The Resurrection meant the re-creation of the world. It will be possible now to hope, and to dream, and to work for good in this world—for equality and for peace. So the things that Jesus stood for are the things that are going to win in this world. That is what you are asked to believe when you believe in the Resurrection of our Lord.

We are called to believe that the stage on which the drama of our life is played is much grander than we ever imagined. I have always found it curious that some who have trouble believing in life after death have no trouble believing in life on other planets, as if one required a great leap of faith, and the other does not. It seems to me that if they would spend equal time investigating the Scriptures as they do listening for some "beep" from outer space, they would come to the same conclusion as the New Testament writers, who said, we believe that when this life is over there is another life waiting for us. The God who created life in the first place can create it again.

The Resurrection means that God is concerned for us forever and always, unto ages and ages, for all of us, every single one of us, no matter what we think or believe or deny.—Mark Trotter

SUNDAY, APRIL 22, 2007
Lectionary Message

Topic: New Creations in Christ
TEXT: Acts 9:1–20
Other Readings: Ps. 30; Rev. 5:11–14; John 21:1–19

I. Paul was such an incredible apostle that we tend to overlook his humanity. He was such an amazing disciple that we can forget he was a person. Renewed awareness of how, with his flesh-and-blood humanity, he became a *"new creation in Christ"* inspires and instructs us to trust that God re-creates us through discipleship.

Paul felt what he wrote: "I am not ashamed of the gospel of Christ for it is the power of God unto salvation." Paul had been saved from his sinfulness, including his self-righteousness and his need "to control" other people, as well as himself. His self-righteousness caused him to participate in the murder of the Lord's disciples. On his way to Damascus, "breathing murderous threats," motivated to kill others through his ever-growing hunger for power, the saving grace of the Lord Jesus Christ blazed into his life. Paul was saved from himself, and followers of the Way were saved from his blind ambition.

Paul was never ashamed of what saved him. The saving even made it possible for him not to be ashamed of his need to be saved. In our weakness, false pride (hubris) is lowered, and the Spirit is given freedom to roam with healing power. Through God's holy kiss, our wounds are transformed into wisdom. And we come to know ourselves for the first time.

II. Paul later wrote, "Anyone in Christ is a new creation where the old is transformed by the new." Through his new identity he could see his real identity. Through Christ, his life came into view. During his years as a youth, Paul was raised in the cultural city of Tarsus. His father was a Pharisee and Roman citizen. His mother was Jewish. He had at least one sibling, a sister. His Hebrew name was Saul, and his Greco-Roman name was Paul. Still living in Tarsus, Paul was educated in the Torah and Jewish tradition; he studied Greek philosophy and literature.

Paul entered his adulthood by living with his married sister and studying with the great Jewish teacher Gamaliel. He also then learned the occupation of tent making.

Paul decided not to marry and aspired to be an emerging leader of Judaism. So he debated disciples of Jesus in Greek-speaking synagogues; he participated in Stephen's martyrdom. Rationally assured but emotionally confused, Paul traveled to Damascus in zealous pursuit of his opponents: Jesus' followers. He chose this enterprise as the avenue to fulfill his youthful dreams and ambitions.

Paul's career advancement was not as fulfilling as he thought it would be. His conversion experience awakened him to what he had never experienced—God's transforming grace. He became "his own man" by becoming a new person in Christ.

The gospel of Christ was Paul's life source. He was not ashamed of what gave him life. Paul grew as an apostle by growing as a disciple. Paul became strong by successfully trusting God in stressful situations. A scene that reveals this sweaty work of successfully trusting is revealed in the pivotal scene of being healed of his physical blindness by the bold faith and kindness of Annanias. Saul became Paul and learned to trust that God would lead him in knowing what to do and how to do it.

III. Guilt is what we feel when we know we've sinned. When our sin becomes public, we feel shame. Guilt and shame have served their purpose once they have motivated us to learn from our mistakes and commit to change. God doesn't want us to feel guilty just for the sake of feeling guilty or to let every threat of public exposure control us through shame. False forms of guilt and shame are oppressive, and the world is full of people who falsely try to liberate us from them. So on several occasions Paul retold his conversion experience as a witness of Christ's transforming power.

God wants us to feel the twin forces of guilt and shame when we've knowingly walked away from his best. This "best" is called *God's will.* The inner feeling of having done wrong flows from a Christ-formed conscience. Guilt functions as a warning signal to pay attention and repent as a corrective course.

Attempting to lie ourselves out of a guilty conscience only makes matters worse, because the lie (whether to ourselves, to others, or to God) intensifies the sin's power. Enough of these lies create an addiction. Then our lives really get out of whack.

Christ-filled hope clears up our vision so we can see life beyond sin. Our life can recover. Christ gives us strength to make U-turns in our life. Hope shows us there is another way to go when we realize the way we are traveling is taking us in the wrong direction. Repentance means to do just that: "turn around."

Hope is powerful. Without hope, faith stalls. Without hope, love stutters. Without hope, tomorrow appears as an enemy. Hope is our vision for the future by which we live in the present. After we have stumbled, hope enables us to get up.

Paul left Damascus a changed man because of the gospel, and the world would feel the gospel's impact from Paul's ministry. Has the gospel of Christ exposed your spiritual blindness? Are you seeing with corrected eyesight? Have you asked, "Who are you, Lord?" The world needs from you what you need for yourself: "to be a new person in Christ."—D. Leslie Hollon

ILLUSTRATIONS

HUMILITY BEFORE THE CROSS.   The Associated Press carried this story about a man who lost hope. The corporate life of Enron had dealt him a tough blow, and in response he committed suicide. Before he ended his earthly life, he wrote this note addressed to his wife. The seven-sentence statement read:

> I am so sorry for this. I feel I just can't go on. I have always tried to do the right thing but where there was once pride now it's gone. I love you and the children so much. I just can't be good to you or myself. The pain is overwhelming. Please try to forgive me.

Humility before God keeps us honest and true to ourselves and each other. The spiritual giant, St. Bonaventure, "warned" in an example from the monkey: "The higher it climbs the more you see its behind." No one stands taller than when kneeling at the cross.—D. Leslie Hollon

ADVENTURE IN GOD'S WORLD.   I enjoy traveling, whether it's down the street or around the world. Every step, every drive, every flight, every ride is an adventure in God's world. Sometimes I'll consult a map designed by a person who has been where I want to go. I will see what their approach is and learn from their efforts. Along the journey, I'll make adjustments to personalize the experience. I continue to learn from the road map by which Saul became Paul.—D. Leslie Hollon

SERMON SUGGESTIONS

Topic: The Wisdom of Worship
Text: Ps. 95
(1) The Creator God is the object of our worship. (2) In worship, we are reminded of things spiritual and eternal. (3) Worship also rebukes and challenges us. (4) Worship restores us.—Perry F. Webb

Topic: Why People Go to Church
Text: Eph. 4:11–13
(1) People go to church to worship God. (2) People go to find forgiveness. (3) People go to find fellowship. (4) People go to find spiritual power.—Leslie Weatherhead

WORSHIP AIDS

CALL TO WORSHIP.   "How beautiful on the mountains are the feet of those who bring good news, who proclaim peace, who bring good tidings, who proclaim salvation, who say to Zion, 'Your God reigns!'" (Isa. 52:7 NIV).

INVOCATION.   Eternal God, in whom we live and move and have our being, who has created us for yourself, grant unto us such purity of heart and strength of character that no selfish passion will hinder us from knowing your will. May this hour of worship empower us for service. May we find in you perfect peace and freedom.

OFFERTORY SENTENCE.   "Therefore, my beloved brethren, be ye steadfast, unmovable, always abounding in the work of the Lord, forasmuch as ye know that your labor is not in vain in the Lord" (1 Cor. 15:58 KJV).

OFFERTORY PRAYER.   Lord, help us to become unobstructed channels through which your love and light can be channeled to a world in need. May these gifts be used for preaching the good news of Jesus Christ to all persons everywhere.

PRAYER.   Loving God, we give thanks for the gift of the Holy Spirit that you have sent to us, drawing us into the body of Christ and making holy the commonplace. The fresh winds of your Spirit are like a cool, refreshing breeze that flows over our hungry souls. You bestow upon us a variety of gifts that we might carry on the work of Christ in this hurting world. We confess, O God, that often we have difficulty even recognizing and acknowledging our gifts. We confess that sometimes we misuse the gifts you grant us. And we confess that, at times, we are reluctant to use our gifts to build up the body of Christ, thinking others will carry on your work in our place. And so, this morning, we recommit ourselves to be Christ's body in the world. We recommit ourselves to seek healing in relationships—mind, body, and spirit. We recommit ourselves to speak the words of justice and compassion. We recommit ourselves to work for unity and reconciliation in difficult situations. We lift up and remember those who have gone before us, who have fought the good fight, who have finished the race and who now celebrate life eternal. And we recommit ourselves to move forward in their memory, to make the vision of your Kingdom a reality for all of your children. We pray that you would come to us and empower us with your Spirit, which unites your people everywhere—people of every color and of every nation. May the mighty winds of your Spirit lift all of us to higher visions, to greater dreams, and to a renewed strength to make those dreams a reality in this world. May we be open today to the new creation you seek to bring about within and among us, through Jesus Christ our Lord.—Susan Gregg-Schroeder

SERMON
Topic: Do We Have a Choice?
TEXT: Deut. 1:1–8

God's people found themselves in a situation where they really had no choice. They had to make some changes. They had to move ahead, no matter how uncertain or frightening those changes were.

I. Let's review for just a moment the situation in which the people of God found themselves (6:1–4). According to the opening verse, Deuteronomy is a collection of Moses' sermons to the people of God. Moses' most significant contribution in his role as the leader of God's people at the most indisputably crucial time in their history was primarily as a preacher—a faithful communicator of the Word of God. Verses 2 and 3 serve as an intentionally stark reminder of the necessity for a preacher like Moses. God's Word is a vital ingredient in life because men and women are, by nature, stubborn and willful. God has to tell them again and again about things they have already repeatedly heard.

As the text demonstrates, it's even possible for a whole group of people to become stuck in place and to make little or no discernible progress on their journey. It certainly happened to the people Moses led—the people of God. Moses stood before the people of Israel, and he spoke the Word of the Lord. "You've been here long enough. Break camp and get on with the journey. The Promised Land is not going to come to you. You've got to go and claim it!"

II. That's the second thing I want you to notice about Moses' challenge to the people of God. He called them to resolve to get on with it (vv. 6–7). The price for staying where they were was simply too high. There's a time for caution and a time for patience. In fact, patience will do wonders in some situations. But patience won't be much help to a man who plants an orange grove in Alaska, will it? He can wait until the Lord returns, and he'll never pick an orange from one of his trees. And a "let's-wait-and-see" attitude is not much help when you're trying to reach people with the gospel of Jesus Christ and change their lives by its power. When you take that kind of approach to reaching people, things and people just go from bad to worse, and they do it more quickly than you would ever imagine.

Across the years, I've noticed some things about churches and people who make a difference, who leave a significant mark on their community and on the lives of other people. They know what's worth more and what's worth less in life. I've also noticed that at key times, when they made crucial decisions, they acted out of a sense of urgency, as well as in the confidence that God has led them to do what they have done.

III. That brings us to the third part of Moses' challenge to the people: he called them to learn how to rely upon God, how to depend on his ability to keep his Word, and how to trust him for the outcome (v. 8). "God told you," he said, "that the land is yours. He has given it to you. What are you waiting for? Why are you still standing here?"

Everything that I've said to you today adds up to simply trusting God. We are his people. He is in charge, and we are ultimately responsible to him. That means that you and I are not responsible for the outcome. The outcome is up to God, and there's no need to worry. God always does his job well. We are responsible only for obedience and faithfulness to him. God has already determined the outcome.—Gary C. Redding

SUNDAY, APRIL 29, 2007
Lectionary Message

Topic: Who Am I?
TEXT: John 10:22–30
Other Readings: Acts 9:36–43; Ps. 23; Rev. 7:9–17

I. We ask questions to get answers, usually. Sometimes we ask questions to demonstrate what we know. When we ask questions of God to parade our sense of self-importance, the question boomerangs into a judgment upon ourselves. When the Temple leaders asked of Jesus to again say who he was, Jesus turned their question into a shepherd image, which exposed arrogance as the illness that blinded them from recognizing Jesus as the Messiah.

Jesus made it clear that to understand him we are required to listen and follow. Through obedience we also reveal our identity of belonging to him as sheep who belong to the Good Shepherd, who came "to give life, and life abundantly."

Jesus chose to offer up himself with obedience unto death, even death on the cross, as the sacrificial Lamb of God. He is "the Alpha and the Omega, the First and the Last, the Beginning and the End." With amazing grace, he offers us the opportunity to join in his King-dom, but we must join on his terms. We are to be obedient sheep to the Shepherd.

George Bernard Shaw was a caustic critic of the arts and society. He was, however, inspired by Mozart's music. On the hundredth anniversary of the composer's death, he wrote: "In art the highest success is to be the last of your race, not the first. Anybody, almost, can make a beginning: the difficulty is to make an end—to do what cannot be bettered." Christ, as the Son of Man, did both. He was the culmination and the beginning of a new humanity.

II. Walking along Solomon's colonnade during Hanukkah, Jesus was surrounded by Tem-ple authorities. Their persistent questions revealed their purpose. They were not interested in knowing whether Jesus was the real Christ. They wanted to push Jesus around by their agendas of power and control.

Nicodemus had shown that a respected religious leader could humbly come to Jesus with soulful questions and get answers that transform the seeker into a believer. Joseph of Ari-mathea would show that Jesus' Temple teachings could connect with a person who yearned for more than positional power, who would then use his power for good, not evil.

Jesus' being the Son of God enabled him to do the Father's business. Jesus' miracles had revealed his authority to speak in the Father's name. The miracles revealed the connection between his being and doing. For instance, as the bread of life, he can feed the multitudes. Jesus, as the bread of life, can feed every people's hunger. As the light of the world, Jesus can shine the gospel into humanity's darkness and not be extinguished. As the truth, he can set people free. As the living water, he can quench spiritual thirst.

The Temple authorities did not believe Jesus because they were not of his sheep, mean-ing they did not listen to Jesus to understand his teachings. They sought to rebuke him, not to receive him. Consequently, they brought judgment upon themselves. They would perish and never know the joy of eternal life.

III. During a pivotal period of Jesus' ministry, he took the apostles to the northern sector of Israel. Near the border, Jesus stopped at Caesarea Philippi. Having taken them to the edge, where the familiar greets the unfamiliar, he asked them two questions: "Who do people say the Son of Man is?" and "But what about you, who do you say I am?" Then was the time and that was the place Jesus chose to call out the faith commitment of those who were ready to give it.

Thinking out loud, the disciples said, "The people think you are a dead prophet come back to life." Some thought he was the beheaded John the Baptist. The one who had executed John (Herod Antipas) feared that Jesus was John come back to haunt him. The crowds whom the Baptist had baptized hoped for such. Others had asked the disciples if Jesus was Elijah, the prophet who had ascended to heaven without dying. The great Elijah had stood up for God and the people against the evil practices of King Ahab and Queen Jezebel.

Others hoped Jesus was the Jeremiah who faithfully prophesied for God when the Israelites were being exiled to Babylon. The troubled people of Jesus' day wanted to hear again that the Lord declares, "I know the plans I have for you. Plans to prosper you and not to harm you. Plans to give you hope and a future" (Jer. 29:11).

With mounting expectation, Jesus seemed to be asking, "What about yourselves? You have been with me. You have heard my teachings, seen my miracles, slept beside me, walked with me, asked me questions, calmed your fears by my presence, been shocked, humbled, and bewildered by me. We have prayed and worshiped together. *You need to know that you know who I am!* So give me your best answer."

The best of the rest in that moment was Peter. He spoke with a faith that he knew was true: "You are the Christ, the Son of the Living God." There, it was said. Peter was glad and proud that he could boldly speak what the others were thinking but were unable or unwilling to say. "You, Jesus," Peter was saying, "are the anointed Messiah, and you are doing this as the sign of God's living presence. You are his Son."—D. Leslie Hollon

ILLUSTRATION

RENEWAL.   Hearing the Shepherd's voice, one day at a time, is the key to obedience. For instance, when my morning alarm clock goes off, I hit the snooze button. Half awake and half asleep, while turning over in bed, I utter, in the morning, "God, I give you my life this day. I give my heart, my mind, my body to you this day. Go before me into the daily schedule and surprises. Guide me through the challenges and help me to seize the opportunities. Let me serve you and be helpful to people." The intent of these words is prayed before the alarm rings again.

Bzzzz—I hit the snooze button and stay horizontal, glad for the bed's comfort. I recall my night's dreams and ask God to reveal their message. I remember if any phone calls came during my night's sleep and pray through what needs to be done.

As the alarm rings a third time, I am glad for my family's patience with the noisiness of my morning routine. A biblical story or verse comes to my mind. As the Shepherd awakens me to a new day, I know afresh the meaning of hearing his voice.

Renewed by a night of rest and moments of meditation, I am ready to get up. The Spirit has made me safe for others. My flesh and bones have rested in God's presence. Touched from heaven, I am ready to live on earth. And thus I pray for God to bless all the people I will see during the coming day. With feet on the floor, I set the alarm to "off" and live the day before me. Through this exercise, I focus to see more clearly how God's best comes to us one day at a time and leads to eternity.—D. Leslie Hollon

SERMON SUGGESTIONS

Topic: Journeying Through the Jungle

TEXT: Matt. 3:1

(1) We are journeying through a jungle in our present day. (2) There is an oasis in the jungle: a word from the Lord that penetrates our darkness. (3) There are dangers in the jungle, including being satisfied living there. (4) There is a way out of the jungle: our Lord entered there to bring us out.—Sandy F. Ray

Topic: How to Become a Peacemaker

TEXT: Matt. 5:9

(1) Disarm yourself. (2) Embrace the suffering of your fellow human beings. (3) Recognize the stranger as your brother.—Clarence Forsberg

WORSHIP AIDS

CALL TO WORSHIP.   "Let us search and try our ways, and turn again to the Lord. Let us lift up our heart with our hands unto God in the heavens" (Lam. 3:40–41 KJV).

INVOCATION.   Kind Father, we gather to worship and to give thanks for the true faith and sure hope you have provided in Christ Jesus. May in this hour our spirits be so challenged and strengthened that we will serve you victoriously all the days of life.

OFFERTORY SENTENCE.   "So then, each of us will give an account of himself to God" (Rom. 14:12 NIV).

OFFERTORY PRAYER.   Lord, we thank you that you are so very gracious and generous to us. All that we possess is a gift from you. Help us to reflect your spirit of goodness and grace, as we commit these gifts for the furtherance of your Kingdom's rule.

PRAYER.   Dear Father, we praise you for your good character. We praise you for your faithfulness, when so many of those around us do not seem to be so faithful. Your constant love surrounds us, even when we do not clearly sense it. We are confident in your complete provision for our needs, even when it is not yet obvious to us. Father, we pray for the many hurts that we have—some known only by you. For those in marriage near divorce, for those whose loved ones are very sick, for those whose emotions have been deeply wounded by those we dearly love, for those needing money and seeking employment where, we believe, you have called us; for those of us who need to express our deep personal emotions, let us be near you now. This morning touch our lives with your strong and powerful hand. Help us to see ourselves, your provision for us, and your everlasting love for us through your caring eyes and sensitive heart. Prepare our minds, wills, and emotions, as well as our spirits, for worship of you this morning. Look clearly into our hearts as we sing and speak praise to you. We pray to receive all that you have to give us this morning. May our lips and lives glorify you, through Jesus Christ our Lord.—Larry Ellis

SERMON
Topic: Jesus' Trial
TEXT: Matt. 26:57–68

Did you know that nowhere in the Gospels of Matthew or Mark or Luke did Jesus ever directly call himself Messiah or Son of God? The only thing he ever called himself is what he said in the last part of verse 64: Son of Man. So who was he? Was he the Messiah?

I. He was the Son of Man. Jesus used that description in three ways to talk about himself. First, he used it to speak of his ministry. *Son of Man*—person—meant that he was the person who made the presence of God felt and known in the world. He was the one who had power to forgive sins; he was the one who sacrificed home and family to show the face of God to the world. When Jesus says that God's will is not to resist evil with evil but to forgive our enemies, do we take his word for it? Or do we know better: surely, God would want me to stamp out these wicked people or to strike back against my enemies. When Jesus says that God's will is for us not to be anxious about tomorrow but to seek the Kingdom of God and let the rest take care of itself, do we believe him? Or do we say, "Well, you can't take that too far or too literally." Jesus, we say, revealed God better, more clearly, more perfectly than any other revelation ever did or could.

II. Second, Jesus used "Son of Man" to talk about his own death. Whenever he predicted his death, he used this term. So *Son of Man* not only means that Jesus reveals God; it also means that Jesus' death seals the relationship between God and the people. People were being destroyed by sin, by things like greed and lust and ambition and hatred, things that fuel wars and prejudice and injustice. He was willing to die to save the world from those sorts of things, willing to die in order to set us free from the bondage of our own mistakes. Jesus was willing to die to change that picture. He was willing, as Son of Man, to create a relationship between God and people out on little ledges, cut off from hope. He knew his death was necessary, so he did it for us.

III. Jesus also used "Son of Man" to speak of his future role as judge of the world. "After this," he said, "you will see the Son of Man seated at God's right hand and coming with the clouds of heaven." The implication is plain: You may condemn me to death today, but eventually I will be your judge. There will be a day of judgment, where all our deeds will be judged. We believe that Jesus will be that standard of judgment. Jesus, the man who showed us God, who died to bring us to God, will also be the one to judge who is guilty and who is innocent on that great day. The Son of Man, who helped the poor and who suffered greatly in his death, will be the one to judge all the great and powerful, all the wealthy and all the sinful.

What we'd better be certain of, then, is that when the final verdict comes down on this world, we are standing on Jesus' side of the courtroom. This morning, what will the verdict be? Do we live by his teachings? Are we identifiable as his disciples?—Richard B. Vinson

SUNDAY, MAY 6, 2007
Lectionary Message

Topic: A New Commandment
TEXT: John 13:31–35
Other Readings: Acts 11:1–18; Ps. 148; Rev. 21:1–6

If someone were to ask you to sum up the message of Jesus to us, his Church, and his disciples, what would you say? There is no better summation of the message of Jesus than this one, found in John 13. With a towel in his hand as he washed the feet of his disciples, he said, "A new commandment I give to you: that you love one another. Just as I have loved you, you also should love one another. By this all people will know that you are my disciples, if you have love for one another."

This is a part of Jesus' farewell speech to his disciples. It is common in Scripture for some announcement to be made at a time of departure. Was this really new? Loving is stressed throughout Scripture, especially by Jesus and Paul. Love is the central theme in the life of the Christian. Nothing else comes close, and nothing else in the Christian life matters without love.

A part of the newness of this commandment is the emphasis on *one another*. He had already announced another commandment: "You shall love your neighbor as yourself." This is a new commandment in that we are to love not just our enemy but one another. It is a new way of relating that often becomes difficult, even for the Church. "Brotherly love," we call it. This new love is the fruit of the Holy Spirit dwelling in the Church. Perhaps the "newness" of Jesus' commandment lay not just in the commandment itself but in the motivational clause attached to it: "Love one another *as I have loved you.*"[1]

I. The measure of discipleship is simply obedience—that we love as we have been loved! This is not something Jesus just *commends* but what Jesus *commands.* And this love is the central command of Jesus. This love then becomes the mark of discipleship. "If there is this love among you, then all will know that you are my disciples" (John 13:35 NEB). Discipleship had previously been recognized by various tests and deeds, but no one had imposed such a responsibility or created such a characteristic. Some disciples of other leaders had been known by reasoning abilities or attachment to certain theories. Some were recognized by their distinctive dress or language or by what they ate or by the work they performed. Their manner of oratory or storytelling was their distinctive mark. But here is Jesus saying the way the disciples will be recognized as his followers is by their love for one another!

Years ago a chorus was circulating among the churches that ended this way: "They will know we are Christians by our love, by our love. Yes, they will know we are Christians by our love."

II. This commandment is especially significant for the Church today. It seems we may have forgotten this message of Jesus. He is, in effect, saying we must not manipulate each other, not treat each other carelessly, not undermine personal character. Treat each other with respect and listen—listen for what the Spirit may be directing us to do and be. Often we have let our theology, politics, and financial positions and stations determine how we will act toward each other. Jesus was emphatic in commanding us to "love one another, as I have loved you." Church groups, denominations, organizations would do well to heed these words. Remember, they will know we are Christians by our love. It is a primary source of witness to the world. "If our discipleship is to be known in the world by the quality of our love for one another, can we wonder that, to a world walking in shadowed valleys, the church does not look like a city set on a hill?" Richard Raines said this back in 1964, in a book titled *Reshaping the Christian Life.* This indicates to me that keeping this commandment of Jesus is an ongoing, but necessary, struggle in our generation.

III. To help us along the way in the *how* of this command to love one another is the clue and direction, "as I have loved you." This becomes our motivation, just as the motivation for following the commandments was the one who gave them with the words, "I am the Lord your God" (Exod. 20:2). That's the motivation!

How are we motivated to love, and how are we to go about loving? Barclay suggests that Jesus loved his disciples "sacrificially, understandingly, and forgivingly." Sometimes love is costly in time, energy, resources. It is loving people when they are not at their best, in fact, when they may be at their worst. It is no great effort to love the "loveable," but we are called to love, even when some are not so lovable. To love forgivingly may be the most difficult love of all, yet we are called to do so. Barclay says that "the love which has not learned to forgive cannot do anything but shrivel and die."

---

[1]Stuart Briscoe, *Happiness Beyond Our Happenings* (Wheaton, IL: Harold Shaw Publishers, 1993), p. 103. In one short paragraph Briscoe lists some of the things that happened when Paul became a Christian: a new perspective, a new position, and a new possession.

Conclusion: this Scripture calls for soul-searching as individuals, churches, and denominations. The proof of discipleship has been given. Hatred is positive proof that one is not a disciple. Tertullian (220 A.D.) said the heathen remarked, "See how the Christians love one another." Hopefully, we can sing again in full voice, "They will know we are Christians by our love, by our love, yes, they will know we are Christians by our love."—Louis Twyman

SERMON SUGGESTIONS

Topic: The Shout of a King
TEXT: Num. 23:21
(1) "The Lord their God is with them": a declaration of divine presence. (2) "The shout of a King is among them": the promise of Christ's victory.—James S. Stewart

Topic: Knowing God's Will
TEXT: Exod. 19:1–8, 20:1–17
(1) Let's not confuse God's will with what we want to know. Much remains hidden. (2) God provides what we need to know. The Ten Commandments reveal God's way for us. (3) Our challenge is to obey what we already know.—David Matthews

WORSHIP AIDS

CALL TO WORSHIP.   "Trust in him at all times, O people; pour out your hearts to him, for God is our refuge" (Ps. 62:8 NIV).

INVOCATION.   Eternal God, grant, this day, light to darkened minds and peace to troubled hearts. Give strength to those who have hard duties to do and courage to those who face severe temptations. May we now, in this time of worship, experience your presence and go forth prepared to serve.

OFFERTORY SENTENCE.   "For ye know the grace of our Lord Jesus Christ, that though he was rich, yet for your sakes he became poor, that ye through his poverty might be rich" (2 Cor. 8:9 KJV).

OFFERTORY PRAYER.   Almighty God, whose gracious hand has provided for our sustenance, grant us grace that we may honor you with our gifts. Remind us, O Lord, that we must give account for all things. May we be found as faithful stewards of your bounty.

PRAYER.   Hear our prayers, God, the ones we say aloud, the silent ones that fill our hearts, and those other ones, only half-formed, the ones we don't even know yet how to pray. Help us to apprehend what is stirring in us this wet, green spring, what is waiting to be born, what is yet to unfold and bloom. God of our hopes and dreams, our disappointments and our fears, hold us, support us when we are here, together, and all the day long. Help us to sense your presence, in this moment, and in our daily lives. Spirit of life and love, we pray today for those who need our prayers, who need your help—for those who are ill, and those who are dying, and those who are facing difficult times ahead. We pray for those we have loved and lost; we pray for all who mourn; we pray for the hungry and the homeless, for prisoners and refugees, for soldiers and civilians who are in harm's way.

Loving God, help us to acknowledge those things in our lives that are painful and uncomfortable and real—the ache of disappointment that what we have hoped for has not come to pass and the guilt and grief from things we have done that we now regret. Help us to face these things, God, and then to let them go and feel renewed and refreshed and forgiven, and able to begin again.

And we thank you, God, for all that we have been given. For our lives, for the sun that shines and warms our soggy spirits, for our friends and family, for this church community, this place of love and warmth and welcome—for all these things, and more, we are grateful. On this Sunday, as lilacs bloom again, we remember those who have died in war—those who in their lives fought for life. We honor their memory and their sacrifice, and we pray for the day when war shall be no more. Hear our prayers, God; gather them all up, gather up the prayers of your people, and let them go forth, out over the hills and the fields, over the towns and the cities, and let them be blessings, on this earth and all its creatures, now and forever.— Frank Clarkson

SERMON
Topic: The Whisper of God
TEXT: 1 Sam. 3:1–10; 1 Kings 19:9–12

The fullest revelation of God comes to us in a conversational relationship, as we get to know God and God gets to know us, and we dialogue back and forth. Today, I want us to look at some Scripture passages that help us see how the Word of God comes to us.

I. There are six categories we will look at quickly. The first is that God uses phenomenal acts and a voice together. In Genesis 15, God sends fire down upon an altar that Abraham has built but, at the same time, speaks a word of promise to Abraham and all his descendants. The second way that God speaks his Word to us is through an angel or some other supernatural messenger. In the first chapter of Mark, an angel speaks to Zechariah as he ministers in the Temple and says, "To you and Elizabeth is born a son, and his name will be John." Later on in that same chapter another angel, Gabriel, speaks to Mary, and says, "To you will be born a son, and his name will be Jesus." A third way that God speaks to us is through a dream or a vision. Remember the story of Jacob's ladder (Gen. 28)? He has a dream at night. In the first chapter of Matthew, Joseph has three dreams in which God speaks to him. In Acts 10, Peter has a dream.

Fourth, God speaks through an audible voice. In Genesis 22, God says to Abraham, "Sacrifice your son, your only son." But then before Abraham can do it, God speaks again and says, "No Abraham, don't do that." God intervenes through an audible voice. God speaks also through a human voice. In the call of Moses, Moses says, "Don't call on me. I can't talk right." God says to him, "I will be your mouth, and I will teach you what to say." Paul says the same thing in 1 Corinthians 2: "It's not I who speaks, it's God who is speaking through me."

The last way that God speaks God's Word is through the human spirit, or what the Scriptures call "the still, small voice." The classical example is the one from 1 Kings that deals with Elijah. Those are all phenomenal ways in which God has spoken to people. But then we are told there is the "still, small voice." That voice says, "Go and return." It is not a word that Elijah wanted to hear, but it's God's word and Elijah does it.

II. What do we learn from these six methods that God has used with people in Scripture to communicate God's word? First of all the foundational affirmation is, obviously, God wants to talk with us. That is absolutely clear. God will use any means possible to bring that about, and God is infinitely creative in doing it. God wants to be in relationship with us. God wants to communicate with us. But what the "still, small voice" says to me more than anything else is that God doesn't overpower us. God doesn't use the supernatural phenomenal ways, or out-of-body experiences, or any other kind of strange situation to speak to us if normal ways of communicating will bring it about.

So what does that mean for us today? I think we look at the life of Jesus, and we see it absolutely clearly lived for us the way God would speak with us today. Jesus' life was one of intense engagement in the world. Jesus was involved in individual people's lives; he was involved with groups of people. And as he would listen to God, he would listen to the "still, small voice" in prayer. I am convinced he took his Scriptures with him and read them. He also took his friends with him on occasion.

III. Why does God speak to us? Maybe that is the better question for us to think about now. There is a great tradition in Christian history called, "The Candle of the Lord." It's an image. The saying goes like this: The Word of God is a candle. It comes and it shines in our lives. God walks with God's word up and down the passageways, the alleys, the byways, and the main streets of our personalities, so we can see who we truly are, but also so we can see our neighbor and our relationship with God. That's why God speaks to us—so we can see ourselves, we can see our neighbor, and we can see God. It goes back to relationships once again. That's the foundation. That's the core, over and over again, in this dialogical life we share with each other and with God.—Jim Standiford

SUNDAY, MAY 13, 2007
Lectionary Message

Topic: The Gift of Peace

TEXT: John 14:23–29

Other Readings: Acts 16:9–15; Ps. 67; Rev. 21:10, 22–22:5

This is Jesus' farewell address to his disciples. He is leaving a legacy for his followers, which includes us. He leaves but promises that his Spirit will be with us and, just as important, he gives us the gift of peace.

Often in our churches we will experience what we call the "Passing of the Peace," which is when one says to another, perhaps during communion or in greeting we will say to those nearby, "May the Peace of God be with you." And the return is, "And also with you." This familiar greeting sounds simple enough but reflects a profound Christian teaching and ministry for all of us. The legacy of love left to the followers of Jesus is peace! This is a vital part of who we are and what our ministry is all about: declaring and sharing the peace we have found in Christ. Peace in the midst of strife, confusion, and hurt. It is different from what the world speaks when it talks of peace. This is part of who we are and part of the mission and message we share with the world.

I. We are anointed through the Spirit to do the work of peace and reconciliation. "God was in Christ reconciling the world to himself . . . and he has entrusted us with the message of reconciliation" (2 Cor. 5:19 NEB). Peace and reconciliation often go together. Steve Shoemaker[2] points out that what we proclaim is reconciliation: first of all with God, for without reconciliation with God there is no other reconciliation possible; reconciliation with our own true self created in God's image, and reconciliation with our brothers and sisters. This is our proclamation; this is what we are about. There is a lot that goes on in the Church today that does not bring about reconciliation and peace and joy. But this is what the Spirit of God is about.

There is a church in our community that works hard at the concept of peace and reconciliation. A couple of years ago I attended their International Reconciliation Conference. People from around the world gathered, and we were fortunate to have one of the visitors as a guest in our home. One of the most impressive parts of the conference was listening to a person from South Africa discuss what the black people had been through and how, in order for them to have real peace, they must first espouse and experience reconciliation with the whites. The oppressor and the oppressed, working with each other for peace!

II. Jesus is leaving a legacy of love and peace. In verse 27 this legacy is explained. The peace that Jesus gives is contrasted with the peace of the world. The world's concept is negative—the absence of war or strife. Christ's concept of peace is positive—peace in the midst of strife and difficulty. Jesus is pointing out to us this distinctive peace that can even be present in the midst of conflict and difficulty.

This gift of peace is a priceless inheritance, a precious possession that passes all understanding. "The peace of God, which is beyond our utmost understanding, will keep guard over your hearts and thoughts, in Christ Jesus" (Phil. 4:7 NEB).

III. This peace is not just the absence of trouble. Barclay points out that the peace the world offers us is the peace of escape, the peace that comes from the avoidance of trouble, the peace that comes from the refusal to face things. The peace Jesus talks about is the peace that no experience in life can ever take from us. It is the peace that no sorrow, no danger, no suffering can make less. It is the peace that is independent of outward circumstances.

IV. This peace can be defined. Jesus is saying he wants us to have the peace he experienced: "My peace I give unto you." He wants his disciples to experience the same peace he had, that is, serenity in danger, evenness in troubling circumstances, freedom from anxiety about results, the ability to have a speedy recovery after being ruffled. Part of the ability to experience this peace is to have within our character and makeup *resiliency*—the ability to bounce back.

A study was done several years ago attempting to determine the difference in people who had experienced difficulties in life or difficult lives. The summation of the study determined that the ability to overcome difficulties was greater in those persons who had *someone who believed in them*. I believe this is a part of what Jesus is saying to us when he gives us the gift of peace: "I believe in you."

Jesus says this is not the peace that the world gives us—not the peace of ease, but of struggle; not of self-content, but of self-sacrifice; not of yielding to the evil, but the conflict with it. He adds, "I have overcome the world."

---

[2]Sermon by Steve Shoemaker, 1999.

This peace comes to us when we come in harmony with God, believing that God believes in us. Christ's peace is the foundation of our peace with our fellow man. It will be difficult to find peace with others when we are not at peace with ourselves and with our God.

V. Finally, we talk about the power of peace. When we have found this peace of God, we are able to face and deal with difficulties and find peace within ourselves. Many today feel powerless, to a great extent because of the inner struggles and division, and thus feel and experience weakness. When our spirits are united and we are at peace with ourselves and our neighbor and our God, we begin to experience a sense of power that enables us to serve, accomplish, love deeply, relate, and on and on.

Conclusion: Jesus said, "Peace is my parting gift to you, my own peace, such as the world cannot give. Set your troubled hearts at rest, and banish your fears" (John 14:27). I say to you: May the peace of God be with you!—Louis Twyman

SERMON SUGGESTIONS

Topic: Christian Parenting

TEXT: Deut. 6:5–9

(1) Christian parents have a great opportunity—and responsibility. (2) We are to love the Word of God: "love these words." (3) We are to teach the Word of God: "and teach them diligently." (4) We are to keep the Word of God: "write them on the doorpost and on the gates."—Lawrence Vowan

Topic: The Home That Pleases God

TEXT: Prov. 12:5–7

(1) Such a home delights in a spiritual presence. (2) It serves as the foundation and strength for all of society. (3) Through loving discipline, it provides protection and care. (4) It is the nearest thing to paradise on earth we can know.—Perry Webb

WORSHIP AIDS

CALL TO WORSHIP.   "Know therefore that the Lord your God is God; he is the faithful God, keeping his covenant of love to a thousand generations of those who love him and keep his commands" (Deut. 7:9 NIV).

INVOCATION.   Exalted Father, in worship today we magnify you, and give thanks to you, and praise you for your overwhelming grace. May we be reminded of your provisions for this present life and for the assurance of a greater life that is to come. Let the memory of your goodness fill our hearts with joy.

OFFERTORY SENTENCE.   "What shall I render unto the Lord for all his benefits toward me? I will pay my vows unto the Lord now in the presence of all his people" (Ps. 116:12–14 KJV).

OFFERTORY PRAYER.   Heavenly Father, remind us that though Christ offers us companionship we must each decide to rise and follow him. May these gifts represent our commitment to witness and to share with the world the goodness of your grace. To this end we dedicate these tithes and offerings.

PRAYER.   Eternal Creator, we come to you this day, thanking you for the wonder, mystery, and beauty of the home. We thank you for what our home has meant, for the nurture of good parents, and for the faithfulness of children who have responded to life and committed themselves to causes with meaning and purpose. Give to us a willingness to listen openly to our parents and children, even when they have failed. Forgive us for wallowing in self-pity or condemning or blaming instead of being willing to lift others up and understand them. We thank you for the joys we have shared together within our home. Teach us how to celebrate these times more fully. We also thank you for your presence with us in the sorrows that we have experienced. Teach us how to embrace each other more fully and lift each other up in times of difficulties and when burdens are heavy. Teach us how to love one another, to be good parents, and to be faithful in our relationship to each other. For we pray in his strong name.—William Powell Tuck

SERMON
Topic: Mothers of the Bible
TEXT: Prov. 1:10–30

I suggest that we take the inductive approach this morning and examine a few of the many examples of motherhood that parade across these pages of Holy Scripture. You will recognize immediately that the Bible is not the least bit sentimental about motherhood. In terms of motherhood, the Bible tells it like it is; the Bible acknowledges openly that some women have succeeded wonderfully in this important vocation, while others have tragically failed, and there is something to be learned from all of this. After all, I can be helped just as much by seeing what not to do as from having positive examples to imitate. Therefore, I suggest we use this particular day of the year to look at how several women of the Bible handled the challenge of motherhood.

I. The first individual to whom I would direct your attention is a woman named Rebecca. She was the wife of Isaac and the mother of twin sons, Esau and Jacob. The one word that sums up the shape of her motherhood is the word *deception.* Unfortunately, both Rebecca and Isaac let the favoritism that is always something of a problem where there are several children get out of hand and shape the whole of their family life. Rebecca liked Jacob more than Esau, and Isaac was just the opposite, and so a deadly game of competition and one-upmanship began. Blind old Isaac and dim-witted Esau were no match for this enterprising Jewish mother and wily son, and together they managed to deceive Isaac and cheat Esau out of his birthright and the family blessing and all that really mattered in terms of heritage. At first, it seemed that Rebecca and her son had won, yet years later the seeds of this way of relating came to flower, for both Jacob and his sons had tremendous problems in the area of personal honesty. Jacob went from one scrape to another, as he continued to follow the patterns of trickery that Rebecca had instilled in him; later in his life, ironically, he was deceived by his own sons, much as he had deceived his old father. The lesson to be learned here is basic: namely, the shadow of our influence as parents is long and powerful indeed.

II. The second mother I want us to look at is a woman named Jochebed. You will probably not recognize her name until I identify her son: the famous Moses. The best word to describe her motherhood is *resourceful.* At the time Moses was born, she was living as a slave in a foreign country, and an edict was out that all male babies born to the Hebrews were to be killed at the moment of birth. Somehow, Jochebed managed to evade this stricture. For three months, she hid the infant in her home and then made a little float and kept him in a nearby river so that he would not be detected. As you may remember the story, Pharaoh's daughter found the baby in this place and was so attracted to him and impressed by the mother's ingenuity that she did not have him killed but adopted him as her own son. The thing that interests me here is the creative resourcefulness of this Hebrew slave woman.

I can think of no quality that is more needed today on the part of all parents than creative resourcefulness. You talk about a challenge to creativity! There is no more demanding one than the twenty-year stint of parenting that goes with birthing a child into this world. This needs to be an intentional vocation, not something one stumbles into without thought, precisely because it is so awesome. The way Jochebed dedicated herself to the challenge of being a mother in ancient Egypt is a positive example of what is desperately needed in our own time.

III. The third case study I would have us look at is a rather infamous mother. Her name is Herodias, and she lived during the time of Christ. She had a rather checkered marital career, having divorced Phillip in order to marry his brother Herod, who at that time was the ruler of much of Palestine. When John the Baptist publicly condemned Herodias for this act, she developed a burning hatred for him. In fact, she could not wait to find occasion to have him eliminated, and when the opportunity finally came, it revealed an awesome aspect of her motherhood. The best word to describe her is *manipulative.* You may recall the story of how her daughter, Salome, danced for the king, and in his drunken stupor he offered to give her anything she wanted, up to half his kingdom. Evidently, the girl had never been allowed to function on her own, because she went straight to her mother to ask what to request, and Herodias used her daughter as a tool in her own diabolical plot. She not only had John the Baptist beheaded, but she also demonstrated a willingness to manipulate her daughter ruthlessly to serve her own purposes.

Now, of course, this is an extreme example, but it does represent one of the real pitfalls of parenthood. It is easy to confuse love for a child with the tendency to absorb that one utterly and make him or her a part of one's own personality. The hardest thing in the world for strong-minded parents to do is to recognize that while there is a unity in love, there must also be space separating the "I" and the "thou," which does not reduce the child into an "it" or a thing. Herodias stands as an awesome example of the manipulative, domineering mother who not only warped the life of her child but did great harm to others in the process.

IV. The last mother at whom I want us to look is unnamed in the Biblical record, but her attitude epitomizes motherhood at its best. This one appeared before King Solomon in a most unusual dispute. It seems that she and another woman shared a house together, and each had a tiny infant approximately the same age. One night one of the women rolled over and smothered her child, and when she realized what she had done, she got up and put the dead child by the other woman's side and took the living child for her own. The next morning a terrific conflict erupted as to whose child was whose. This dispute was finally brought to Solomon, and the young king displayed unusual wisdom by calling for a sword and proposing to cut the living child in two and give half to each of the disputants. The split-second reactions of the two women gave Solomon his clue. The real mother reacted in horror to such a suggestion and offered to relinquish her claim if the infant could be spared. The other woman found no fault with Solomon's suggestion. Such a response enabled the king to discern the identity of the true mother and to award her custody of her child. This incident lays bare not only the wisdom of Solomon but also a quality that is characterized in motherhood at its best, namely, a willingness to sacrifice one's own desire for the well-being of the child.

V. The final point I want to make is that motherhood, like any condition in the human saga, is nothing more than an occasion for challenge. The question becomes, What will one do with this opportunity? It is easy to grow sentimental at this point and to delude ourselves into thinking that the physical act of having a baby automatically transforms a woman into a saint, but this is not true. The quality of motherhood, like everything else in life, is ultimately determined by what a person brings to it and what one is willing to make of it. It is a vocation that must be lived out intentionally. There is nothing automatic or simple about it. Motherhood is what one chooses to make it. What kind of mother will you be, then? The answer is in your hands.—John R. Claypool

SUNDAY, MAY 20, 2007
Lectionary Message

Topic: Jesus' Desire for Us
TEXT: John 17:20–26
Other Readings: Acts 16:16–34; Ps. 97; Rev. 22:1–14, 16–17, 20–21

If we could think of Jesus praying for us today, what do you suppose that prayer would be? We have discussed previously his desire for us to have peace. Also we have mentioned that he wanted us "to love one another."

Now in this Scripture he speaks of us as "being one"—wanting us to have "unity." What would that unity look like?

I. First, it seems that it is not some type of organizational or ecclesiastical unity. If that were the case, then we have failed miserably. There are too many issues that divide us— ecclesiastical style and worship style, just to name a couple for examples of our division.

Could it be that he is calling for a unity based on our relationship with him? As Barclay points out, it is a unity in which men love each other because they love God. It is to be unity based on the relationship between heart and heart. He says, "It will never be that Christians will organize their churches all the same way. It will never be that they will worship God all in the same way. It will never be that they will all believe precisely and exactly the same things." He points out that we often have loved our creeds, organizations, and rituals more than we have loved each other. Only love can tear down the walls we have built around us. This unity is what has convinced the world of the truth of Christ and Christianity.[3]

Is this possible? Yes, but it will come when we realize that this is Christ's wish and prayer for us.

II. It is becoming increasingly necessary that we move in that direction as a witness. Listen again to the prayer of Jesus (vv. 22–23): "The glory which thou hast given me I have given to them, that they may be one even as we are one, I in them and thou in me, that they may become perfectly one, so that the world may know that thou hast sent me and hast loved them even as thou hast loved me."

---

[3]William Barclay, *Daily Bible Studies Series: Gospel of John,* vol. 2 (Edinburgh: The Saint Andrew Press, 2001), p. 161.

Some have indicated that this is our great duty for Jesus:

1. *To walk in unity.* The New Testament speaks a great deal about our preserving the unity of the Spirit, attaining unity of mind and judgment that the world may know that God loves them (Eph. 4:3–6; 1 Cor. 1:10–13; Phil. 2:1–5).
2. *To walk in faith.* To remain steadfast.
3. *To walk in love.* That they may know we are followers of Christ.

Therefore, we may well assume that one of the primary purposes of the prayer for unity is *evangelistic.*

We so often are sharing our differences with the world. "They" do that; "we" don't. "We" believe this; "they" don't. It is so much easier to emphasize differences rather than ways we are alike: Jesus Christ is central to who we are, and the Bible, simply put, is God's Word to and for us.

III. There is some concern that we may be going in the opposite direction. Where there was once a great sense of cooperation and sharing among local and regional churches and church groups, there now seems to be an increased contest for members, competing over what our church offers that yours doesn't. Many churches seem to be almost market-driven, looking for what works and viewing the worshippers as customers.

We wonder what pain Christ may feel, looking upon the competition among us. Have we become more like competing car dealers or gas stations, seeing who has the best deal?

Now we understand that just being united together is not enough. Even forces of hate and violence can be united around their cause. We have had experiences with hate groups—terrorist activists who are united in their cause. So just being united is not the point. Being united around love and peace is the point.

The message and motive for us is love—not just any love but the "love with which God has loved us." The ultimate reason for the Church "to be as one" is that the world may know the nature of God, that is, a God of love, mercy, forgiveness, acceptance, and hope.

Conclusion: now as we speak of this unity in a global, national, and regional way that cuts across ecclesiastical lines, we must keep in mind the oneness in the local church. We must bring it down to where we worship on a regular basis. The local congregation—*that* is where true unity becomes real. We can talk all day long about unity, about oneness in the universal Church. But all begins where we live, where we can taste it and feel it, where we truly learn what it means to be a Christian community, learning to share the love of Christ in the local setting. It is so, is it not, that a love exists strong enough to embrace the differences that separate us and to overcome the barriers of personal preferences and value judgments that exclude others? This love is empowered by Christ's strong spirit, which embraces all people and draws us together.

We can start right where we are today being the answer to Christ's prayer.—Louis Twyman

SERMON SUGGESTIONS

Topic: This Is the Church's Hour

Text: Matt. 5:13–16

(1) We must get serious about our lives with God. (2) We must be repentant people. (3) We must take our stand on the Word of God. (4) We must think as Christians. (5) We must live obediently. (6) We must be holy.—Charles Colson

Topic: Herod, Peter, and James
TEXT: Acts 12:1–11, 21–24
(1) Herod exemplifies arrogance that leads to a fall. (2) Peter exemplifies the miracle of freedom that comes through faith. (3) James exemplifies the blood of the martyrs whose faithfulness to the end inspires and challenges.—Jan M. Lochman

WORSHIP AIDS

CALL TO WORSHIP.   "Come, all you who are thirsty, come to the waters. . . . Give ear and come to me; hear me, that your soul may live" (Isa. 55:1, 3 NIV).

INVOCATION.   Lord God, holy and eternal, who dwells in the high and lofty places and in the places of the contrite and humble, we come before you seeking to be cleansed by the power of your grace that we may give you praise, both now and forevermore.

OFFERTORY SENTENCE.   "Offer the sacrifices of righteousness, and put your trust in the Lord" (Ps. 4:5 KJV).

OFFERTORY PRAYER.   Dearest God, you who are Father of all, may we so live as your children—brothers and sisters in Christ—that your kindness will be born in our hearts. Give us generous and cheerful spirits that our witness will be born to the uttermost parts of the world.

PRAYER.   In our walk to the cross and beyond, who will roll the stone away and show us the empty tomb? Only you, Lord, as you revealed yourself to three women early on that Resurrection morning. Only you, Lord, as you revealed yourself to hesitant and frightened disciples in the Upper Room and showed your wounded side. Only you, Lord, as you revealed yourself through the power of your Holy Spirit on that Pentecost morning and reveal yourself today through tongues of fire and through the gentlest of breeze, through revelation and revolution in hearts and souls. In our walk to the cross and beyond, who will roll the stone away? Show us the empty tomb, our Risen Messiah. Only you, Lord. Only you.—John Birch

SERMON
Topic: Dream When You're Feeling Blue
TEXT: Ezek. 37:1–14

To believe in God is to believe that God is the Lord over the future. So you can be the best informed, you can know all the facts of despair, you can know all the statistics of gloom and still conclude that things are going to get better, because God is in control of history. You cannot believe in God and be a pessimist.

    I. That's what our lessons this morning are saying to us, beginning with the Old Testament lesson from Ezekiel, the famous "dry bones" passage in the thirty-seventh chapter. It's a vision of resurrection—not resurrection into the next life but resurrection in this life: being reborn now, receiving new life now, being renewed now. He said God took him to a valley filled with dry bones. God asked him, "Can these bones live?" And Ezekiel said to God, "O Lord God, you know." And God said to Ezekiel, "These bones shall live."

You see what's happening here? Ezekiel had a vision of the unimaginable, the utterly impossible. Ezekiel went to his people and said, imagine the future. Have hope. The definition of "hope" in Hebrews is "the assurance of things not seen." Don't dwell on the past. Look toward the future. Don't dwell on what we have done or what has been done to us. Dwell on what God can do. Have hope for the future.

II. Now go to the New Testament lesson: Peter's sermon at Pentecost. So on Pentecost, fifty days after the Passover and the Resurrection, they are gathered together. And the Spirit of Jesus came upon them with power, and they poured out of that Upper Room onto the streets of Jerusalem and started telling people about Jesus and his Resurrection. This is what the world is waiting for—the news of Jesus and his Resurrection.

Some people asked Peter, "What's going on here?" Our text for this morning is Peter's answer in the form of a sermon. So what we have before us in our text this morning is the first Christian sermon. Peter said that is what is happening here now, today. This is the beginning of the age that Joel was talking about, when we are all like Ezekiel. The Church is that community with a vision of what the world is supposed to be like. The Church is that community on earth that is to keep alive a vision of what life is supposed to be like and then act on that vision.

III. What an image of the Church that would be. Can you imagine people walking by a church, hearing the laughter inside, then the singing? Can you imagine hearing the sounds of joy and then hearing somebody inside saying, "But that's preposterous. That could never be. It could never happen, not in this world."

Maybe Pentecost is saying this to us. If the Church's plans aren't big enough to be impossible, then you're not the Church. Because according to Pentecost that's how you know it's the Church: people joyful, singing, laughing because they have been given a vision of Resurrection of life. New life is always possible, which is preposterous, given the facts as we see them in the present. But that's our vision. Resurrection of life is our vision. And vision produces hope, and hope produces anticipation, and anticipation motivates action.

The future doesn't belong to those who have all the facts but to those who have a vision and act on it.—Mark Trotter

SUNDAY, MAY 27, 2007
Lectionary Message

Topic: Anointing of the Spirit
TEXT: John 14:8–17, 25–27
Other Readings: Acts 2:1–21 or Gen. 11:1–9; Ps. 104:24–34, 35b; Rom. 8:14–17

On this Pentecost Sunday the focus is on the concept of the anointing of the Holy Spirit. This concept sometimes makes some of us uneasy, and we have difficulty preaching on this topic because of images of "speaking in tongues" and other so-called manifestations of the Spirit. In staying away from this topic, we miss a vital and important aspect of the work of the Church. That is what this Scripture is about, as Jesus talks with his disciples prior to his departure and declares that his Spirit will continue on with them—and us—to continue his work.

What is this work of Christ? First, it's the work of reconciliation. Paul said in 2 Corinthians 5:19, "God was in Christ reconciling the world to himself."

What we proclaim is reconciliation: reconciliation with God, for without reconciliation with God there is no other reconciliation possible; reconciliation with our own true self, created in God's image; and reconciliation with our brothers and sisters.[4]

Second, in the Gospel we hear, "If you love me, keep my commandments; and I will ask the Father and He will give you another helper." In other words, there is only one test of love, and that test is obedience. But obedience is not easy, just as loving is not always easy. But Jesus is saying, "I will not leave you in your struggle alone." This is where he says I will send you a comforter, but Barclay points out that the better translation is "Helper."[5]

Obedience is not easy; we are not left alone. Often we hear and know of people talking about not being able to cope or about having difficulty coping with one thing or another. This is what Jesus is giving us when he speaks of this gift of the Spirit or the anointing of the Spirit—you will be able to cope with the difficulties and challenges of life.

Barclay paraphrases this saying of Jesus in this way: "I am setting you a hard task, and I am sending you out on an engagement very difficult. But I am going to send you someone, the *Helper*, who will guide you in what to do and who will make you able to do it. The Holy Spirit will bring you truth and you are able to cope with the battle for the truth."[6]

Third, this anointing of the Spirit is also to be anointed with the Spirit of Truth.

The Spirit of Truth given to the Church is the living presence, wisdom, power, and love that Christ brought to the world. When we have received the "anointing" of the Spirit, our minds are opened. Sometimes we wonder why some minds seemed closed and unwilling to see and hear truth. Could it be that we have not been open in prayer to receive the promises that Christ made to us and to receive the Spirit? How often have we prayed to be filled with the Spirit and included in that prayer the need to know the truth? As we read through the New Testament we begin to see, little by little, how the followers were beginning to see and apply the truths of Christ. That is the Spirit at work.

The anointing of the Spirit helps us to "open our eyes," as the old hymn goes: "Open my eyes that I may see glimpses of truth thou hast for me, open my mouth. . . ." This is a prayer for the Spirit to be with us during our daily living, to be able to apply the lessons and spirit of Christ to our daily lives, to help us overcome sin and grow as Christians.

So when we are anointed by the Spirit, our minds are enlightened, and we are given strength for service.

Conclusion: obedience and service are not easy. Loving is not always easy; reconciliation is often difficult. But as it often is in daily life, knowing that I am not alone as I go through challenges of daily Christian living, the Spirit of the Living Christ is with us.

We must not just think that the gift of the Spirit is just for special occasions or special times of worship. The Spirit that Christ is speaking about is with us at all times to offer guidance, strength, hope.

In the field of mental health we often talk about a healthy person as one who is able to be *intimate,* that is, one who can open up to another person and get close. Or we might say the person has *awareness*—is aware of his or her own strengths and weaknesses and impact on others, whether negative or positive. Or we might say a healthy person is one who has

---

[4]Sermon by Steve Shoemaker, 1998.
[5]Barclay, *The Daily Study Bible: Gospel of John,* vol. 2, 2001, p. 96.
[6]Barclay, *The Daily Study Bible: Gospel of John,* vol. 2, 2001, p. 96.

spontaneity, meaning the person is not stuck in a rut but is open to seeing things differently and responding differently.

I believe this is close to what Jesus is calling us to when he says the Holy Spirit will be with you. He is saying that we are willing to be intimate with his Spirit and open ourselves to him, that we seek to become more aware of our strengths and needs so that we can respond better to the leading of God's Spirit, and, finally, that we are called to be more spontaneous in our living, meaning we are not stuck in only one way of experiencing life, or God, or ourselves and others.

Jesus is saying his Spirit is with us. It is part of his promise to us. But we must be aware of our strengths and needs; we must desire to be closer in our walk, and we must be willing to step "outside the box" in spontaneity to follow his Spirit.—Louis Twyman

SERMON SUGGESTIONS

Topic: Dives and Lazarus: Neighbors Who Never Meet
TEXT: Luke 16:19–31
(1) Notice the contrasting lifestyles. (2) Then see the surprising reversal in eternity. (3) Then see the blindness that the brothers chose. (4) We are to notice the neighbor at our gate.—Joe E. Trull

Topic: The Principle of Substitution
TEXT: Matt. 27:15–26
(1) Christ voluntarily yielded himself as a substitute for others. (2) It came as obedience to the Father. (3) The substitution was for the forgiveness of our sin.—Glen Charles Knecht

WORSHIP AIDS
CALL TO WORSHIP.   "Both young men and maidens, old men and children: let them praise the name of the Lord: for his name alone is excellent; his glory is above the earth and heaven" (Ps. 148:12–13 KJV).

INVOCATION.   Kind Father, as we worship may your Presence be made known to us. Fill us afresh with your Spirit that we may be strong in a world full of complexities and constant change. May we today boldly bear witness to the claims of your Kingdom, and may we look forward to the day when your knowledge covers the earth as waters cover the sea.

OFFERTORY SENTENCE.   "Go, sell your possessions and give to the poor, and you will have treasure in heaven. Then come, follow me" (Matt. 19:21 NIV).

OFFERTORY PRAYER.   God of our fathers, we cherish the blessings your Church brings to us. We are indeed grateful for the privilege of sharing, through these gifts, the proclamation of your Word to the uttermost parts of the world, until that day when all earth praises you.

PRAYER.   O God, the fresh winds of your spirit are like a cool, refreshing breeze that flows over our hungry souls. But we have to admit, Loving God, that sometimes we are left wondering when we experience the mystery of your presence with us. You tell us that unless we are born again, we cannot see the Kingdom of God. Help us to understand that we are constantly given opportunities to begin again. Teach us again how to see, but this time through your eyes. Teach us again to walk, this time in your shoes. Teach us again to feel, this time through your senses. Teach us again to love, this time with your heart.

Help us to be born from above and inspire us with the confidence that you will be with us in our life journey. Help us to let go of those things that hold us down. Comfort those among us who struggle with illness, who anxiously await the outcome of medical testing, who are overcome with loss, who are held prisoner by addictions, who are despondent over their present life situation. And on this Memorial Day weekend, we especially remember those who have gone before us, who have fought the good fight, who have finished the race and now celebrate life eternal. We ask for your special guidance for the leaders of our country, and we pray for peace throughout the world. You, Loving God, come to offer hope, to change the circumstances of our lives and to offer to us the promise of eternal life. As your grateful children, we boldly pray the prayer Jesus taught to his disciples.—Susan Gregg Schroeder

SERMON
Topic: Stones from the River
TEXT: Josh. 4:1–7

Tomorrow is Memorial Day. Specifically, it's a day for remembering those who served in our nation's armed services. More generally, Memorial Day calls us to remember and to give thanks for the person, the events, and the experiences that have shaped us and formed us. We pause at times like these, not only to give thanks for God's mercy and for those who have been agents of God's mercy in our lives but to *organize* our memories and our thanksgiving.

I. Our Scripture text today recalls an act of remembrance undertaken by the children of Israel, as they prepared to cross over the Jordan River and take possession of the Promised Land. The story begins in Joshua 3. The Leviticus priests bore the Ark of the Covenant to the edge of the Jordan. As their feet dipped into the river, the waters piled up upstream, and the riverbed became dry and empty. While the priests stood in the middle of the riverbed holding the ark, the whole nation crossed the Jordan. Then last of all, the priests came out on the other side. But before the crossing was complete, a representative of each of the twelve tribes of Israel hoisted a stone from the riverbed, from the spot where the priests had stood, and carried it over to the encampment on the far side of Jordan.

II. And the stones "are there to this day," the book of Joshua tells us (Josh. 4:9), reminding Israel that their life as God's covenant people, freed from slavery and living in a new land, was the result of one miracle of God's grace after another.

And what about us? Where have you and I experienced God's uncanny grace? Do you have "stones from the river" set up somewhere, to remind you, to organize your memories? These "memory stones" can be pictures, letters, videos, scrapbooks, special songs, special vacation spots, special family rituals (almost every family has them). Our memory stones may be personal. Where did you meet your spouse? Do you go back there from time to time, to eat at the special restaurant and look at the special view? How did you find your career? How did you meet Christ? Do you have a way to mark the times and places? Our memory stones may belong to the family. Of course, our nation has memory stones as well, among them the flag displays, patriotic speeches, parades, and cemetery visits of Memorial Day. That's what started us off on this train of thought.

III. We've asked about the identity of our memory stones; they're as varied as our unique identities and life histories. I want to conclude with another question: How do our memory stones function? Obviously, they help us to *look back* and remember where we've come from and how we became who we are. "When your children ask their parents in time to come, 'What do these stones mean?' then you shall let your children know. . . . The Lord your God dried up the waters of the Jordan for you until you crossed over, as the Lord your God did to the Red Sea (Josh. 4:21–23).

Our memory stones also help us to *keep our bearings.* Life can be tough; people can be cruel; it's easy to doubt and lose our grip on our faith. But I remember what Martin Luther said: "When the devil assaults you, remember your baptism."

And finally, our memory stones help us to continue *moving ahead.* I carry with me a life-time of Bible narratives, taught to me from infancy, modeled for me by godly parents, Sunday school teachers, and youth leaders, and absorbed and pondered on my own. When I doubt or worry, I remember the heroes and heroines of the Bible stories. And I remember the God who brought the people over Jordan on dry land and kept them moving until they got to the Promised Land. Our memory stones remind us that the One who has brought us this far will never let us go. "Jesus Christ is the same yesterday and today and forever" (Heb. 13:8).—David L. Wheeler

SUNDAY, JUNE 3, 2007
Lectionary Message

Topic: Always Another Hill
Text: Rom. 5:1–5
Other Readings: Prov. 8:1–4, 22–31; Ps. 8; John 16:12–15

I. Does this hill ever end? I love to go hiking, but there's ordinarily a point on the hike where somebody says, "Who thought this was a good idea?" Often that comes on a trail that has been ascending for a long time, and you have had several false bursts of hope that you've reached the top of the ridge, only to find that the trail made a switchback and you were still on your way up. Bill Bryson, in his hilarious *A Walk in the Woods,* says "the elusive summit continually retreats by whatever distance you press forward, so that each time the canopy parts enough to give you a view you are dismayed to see that the topmost trees are as remote, as unattainable, as before. Still you stagger on. What else can you do?"[1]

A much more serious analogy to that feeling comes as we think about how hard we struggle against sin—against either our own tendencies to do evil or the systematic evil that presses down on us—and how little progress we make. We pray to make some progress on dealing with our own hot tempers but find ourselves muttering in the shower about what he said or she did. We work and pray to relieve poverty in our communities, only to find that government policies or the soaring price of oil will undo our efforts. Why keep trying to make it up

---

[1]Bill Bryson, *A Walk in the Woods* (New York: Broadway, 1998), p. 35.

the hill? Sisyphus, in the Greek myth, pushed the boulder up, only to have it roll back; maybe we feel like him, or more than a little like Bryson on the AT. The author of Second Esdras complained to God that a more sensible creation either would have omitted people or would have prevented them from sinning: "For what good is it to all that they live in sorrow now and expect punishment after death? What good is it that everlasting hope has been promised us, but we have miserably failed?" (2 Esd. 7:117, 120).

II. *Where we are:* Paul has already argued, in Romans 1–4, that Christ's death brings freedom from eternal death and eternal punishment. In Romans 5:1–5, he amplifies what Christ's death does for the believer.

Being in Christ, he says, brings us peace with God, access to God, hope of sharing God's glory, and a heart filled with God's love. Peace with God is more than what we mean by "peace of mind." A good insurance policy brings peace of mind—the assurance that if disaster strikes, you can replace your things or your income. Peace with God looks ahead to Judgment Day, promising that because we are in Christ, we don't need to fear eternal punishment. But peace with God also means that we need not interpret every hill, every struggle, every catastrophe as God's punishment on us. The road is tough, but God isn't up there making it harder on you. That's good to know.

Being in Christ brings us access to God as well. We have, literally, "an entrance into this grace in which we stand"; the image is of an open door or, more precisely, of God's open-door policy with us. We are part of God's family by God's gift and invitation; God's presence, from which we often wander, is always available if we will seek it.

Christ's gift is also a heart full of God's love—love for God, love of God for us—because God's very Spirit has been poured into us. Peace is nice (knowing that God isn't at odds with us), and access is also nice (knowing that God's door is always open), but love means that God wants us there and that we want to be there, too. And what about when we're so tired from walking up those endless hills that we're not certain we feel anything, much less love? The heart full of love doesn't depend solely on us; it's the gift and the work of God's Spirit.

III. *Where we are headed:* All that is very sweet, but there is the matter of the hills. It hurts to keep walking uphill, and eventually we begin to despair. One hike involving several miles of steep ascents at high altitude left me gasping for air, unable to walk more than twenty-five paces at a time. And then, just as we were getting close to the top, a dark cloud formed over us and dropped hail on our heads. Life is often full of suffering, and often suffering seems to beget more suffering.

"We boast in our sufferings," says Paul, in the same way we "boast in our hope of sharing God's glory." Boasting means, first, being confident of something; we certainly know that we suffer, so we know, Paul argues, that we are on the way to the top, where we will share in God's glory. Suffering produces (the verb implies a lot of work involved) endurance, or the ability to hold up under pressure. Endurance produces character, or "proven-ness." Paul wasn't thinking about just any character but the character of Christ: suffering in order to stay on the path God has laid for us makes us more like Christ. Being more like Christ increases our hope of sharing God's glory, naturally, since we're talking about the man who went to the cross out of love for and obedience to God. As long as we keep on moving, then, keep on walking up the hill, we can know, just as certainly as we are hurting and sweating and struggling, that there will be a positive outcome. God's hope does not trick us or leave us empty at the end of the path.

There is always another hill, but for those in Christ, who stand in grace, whose hearts God fills with love, and whose sufferings can bring us close to Christ, we don't have to think of the hill as punishment. And we walk up knowing that the ascent itself is proof of the summit; we can live in the hope of sharing in God's blessings.—Richard B. Vinson

ILLUSTRATIONS

FINDING DELIVERANCE.   "When the holy abbot Anthony was living in the desert, his soul fell into a weariness and confusion of thought, and he began saying to God, 'Lord, I would be made whole and my thoughts will not suffer me. What shall I do in this tribulation, and how shall I be made whole?' And in a little while, rising up, he began to walk in the open, and he saw someone, as it might be himself, sitting and working: and then rising from his work and praying; and again sitting down and making a plait of palm-leaves, and then rising once again to prayer. Now it was an angel of the Lord sent to the reproof and warning of Anthony. And he heard the voice of the angel, saying, 'This do, and thou shalt be whole.' And hearing it, he took great joy of it and courage. And in so doing, he found the deliverance that he sought."[2]—Richard B. Vinson

OFFERING ONESELF.   "I am constantly guilty of the sin of words. Vulgarity is not my downfall, though I am vulgar. My sin is having words that are far more beautiful than my life. . . . I have nothing to offer the Creator but myself. Here I am. I have nothing to claim but grace."[3]—Richard B. Vinson

SERMON SUGGESTIONS

Topic: Creation and/or Evolution
TEXT: Gen. 1:1–2:3
(1) The Creation account in Genesis emphasizes the divine prerogative to act. (2) Genesis 1 is not about science and does not speak scientific language. (3) *Evolution* and *evolutionism* are not the same thing. Evolution speaks of natural change as one of the ways God works in the world. Evolutionism dismisses God's activity in change, that is, that God is absent from the world.—John D. Suk

Topic: Life's Single Constant
TEXT: Heb. 13:8
(1) Jesus Christ is the Lord of yesterday. (2) He is the Lord of today. (3). He is the Lord of tomorrow.—Frank Pollard

WORSHIP AIDS

CALL TO WORSHIP.   "But let all who take refuge in you be glad; let them ever sing for joy. Spread your protection over them, that those who love your name may rejoice in you" (Ps. 5:11 NIV).

---

[2]Helen Waddell, *The Desert Fathers* (Ann Arbor: University of Michigan Press, 1957), pp. 86–87.
[3]Gordon Atkinson, *RealLivePreacher.com* (Grand Rapids, MI: Eerdmans, 2004), pp. 38–39.

INVOCATION.   Gracious God, out of darkness we come to you for light; out of sorrow we come for joy; out of doubt we come for certainty; out of fear we come for security; out of sin we come for pardon. Open your hand this day to satisfy our every need.

OFFERTORY SENTENCE.   "Seek ye first the kingdom of God, and his righteousness, and all these things shall be added unto you" (Matt. 6:33 KJV).

OFFERTORY PRAYER.   Lord, as we give the gifts of tithes and offerings, open our eyes to the glorious opportunities for work and witness they avail for your Kingdom. How gladly we give in order to extend the boundaries of your witness—the witness of loving fellowship with you and with each other.

PRAYER.   God of grace and God of power, our hearts rejoice on this special day when we celebrate the greatest of all gifts bestowed upon your Church—the gift of your Holy Spirit. We give you thanks for all the manifestations of your love and mercy to us. Unite us, O God, by the power of your Spirit, and empower us to go into the world to proclaim the good news of Jesus Christ to those who still live not knowing who he is.

Revive us with a new Pentecost, and break the walls that separate us. Give us the conviction that we are indeed your Church—the body of Christ—and that ours is one faith, one Church, one baptism, and one Spirit. O God, Holy Spirit, come to us and among us. Come as the wind and cleanse us. Come as the fire and burn us. Come as the dew and refresh us. Convict, convert, and consecrate our hearts and lives to thy greater glory. For this is our prayer, which we lift unto you in the name of Jesus Christ.—Djalma Araujo

SERMON
Topic: Living from a Benediction
Text: 2 Cor. 13:5–14

Today is Trinity Sunday. It is one of the few Sundays of the year named after a doctrine of the Church rather than recognizing one of the great redeeming events of the Christian story, such as Christmas, Easter, or Pentecost. The doctrine of the Trinity is the most controversial, as well as the most unassailable, of Christian doctrines. It tries to describe the fullness of the being of God. It makes an attempt, through language, to point to the depth and breadth and height of the God whom Christians worship.

I. You see, the Trinity begins not as a doctrine but as an experience. When Paul closes his letter to that argumentative, clashing, ever-divided Corinthian congregation, he urges them to join in a common purpose; he begs them to restore a sense of unity; he closes his letter not with medieval dogma but with a blessing, a benediction: "The grace of our Lord Jesus Christ, the love of God and the communion of the Holy Spirit be with you all." Paul offers a prayer that grace will transform him from an antagonist—hostile and resistant to Christ—to one devoted to the service of Christ. He hopes the same Spirit uniting him with men and women in churches across the ancient world might bind, restore, reconcile, and forge unity among that cantankerous and splintered Corinthian fellowship.

II. And thus, the question facing us on this and every Trinity Sunday is not so much whether we can make sense of the doctrine of the Trinity but whether Paul's experience can be ours. Can this benediction—the grace of our Lord Jesus Christ—be the source of our life as well? Look at it this way. Some of us here know what it is to be imprisoned by demons from our past. Others of us have been haunted by memories paralyzing us and keeping us from tackling even the simplest matters. But as we wrestled with those demons, perhaps through prayer or alongside others or through a radiant encounter, light broke through, the dawn came, the demons subsided. Something or someone beyond ourselves granted peace; someone bestowed what we can only call grace, and we were changed, released, freed, transformed, renewed. And we can thank the grace of our Lord Jesus Christ.

III. Any number of us here can stand with others who, through the ages in face of the stupid, capricious, malicious things life can do to us, questioned love at the heart of creation. "Don't tell me God's love is in control," we cry. "Everywhere I look I see only chaos, chance, dog-eat-dog, life-as-a-lottery, a world where might makes right. Where do we begin to resolve this terrible question of the love of God? Well, we look where Paul looks. Every Sunday we face this cross in the heart of our sanctuary where love encounters the worst that life can do to it, and our faith says, "There. Love wins. There, death and life engage, and life wins."

IV. The grace of our Lord Jesus Christ, the love of God, and the communion of the Holy Spirit: this communion table illustrates our oneness in the Spirit. For here, at this table we gather, you and I: you and I with one another, you and I with Christians around the world, you and I with the saints of the ages—we gather here in what Paul names and what for him proclaims the communion of the Holy Spirit.

It is Trinity Sunday, friends. Today, we receive a benediction we can live from. And this morning I pray, as we join in the sacred and common meal, the grace of our Lord Jesus Christ, the love of God, and the communion of the Holy Spirit be with us all.—James W. Crawford

SUNDAY, JUNE 10, 2007
Lectionary Message

Topic: He Gave Him to His Mother
TEXT: Luke 7:11–17
Other Readings: 1 Kings 17:8–16 (17–24); Ps. 146; Gal. 1:11–24

I. Jesus is the miracle-working prophet. Luke's Jesus is an honest-to-God prophet, even more so than in the other Gospels, and in this part of the Gospel, he is working miracles that are meant to make us think of famous rip-snorting, king-baiting preachers from Israel's past. In the story just before this one, he heals the slave of a Gentile centurion, reminding us of how Elisha cured Naaman the Syrian of leprosy (2 Kings 5:1–14). In this second story, Jesus gives life to the only son of a widow, reminding us of Elijah's similar miracle (1 Kings 17:1–16). The crowd at the end gets the point, and their reaction makes sure Luke's readers get it, too: "A great prophet has risen among us! God has looked favorably on God's people!"

Both are prophet-miracles for other reasons as well. In the first one, Jesus does a good deed for a Gentile, and until the centurion stops him, Jesus seems perfectly willing to come into his home to cure his slave. When the centurion's friends tell him that he need only to speak a word, Jesus commends this sort of faith as being greater than any he had seen so far. Here's a miracle that looks ahead to the success of the gospel in the wider Roman world—the part of the story Luke addresses in his second volume, Acts.

II. The prophet has compassion. The widow story, though, gets at the very core of what's prophetic about Jesus in Luke. Unlike the centurion, she has no money to use to gain influence in her community; she has no clients she can order to go ask Jesus for a favor; she has no friends to send to intercede for her, as Jesus approaches her town. She has only her dead son, and the way Luke constructs the scene really directs our attention to her loss. There is a procession coming out of the little hamlet of Nain: first the corpse, carried by mourners; then the grieving mother, who is also a widow bereft of her only family; and then a large, undifferentiated crowd from the town. Note: they were not clients (as 7:4), not friends (7:6), and not family, but just townsfolk. She's all alone, and in her society as in ours, she is vulnerable.

On the other side of the entrance to the village is Jesus, who has a retinue of his own: his disciples and a large crowd of onlookers are with him. Jesus and the widow meet over her son's funeral bier, and Jesus was "moved with compassion." This is the only time Luke uses that expression to describe Jesus having that emotion. Think about what that says. Out of all the folks Jesus helps in Luke, it is the plight of this one bereaved widow that turns the Lord's heart over and moves him to do what he does next. "Don't weep," he says, and then he commands the son to be raised. When the young man sits up and talks, Jesus gives him back to his mother.

III. Give him back to his mother: "Blessed are those who weep now, said Jesus, for they will laugh" (6:21), but that is little consolation for those who experience the deep loss of losing a child. "O God—please give him back! I shall keep asking you." The last line of John Irving's novel *A Prayer for Owen Meany* is the heart's testimony of so many parents; such a loss is never erased, never filled by other things, even if the sharpness of the pain eases in time.

We cannot in good conscience promise that if we pray hard enough, God will restore the dead, as Jesus did on that day. But the church that ministers in Jesus' name can certainly become family to those who suffer so much. We cannot give their sons and daughters back to them now, but we can be brothers and sisters and children to them, if we choose, and enfold them in God's love.

And a ministry in the name of Jesus, who gave the widow her son back, could also challenge some of the structures that make life vulnerable for widows and orphans and strangers. Why is it that, given the entire biblical witness about charity to the poorest and most vulnerable among us, American Christians continue to spend more on pet food, chewing gum, video rentals, and so on, than they give to the poor? Why is it that so few followers of Jesus are engaged on a regular basis in hands-on ministry to the poor? We can, if we so choose, make life much less dangerous and much more secure for the vulnerable groups: the widows, the orphans, and the strangers.

And although this moves from preaching to meddling, I'm afraid, a prophetic ministry in Jesus' name would certainly challenge some of the causes that kill young men and women, leaving their mothers bereaved. Too many are dying, as I write this, in a war begun on false premises and mistaken assumptions. Too many are incarcerated, too many killed or ruined by drugs. Can we, like Jesus the prophet from Nazareth, give some of these back to their families by working to change the factors that took them away?

On that day in Nain, the Lord met the widow over her son's bier; life met death, God's grace met poverty, compassion met grief and loss, and all who saw it were amazed. Let Jesus' followers look and learn—learn to be heartbroken and learn where our emphasis should be: "give him back to his mother."—Richard B. Vinson

ILLUSTRATION

COMPASSION.   Early Christian ministry to widows:

"Instead of fields, then, purchase souls that have been afflicted, insofar as you can, and take care of widows and orphans and do not neglect them."

"Taste nothing but bread and water on the day you fast. Then estimate the cost of the food you would have eaten on that day and give that amount to a widow or orphan or someone in need" (Shepherd of Hermas Similitudes 1.8, 5, 3, 7).

"Do not allow the widows to be neglected. After the Lord, it is you [he is writing to a local bishop] who must be mindful of them" (Ignatius to Polycarp, 4.1).

"The presbyters also should be compassionate, merciful to all, turning back those who have gone astray, caring for all who are sick, not neglecting the widow, the orphan, or the poor, but always taking thought for what is good before both God and others" (Polycarp to the Philippians, 6.1).—Richard B. Vinson

SERMON SUGGESTIONS

Topic: Hell Is Not to Love Anymore

TEXT: Jon. 4:1–5, 10; 1 Cor. 7:29–31; Mark 1:14–20

(1) Repentance is turning away from sin and toward our true selves. (2) Repentance is to turn to Christ once—and then day-by-day. (3) Repentance is turning to each other in love and in caring community.—Walter J. Burghardt

Topic: Christianity at Its Best

TEXT: Acts 27

(1) The story tells of a shipwreck and the courage that faith provided. (2) The shipwreck illustrates the world at its worst, heading for destruction. (3) The Church, though imperfect, is the instrument through which grace arrives to set people free. (4) Such a need comes through the dedicated obedience of God's people.—Leonard Griffith

WORSHIP AIDS

CALL TO WORSHIP.   "Behold, how good and how pleasant it is for brethren to dwell together in unity!" (Ps. 133:1 KJV).

INVOCATION.   Father, as we worship, may authentic praise rise within, expressing our gratitude for the salvation we know in Christ Jesus, the Lord. Give us the grace to live joyfully, obediently, and triumphantly as your children in this world. May your Spirit reign within our hearts.

OFFERTORY SENTENCE.   "I will freely sacrifice unto thee: I will praise thy name, O Lord; for it is good" (Ps. 54:6 KJV).

OFFERTORY PRAYER.   Lord, as we return to you a portion of the bounty you have provided, may our gifts reflect the glad heart of your people. We rejoice in your favor and celebrate together our participation in the gospel, from the first day until now.

PRAYER.   Loving God, sometimes it feels like our dreams have dried up and our hopes are lost. We sometimes feel that your Spirit, which blows where it will, has passed us by. We confess, O God, that we often find ourselves in such a predicament because we have not been receptive to your presence. We ignore the winds of your Spirit and the light of your promise to be with us in all the times of our lives. And so this morning, we seek to be open to your presence and to be receptive to your Spirit that dwells in our midst. For you, O God, create life, overcome darkness, and conquer death. We know this in our hearts, but sometimes we can't comprehend what that means for our lives at this moment. Violent events in the world frighten us. The magnitude of problems weakens our resolve to take positive action for constructive change. Yet we want to be made new. And so give us hearts of courage that we may not hide from those who suffer but rather walk up to their tombs and call out for new life. Give us strength to walk with and, if need be, to hold up those among us who are surrounded by grief, illness, broken relationships, depression, unemployment, or simply a sense of having lost their way. Our souls rest in you, in the promise of new possibilities and in the newness of life that you continually make available to us. We open ourselves to the wind of your Spirit that blows where it will.—Susan Gregg-Schroeder

SERMON
Topic: Teach Your Children Well
TEXT: John 3:1–17

The Church is different from the world. The values that we hold are different from the values of the world. We live by a different standard of behavior. In the world all things are permissible. In the Church not all things are permissible. To be Christian is to be different.

I. Early on, churches began to baptize children because parents said, "We want to raise our children in the church, with the values of the Kingdom." Children are in the church because raising children in this kind of a world is not only a parental responsibility, it is a community responsibility. Children have always been part of the church. Every so often I run into somebody who says, "We chose not to raise our children in the church because we wanted them to make up their own minds about religion." But the problem is that you cannot raise children in a neutral environment. Children learn what the world is all about from the environment in which they are raised, which means that they will learn from everything else except the church. To raise a child in the church is to at least give them a choice.

Children learn from the communities in which they are raised. Throughout childhood there is a tremendous capacity to learn. The brain is constantly building structures, circuits, to process information from the world. In the first six months, a child's brain doubles in size. It's in childhood that children are learning what the world is all about. You see the world through eyes that have been trained by the environment in which were raised.

II. Now turn to our lesson this morning—the famous story of Nicodemus. Jesus says to Nicodemus, "Unless you are born anew you cannot see the kingdom of God." We often say,

"Seeing is believing." It's true to say, "Believing is seeing" because our beliefs, our values, our morality will determine what we see. Unless one is born anew, one cannot see the Kingdom of God. Nicodemus was raised in a different world. He saw things differently. Therefore, in adulthood he had to be jarred loose, to go back, as it were, to childhood to learn how to see the world all over again. There is a Christian way of seeing the world, and it is the church's job to teach it and to model it. That's why we are here.

The way you teach children well is to get them into a community of adults who will surround them with love and forgiveness, show their care for them, and model for them what life is all about. It is then that it will probably happen. They will be born anew and see the Kingdom of God.—Mark Trotter

SUNDAY, JUNE 17, 2007
Lectionary Message

Topic: Do You See This Woman?
TEXT: Luke 7:36–8:3
Other Readings: 1 Kings 2:1–10 (11–14), 15–21a; Ps. 5:1–8; Gal. 2:15–21

I. *False first impressions:* First, let's get our facts straight, because there are three versions of this story in our four Gospels. In Mark and Matthew, in the house of Simon the leper, a nameless woman anoints Jesus' head a few days before his death. In John, in Lazarus' house, Mary of Bethany anoints Jesus' feet, also just a few days before the Crucifixion. Luke's story has a different setting—a dinner party at Simon the Pharisee's house early in Jesus' ministry. An anonymous woman, as in Mark and Matthew, anoints Jesus' feet, as in John. Luke's phrase, "a sinful woman in that city," does not imply that this anointing woman is a prostitute, and there is nothing to connect her to Mary Magdalene except a poor job of exegesis by some early Christians. For Luke, the woman is precisely what the text says: a sinner, like so many others in the Gospel, who comes to repent with her whole heart.

But Luke lets us start the story by looking at her from the Pharisee's point of view. Simon the Pharisee invites Jesus to dinner (Jesus eats with Pharisees three times in Luke, which he never does in the other Gospels), and Jesus comes. At formal dinners in those days, people reclined on couches or on floor cushions, propping themselves up on one elbow and eating from dishes in front of them with the other hand. Somewhere during the meal, a woman comes into the dining room and begins to do strange things to Jesus' feet: she wets them down with her tears, wiping them off with her hair, and then puts scented oil on his feet and kisses them all over. The vocabulary Luke uses here is meant to make us squirm, to imagine low lights and Barry White on the CD player. What in the world is she doing down there, messing with his feet? And why is he letting her do it? Isn't it obvious the kind of woman she is? Jesus is obviously not the man of God that he has been reported to be.

II. *Jesus' viewpoint:* But it's all a trick of the eye, as we've only seen from the Pharisee's point of view. When we get to Jesus in verse 40, we find he has another way of seeing things. Turns out, from what he says, that old Simon has been pretty rude to him. He invited Jesus over, but he didn't meet him at the door and didn't give him the traditional kiss of greeting. It's hard to imagine going to a home in the Middle East and not being kissed on each cheek by everyone present; if Simon didn't do it, he was being deliberately inhospitable to his guest.

Then he didn't invite Jesus to sit in a chair while he had his servants bring water to wash his feet—another rude act that meant that Jesus had to stick his dirty feet out on the couch for everyone to see. Shameful! And then he didn't bring oil to put on his head, which would have shown Jesus that he was a valued and welcome guest. Does Simon love Jesus? Not at all, to judge by the way he acts.

The woman steps into the gap. Big fancy homes like Simon's were made so that passers-by could look from the street into the beautifully decorated courtyards and dining rooms. She lives in that city; she knows Jesus has been invited, and something makes her wonder if Simon will do right by him. She looks in and sees what is being done, and then she steps in, providing what's needed from her own body: tears to wash his feet, hair to dry them, oil she bought with her money to perfume him, and kisses of apology and devotion. "Do you see this woman?" Jesus asks Simon. Well, no, actually. Simon thinks he sees something outrageous—a sinner smooching all over a false prophet, on his couch and at his table! But Jesus sees a penitent filled with gratitude and love, who wants to give what she can to make up for Simon's disrespectful treatment.

III. *How the women see Jesus:* And this woman isn't the only one to act like this. As Jesus makes his way village-by-village through Galilee, preaching the good news of the Kingdom, he is accompanied by others. The twelve are there—just there, that's all. But there are women—three named—and then a whole group of anonymous women like the one weeping over Jesus' feet—who "provided for them" out of their own resources. That's a weak translation; "they [the women] 'deaconized' them" is awkward but gets at what they were doing. These women, who gave freely from their resources, were the ministry core of the early Jesus movement. They weren't cooking and cleaning so that Jesus and the boys could do the real work. They were serving, ministering, deaconizing, just as the whole company of disciples did in Acts 2–4.

Simon saw a disreputable man—a "friend of tax collectors and sinners," whom he did not need to treat with respect. The man turned out to be Jesus. Simon saw a disreputable woman doing salacious things to Jesus' feet. She turned out to be a better host than he and a model for Christian ministry. Jesus saw a penitent whose love was more than admirable. He saw other women whose dedication to his calling led them to minister out of what they had. Jesus' vision was better, of course; he saw these people for what they could become.

A female Baptist pastor testifies of volunteering, as a teenager, to preach the sermon on Youth Sunday, when nobody else would do it, and being told that ministry was only for men. Thank God that God had other ways of speaking to her and that others could see what Jesus saw. Do you see this woman in your congregation?—Richard B. Vinson

ILLUSTRATIONS

THE GRACIOUS HOST.   In the following excerpt from *The Odyssey*, Telemachus (Odysseus' son) demonstrates the role of a good host to the goddess Athena, who appears at his door in disguise. Keep in mind that he is standing in for his father, who is far away and feared dead, and that his house is already full of boorish suitors who are very unpleasant house guests.

No one noticed her at first but Telemachus, who was sitting disconsolate among the Suitors, dreaming of how his noble father might come back from out of the blue, drive all these gallants pell-mell from the house . . . he caught sight of Athene and set off at once for the porch,

thinking it a shame that a stranger should be kept standing at the gates. He went straight up to his visitor, shook hands, relieved him of his bronze spear and gave him cordial greetings. "Welcome, sir, to our hospitality!" he said. "You can tell us what has brought you when you have had some food." With this he led the way and Pallas Athene followed. . . . He conducted her to a carved chair, over which he spread a rug, and seated her there with a stool for her feet. . . . Presently a maid came with water in a handsome golden jug and poured it out over a silver basin so that they could rinse their hands. She then drew a polished table to their side, and the staid housekeeper brought some bread and set it by them with a choice of dainties, helping them liberally to all she could offer.[4]
—Richard B. Vinson

THE OFFERING OF PRAYER.　　"Of the Reception of Guests" from the Rule of St. Benedict, section 53:

All guests are to be received as Christ himself . . . When, therefore, a guest is announced, the prior or the brothers shall run to meet him, with every service of love. And first they shall pray together; and thus they shall be joined together in peace. Which kiss of peace shall not first be offered, unless a prayer has preceded, on account of the wiles of the devil.
—Richard B. Vinson

SERMON SUGGESTIONS

Topic: God's Mercy Exemplified
TEXT: Mark 10:47
(1) The blind man was in need of urgent help. (2) As opportunity came, he called upon Jesus: "have mercy on me." (3) He refused to be quieted by the crowds. (4) Jesus responded mercifully: "Bring the seeker to me. What do you want?" (5) Mercy and compassion meet: "that I may receive my sight." And he went away rejoicing.—Lawrence Vowan

Topic: Jesus' Messiahship and Our Discipleship
TEXT: Mark 8:31–38; Rom. 8:31–39
(1) Our discipleship grows out of Christ's Messiahship. (2) Discipleship struggles in the face of personal goals and obligations. (3) We must yield to God's purpose for our lives. (4) Only God's action, specifically the cross of Christ, can energize authentic discipleship.—Allan M. Parrent

WORSHIP AIDS
CALL TO WORSHIP.　　"Within your temple, O God, we meditate on your unfailing love. Like your name, O God, your praise reaches to the ends of the earth" (Ps. 48:9–10 NIV).

INVOCATION.　　Teach us, dearest Lord, the ever-present need of gathering together to worship as the community of faith. Keep before us the vision of your son, Jesus Christ, who as a child worshipped with his family. May that vision inspire us, as members of your Church, to maintain the joy of our witness—in worship and love.

---

[4]From *The Odyssey*, I, 105–181, E. V. Rieu, trans. (New York: Penguin, 1946), p. 27.

OFFERTORY SENTENCE.   "You are to receive an offering for me from each man whose heart prompts him to give" (Exod. 25:2 NIV).

OFFERTORY PRAYER.   Living Savior, help us to know the ecstasy of your eternal Lordship, that we may be cheerful givers. Bless these gifts to the building of your Kingdom.

PRAYER.   Heavenly Father, we will be listening to your word today. Our hearts will be listening to your Spirit this morning. Those of us who are fathers particularly will be listening. Because we love our sons and daughters, like you, our heavenly parent, we want our children to be strong, wise, mature, gentle, and loving. Daily bring to our hearts what and how our roles as fathers mean to these children in our lives. For those men among us who are not fathers, give us the vision and the heart to love these children as our very own. For all of us—children, women, and men—accept our thanks for the gift of our very own lives in which each of our own fathers played a part. Some of us can easily thank you for our fathers, remembering many wonderful experiences. Others of us may not be so fortunate. Hear us as we express our thanks to you for giving us those loving fathers and whoever else has loved, initiated with us, and encouraged us throughout our lives. [*A silence is kept to permit silent prayers of thanks.*] Father, enable us not to exasperate our children, yet to discipline wisely. We pray that we will not be too busy to see, play with, talk with, and be completely present with our children for however long they are in our care. It always seems much too short. Teach us the joy of learning from our children, for they too are made by you in your image. Help us to learn about faith, trust, innocence, quick forgiveness, and love. [*A silence is kept.*] It is in the strong name of Jesus our Savior that we pray.—Larry Ellis

SERMON
Topic: Top Men!
TEXT: 1 John 2:13

It is not customary to advertise for fathers. If society did such a thing, it would seek only top men! Fathers are not just men who beget children but men to whom God entrusts a holy role: to rear the next generation and to do so with the spirit required and the urgency demanded.

I. Of course, fathers do not stand alone. They cannot supplant mothers, nor are they equipped to do so, albeit some fathers must be mothers to their children as well. Some mothers must be fathers to their offspring also. In the design of God, however, it is intended that each shall have their role, while blending their gifts so that the family knows not only unity but similar aims that arise from common hopes. Nevertheless, if we were to circulate handbills and publish advertising and invest in television commercials, we would all insist that we want only top men for the role of fathers for the world's children.

II. That does not mean that the men must have means or dashing good looks necessarily. It does not mean they must be academic geniuses or particularly gifted leaders. The top men this world needs to succor its offspring are not human gods but God's humans—those who know him and are open to his will for themselves and the progeny. Top men are those men who fall to their knees in prayer and rise to acclaim the Risen Christ by faith. Top men are those who have seen the bottom's failings and yearn for the heights of joy for their families.

Top men are sinners saved by grace, who are not perfect in themselves but who strive, in love, to be the best they can be for God, for their wives, for their children, and for themselves.

Fathers who succeed implant in their children something more than a family likeness; they implant a love for Christ and his Church. These are top men, for they have given their sons and daughters him who is the Eternal Father as the family's supreme head. They have given them more than life now; they have given life forever.

III. Fathers have a significant role to play in the rearing of their children. If mothers have a more formative role early in the lives of their children, fathers are not excused from the roles they are to play in encouraging their little ones in faith and thereby helping them meet the demands of life. Many of the nations from which we come have been strengthened by the commitment of simple homes to the truth of Scripture and the joy of Jesus. It takes many families of faith to build a strong nation. Whether fathers and children are bricklayers or politicians, educators or farmers, artists or mechanics, the importance is in whom they serve because that affects what they do and how they live, and that affects the whole nation and the entire world.

It is your home and my home and the homes of people like us that must pass on the vitality of Christ's gospel to the generations ahead. It requires top men to handle this top role of spiritual nurturer to the offspring of our nations.

IV. Let us, on this Father's Day, consider the whole worldwide realm of the Christian family. Let us come to the altar to be nurtured, so we may return to our homes to ensure that this generation and all those ahead will have something more than materialism to live for or sports titles to claim. Let us show that life is full and purposeful, ensured by the cross and encouraged by Christ's crown.—Richard Andersen

SUNDAY, JUNE 24, 2007
Lectionary Message

Topic: Driven into the Wilds
TEXT: Luke 8:26–39
Other Readings: 1 Kings 19:1–4, 5–7, 8:15a; Ps. 42; Gal. 3:23–29

I. *He lived by himself:* When 739 people died in Chicago in July 1995, the result of a killing heat wave, one of the most heart-wrenching aspects of the tragedy was how many died because there was no one checking up on them. Many of the victims were ill or elderly, or both, living in small apartments with inadequate ventilation, and they simply smothered. Others, weakened by the heat, died of dehydration and because their body temperatures stayed too high for too long. Many, perhaps most, of these deaths could have been prevented by moving the person to a cooler spot or by making sure that they sat in a tub of water and drank enough liquids. But no one was there to intervene, and they perished.

Luke's demoniac is a loner, like Kipling's cat, walking by himself, escaping all attempts to restrain him. The demons inside him drive him, says Luke, so that he lives naked, exposed to the elements and the insects and the thorns and the rocks, without a shred of self-respect left. He lives naked "among the tombs," some translations have it; more precisely, he lives among the grave markers, the things people have left as memorials to their departed loved ones. Ironically, he has no marker, no name, and no community who cares to think about him; the corpses below him are dressed and tended with more care than he is. His attitude toward his community comes out in his first words to Jesus: "What am I to you, Jesus Son of the Most High? I beg you, do not torture me." The binding and chaining and shackling that his town has attempted to force on him leave him justifiably wary of any further human touch. He may be demon-possessed, but he understands torture when he feels it.

II. *His community preferred it that way:* Nobody in his or her right mind would choose to live like that, or like the Chicagoans who perished. Jesus first addresses the mental health issues with this man. The incident with the pigs is another ironic element in the story. If these are Gentiles, Luke doesn't tell us, and if they are Jews, why do they have herds of pigs? In any event, the band of unclean spirits that has forced the man to live in a graveyard, making him perpetually unclean, begs Jesus for a spot in the unclean pigs. But the pigs immediately destroy themselves, clearing the way for the town to live more in line with Torah. The towns-people, however, want no part of any of this: they don't want the newly healed former demoniac or his healer. They prefer the former state of things, where the crazy man lives out of their sight, and their pigs are safe in the care of the swineherds.

Hmm—that touches a nerve, doesn't it? Let's see—in your city, how many folks are elderly or sick or of "diminished capacity," and how many of them would be vulnerable, just like the 739 Chicagoans, to some event that put extra stress on them? How has the skyrocketing price of fuel, for example, affected their ability to provide for themselves? How have the new government policies on drug pricing affected their ability to medicate themselves? Is there a community that knows enough about them to make certain that they do not die from neglect?

The Gerasene community learned nothing, it seems, from the events Luke describes. They did not seem interested in facing their failure to care for the poor and the sick in their midst; they seemed most interested in their economic loss and most concerned to make certain that Jesus never threatened them again. They ask him to leave, and he obliges. Later in Luke, Jesus warns about how a house can be cleansed of demonic possession and then re-infested (in systems theory terms, if the system is perverse, then changing the players will not prevent abuse from recurring). Had Jesus returned to their region sometime later, would he have found someone else naked among the gravestones?

III. *Jesus hoped to heal the sick town:* The former demoniac, however, who at first begged Jesus to leave him be, now begs Jesus to take him along. Jesus, however, sends him back to the community to be an advocate for the work of God that needs to take place there. However little the Gerasenes have learned, and however little they seem to want to change, Jesus has not given up on them. Maybe the former demoniac can go home and, by refusing to operate according to a demonic system, begin to force the system to change.

No one in his or her right mind would choose to live naked in the graveyard or to die alone, suffocating in a tiny airless apartment. No one in that condition will be able to step forward and ask for help or to advocate for themselves. We followers of Jesus, the prophet from Nazareth, will need to go and find them and will need to be prepared to be met with skepticism, anger, and fear—"please don't hurt me—just leave me alone." But we followers of Jesus know that, just as we have been healed and nurtured by the beloved community, so we can offer that same healing to others, if we choose.—Richard B. Vinson

ILLUSTRATION

LACK OF COMMUNITY.   "The absence of a community does not require a heat wave or a cold spell, much less hundreds of deaths, to make its presence known. It surrounds us in a daily way—in our neighborhoods, our work lives, and the anguish of our own souls. We may not always be aware of this void. But the scarcity of a deep sense of community can wreak havoc below the surface of outwardly busy lives, just as it occasionally makes the ultimate claim on an elderly individual living alone."[5]

> "Be our primary disease, and infect us with your justice; be our night visitor, and haunt us with your peace; be our moth that consumes, and eat away at our unfreedom . . . until we are toward you and with you and for you, away from our injustice, our anti-peace, our unfreedom."[6]

SERMON SUGGESTIONS

Topic: Heaven

TEXT: Rev. 21; Num. 13:17–14:3; John 14:1–7

(1) Today, many view heaven as the Israelites viewed the Promised Land: they look into it but aren't inspired by it. (2) But to think of heaven as unimportant denies the living hope God has for creation. (3) The vision of heaven empowers the best of living in this world.—Daniel Aleshire

Topic: The Final Giants

TEXT: 2 Sam. 21:14–22

(1) We must bury the giants of yesterday (v. 14). (2) We overcome the giant of exhaustion and age (v. 15). (3) We allow others to come to our aid (v. 17). (4) We admit to new giants along the way and rise up to new challenges.—Calvin Miller

WORSHIP AIDS

CALL TO WORSHIP.   "I will lift up mine eyes unto the hills, from whence cometh my help. My help cometh from the Lord, which made heaven and earth" (Ps. 121:1–2 KJV).

INVOCATION.   Kind, divine, Heavenly Father, who reigns over all things in wisdom, power, and love, we adore you for your glory and majesty. We praise you for your grace and truth, which come to us through Christ our Savior. Grant the moving of your Spirit that we may worship you in spirit and in truth.

OFFERTORY SENTENCE.   "Honor the Lord with thy substance, and with the first fruits of all thine increase" (Prov. 3:9 KJV).

OFFERTORY PRAYER.   O Lord, may we trust more and more in the provisions of your love and care. And may our devotion to you be expressed in the sincerity of our giving. Receive, magnify, and bless these tithes and offerings for your glory.

---

[5]Peter W. Marty, "Breathing Together," *The Christian Century*, Aug. 23, 2005, p. 8.
[6]Walter Brueggemann, *Awed to Heaven, Rooted in Earth* (Minneapolis: Fortress, 2003), p. 99.

PRAYER.   O Divine Love, who everlastingly stands outside the closed doors of the minds and hearts of persons, grant us grace to throw open our soul's door. Let every bolt and bar be drawn that has hitherto robbed life of air and light and love.

Give us open eyes, O God, eyes quick to discover your indwelling in the world that you have made. Forgive all our past blindness to the grandeur and glory of nature, to the charm of little children, to the sublimities of human society, and to all the intimations of your presence in and around us. Give us an open ear, O God, that we may hear your voice calling us to higher ground. Give us an open mind, O God, ready to receive and welcome such new light of knowledge as is your will to reveal. Let not the past ever be so dear to us as to set a limit to the future. Give us courage to change our minds. Give us open hands, O God, ready to share with all who are in need the blessings with which you have enriched our life. Let us hold our monies in stewardship and all our worldly goods in trust for thee.

We pray not only for the overcoming of personal estrangements but for the healing of the nations. Grant to us the wisdom, the courage, the faith, to be bridge builders, as we share the bread and the Bread of Life, with which we have been so richly blessed.—John Thompson

SERMON
Topic: Learning to Live
TEXT: Ps. 23; Matt. 6:25–34

If you had the chance to go back and live life all over again, would you make some changes? Would you approach life differently? We have often heard it said, and we may have said it ourselves, "If I could only go back knowing what I know now." This is precisely what Jesus is talking about in the Scripture that we heard read from Matthew in the Sermon on the Mount: learning how to live.

I. Life should not be dominated by worry. "Do not worry about your life," Jesus tells us. It is natural for us to worry a little. But worry should not be the dominating force in our lives. We should not live to worry. It has been said that people spend the most time worrying about things that never happen anyway. And worrying about something doesn't change it a bit. Jesus is encouraging us to relax and trust in God. Our heavenly Father loves us very much and wants to supply our needs. A good relaxing exercise for us would be reading or reciting the twenty-third Psalm whenever we begin to feel stressed or feel worry or anxiety coming on. I think this is the kind of thing Jesus had in mind—relaxing and trusting the Good Shepherd to take care of us.

II. Life should be lived and enjoyed to its fullest. Some people learn late in life how to live. Others never learn how to live at all. Jesus encourages us to take time to look at the birds of the air and consider the beautiful lilies of the field. We need to learn how to stop and smell life's roses. To really live life to its fullest and to find true happiness is to come follow Christ and the way he laid out for us in the Sermon on the Mount. For in the Sermon on the Mount, Jesus teaches us of love, forgiveness, patience, prayer, faithfulness, service, and trust.

III. Life gives us one day at a time; that is what we have to work with. Taking care of the present is what should concern us, not the mistakes of the past and not what might happen in the future. God gives us life in one-hour segments. "Do not worry about tomorrow," Jesus says. Today's concerns are enough for today. Such is a good philosophy and approach to life.

IV. We would do well to ask ourselves three questions each morning: (1) What can I do this day to better myself? (2) What can I do this day to show my love for my family? (3) What can I do this day in my job to improve my productivity and give my employer his money's worth? Learning to live: relaxing and trusting the goodness of God, living life to its fullest by loving and serving others, and taking life one day at a time.—Randy Hammer

SUNDAY, JULY 1, 2007
Lectionary Message

Topic: The Cost of Discipleship
TEXT: Luke 9:51–62
Other Readings: 2 Kings 2:1–2, 6–14; Ps. 77:1–2, 11–20; Gal. 5:1, 13–25

Verse 51 begins Luke's center section focused on Jesus' journey to Jerusalem. The time is drawing near for the fulfillment of Jesus' mission. Luke makes it clear in the very first verses of this section that people must now make a choice: they can reject Jesus as the Samaritan villagers do in verse 53, or they can accept Jesus and become his disciples. But it is made quite clear that following Jesus will be costly. There is no cheap grace.

I. *Rejection* (one choice—9:51–53): Jesus sends his disciples ahead to find a village in Samaria where he could stay the night. The long-time Samaritan animosity toward the Jews seems to surface quickly when the disciples ask for shelter for the night. The Scripture says they rejected Jesus because his face was set toward Jerusalem. Practically every commentary says this rejection dates back to the rejection of the Samaritans when they offered to help rebuild the Temple when the Jews returned from exile. The rejection of Jesus because of the actions of others has been a common occurrence throughout the history of the Church. It is just as present today as it was in the first century. Every pastor has heard something similar to the following at one time or another: "Preacher, my father was a member of your church, and he got fed up with all the unchristian actions of the folks down there. He left while I was a boy and, to be honest, I never have wanted to be a Christian after that." We all have the option of rejecting the Messiah, but that decision has eternal consequences.

One probably should not question the wisdom of the New Testament scholars' interpretation of verses 51–53, but there may be another possibility. Luke puts this story immediately after Jesus sets his face toward Jerusalem, which will certainly mean his death. Luke states that the rejection in Samaria comes because he has set his face toward Jerusalem. It is quite possible that the rejection is simply out of fear. Any connection with this religious rebel could mean their death or at least some punishment. It would be too costly to give him shelter for the night. Fear has been a motivating emotion in the rejection of Jesus for centuries. In the beginning, it was fear of losing one's life. Today, fear comes cloaked in a variety of ways. Some of these are addressed by Jesus in verses 57–62.

II. *Acceptance* (the other choice—9:57–62): The rejection-acceptance motif is quite clear in this brief passage. Neither is made without cost. Jesus never extended a call to easy discipleship. His brief encounters with three would-be disciples, like the Sermon on the Mount, highlight the demands of being a Kingdom person.

First (vv. 57–58), following Jesus may mean giving up physical comforts. The first encounter is with an overzealous volunteer. "I will follow you wherever you go," were his first words of commitment. Jesus has just been denied a place to stay the night, so he reminds the would-be disciple that he may have to sleep on the ground out under the stars. Going where the Father led him didn't always provide Jesus with physical comforts. Why would Jesus discourage this obvious enthusiasm? Because there is no cheap grace.

Second (vv. 59–60), following Jesus may mean giving up long-held ways of living. In the second encounter, Jesus takes the initiative by issuing an invitation to a man that was similar to ones he gave James and John and Peter and Andrew: "Follow me." It would appear that Jesus expected the man to follow the example of the fishermen and cut all ties and join the journey to Jerusalem immediately. But the man replied that he must first bury his father. Jesus' reply seems rather harsh: "Let the dead bury the dead; you need to be about proclaiming the kingdom of God." Even the "age-old" custom of the older son remaining at home until his father died so he could provide a proper burial was not sufficient to postpone discipleship. One may have to give up old ways of living if one is to follow Jesus. The most important and first responsibility is the proclamation of the Kingdom of God.

Third (vv. 61–62), following Jesus may mean turning your back on the past. Another responds to the call of Jesus by simply saying, "Lord, could you wait until I first go home and bid farewell to my family?" Sounds good until you realize that it probably involved a farewell festival that could last a couple of weeks. Probably the word *first* prompted Jesus' reply: "No one who puts his hand to the plow and looks back is fit for the kingdom of God." If a farmer is to plow a straight furrow, he must keep his eye on the target point ahead. Becoming a Kingdom person meant cutting ties that bind one to the past and turning one's face to the future.

God has given every individual the freedom to accept or reject the salvation offered in Jesus Christ. Rejection is costly because it has earthly and eternal consequences. Acceptance is also costly because there is no cheap grace, but the consequences are also earthly and eternal. To join Jesus as a joint heir of the Kingdom of God certainly offers the better alternative.—John Dever

ILLUSTRATIONS

GRACE.   Dietrich Bonhoeffer's book, *The Cost of Discipleship,* is an excellent essay on what it means to be true followers of Jesus. The section on cheap grace and costly grace is of particular importance. Bonhoeffer defines *cheap grace* as the justification of sin without the justification of the sinner. He sees preachers preaching forgiveness without requiring repentance, priests offering absolution without personal confession, disciples proclaiming to follow Jesus without a willingness to take up their cross. This, he proclaims, is cheap grace.

Bonhoeffer's life became a living mirror of costly grace. He was arrested for helping some Jews escape Nazi Germany and later was implicated in a plot to assassinate Hitler. He was hanged just three days before the Allied forces arrived. Bonhoeffer was willing to take up his cross and follow Jesus, no matter the cost.—John Dever

A REFERENCE POINT.   I grew up in southeast Missouri, which is blessed with some of the richest farm land in the nation. Although I did not live on a farm, I was a member of the FFA and spent many long hours helping my friend Robert on his small farm—small in comparison to many others. I remember riding the tractor with him one day when we were planting corn in a rather large field behind his house. We loaded the seed in the planter and proceeded to lay off the first row, which was the most important because it determined the direction of every row afterwards. Robert turned on the planter and then proceeded to pick out a point of reference about a quarter of a mile off at the end of the field. For the next five minutes Robert was absolutely quiet—a miracle for him—as he steered toward the end of the field, never taking his eyes off the marker. When he was finished he had laid out a straight corn row, a quarter of a mile long.—John Dever

SERMON SUGGESTIONS

Topic: Freedom's Message
TEXT: Acts 1:8, 17:19–23; Rom. 10:13–17
(1) A renewed faith in the gospel. (2) A deepened commitment to a life of love. (3) A powerful experience of prayer. (4) A clear calling to bold proclamation. (5) A willing dependence on the Holy Spirit.—Lawrence Vowan

Topic: Being a Christian in America
TEXT: Rom. 13:1–7; Rev. 13:1–10
(1) In Romans 13, the call is to respect government and to obey the laws of the land. (2) In Revelation 13, it is clear that at times God and government are not in agreement, and decisions about obedience must be made. (3) Christians cannot ignore either passage. We yield to both and keep our eyes wide open.—Thomas D. Campbell

WORSHIP AIDS
CALL TO WORSHIP.   "From the rising of the sun to its setting, my name is great among the nations" (Mal. 1:11 RSV).

INVOCATION.   As we gather to worship on this day before Independence Day, hear our words of thanksgiving for the freedom we celebrate. Let our words ring a glad note of celebration that today we come to this place guaranteed the right of freedom to do so and remind us that such a gift does not exist everywhere. May we never take for granted the blessings we enjoy as a nation.

OFFERTORY SENTENCE.   "Give unto the Lord the glory due unto his name: bring an offering, and come before him: worship the Lord in the beauty of holiness" (1 Chron. 16:29).

OFFERTORY PRAYER.   We thank you, dear Father, for another anniversary of our nation's independence. We pray that this gift to us may be understood as an opportunity to serve the whole world in love. Bless our gifts to this great end.

PRAYER.   Father, we come with a peculiar recognition of community. We see that we are not simply individuals, even though we realize that we have been tended to with the special care of your grace. Yet we sense that our individuality must touch others of your children. We are called to serve, to love, and to form into communities of all kinds. Sometimes our formations become selfish clusters. We use others, and we seek out vested interests. We easily become ghettos and force others to retreat from us. We know that true loving community is your deepest will for all on this earth. We come today with the fragments of communities within us—as couples in marriage, as families, and as peer groups, neighbors, and races. And we come as communities of the mind and spirit: big and little communities, sometimes loving, sometimes forgetting, but asking this day for the vision that comes through Christ to be able to perceive the brothers and sisters in our midst and to reach out for their hands and spirits and, in so doing, find your own.—Richard Andersen

SERMON
Topic: The Almost Chosen People
Text: Gal. 5:1

Abraham Lincoln, in addressing the Illinois (and later the New Jersey) senate, used two phrases that came to be almost a hallmark for the kind of administration, the kind of memory that he would give to the nation. He said that America was the almost chosen people—the last, best hope of earth. We are not the old Israel, but there is some kind of destiny that many believe is here in America. Since 1776, millions have looked to the United States for help. Our soldiers have fought in every part of the world to bring peace and democracy there. Many of you served in World Wars I and II, or the Korean and the Vietnam conflicts, knowing that you were doing it for high moral reasons. You were, to many people around the world, hope—hope of what they could be. And you were giving them some sense that there could be a stable government for them also. You were also giving them a sense that in the midst of all kinds of pressures upon the world, men have the kind of personal dignity that will allow mankind to rule itself.

I have traveled in the land of the Rising Sun. I have seen the sights in Singapore, but I must tell you that down deep in this preacher's heart is a special affection when I see the waving of Old Glory. I love it, not because of some kind of civil religion in America, but I love it because we are God's almost chosen people. We are not the old Israel. We may not be the new Israel. But there is a distinctive message that we have taken to the world that the world needs to hear.

I. The liberty to worship and to proclaim and to persuade in the name of Jesus Christ is a liberty that is found rarely across the face of this earth and has been found rarely in the history of mankind. Under God we have been given the privilege and the responsibility and the right and the joy to freely, without any kind of coercion, worship our God, proclaim the gospel, and call other men to repentance in the name of the Lord Jesus Christ. What a sacred heritage that is.

Why do we believe so strongly in religious liberty? It is not anti-anything. It is pro-gospel. We believe in freedom of religion or religious liberty for these reasons. First of all, we believe it because it is built into the creation of this universe. We are created free beings. We believe it because of the doctrine of God. He is omnipotent, but he does not force his will on anyone. He did not even force his will on Adam and Eve. We believe in freedom of religious liberty because of the doctrine of man. All are made in God's image. We believe in religious liberty because of the absolute lordship of Jesus Christ. The absolute lordship of Jesus Christ is the dominant fact in his religious experience. We believe in religious liberty also because the Bible is the absolute rule for our lives. Every invitation of the Bible involves an individual choice. We believe in religious liberty because our evangelism demands it.

II. Freedom is not toleration. Freedom of religion is different from toleration. Toleration is one thing, but freedom is another. Toleration is a concession by the state. Liberty is a right of the individual. Toleration somehow comes to be an expediency for the state, but liberty is a principle that guides it. Toleration is a gift of man. Liberty is a gift of God.

We are silent about this today. Three decades have gone by when we have had little or no preaching about religious liberty. Church and state must be separate. What this means is that the state will not tell us what to teach or preach, and the state does not use our tax dollars to teach religion. It does not mean that the Church does not speak prophetically to the state.

III. Now, what must we do? Here we are, free men in a free society, living almost in two kingdoms. How do we do this? I'll guarantee you that a good and sensitive and mature Christian will be a mature citizen. So I ask you to do two things. First of all, if you are a believer in Jesus Christ, I ask you to be a better citizen. A Christian needs to be as good a citizen as he or she can be. I believe good Christians can run for public office. I believe good Christians can support men and women running for office and can be involved in the public process.

The second thing is that you need to understand that because you're a citizen of two worlds, you live in one and exercise citizenship in the other. You need to be a good citizen as well as a good Christian. You're a good Christian, a good citizen, and you will participate in the governmental process, and you will participate vigorously in the life of your community of faith—witnessing, studying the Bible study, giving all these things together—because you have a dual responsibility.

IV. We are citizens of two lands. When we talk about liberty and freedom, it has a special note in the heart of a Bible-believing, blood-washed, repentant, born-again Christian. And because it has a special meaning for us, the land is made better because we're here. We thank God for the privilege and will fight for the privilege of preaching the gospel as free men, freed under the Spirit of Jesus Christ and a free nation.—William C. Self

SUNDAY, JULY 8, 2007
Lectionary Message

Topic: Ambassadors for Christ
TEXT: Luke 10:1–11, 16–20
Other Readings: 2 Kings 5:1–14; Ps. 30; Gal. 6:1–6, 7–16

I picked up my grandson from school last week, and he was brimming with pride. He had been appointed by his second-grade teacher to be a "bin buddy" for the week. He and one of his classmates had been given the authority to go to the other second-grade classes and announce that they were the bin buddies for the week and they were there to pick up all the recyclable materials. There was little doubt that he was taking this appointment seriously. The pride carried over to the next week, when he helped train the new bin buddies.

The text for today is about Christ appointing seventy of his disciples to a special task. He was giving them the authority to be his ambassadors to the surrounding communities. The story indicates that they accepted the appointment with pride and determination to carry the good news that the Kingdom of God was at hand. But this is not just a story of seventy first-century Christians. It is the story about Christ's appointment of you and me as his ambassadors to the twenty-first century.

I. *The charge:*

(a) *The harvest is great.* As their names were called, Jesus reminded the ambassadors that the harvest was great. People were ready to hear the good news of the Kingdom. It had been a long time since the people of Israel had heard a direct word from God. They had struggled with the false promises of the Temple priests; life had become burdensome and meaningless. As Paul wrote later, "the fullness of time was at hand." The people were ready to listen to the ambassadors as they spread the good news Christ had proclaimed.

The harvest is truly ready for twenty-first century ambassadors. Life has become burdensome and meaningless for millions in the United States and around the world. The false "isms" of the world have not proven to meet the real needs of life. People are just as ready to hear the good news of the gospel today as they were in the first century.

(b) *It won't be easy.* Jesus reminded them that they were going out like lambs among wolves. It wouldn't be easy. The task of spreading the gospel is never easy. It wasn't in the first century, and it isn't today. Competing world religions, worldviews, and secular materialism all become barriers to the gospel message. Satan is still at work in the world, and anyone who becomes an ambassador for Christ will encounter him.

(c) *Travel light.* Don't burden yourself down with material things, Jesus instructed them. Don't carry a purse, a bag, or even extra sandals, he said. I really wonder what Jesus would say to his twenty-first-century ambassadors. What are the things he would instruct us to leave behind? What are the material things that hinder the spreading of the message in the twenty-first century?

(d) *Don't be diverted from the task.* Don't stop for small talk along the way. Keep your mind focused on the task. It is so easy to get sidetracked, particularly when we are not overly anxious to perform the task in the first place. But even when we are determined to complete the task, it is amazing how many things can distract us. As I prepared this message, it seemed like a dozen things demanded my attention. In a busy world, it is very easy to get diverted from the task of sharing the good news with those around us.

II. *The task:* Jesus instructs his ambassadors to go directly to the people in the communities along the way and bear witness to the Kingdom of God, which he, Jesus, had proclaimed. This was their evangelistic message at that time. We, as twenty-first-century ambassadors, are even more blessed to be able to share the full gospel message of the life, death, burial, and Resurrection of Jesus. As they entered the homes of those who were receptive, they were to bless the house by sharing their story and offering the new salvation to all who would receive it. But Jesus reminded them that they could not force people to receive the good news. If people refused, the ambassadors were to simply move on to the next town. But they were to remind the folks that the Kingdom had come near to them and they had refused to join it.

III. *The results:* I think one of the most exciting affirmations in this passage is Jesus' proclamation that whoever hears his ambassadors' message hears him. We truly become coworkers with Christ. He entrusts the message of salvation to us, with the promise that those who hear and accept the message we proclaim also hear and accept him. And the opposite is also true. Those who reject the message we proclaim reject Christ. What an awesome responsibility is given to us. I can only hope that we receive this appointment with the same depth of pride that my grandson felt after his appointment as a bin buddy.

When the seventy returned, they rejoiced saying, "Lord, even the demons are subject to us in your name!" To which the Lord replies, "I saw Satan fall like lighting from heaven."

Satan retreats when we go in the name of Christ. In many ways, as ambassadors we become soldiers of God in spiritual warfare.

Jesus ends his debriefing session with the seventy with these words: "Behold, I have given you authority . . . over all the power of the enemy; and nothing shall hurt you. Nevertheless do not rejoice in this, that the spirits are subject to you; but rejoice that your names are written in heaven." This warning is still very contemporary. We should never become prideful when we experience victories in the name of Jesus. Our only pride should come in the salvation that is ours in Jesus the Christ.—John Dever

ILLUSTRATIONS

THE CALL TO JOIN.   Frodo the hobbit receives a "call" to destroy the evil "one ring" before its power is able to corrupt and destroy all of Middle Earth. This call involves a long and extremely dangerous journey, and the likelihood that Frodo will not return alive. In one scene, Frodo expresses his fear and his wish that the ring had never come to him. Gandalf the wizard tells Frodo, "We cannot choose the time we live in. We can only choose what we do with the time we are given."[1]

A VISION FOR CHANGE.   From a sermon by William Loader:

> It is a long way from this strategy of mission to our modern day. The architecture of houses in most societies does not lend themselves to this plan. But I wonder if the invitation to join the movement of God's kingdom does not sometimes work like this. It is not about selling a brand name ("Christian"), but sharing a vision of change is such a way that means real participation in making it real in the here and now.[2]

—John Dever

SERMON SUGGESTIONS

Topic: The First Recorded Song

TEXT: Exod. 15:2

(1) This song sings of the Lord, who is our salvation. (2) It sings of the Lord, who is our strength. (3) It sings of the Lord, who redeems us from sin and leaves us with praise.—Perry F. Webb

Topic: The Days of Our Years

TEXT: Ps. 90:12

(1) Wisdom is found as we embrace God's design for human mortality: we are to number our days. (2) God provides the answer to our quest in the death of Jesus: in Christ, sin and death are destroyed. (3) Because life is now lived in Christ, our days are to be lived wisely.—Joseph A. Hill

---

[1]From *Lord of the Rings: The Fellowship of the Ring*, 2001 (available at http://www.textweek.com/movies/call.htm).
[2]William Loader, "First Thoughts on Year C: Gospel Passages from the Lectionary" (sermon), Murdoch University, Uniting Church in Australia (available at http://wwwstaff.murdoch.edu.au/ ~ loader/LKPentecost5.htm).

WORSHIP AIDS

CALL TO WORSHIP.   "I am still confident of this: I will see the goodness of the Lord in the land of the living. Wait for the Lord; be strong and take heart and wait for the Lord" (Ps. 27:13–14 NIV).

INVOCATION.   Eternal God, who is worshiped by all the hosts of heaven, touch our hearts today. Search our consciences and remove from us any evil that hinders our worship. Give us pure hearts, O God, that we may rightly speak the words of praise.

OFFERTORY SENTENCE.   "God was reconciling the world unto him in Christ, not counting men's sins against them. And he has committed to us the message of reconciliation" (2 Cor. 5:19 NIV).

OFFERTORY PRAYER.   Father, we pray that your blessings, which are as numerous as the stars of the sky, may be so received with grace that in turn they will be used to bring light and love to people everywhere. Bless these gifts, for Christ's sake.

PRAYER.   Eternal and glorious God, as we gather together in this holy place we come to you humbly to glorify your name. As we recognize our faults before you, we stand ready to open our hearts and hear your voice. We give you thanks for your continuing presence in the world, for your guidance to the nations, for the acts of transformation in the human heart.

This morning, O God, we lift unto you the condition of the members of this congregation. We pray that new signs of hope, comfort, and consolation will be brought into their lives. Give them the comfort of your presence and the assurance of your promises. Strengthen their faith so that whenever they feel weak they might be empowered by your grace. Whenever fear comes to their lives, give them courage. In their affliction, afford them the patience you gave your servant Job.

We give you thanks for the ministries of this great church. For all the saints who now rest in your presence, we give you thanks and praise your holy name. Bless this worship. Speak to us through your Word. Anoint your prophet, and let him be free to speak with authority and power. Lift our hearts, open our minds, and give us wisdom to live day-by-day in your presence as children of light. Help us to be a faithful church and renew our discipleship. This is our prayer.—Djalma Araujo

SERMON
Topic: Against All Odds
TEXT: John 1:43–51

I. How many times will you get to live this life? Why not live life to the fullest? The presence of so much boredom in our world is the result of refusing to take risks and not having any purpose outside our own meager existence. This is the very opposite of our risk-taking God. God took a risk in creating human beings as free moral creatures. God took a risk in making covenants with Abraham, Isaac, and Jacob. God took a risk in using Moses—a fugitive from justice—to liberate his people. God took the ultimate risk in coming as Jesus, knowing that in coming as a human being he could be rejected and murdered—which happened. God took a risk in entrusting the good news of Jesus Christ to humankind, knowing that we could distort it and use it for our own purposes—which happened.

If we are to be God's people, then we must be about risk taking as well. Faith as risk taking involves seeing what needs to be done in this world and getting involved in it—for Christ's sake. When we are not living life with risk, we are confining ourselves in a prison of our own making, and prisons are rarely productive for human growth.

II. Our text speaks of the calling of Philip and Nathaniel. Jesus calls Philip, and he immediately responds by finding Nathaniel and bringing him to Jesus. Philip believed immediately; Nathaniel was a bit more skeptical. However, both took a risk in following Jesus. Both were betting that Jesus was who they thought he was: the Messiah. Serving our Lord is not always a matter of having life nice and easy. There are defining moments—those times in our lives when we are faced with momentous decisions. They are not necessarily the big economic decisions but are those that keep us awake at night—the ones that hinge on our values and beliefs, that reveal our true character.

III. Jesus took risks all the time. Calling disciples was a risk. When others focused on saying no to the wrong things, Jesus dared to say yes to the right things. In so doing, he empowered all around him to be liberated from the cultural prisons in which they found themselves and live life positively, not negatively. What about us? Are we living life to its fullest, or are we being cautious and careful? When we live life in "safe mode," we miss so much of what life is about.—Robert U. Ferguson

SUNDAY, JULY 15, 2007
Lectionary Message

Topic: Christianity—A Way of Life
Text: Luke 10:25–37
Other Readings: Amos 7:7–17; Ps. 82; Col. 1:1–14

It was vacation time, and as usual I bought a book to be my relaxing companion on the beach. Richard Carlson's *Don't Sweat the Small Stuff—and It's All Small Stuff*[3] was this year's best-selling choice. The basic thesis was that we overreact to small things, and by doing so we make them big deals. This, in turn, causes us to lose the bigger picture. Carlson offers another way of living that involves replacing old habits of "reaction" with new habits of "perspection." In the remainder of the book he introduces us to one hundred ways to replace the old habits. Here are just a few:

Make peace with your imperfections.
Be the first one to act loving or reach out.
Set aside quiet time, every day.
Fill your life with love.

---

[3]Richard Carlson, *Don't Sweat the Small Stuff—and It's All Small Stuff: Simple Ways to Keep the Little Things from Taking Over Your Life* (New York: Hyperion, 1997).

I was just one of millions who had purchased the book within a very brief period of time. The reviews and the reports of individuals concerning the book were overwhelmingly positive. This was "Something New," "a New Discovery," "a Marvelous Book." It struck me as not being new at all. It fact, in the terminology I know best, it was a basic course in Christianity 101. I know your first reaction is, "You are biased; you see everything through the eyes of a minister." Let me try to explain what I mean.

I. Let's begin with a question: What is Christianity? Answers vary. From an evangelical perspective one might say that Christianity is the good news of salvation, provided for us through the death, burial, and Resurrection of Jesus. A more mainline definition might emphasize that Christianity is the coming of the Kingdom of God. After all Jesus began his ministry saying, "The time is fulfilled and the Kingdom of God is at hand." Those from a more liturgical perspective might equate Christianity to the worshipping of God through Jesus Christ. "After all," they would say, "you should worship the Lord your God with all your heart, mind, and strength."

I would like to present a little different definition. I really think the Bible teaches us that Christianity is a way of life. It is a way of life based on right relationships. It all begins with the Genesis stories. There are the ideal relationships presented in the garden of Eden story. The relationships are broken in the Fall stories. These broken relationships are reflected in the Cain and Abel stories and the Tower of Babel and flood accounts. This sets the stage for the rest of the Old and New Testaments. They become the story of God's initiative to reestablish right relationships. The Ten Commandments are directions for right relationships between God and human beings and among human beings themselves. Jesus, in the Sermon on the Mount, gives us guidance for right relationships. The model prayer addresses our relationship with God and our fellow human beings. To be a Christian is to have a right relationship with God—a relationship that is reflected in our everyday lives.

II. A right relationship with God is the first priority. Sin is basically a broken relationship with God. David's great desire was to restore a right relationship with God. His sin had severed that relationship, and now he longed for a renewal of the bond that would hold him close to God. For the Christian, that relationship is restored through a belief and trust in the atonement of Jesus Christ. It is believing that he died for our sins and that, through him, we can once again have a right relationship with God. Our sins are forgiven, and we are born again to a new relationship.

III. This must be reflected in our relationships with each other. I cannot be too emphatic about this. Over and over the Scriptures indicate that if we say we love God and do not love each other, we are liars. The Sermon on the Mount is primarily directed toward this aspect of the Christian life. Our relationship to God is to be reflected in our relationships with our family, our friends, and with others. And maybe most of all, it is to be reflected in our relationships with fellow Christians. This was a distinguishing characteristic of the early Church. "See how they love one another" was the pagan community's reaction.

One of the best illustrations of living in right relationships with others is the story of the Good Samaritan. One day a lawyer asked Jesus, "What must I do to inherit eternal life." "What does the Scripture say?" Jesus replied. The lawyer answered, "You shall love the Lord your God with all your heart, and with all your soul, and with all your strength, and with all your mind; and your neighbor as your self."

In reply to a lawyer's inquiry as to who is my neighbor, Jesus relates the parable of the Jewish man who fell among thieves on the road to Jericho. They robbed him, beat him, and left him half-dead. A priest passed by and ignored him. Later, a Levite saw him, pitied him, and went on his way. Finally, a despised Samaritan came by. He stopped, bound his wounds, took him to an inn, and paid for his stay. "Who proved to be the neighbor?" Jesus asked. And of course the answer was, "The Samaritan."

I think we could modernize this parable by substituting rabbi for priest, member of the Knesset for Levite, and Palestinian for Samaritan. The result would be the same. Jesus facilitated a great reversal in telling the story. He turned the question, "Who is my neighbor?" into "To whom can I be a neighbor?" And in doing so, he instructed us to live out our relationship to God in our everyday lives with others. Christianity is a way of life.

IV. Back to Richard Carlson and *Don't Sweat the Small Stuff*. There is really nothing new here. It incorporates the basics of Christianity 101

Carlson	*Jesus*
Fill your life with love.	(John 15:12) "This is my commandment, That you love one another, as I have loved you."
Resist the urge to criticize.	(Luke 1:3) "Why do you see the speck in your brother's eye, but do not notice the log that is in your own eye?"
Try to understand one another.	Jesus' whole life was one of understanding others: the woman at the well, the woman caught in adultery, Peter. "Father forgive them for they know not what they do."
Quiet the mind.	Jesus often quieted the mind with prayer.
Develop your compassion.	Jesus lived a life of compassionate relationships.

I could go on. But it becomes quite clear that Carlson has incorporated the essential elements of what Jesus taught. And it is this: Christianity is a way of life. It is a way of relating to God, self, and others—in that order. When we really experience this, life becomes a joy. It is exciting. It is life lived in perspective. It is a life lived where we don't sweat the small stuff, because in relation to God, it is all small stuff.—John Dever

ILLUSTRATIONS

GOD'S LOVE.   My teaching colleague and I had taken a group of seminary students to New York City to study and observe intercity missions. When we arrived, we gave the students $5 and instructed them to buy a street person a meal while they were there. We also gave ourselves $5 and the same challenge. The time passed quickly, and I had not fulfilled my vow. So I went down to the nearby park to search for a person in need. There she was, a typical bag lady, sitting on a park bench. In the middle of July she was wearing four dresses and holding on to her shopping cart that contained her earthly possessions. I struck up a conversation and discovered that she was a former telephone operator who had been phased out by technology. She had been living on the streets for seven years. I asked her if she was hungry, and she replied that she would like to have a hot dog. I invited her to go across the street to the vendor and I would buy her what she wanted. She declined, insisting that I would be embarrassed to be with her. I proceeded to buy the meal and continued to talk. At the end I said to her, "I have to go, but before I do, I want you to know that God loves you and so do I." She sat up straighter and brushed her hair back and replied, "Thank you. You don't know how long it has been since someone told me they loved me." There are a lot of hurting people in the world who need to hear, "God loves you, and so do I."—John Dever

UNEXPECTED COMPASSION.   A minister riding the subway noticed that an old woman shuffled into the subway wearing only ragged clothes to protect her from the bitter Chicago winter wind. Her white, cracked, bony hands clutched a worn shawl tightly around her. The minister watched with wonder and pity. At the next stop, an energetic young man strode confidently onto the train. His warm, high-fashion clothes offered a stark contrast to the rider from the last stop. As he made his way to his seat, his eyes lingered just a moment on the old woman. Three stops later, as the train slowed, he glided by her to the other door and disappeared into the tunnel. On the woman's lap lay his brown leather gloves. The minister observed, "I don't know if he was a believer in Christ or not. But I do know this: He saw her need and responded with compassion—while I just sat there. It never occurred to me to give her my gloves. That young man showed compassion in a way I'll never forget."[4]—John Dever

SERMON SUGGESTIONS

Topic: Why So Tense?
Text: Job 22:21
(1) We are tense because of the general insecurity of our time. (2) We can help to remove the tension by getting our minds off ourselves. (3) We should not dwell on the future, which we cannot control. (4) But most of all, we should place ourselves in the energy of our faith, grounded on belief in God.—Robert McCracken

Topic: Overcoming Emotional Depression
Text: Ps. 130:1
(1) Depression may result from physical exhaustion, tension, or ethical conflict. (2) But let's not accept any present mood as permanent. (3) Talk with others about it. (4) Practice tension-reducing devices. (5) Link our present thoughts with the power and goodness of God. (6) Think through a reasonable program of action. (7) Help someone else.—J. Wallace Hamilton

WORSHIP AIDS
CALL TO WORSHIP.   "The Lord will be the sure foundation for your times, a rich store of salvation and wisdom and knowledge; the fear of the Lord is the key to his treasure" (Isa. 33:6 NIV).

INVOCATION.   Father God, we gather today and ask for a renewed vision of your Presence, for a resurrected spirit of life in history and beyond. We humbly come to worship seeking you. May we so know you that we may live in your world in joy and peace.

---

[4]*Our Daily Bread,* February 6, 1997, quoted in *The Abingdon Preaching Annual,* 2001, p. 263.

OFFERTORY SENTENCE.   "To do good and to communicate forget not: for with such sacrifices God is well pleased" (Heb. 13:16 KJV).

OFFERTORY PRAYER.   Dearest Lord and Savior, receive these gifts as expressions of our love, trust, and joy in participating with you in the work of the Kingdom. May we forever be obedient in dedicating all that we have—and are—to you.

PRAYER.   Eternal Father, we confess that we do not always find life easy. Break in upon us in our worship this hour with the reality of your presence. May the power of your presence be so strong within us that our faith will come alive with meaning, with power and strength, love, hope, and courage.

O God, teach us to hate evil and to love the good, to be willing to take the hard and difficult way when it is your way and not the easy path when it is the popular or softer way. May we remember the way of the crucified Christ. Give us then courage to take up our crosses and follow him in the war against evil, in the battle of truth over ignorance, justice over inequity, and righteousness over corruption. Help us, O God, to bring light where there is darkness, hope where there is fear, concern where there is apathy, victory where there is defeat, and redemption where there is division.

Guide us to draw upon the strength of your abiding presence, which can enable us to become what you have created us to be. Let us not grow weary then in well-doing. Inspire us with confidence to continue to follow the way of Christ wherever it leads us. For we pray it in his strong name.—William Powell Tuck

SERMON
Topic: A Child's Eye View of Jesus
TEXT: Col. 1:15–23

Jesus is told about in every book of the Bible. To fully understand about him, you have to study the whole Bible. I have chosen a passage of Scripture in one of the letters Paul wrote. In this passage we have one of the more beautiful descriptions of Christ in the entire Bible. Turn to Colossians 1, and let me read to you verses 15 through 20. In this passage Paul tells us four very important facts about Jesus.

I. Paul says that Jesus is the one who teaches us the truth about God. "And he is the image of the invisible God." That word, translated "image," is a word meaning "an exact likeness." Paul says that he is an "exact likeness" of God. What does this mean? It tells us that the place to look to find out about God (what he thinks, what he desires, how he acts, what his attitudes are)—is to look at Jesus.

II. There is a second fact about Jesus that Paul gives us in our text. "In Him all things hold together," Paul said. He is the magnet that holds it together. The universe in which we live is not geocentric. The universe is not heliocentric. The universe is Christo-centric, that is, it revolves around and is centered in and is held together by Jesus Christ.

III. Paul says in verse 18 that Jesus also directs the Church: "He is also the head of the body, the church." He is the one who gives direction to the Church and who sets out the limits within which the Church is to do its work. It is not the pastor who rules, it is not the deacons who rule, it is not the majority who rule. It is Christ who rules the Church. He is the one who directs us.

IV. Then the Bible says that Jesus also saves the sinner. "Through Jesus, God can reconcile all things to himself." That word—*reconcile*—means to bring together two things or two people who have been separate. This is what Jesus does for us. He puts one hand on our life and one hand on God, and he brings us together. He forgives our sin. He removes our guilt. He gives us power. He brings us into the family of God. Jesus saves us. Will you let Jesus be your Savior today?—Brian L. Harbour

SUNDAY, JULY 22, 2007
Lectionary Message

Topic: The Hazards of Privilege
TEXT: Amos 8:1–12
Other Readings: Ps. 52; Col. 1:15–28; Luke 10:38–42

When I taught Bible courses in college, I often mentioned to the students that they could not fully understand the New Testament unless they understood the Old Testament. I'm not sure this always served as sufficient motivation to get them involved in a study of the first half of the Bible, but there is a great deal of truth in the statement. One might even make a chain of these types of statements: We cannot understand what the ministry of God's people should be unless we understand the ministry of Jesus. Further, we cannot fully understand the ministry of Jesus unless we understand the ministry of the prophets. And to go one step further, Limburg in his book, *The Prophets and the Powerless,* insists that there is an antecedent to the prophets. He notes that the prophets are calling the people of God back to the basic teaching of the law and the covenant.

The messengers of God—the prophets—trumpeted words of condemnation and words of hope for Israel. But the message was always a call back to the covenant with God. This was not so much a call to renew their fidelity to the law as it was a summons to a renewed response to their covenant relationship with God. God had delivered them from their bondage in Egypt and had established a special relationship with them. He would be their God, and they would be his people. Their response to this relationship was to be expressed in their attitude toward God and in their attitude toward others. The first four commandments gave guidance to Israel's response to God, and the remaining six provided general guidelines for living in relation to others. Israel had failed in both areas of responsibility, and the prophets spoke passionately concerning those sins.

I. *Responsibility—justice and righteousness:* The book of Amos has two themes interwoven in its chapters. God's people are to live righteous lives. Righteousness was to be in a right relationship with God. They were to live by the standards that God holds before a moral society. When they exhibited this righteousness, justice would be the inevitable result. When righteousness and justice are not present, even the worship of God's people is not acceptable. Amos writes, "I hate, I despise your feasts, and I take no delight in your solemn assemblies. Even though you offer me your burnt offerings and cereal offerings, I will not accept them. . . . Take away from me the noise of your songs; to the melody of your harps, I will not listen" (Amos 5:21–23).

Amos makes it quite clear that God expects justice to be practiced in relation to the poor, and when this is not done, God is angry with his children. The condemnation is made clear in the eighth chapter of Amos. Amos cries out in disgust over the way the poor and needy had been treated. "You trample on the needy. You can't wait for the religious festivals to end, so you can get back to cheating the helpless. You mix the wheat you sell with chaff swept from the floor. You enslave poor people for a debt of one piece of silver or a pair of sandals" (Amos 8:4–6 [paraphrase]).

Have things changed in an affluent United States of America? If the Old Testament prophets were to become prophets on main street U.S.A., what would their message be? Would they still cry out, "You oppress the poor and crush the needy. You get wealthy at the expense of the helpless. Therefore, let justice roll down like waters, and righteousness like an ever-flowing stream"?

II. *The hazards of privilege:* With the privilege of being God's people comes responsibility. That responsibility is to be lived out in community. It is interesting that in the prophet's relationship to God, responsibility is never mentioned outside of communal relationships. It is only in the arena of life that one's faith may find expression. And when that responsibility is neglected, then the wrath of God will bring justice to bear upon those who refuse to live righteously and practice justice in their everyday lives.

Time and time again, Amos pronounces God's judgment on his people. This judgment is expressed in at least two ways. First, God will no longer hear the songs of the Temple. He will not listen to their voices of worship, because the words are hollow and meaningless. Second, God will withdraw his sustaining word, and the people will experience a famine of the Word of the Lord. Earlier, Amos indicates that God will withdraw and allow the people to reap the results of their sinful ways.

III. Donald Williams has said it clearly:

For too long many have been frightened away from the phrases "social righteousness," "social responsibility," or "social action," because of our fear that we might tarnish the central doctrine of justification by faith. There is no contradiction between the two. Let us erase, therefore, our fear of the word *social*, whether social responsibility, social righteousness, or social action. It means no more (dare we say "no more" when the concept means "so much" to biblical faith) than the practice of justice and righteousness in every action as we deal with other persons and to live by the will of God in determining our thoughts, words, and deeds. Is this too much to ask of one who knows the Lord?[5]

There really isn't a "social gospel" and a "salvation gospel." There is one gospel that is concerned with the whole person. This is the gospel that the Church and individuals should be about in the world.—John Dever

ILLUSTRATIONS

OUR RESPONSIBILITY.   Hear this word, you who while away the idle hours, saying, "When will the next bingo game be played?" or "What club shall we go to tonight?" Woe unto you who go to deep freezers, saying, "Shall it be steak or chicken?" But care little for

---

[5]Source unknown.

my children in India who have no rice. For I will take away what you think you have, and give it to those who have none.[6]—John Dever

OUR WEALTH.   Did you know that (1) The world's 225 richest individuals of whom 60 are Americans with total assets of $311 billion, have a combined wealth of over $1 trillion—equal to the combined wealth of the poorest 47% of the entire world's population. (2) The three richest people in the world have assets that exceed the combined gross domestic product of the 48 poorest countries. (3) The average African household is some 20% poorer today than it was 25 years ago. (4) The richest 20% of the world's people consume 86% of all goods and services. The poorest 20% consume 1.3%. (5) Americans and Europeans spend $17 billion a year on pet food. This is $4 billion more than the estimated annual total needed to provide health and nutrition for everyone in the world. (6) Americans spend $8 billion a year on cosmetics—$2 billion more than the estimated annual total needed to provide basic education for everyone in the world.[7]—John Dever

SERMON SUGGESTIONS

Topic: Stand Up to Life

TEXT: Neh. 2:10–19, 4:7, 6:1–11

(1) The world is full of people who flee from work, responsibilities, and troubles of life. (2) We can handle the problems of life by standing up to them. (3) We must discover reinforcements beyond ourselves: "Such a man as I," speaks of a pride deeper than Nehemiah's own ego.—J. Wallace Hamilton

Topic: The Christian Pilgrim

TEXT: Heb. 11:13–14

(1) The Christian life is to be seen as a pilgrimage toward heaven. (2) It is a journey, for earth is not our eternal home. (3) We may mourn the loss of family and friends who die but rejoice that their journey has ended. (4) We are to labor during our earthly days of our journey that heaven will be our inheritance.—Jonathan Edwards

WORSHIP AIDS

CALL TO WORSHIP.   "Lift up your heads in the sanctuary, and bless the Lord. The Lord that made heaven and earth bless thee out of Zion" (Ps. 134:2–3 KJV).

INVOCATION.   Kind Father, who keeps no good thing from your children, and in your wisdom draws us to this day of worship, we give you thanks for the world that you made and prepared as our dwelling place. We ask that your steadfast love will forever hold us close and allow no evil thing ever to gain mastery in our lives. Give us peace and joy in the Holy Spirit.

OFFERTORY SENTENCE.   "Therefore, as we have opportunity, let us do good to all people, especially to those who belong to the family of believers" (Gal. 6:10 NIV).

---

[6]J. Elliott Corbett, *The Prophets on Main St.* (Richmond: John Knox, 1969), p. 28.
[7]*New York Times,* September 5, 1999, p. 16.

OFFERTORY PRAYER.   Lord, as we dedicate these gifts to you, we pray that we will ever seek to discover your way and will for our lives. Let us never be satisfied to give you our second best in return for your gift of love.

PRAYER.   Our gracious and loving Heavenly Father, we come to you in Jesus' name—the name that's above every name in heaven and on earth. How comforting it is to know that you're in control of the world and even the whole universe, however vast and big it is! Help us to trust you, even when we can't see, because with our hand in yours, we'll make it through. We're thinking especially today about those that have lost loved ones in recent days. We pray for the comfort of the Holy Spirit, the Comforter, and may they find in you their source of strength and the courage to go on. We pray, too, for those with sicknesses and physical problems. We pray for our president and his cabinet. We pray for the men and women of Congress and those of the courts of our land. We pray for your influence in the affairs of our nation.

Thank you for your presence in this service. We sense that you are here. We want to be drawn closer to you. We want to be encouraged and uplifted and challenged in our personal lives. We pray for our pastor as he ministers this morning. You have already spoken to him, and now we expect you to speak to us through him. We pray in the name of Jesus our Savior.—Paul Meeks

SERMON
Topic: The Answer to Broken Homes
TEXT: Gen. 2:24; Matt. 19:6

The broken home has become the number-one social problem of North America and could ultimately lead to the destruction of our civilization. This problem does not make screaming headlines, but, like termites, it is eating away at the heart and core of our social and moral structure.

I. For some one hundred years our educational system has been subject to a psychology that has taught that humans are little more than animals. Our young people have been led to believe that the achievement of happiness is based on physical compatibility and that spiritual issues are incidental. It is becoming increasingly obvious that such psychology, having been sown to the wind for years, is now being reaped in the whirlwind of broken homes and tragic lives. If the love that binds husband and wife together and builds the home is but the refinement of animal art, then the natural consequences would be these: Down with decency and purity! Let conscience perish and agreements crash! Abandon restraint! Give us a perpetual carnival of promiscuity and a lifelong sensuality of sin!

II. It is time that our experts in marriage, the family, and the home turn to the Bible. The One who performed the first marriage in the Garden of Eden and instituted the union between husband and wife has been left out. It was God himself who brought the bride to her husband in the first marriage. It was God's Word that declared for all ages, "Therefore shall a man leave his father and his mother, and shall cleave unto his wife: and they shall be one flesh" (Gen. 2:24). We speak of "holy matrimony," and holy it is, for it is the oldest of God's institutions. All through the Old and New Testaments, marriage is exalted as the very highest of relationships.

III. When God instituted matrimony, he made no provision for the separation of husband and wife. They are to cleave together. Christ ruled, after directing their attention to the divine institution of marriage, "What therefore God hath joined together, let not man put asunder" (Matt. 19:6). To emphasize the words of Jesus, Paul says in Romans 7:2, "The woman which hath a husband is bound by the law to her husband so long as he liveth." According to some experts, children of single or divorced parents are more likely to drop out of high school, become pregnant as teenagers, have poor relationships with their parents, abuse drugs, and get into trouble than those living with both parents.

IV. Tens of thousands of homes are almost on the rocks. There is one great insurance policy that you can take out in order to guarantee the unity and happiness of your home. It is simple: Make Christ the center of your home. A home is like a solar system. The center—the great sun—holds the solar system together. If it were not for the sun, the solar system would fly to pieces. Unless the Son of God is put at the center of your home, it, too, may fly to pieces. Make the Son of God the center of your home.

If the foundations of your home are about to break, make sure that you yourself are a believer in Christ, having had your sins washed away through faith in him. Then ask God for the patience and love to win that wayward husband or unfaithful wife. That husband or wife can be gloriously changed by the power of God. Your home can be so completely transformed that it will have been worth waiting all these months or years. "Believe on the Lord Jesus Christ, and thou shalt be saved, and thy house" (Acts 16:31).—Billy Graham

SUNDAY, JULY 29, 2007
Lectionary Message

Topic: Principles of Prayer
TEXT: Luke 11:1–13
Other Readings: Hos. 1:2–10; Ps. 85; Col. 2:6–15, 16–19

Have you ever wondered what it must have been like to walk beside Jesus daily during his ministry here on earth? It must have been exhilarating for the disciples as they discovered week-by-week and month-by-month the depth, the power, and the spiritual insights that radiated from this man, Jesus. It took a long time, but it finally became clear, this was "the Christ, the Son of the living God." It had been clear from the beginning that Jesus' whole life was different: his words, his personality, his vision, his control over demons, his miraculous acts. Surely, this man could give them anything they wanted, but Luke does not record any such requests from the disciples up to the time of this passage in Luke 11. "Lord, teach us to pray" is their request.

Why would the disciples ask Jesus to teach them to pray at this particular time in their journey with him? I would suggest that over the long journey they had come to realize that prayer literally saturated Jesus' whole life. Every significant decision, every miraculous event, every movement in his ministry was preceded with prayer. In the midst of a busy schedule, he always found time to retire for prayer. He sought the Father's direction in choosing his disciples. He demonstrated prayerful dependence on the Father by "looking up toward heaven" before he fed the five thousand or raised Lazarus from the grave. Prayer had made a difference, and they wanted to learn how to pray the way Jesus did.

It seems worth noting that the disciples didn't ask Jesus to show them *how* to pray; they knew how. There was something more about Jesus' prayer life they need to emulate. His prayer life was so endowed by the very spirit of God that it stood apart from anything they had experienced before. They knew by now that if Jesus could "teach" them to pray, they could become true disciples. Jesus' answer to his disciples' request gives us a guide to true spiritual depth. It directs us to a life centered in God.

I. *A pattern for prayer.* It would appear that Jesus did not mean for his words to become a rote prayer that the disciples should learn and repeat continuously; rather, he gave them a pattern for prayer. First, begin with God, not ourselves. Prayer should be centered on God. How often do we begin our prayers with our thoughts centered on ourselves? I think Jesus is saying, "If you start with your thoughts and mind centered on God, everything will be in the right perspective."

Second, pray as a child. By praying to God as Father, we place ourselves in our born-again relationship to him. We proclaim our dependence on him as our Heavenly Father. The heavenly family relationship is affirmed.

Third, pray to honor God's name: "Hallowed be thy name." *Hallowed* means "to make holy." Far too often we take the commandment that forbids taking the Lord's name in vain to mean that we should not to curse or swear. I don't think that is what it means. Rather, it means don't claim to follow God and then fail to act accordingly. In some ways, "hallowed be thy name" is the same idea. May my life proclaim the holiness of God. Pray for God's will on earth. Pray that the Kingdom of God will come to earth and, as Matthew puts it, "thy will be done." Maybe it goes a little further and says let the Kingdom live in me. Pray for physical needs. God created us whole persons. He is concerned about us as whole persons. He knows we have physical needs, and it is not wrong to take those needs to him. Pray for spiritual needs. Pray for our own spiritual needs. We have all sinned and fallen short of the glory of God. We all need forgiveness. Pray for our relationship to others. Pray that we will reflect the forgiveness of God in our relationships to others. Finally, pray that we will not be overcome by temptation. Temptation is real, and only with the power of God can we overcome the evil one.

II. *The purpose of prayer.* Jesus is not explicit in teaching his disciples about the purpose of prayer, but it is implicit throughout the prayer. Prayer is about relationships. We have a family relationship with our Heavenly Father. Families need to communicate. This communication can take place as the individual lifts up his or her prayer to heaven, and it can take place as a congregation lifts up its corporate prayer. Our Heavenly Father is ready to give us good gifts if we are willing to ask for them. If an earthly father will not give a scorpion to a child who asks for an egg or a serpent when he asks for a fish, how much more does God want to give his good gifts to his children. And the greatest gift would be the gift of the Holy Spirit.

III. *Persistence in prayer.* Too often we take the parable in Luke 11:5–8 to indicate that we need to keep pounding on the door of heaven until we receive what we want. This is not what Jesus is teaching his disciples. He is teaching them that one who is consistent in prayer will find God's answer. He follows the parable with these words: "Ask, and it will be given you; seek, and you will find; knock, and it will be opened to you." In other words, "pray." James reminds us, "You have not, because you ask not" (James 4:2).

If the disciples could only pray like Jesus, they knew they would be the kind of disciples he had called them to be. The same applies to us. If we can pray like Jesus, we can be the disciples he has called us to be. Jesus gives us the secret in Luke 11.—John Dever

ILLUSTRATIONS

WHAT PRAYER MEANS.   Harry Emerson Fosdick says,

Perhaps the greatest single difficulty in maintaining the habit of prayer is our tendency to make of it a *pious form* and not a *vital transaction*. We begin by trying to pray and end by saying prayers. To urge ourselves to a practice that has thus become a stereotyped and lifeless form is futile. Nobody ever succeeds in praying as a *tour de force;* but if the act of prayer can be seen as the great Christians have seen it—a vital and sustaining friendship with a God who cares for every one of us—praying will cease being a form and become a force and a privilege.[8]

WHAT PRAYER IS.   "Prayer is a relationship, not just a religious activity. Prayer is designed more to adjust you to God than to adjust God to you."[9]

SERMON SUGGESTIONS

Topic: Love and Forgiveness
TEXT: Luke 7:47
(1) There is the unloving and arrogant Pharisee who was ignorant of the love of Christ. (2) There is "this woman," who represents the penitent sinner who lovingly recognizes divine love. (3) There is Christ, who reveals the divine love as forgiveness to sinners who repent.—Alexander Maclaren

Topic: Breaking the Worry Habit
TEXT: Luke 10:41
(1) Examine our worries carefully. (2) Don't dwell on our troubles. (3) Replace worry with other thoughts that stimulate us. (4) Replace doubting with trust in God.—David J. Davis

WORSHIP AIDS

CALL TO WORSHIP.   "Sing unto the Lord, sing psalms, unto him. Glory ye in his holy name: let the heart of them rejoice that seek the Lord" (Ps. 105:2–3 KJV).

INVOCATION.   Lord Jesus, you are the truth incarnate and the teacher of the faithful. May now your spirit hover over us as we meditate on your Word and seek to learn more of you. May our lives forever be rooted in you, may we forever grow closer to you, and may we live with you, Father, Son, and Holy Spirit—ever one God, world without end.

OFFERTORY SENTENCE.   "Offer unto God thanksgiving; and pay thy vows unto the most High" (Ps. 50:14 KJV).

---

[8]Harry Emerson Fosdick, *The Meaning of Prayer* (New York: Association Press, 1949), p. 37.
[9]Henry Blackby and Claude V. King, *Experiencing God* (Nashville, TN: Life Way, 1990), p. 87.

OFFERTORY PRAYER.   Dearest Father, help us to be cheerful givers of our time, talents, and financial resources—and of our own selves—that we may be useful in the building of your Kingdom. Bless these gifts for your own glory.

PRAYER.   Father, we are *your* people, chosen by you. As we meet together in this place, help us to listen, to understand, and to remember. Make us aware that we are meeting not simply with one another but with *you*. Let your presence be real to each of us. As we pray, may it be just like speaking with you. As we listen, help us to concentrate so that we really hear your Word, and help us to take in and retain all that we hear, see, and experience this morning. Hear our confessions of those things we have done [*silence is kept*]. Hear our confessions of those things we ought *not* to have done [*silence is kept*]. Now hear our confessions of what we could or should have done in a different way to better reflect who you are in us [*silence is kept*]. Hear now our praise and thanksgivings for your blessings and unearned grace that you give to us [*silence is kept*]. It is in the name of Jesus, your beloved Son, that we pray.—Larry Ellis

SERMON
Topic: Jesus in the Marketplace
TEXT: Acts 17:16–34

One of the great challenges for Christians today is holding fast to what we believe in the great marketplace of ideas that is the World in the twenty-first century. It's like living in a superstore of beliefs.

I. Athens was the marketplace of ideas. Just about any philosophy or religion known to the Western mind could be found there. Paul had been sent to spread the gospel of Jesus Christ in Europe. His practice was to speak in the Jewish synagogues of the cities he visited. Paul and the Jews spoke the same language, literally and figuratively. Paul could show his fellow Jews how Jesus was the fulfillment of Hebrew prophecy, the culmination of God's promises to Abraham. They had a common starting point, and they worked from the same Scriptures. In Athens Paul was struck with how religious the non-Jews were. They were what we might call seekers. They were looking for something to fill that empty place in the spirit of every person, and they gave every option a hearing. So Paul began to speak in the agora (marketplace) about Jesus. Some of the leading philosophers of Athens were so intrigued by what Paul said that they invited him to go with them to the Areopagus, also known as Mars Hill.

II. But now Paul wasn't talking to the Jews. The Ten Commandments didn't mean a thing to the Greeks. They didn't have a clue what the prophets had said. Paul couldn't appeal to a tradition they had grown up with—one that their grandparents taught them. Paul had brought Jesus to the ancient marketplace of ideas. He has a lot to teach us who follow Christ in an increasingly diverse world.

First, Paul saw the connection between the questions the Athenians were asking and the answers Jesus gave. Athens was full of statues of gods the Greeks worshiped: Zeus, Athena, Ares, and Artemis. Among those statues, Paul had noticed one labeled, "to an unknown god." They wanted to be sure they hadn't offended some god by overlooking him, so this statue covered their bases. Every religion and every philosophy—every human endeavor—seeks to satisfy the longings of the heart. So that's where Paul started, with what every human being has in common—that need for forgiveness, for acceptance, for love, for purpose, for meaning.

Paul then explained to them that what we hunger and thirst for is God. But we don't have to wander through the marketplace of religions. God sent Jesus to bring us home to God, to that one in whom we live and move and have our being. The proof of that love is that Jesus died for us and that God raised him from the dead so we can share that eternal life. This is what struck the Athenians as so novel. They had never heard of anything like resurrection from the dead.

III. Paul identified the need the Athenians shared with people of every time and every place. He proclaimed the good news that Jesus Christ fills that need. Then he left the results to God. Different reactions shouldn't surprise us. Jesus spoke of the different ways people would react to him in the parable of the soils. Whether it flourishes or withers doesn't depend on the truth of the seed but on the receptivity of the soil. It's easy for us to lament we can't take it for granted that we live in a world where everyone shares our faith. Some people react by trying to force what we believe on others. But Paul started with what everyone has in common: our need for spiritual fulfillment. He wasn't timid about proclaiming the truth of Jesus Christ. And he knew that the results of his efforts didn't depend on him but on the Holy Spirit working in those who heard him. Things haven't changed.—Stephens G. Lytch

SUNDAY, AUGUST 5, 2007
Lectionary Message

Topic: How Far Love Goes
TEXT: Hos. 11:1–11
Other Readings: Ps. 107:1–9, 43; Col. 3:1–11; Luke 12:13–21

You know, there are all kinds of love in the world. There is the love we have for inanimate objects—things such as chocolate and cheesecake. "I *love* chocolate," or "I *love* cheesecake," we are in the habit of saying. Then there is love between friends, designated by the Greek word *phileo,* from which comes the word *Philadelphia,* which means brotherly love. Then there is sensual, romantic, sexual love, signified by the Greek word *eros,* from which comes the word *erotic.* And then there is the Greek form for godlike love—the most perfect love— which is *agape.* This love is sometimes difficult, and it is sometimes costly. It is self-sacrificing love.

I. Love that is difficult and love that is costly—that is the nature of God's love for the world. We read about the great love of God in the book of Hosea. Through this eighth-century B.C.E. prophet, God recounts how Israel was adopted, nurtured, and loved as a parent would adopt, nurture, and love a child. God, Hosea says, went down to Egypt and through Moses adopted and delivered this beloved child from Egyptian bondage. God led them into the land of Canaan and made of them a great nation. "When Israel was a child, I loved him," God says. "I taught them to walk. . . . I took them up in my arms. . . . I bent down to them and fed them." It was as though God gathered the beloved child up in loving arms when there was a scraped knee to heal. It was as though God bent down to feed and cuddle the beloved child. And yet, the more God worked with the child Israel, the more the people of Israel turned aside to fertility gods and idol worship. They refused to follow the instructions of their parent. They strayed from the One who had loved them. They seemed bent on turning away from the Most High. But God says, "How can I give you up, Ephraim? How can I hand you over, O Israel? . . . My heart is torn within me; my compassion grows warm and tender" (NLT). In spite of Israel's wanderings and rebellion, Hosea says, God still loved Israel as a parent loves a child with a self-sacrificing, painful love. Such is the love of God: it is a tolerant and patient, healing and suffering, unconditional love.

The psalmist speaks of this love of God, what he calls a "steadfast love"—a constant, dependable, redeeming, delivering kind of love. The love of God has been shown to us through the person of Jesus of Nazareth. In Jesus, God came looking for us. The God revealed in Jesus Christ is eternal love. None of us (and no one we know) is beyond the reaches of God's love. That is good news for all of us. God's is a love that will go the distance.

II. This *agape* love—self-sacrificing love, love that leads one to go the distance should be our goal. I read a story of a man whose little daughter was killed by a neighbor's dog. The tragic loss turned the entire community against the dog's owner and drove the father of the little girl almost insane. At first the tragedy shattered his faith. Shortly afterward, the region was stricken with a great famine. The grieving father took some of his meager supply of seed corn and planted it in the field of the neighbor whose dog had taken the life of his little girl. Such is the love of God that Hosea talks about—a love that can give even to those who have caused great sorrow. That's how far love goes.

Stephen Brown, in his book *If God Is in Charge,* tells the story of a young couple (she was eighteen and he was nineteen) who fell in love and got married. Some six years and three children later, the wife decided, while standing before a kitchen sink full of dirty dishes and a pile of dirty diapers on the floor, that she just couldn't stand it anymore. She took off her apron and walked out the door. Occasionally, she would call home to check on the children, and when she did, the husband would tell her how much he loved her and would ask her to come home. Each time she refused. And she would not tell him where she was. After a number of days, the husband hired a private detective to find his wife. The report was that she was living in a second-class hotel in Des Moines, Iowa. The husband packed his bags, placed the children under the care of a neighbor, and took a bus to Des Moines. He found the hotel and made his way to her room. When he knocked on the door, his hand trembled because he didn't know the kind of reception he would receive. His wife opened the door, stood for a moment looking at him in shocked silence, then fell apart in his arms. Later at home, when the children were in bed, he asked her a question that had troubled him: "Why wouldn't you tell me where you were when you called? You knew I loved you. Why didn't you come home?" She replied, "Before, your love was just words. Now I know how much you love me because you came looking for me." That's how far love goes.

Agape love is different from the world's conceptions of love. It is a love that leads us to not be concerned about the cost, a love that leads us to gladly make a sacrifice, a love that proves true, even when it is difficult. It is painful to have to confront a relative over an addiction that is destroying her life, perhaps even to insist that she get professional help. But love sometimes necessitates it. It is painful to have to put an aged parent in an assisted living facility, even though that is sometimes the best option. But love sometimes requires it. It is difficult for a mother or father to sit up with a sick child all night. But the parent does not look upon it as a hardship or legal requirement; it is an act of love. Such is the nature of the Christian love we are called to have for our families, for fellow church members, for our neighbors, and even for our enemies. It is a love that, by its very nature, expresses itself in action; otherwise, it is only an empty word. But it is that kind of far-reaching love that makes us most like God.—Randy Hammer

ILLUSTRATIONS

LOVE FOR NOTHING.   Perhaps you have heard the story about a young man named Bradley. One morning Bradley came down to breakfast and put on his mother's plate a piece of neatly folded paper. When his mother opened it, this is what she read: "Mother owes Bradley: for running errands, 25 cents; for being good, 10 cents; for taking music lessons, 15 cents; extras, 5 cents; total, 55 cents." When lunchtime came, the mother placed the bill on Bradley's plate along with the 55 cents. Bradley's eyes danced when he saw the money, and he was proud of his business ability. But with the money he found another bill, a bill which read: "Bradley owes Mother: for being good, 0; for nursing him through his long illness with scarlet fever, 0; for all his meals and his comfortable room, 0." Bradley got the message and went and got the 55 cents, put it in his mother's hand and said, "Take all the money back, Mama, and let me love you for nothing."[1]

GOD'S UNCONDITIONAL LOVE.   For years I struggled to earn God's love. But I could never work hard enough. I could never be at peace. But then when I finally understood the unconditional nature of God's love, it was like a revelation that gave me a new lease on life.—Randy Hammer

ADOPTION FOR LOVE.   We have friends, and you may have, too, who could not have children of their own but who went to China, not once but twice, to adopt children and bring them back to America where they would have a home. Such requires a lot of love.—Randy Hammer

SERMON SUGGESTIONS

Topic: The Grounds of Our Hope

TEXT: Col. 1:15–19

(1) Christ is the image of God who reveals God's love to all mankind. (2) He is the end of the world: "All things were created through him and for him." (3) He is the preserver of the world: "All things hold together in him." (4) He works through the Church for the world's redemption: "He is the head of the church."—Ernest Trice Thompson

Topic: What the Holy Spirit Offers

TEXT: Ps. 51:11; John 14:1–25

(1) He leads us into truth. (2) He brings to memory what Jesus has said. (3) He gives to us comfort. (4) He is our strength. (5) He speaks for us and through us.—Richard M. Cromie

---

[1]John A. Redhead, *Getting to Know God* (Nashville, TN: Abingdon Press, 1954), p. 147.

WORSHIP AIDS

CALL TO WORSHIP.   "Blessed is the man who trusts in the Lord, whose confidence is in him. He shall be like a tree planted by the water that sends out its roots by the stream" (Jer. 17:7–8 NIV).

INVOCATION.   O God, we thank you for leading us to this hour. We gather in your name. May the experience of today's worship prepare us for the living of our days. Grant to us boldness to live faithfully, to recognize our own inadequacy and your sufficiency.

OFFERTORY SENTENCE.   "Each man should give what he has decided in his heart to give, not reluctantly or under compulsion, for God loves a cheerful giver" (2 Cor. 9:7 NIV).

OFFERTORY PRAYER.   Our Father, as we bring to you these gifts, receive them as expressions of our love to you and receive us, along with our human frailties, and develop us after your own heart. May we have sacrificial and loving hearts.

PRAYER.   Almighty God, on this fresh and beautiful morning, we come to your presence with thanksgiving for all the blessings received and for all the signs of your unfailing grace. We humbly confess our faults and sins before you, knowing that you are always merciful and ready to forgive and to accept us as we are. We thank you again for the life of Jesus Christ your Son, the Lamb of God, who came to manifest your salvation and your eternal plan to redeem us.

Once again, O God, we want to affirm our dependency on your power and the great need we have to stay connected with you as a condition for the blessings you have stored in heaven for us. Thanks for the ministry of prayer, for as your Word has taught us, if we abide in you and you in us, our prayers will be answered, indeed.

It is in that spirit that we come to you this morning to pray for the sick, to intercede for those who are in need of love, care, and compassion. Enable us to be healers, agents of reconciliation. Transform our lives, and make us caregivers in the same spirit and manner of those of the apostolic days. Revive us by the power of your Holy Spirit, and place a new song in our mouths. Help us to be true witnesses of the gospel wherever we find ourselves.

As your church, we want to be missional with a clear sense of commitment and a new understanding of your call to your service. Baptize us anew and prepare us for a new day of new beginnings with you, through the power and ministry of your Holy Spirit. This we ask in the name of Jesus Christ.—Djalma Araujo

SERMON
Topic: Don't Miss the Trip
Text: Matt. 17:1–9; 2 Pet. 1:16–18

Have you ever missed a trip? At one time or another we all do. But my question today is more far-reaching than that. Will you miss *the* trip? In Matthew 17, Jesus took three disciples up to the top of a mountain. And there on the mountaintop something happened. We're not sure what occurred, but they called it *transfiguration,* which means change or metamorphosis. Moses and Elijah appeared. Jesus' face shone in a way they had never seen it. And God spoke, saying, as he did at baptism: "This is my beloved Son. . . . Do not be afraid." Simon

Peter wanted to stay there forever. Let's build three temples and just stay! But Jesus wouldn't stay. And Jesus and the three disciples made the winding trip back down the mountain. Jesus called it a "vision" in verse 9. Scholars would call it a "Theophany"—a visitation from God. And the disciples would tell it over and over again—that day, that special day, when God came down, and they beheld his glory.

I. There comes a time when we have to disengage. From time to time we activists need to stop, look, and listen. Don't do anything—just stand there. That's a hard thing for most of us. We think we must be doing something. Have you seen the T-shirt that says: "Jesus is coming back—look busy"? There's more truth to that than we let on. The reason Jesus took his disciples with him was so they could be prepared.

II. We are to open our eyes. On Mount Hermon the disciples told the others: our eyes were opened. Why, we saw things we never saw before. We all need some transfiguring experiences when we see what we never saw before. Second Peter 1:16 reads: "We have been eyewitnesses to the majesty." What a wonderful thing to say about Christians and about the Church. One translation says: "You do well to pay attention. For, you see, when you pay attention, everything changes."

III. One of the things that happens is that our perspective changes. We see the big picture. After it was all over, they saw Jesus only. They remembered God had said: This is my beloved. Do not be afraid. Even if he suffered, they would later piece it together. God was in it. Even if it did not work out the way they thought it would, God was in it. They began to see this was a large thing—this Jesus, his calling of disciples, this thing called Church.

IV. Above everything else, we learn from this story that God was there. That's the big picture that kept the black people going when nobody wanted them to vote or have equal opportunities. God was infinitely concerned about their lives and their futures. At transfiguration, God spoke to Jesus and to the disciples. This is my Son, that voice said, my beloved Son. But they were touched, and they were changed.

V. The story said they couldn't stay on the mountain. Reality intrudes. Visions don't last, unfortunately. You can't stay high forever. They couldn't stay. Reality intrudes here, too. We lose a job. We get depressed. We have a wreck. Our back hurts. And life is sometimes tough and crowded and difficult. But the test of the vision is what we do when we get back down to the bottom of the mountain. This is life. This is not school. We are called to make this a better community. We are called to make this a better church. We are called to be better people. We are called to let justice roll down like waters and righteousness like a mighty stream.

Life is short. It doesn't last long enough. Enjoy the journey. For God's sake, don't miss the trip.—Roger Lovette

SUNDAY, AUGUST 12, 2007
Lectionary Message
Topic: The Importance of the Journey
TEXT: Heb. 11:1–3, 8–16
Other Readings: Isa. 1:1, 10–20; Ps. 50:1–8, 22–23; Luke 12:32–40

Few of us, most likely, hold the same spiritual and religious beliefs that we held fifteen years ago. Or ten years ago. Or even five years ago. If you are anything like me, your faith and beliefs have changed substantially over the years. I sometimes shudder when I think about some of the things I believed as a young Christian and some of the sermons I preached in my early years of ministry. I hope my preaching skills have improved somewhat over the years, as well as my faith and theology.

My faith continues to evolve, change, and grow. For several years I have thought it important to write my own creed or statement of faith. It is a personal and private thing. But I have learned that as soon as I set down my new statement of beliefs and think, "This is it!" I read a couple of new books, and I have to go back and refine it all over again. The truth of the matter is that *faith is a journey*. Faith development is a never-ending process, an inner journey that continues as long as we live. As Dag Hammarskjöld (a Swedish philosopher, of sorts, who won the Nobel Prize) observed, "The longest journey is the journey inward."

I. Journey as a theme is something we see in the eleventh chapter of Hebrews. Take Enoch, for example. Regarding Enoch of old, Genesis says, "Enoch walked with God" (5:24). In other words, Enoch had a close relationship with God—a relationship that might be compared to two friends who take long walks together and talk about anything and everything. As such, Enoch is held up by the writer of Hebrews as a worthy example of one who had faith, one who pleased God (11:5). Walking with God implies movement, progression, and growth. To *not* walk with God is to be left behind, spiritually speaking.

II. Our faith leads us, as it led Abraham and Sarah, to set out with God, not knowing where the journey will take us. "By faith Abraham obeyed when he was called to set out for a place that he was to receive as an inheritance; and he set out, not knowing where he was going" (Heb. 11:8). The writer of Hebrews notes that the saints of old all walked with God in faith. They knew that "they were strangers and pilgrims" (11:13), as the New King James Version translates it. They knew they were on a journey of faith, constantly seeking.

God is not static or staid. On the contrary, God is always at work in the world, and new revelations of God are ongoing. Some churches, you know, years ago set down their faith and beliefs in creeds or confessions, and hundreds of years later they hand their creeds or confessions to prospective members and say, "This is what we believe." And all new members are expected to adopt those beliefs. It matters not that our understanding of God and what God wills for the Church and the world have changed drastically over the years. Granted, at the heart of most creeds and confessions there is some timeless truth. But also included in most creeds and confessions are beliefs that periodically need to be reexamined, reevaluated, and rewritten. I often find inspiration in what pilgrim pastor John Robinson said to the pilgrims just before they set sail for the New World: "The Lord has more truth and light yet to break forth out of his Holy Word."

"God," as the psalmist puts it, "shall not keep silent" (Ps. 50:3 NKJV). Or to put it in more contemporary terms, "God is still speaking."

III. We should never think that our faith journey is over. We should never get to the point when we think that our belief system is set in stone, never to be altered. To cease growing, spiritually speaking, is to begin to die. To not walk with God, as I said earlier, is to get left behind. We need to constantly refine our faith and personal beliefs through biblical and devotional study, attendance at Christian education and spiritual formation classes, and in community worship. Faith involves the willingness to stretch ourselves and be open to new revelations of truth. In other words, we, like Enoch and Abraham and Sarah of old, need to continually walk with God, who is Spirit.

When I set out on a journey of faith as a teenager, I had not the slightest inkling that that journey would take me to a university degree in philosophy and religion, a move across the state of Tennessee to attend seminary, a move to Texas, a move back to Middle Tennessee to start a new church, a three-and-one-half-year commute to Chicago for a Doctor of Ministry degree, and then a move to the state of New York. Had I known all that when I commenced my pilgrimage of faith, I would have been overwhelmed. Furthermore, I had no idea how my theology and beliefs would change drastically over the years. But that is the way it is when we venture out on faith—we know not where the journey will lead us, and we have no map of the twists and turns that our faith and beliefs will take along the way. The kind of faith that we see in Abraham and Sarah has no clear-cut itinerary, but that faith leads us to continue on the journey, nonetheless.

Half the joy of vacation is the journey itself; it is the joy we find in getting there. In a similar way, we do well to always keep in mind that faith is not a destination that we arrive at once and for all. Faith development is ongoing. Faith is a joyous pilgrimage. Faith is a journey.

Are we on a faith journey this day? Does our faith continue to grow? Let us carry home with us the great truth that the journey with God is just as important as the destination.—Randy Hammer

ILLUSTRATIONS

LEARNING TO PREACH.   One sermon that stands out in my mind that I preached at my home church the year I began preparing for the ministry was about the Old Testament character Balaam and his donkey (Num. 22). Balaam was trying to get his donkey to go somewhere the Lord didn't want Balaam to go, so the Lord caused the donkey to balk and not go any further. So Balaam started to beat his donkey. Finally, the donkey got tired of it, and the Lord got tired of it, too. And, as the story goes, the Lord opened the mouth of the donkey, who turned around and spoke to his master. And this is what the donkey said: "What have I done to you that you have struck me these three times?" The point I was trying to make had to do with evangelism and how each of us should be speaking out on behalf of the Lord. And this is what I said: "If the Lord can open the mouth and speak through the mouth of a dumb donkey (although I may not have used the word *donkey*, if you know what I mean), then surely he can open your mouth and speak through you." Well, since I had compared my homefolk to a dumb donkey, I didn't get too many positive comments on that particular sermon.—Randy Hammer

FAITH BECKONING.   I have a habit of collecting beautiful scenic calendars. One of my favorite calendar pictures is of a massive limestone rock gorge in Jasper National Park in Canada. At the bottom of the deep, narrow gorge is a beautiful blue river. The curious thing is that a fallen tree or log high above the river serves as a primitive bridge between the two sides of the limestone gorge. Now, it would take a lot of faith to venture out on that log bridge to cross from one side of the gorge to the other. But doing so would enable one to see the beautiful river gorge from a whole new perspective. That is sort of the way with religious faith. Faith beckons us as individual Christians and as a Church to venture out, take a few risks, give up the comfort of certainty for a while, so that we may experience new heights of spirituality and see God and life from a different perspective. Faith leads us to think outside our intellectual boxes.—Randy Hammer

SERMON SUGGESTIONS

Topic: The Heavenly Walk

TEXT: Gen. 5:22–24

(1) Enoch taught us how to live; he walked with God. (2) That walk is pursued in the midst of an evil world. (3) It is pursued in the prime of life. (4) It is pursued into the very portals of heaven.—Lawrence Vowan

Topic: Religion of Public Opinion

TEXT: John 12:43

(1) There are those who love the praise of others more than the praise of God. (2) They measure themselves by themselves. (3) They think little of encouraging piety. (4) Their public life is different from their private life. (5) They are careful not to do anything considered unpopular. (6) True faith means being governed by God and not by public sentiment.—Charles Grandison Finney

WORSHIP AIDS

CALL TO WORSHIP.   "I will bless the Lord at all times: his praise shall continually be in my mouth. O magnify the Lord with me, and let us exalt his name together" (Ps. 34:1, 3 KJV).

INVOCATION.   Father, open now our eyes that we may see with clear vision. Open our hearts that we may feel with deep conviction. Open our minds that we may know you with certainty. Make us ready to serve you and others with compassion.

OFFERTORY SENTENCE.   "If you spend yourselves in behalf of the hungry and satisfy the needs of the oppressed, then your light will rise in the darkness, and your night will become like the noonday" (Isa. 58:10 NIV).

OFFERTORY PRAYER.   Father, as we walk the pilgrimage of faith, give us generous hearts and willing spirits. Bless and multiply these offerings for the cause of your Kingdom and allow them to be used for the good of all people in every circumstance of life.

PRAYER.   Holy One, to you forever, let all thanks be sung! Father, may we be glad when it is said to us, "Let us go into the house of the Lord!" Let it be our delight, as well as our responsibility, to worship you in the fellowship of your church. Prepare us in mind and spirit for our worship, and tune our hearts to sing and speak your praise. May we receive all that you have to give to us and offer all that you require from us. May our lives, as well as our lips, glorify you. Right now, we come to you in silence, yet shouting for joy. Amidst this silence we are overawed by the thoughts of your love for us; for you love us so much that you gave your only Son to suffer and die for us. Yet to think that you love us like that makes us long to break our silence—to shout for joy and sing your praise. You have given us new birth into a living hope through the Resurrection of Jesus Christ from the dead. In him we are loved, ransomed, healed, restored, and forgiven. This morning give us a heart to praise you, our God and Father. Accept our worship and praise, whether silent, spoken, or sung, to the glory of your holy name.—Larry Ellis

SERMON
Topic: If I Could Just Figure Out What It Means
TEXT: Eccl. 1:16–2:11; John 10:7–10

Every national poll and survey of my lifetime says that upwards of 90 percent of modern, secular Americans believe in the existence of a higher being. The problem is that a lot of us haven't made any real connection between that rational, intellectual assumption and our deeper hunger for a meaningful life center. So we go for other centers—idols—hoping that these substitute gods will work.

We're an awful lot like the philosopher of Ecclesiastes in this way. Ecclesiastes, chapter after chapter, keeps trying to figure out something better, more lasting. The philosopher is hunting a center that will last—a god more durable than his various idolatries have given him. And I submit to you that this is the same restless sound I hear in America's secular soul. So the beat goes on—the stirring in our modern souls, the quest for a lasting center, our searching for some place to land our lives. Let me speak about this hunger, this "figuring out," in a couple of ways.

I. First of all, *look at what's not working any longer.* Modernism is what's not working any longer. This worldview formed about two or three hundred years ago, when modern science, the power of reason, humanism, and the worth of the individual came together to create what historians now call an Enlightenment. That was a powerful and world-changing time. It ushered us into the modern age. But a lot of the assumptions have proven false, and a lot of the centers have broken and will not hold. Trust in science and technology has broken down. They were supposed to explain everything and fix everything. But crime, poverty, racism, pollution, and war have not been fixed.

Our science and technology have just not become our saviors—our centers. Trust in inevitable progress has broken down. Morally, we slip and slide backwards. We are now living in a world of limits, and we know it; there's a real question as to whether or not my children will ever enjoy a standard of living equal to mine.

Trust in secularism has broken down. We thought you could wrap up an empty life in the jeweled robes of career, or acquisition, or a sexual revolution, or activism in some social cause, or just pleasure. Our culture keeps telling us in all our senses that these are the places we can find satisfaction. But the philosopher of Ecclesiastes discovered long ago that these, too, are broken centers. So we learn that this modern mind-set (which is at least as old as Ecclesiastes) isn't working any longer. The surrogate centers won't hold.

II. Look with me at *what will work.* In the tenth chapter of John, Jesus says something like this: "Look, you've lived in a world where a lot of promises are made and broken. Teachers, insurrectionists, revolutionaries, Pharisees, scribes—they've all promised you liberation and abundance . . . what you've gotten is disappointment and destruction and death."

Then he says, very simply and directly, "I've come to give you a more abundant life than any of that." Here is something deeper, more dependable than all the tangled threads and broken promises of work or pleasure or power. Things change, life shifts on you, and nothing lasts. But God didn't design you to run on any of those external realities, anyhow. God designed the human machine to run on God—his grace and our relationship with him.

You don't have to drown in an ocean of relativism and permissiveness. Christian values can be lived in freedom and joy. And life can have meaning. God has acted decisively in Jesus Christ. There's a mission growing out of that for every believer.

Want to "get a life"? Christ offers it in freedom and abundance. Fellowship with him will work. Will you try it?—William L. Turner

SUNDAY, AUGUST 19, 2007
Lectionary Message

Topic: Getting Rid of Excess Baggage

TEXT: Heb. 11:29–12:2

Other Readings: Isa. 5:1–7; Ps. 80:1–2, 8–19; Luke 12:49–56

Perhaps you are one who looks forward to watching the Summer Olympics. The Olympics, as I understand it, are about 2,500 years old, dating back to around the fifth century B.C. The writer of the book of Hebrews was, no doubt, very familiar with the Olympics, and perhaps that is why he uses the metaphor that he does for running the life of faith. In Hebrews 12:1–2 he speaks of laying aside every weight and every sin that clings so closely, that so easily distracts us, so that we may run with patience (perseverance) the race of faith that is set before us. Olympic runners, you know, often train by strapping weights to their wrists and ankles to help them build up strength and endurance. But in the real race they throw off those weights so that they may run the best that they can run.

Spiritually speaking, there are weights—excess baggage—that hinder us from running the race of faith. There is the "sin that clings so closely," as the author of Hebrews puts it, that might include any number of unhealthy desires or addictions. There is the bad habit that threatens to damage our physical or emotional health, relationships, or our good reputation. There is that personal characteristic, such as an uncontrolled temper, that holds us back from spiritual growth and maturity. We may be struggling with the baggage of guilt over past failure. Or the baggage of bitterness, anger, or ill feelings toward another person who has hurt us. Or the baggage of regret over a foolish mistake or broken relationship.

Some years ago I went to Texas to preach a series of renewal services at the church I had previously pastored. When it came time for me to return home, a friend drove me to the Dallas/Ft. Worth airport. That airport is quite large and makes most airports look like miniature scale models. My friend dropped me off at the American Airlines terminal. It turned out that I had to walk a great distance to reach my gate, which happened to be the very last one in the terminal. I had chosen to carry on a clothes bag with my suits, pulpit robe, and some other things, as well as my briefcase. The bad thing was, I had gone to a used bookstore I frequented when we lived in Denton and had purchased three or four books, which I had foolishly packed in my briefcase. It was all I could do to carry the heavy clothes bag and briefcase full of books down the long corridor to my gate. I strained more than I should have to do so. I found myself asking repeatedly, "Why did I bring all this stuff? Why did I choose to carry all this excess baggage?"

Perhaps that is precisely the question that some of us are asking ourselves this morning, spiritually speaking: Why am I carrying all this excess spiritual or emotional baggage? Why do I allow myself to struggle with all these emotional weights and sinful habits that drain the joy from the life of faith? So it is that the author of Hebrews instructs us to look to Jesus, "the pioneer and perfecter of our faith," who, like an athletic coach, stands ready to encourage us, cheer us on, and help us to get rid of the unnecessary weights and baggage that hinder us.

There is a scene in the movie *Forrest Gump,* starring Tom Hanks, that has an encouraging lesson for all of us. You may remember that as a young boy, Forrest had to wear leg braces. One day when bullies were picking on him and his friend Jenny and chasing them down the road, Jenny called out, "Run, Forrest, run!" All of sudden a dramatic thing happened. His leg braces began to pop off his legs, and he started to run faster and faster, leaving the bullies behind. After that day, Forrest was off and running and breaking records for the rest of his life.

Well, we're not Forrest Gump with leg braces, and we're not at the Summer Olympics today, but we all are running the race of faith. We may all be at different points in the journey, but every one of us here is on the Christian pathway—a pathway that is not always easy. We all carry different burdens. We struggle in different ways. The good news is that God wants us to be free of the negative weights and excess baggage so that we can run with joy and faithfulness the race of faith before us. Perhaps it is time to examine our lives and let God help us get rid of some negative excess baggage. Like Forrest Gump, let us throw off those unnecessary weights and shackles—the sin that clings so closely—so that we can joyously run the race of life that is set before us.—Randy Hammer

ILLUSTRATIONS

OUTRUNNING A COUGAR.   Two men were backpacking and camping in the wilderness. Of course, the men had to carry on their backs everything they needed to survive: their food and cooking utensils, tent and sleeping bags, water and extra clothing, and so on. As they were walking down a wilderness path, they heard the nearby cry of a cougar. Both men stopped dead in their tracks. One of the men very slowly began to ease the heavy backpack off his shoulders. The other man looked at him somewhat bewildered and said, "Surely you don't think you can outrun that cougar." "No," the first man replied, "but I don't have to. I only have to outrun you."

SPIRITUAL BARNACLES.   In the New York State Museum there is a bicycle that was pulled from one of the state's waterways. The bicycle is covered in barnacles that had attached themselves over time. It would be virtually impossible to ride the bicycle with all those barnacles attached. Our lives are sort of like that. There are all kinds of negative "barnacles" that will seek to attach themselves to us, detracting from our beauty and slowing us down. Every once in a while we need to throw off the barnacles that cling so closely so that we can freely run the life of faith again.—Randy Hammer

SERMON SUGGESTIONS

Topic: Christ Regenerates Even the Desires
TEXT: Mark 10:35
(1) Human desires are out of keeping with our real possibilities. (2) Christ remolds our desires, thus renewing our character. (3) Herein is found the possibility for the best of life.—Horace Bushnell

Topic: Loving Your Enemies
TEXT: Matt. 5:43–45
(1) Loving our enemies means maintaining the capacity to forgive. (2) Returning hate for hate multiplies hate. (3) Love has the ability to transform an enemy into a friend. (4) Love is the most durable power in the world.—Martin Luther King Jr.

WORSHIP AIDS

CALL TO WORSHIP.   "The Lord is great in Zion; and he is high above all the people. Exalt the Lord our God, and worship at his holy hill; for the Lord our God is holy" (Ps. 99:2, 9 KJV).

INVOCATION.   O Lord our God, who dwells in the high and holy places, and with the lowly and contrite of spirit, grant that our worship may again assure us that our true home is with you. We rejoice that you are ever with us in our daily routines and that your presence gives meaning and beauty to this earth.

OFFERTORY SENTENCE.   "The goal of this command is love, which comes from a pure heart and a good conscience and a sincere faith" (1 Tim. 1:5 NIV).

OFFERTORY PRAYER.   Father, in bringing before you these gifts of tithes and offerings, we express our devotion to you. May we forever give to you definite, consistent, and heart-felt service.

PRAYER.   Dear God, how we need a bridge across the chasm separating us from the rest of the human race—a bridge to span the space between the darkness of loneliness and the light of belonging. How we need to leave the caves of our self-seeking and selfishness, and walk forth into the light of the vision that your love for all persons and peoples inspires. But when we see man's inhumanity to man, it is difficult sometimes for us to hold on to that vision.

For leaders in the community of nations pursuing ways of peace, we pray wisdom and courage that foundations of justice may be laid, that the hungry may receive bread, the naked clothes, the refugees and homeless home and housing. Open our eyes to see the new thing you are doing in our day and rejoice. We pray shalom, well-being, wholeness for all those suffering brokenness of mind, body, and spirit among us. We pray for them an increase of faith that they may be open to receive the healing, the wholeness, the life that you will for them. When life-threatening illnesses threaten any of us, grant to us that "peace that the world cannot give and that the world cannot take away." Through him who is our peace.—John Thompson

SERMON
Topic: Grow Up!
TEXT: 1 Cor. 3

We need to hear again the keynote of this third chapter of Paul's first Corinthian correspondence: conversion is only a beginning. Paul uses the imagery of a building to illustrate this point. He says in verse 11 that in Christ we have been given a foundation. A foundation is laid so that on it you can construct a building or a house. Paul says that the foundation of the Christian life that comes at conversion is only the beginning of the Christian life. When you are converted, Paul says you have before you the challenge to grow. I want to answer two key questions that relate to that idea of spiritual growth: Why should we grow? and How can we grow?

I. First, let's take the why question: Why should you and I, as Christians, be concerned about growing spiritually? For one thing, God wants us to grow up spiritually *for our own sake.* When you remain a baby Christian, you are first of all hurting yourself. By remaining a baby Christian, you are missing out on the greatest joys of life and the deepest understanding of God's purpose and the fullest experiences of his abundant life. For your own sake, you need to grow up.

We also need to grow up *for the world's sake.* We live in a day when baby Christians are simply not going to be able to adequately deal with the perplexing questions of our world. We are living in a day of moral erosion and political corruption and social upheaval and intellectual confusion. People are looking to us as Christians. For the world's sake, God wants us to grow up.

Then we also need to grow up *for judgment's sake.* We need to grow up spiritually because someday our lives will be passed through the fire of God's judgment. You are someday going to be called to give an account of what you have built on that foundation. You can build on the foundation with gold or silver or precious stones—that is, with something that is valuable and enduring. Or you can build with wood, hay, or straw—that is, with something that is cheap and perishable. Someday, you will have to stand before God and account for your life. And there will be no sweeter sound in the entire world than to be welcomed into eternity with God's greeting to the mature: "Well done, thy good and faithful servant."

II. That raises a second question: If spiritual growth is essential for the reasons I have mentioned, then the accompanying question is, How can I grow spiritually? The clearest, simplest answer to that question is found in 1 Timothy 4:7: "Discipline yourself for the purpose of godliness." The key word is *discipline.* There is no other way. In our day of instant fulfillment, when the touch of a button can bring us most of what we desire, we need to remind ourselves that there is no instant spiritual maturity. Christian maturity comes as a result, as the finished product, of a life of daily discipleship.

These are five disciplines that you must apply daily to your life in order for you to grow up spiritually. You must study diligently, worship regularly, pray daily, give systematically, and serve faithfully. It won't be easy. And it won't happen instantaneously. But if you will fit your life into these grooves consistently, the result will be progress and growth in your spiritual life.

Let's make that the motto of our Christian life: "I'm not what I ought to be. I'm not what I'm going to be. But thank God, I'm sure not what I used to be!"—Brian L. Harbour

SUNDAY, AUGUST 26, 2007

Lectionary Message

Topic: The Burden on My Back

Text: Luke 13:10–17

Other Readings: Jer. 1:4–10; Ps. 71:1–6; Heb. 12:18–29

If you have ever suffered extreme back and leg pain from a ruptured disk or have had any of the other possible back ailments, then you surely can relate to and sympathize with the poor woman in Luke's Gospel who was bent over with a debilitating back problem. She couldn't stand up straight. The pain must have been almost unbearable. How difficult it must have been when she tried to get out of bed in the morning. What a tremendous burden weighed her down!

But the woman was bent over emotionally and spiritually as well. Her condition was a source of shame for her and robbed her of her human dignity. But as the woman encountered Jesus, she was set free of the great burden that weighed her down. Jesus enabled her to stand up straight, both physically and emotionally. Jesus restored her dignity as a woman, a daughter of Abraham, and a child of God.

As a pastor, I have often encountered persons who shared with me their story of defeat and told how for years they have carried burdens on their backs that have weighed them down emotionally, spiritually, and, ultimately, physically. Guilt over real or perceived sin, defeat, poor self-image, self-hatred, loneliness—these are just a few of the burdens that God's children are shouldering. As I have told people of God's love, grace, and desire that they be set free of their great burdens, they often have burst into tears and said, "You mean I have been carrying around this great burden all these years for nothing?" The burdens of guilt, defeat, poor self-image, self-hatred, and loneliness are burdens that God wants to help us be free of. We don't have to carry those burdens with us forever.

One of the best resources I found early in my ministry having to do with the burden of unresolved guilt is a book titled *Guilt and Grace* by Dr. Paul Tournier. In *Guilt and Grace,* the author speaks of "the universal problem of guilt and the universal need of forgiveness."

"The question of guilt arises in every man [and woman]," Dr. Tournier observes, "and it demands an answer."[2] He also distinguishes between "true guilt" and "false guilt." True guilt is that genuine feeling that we experience when we know we have done something to offend God or others. It is the kind of guilt experienced by the psalmists. As long as they held on to their sin and guilt, we often read in the psalms, their bodies wasted away. Only after acknowledging and confessing their sin did they feel that their sense of guilt was removed (see, for instance, Psalm 32). False guilt, on the other hand, as Dr. Tournier points out, is unfounded guilt that we impose on ourselves or that we let others impose on us. In either event, guilt is a burden we don't need to carry with us forever. It is a burden that God can remove from us.

In that great Christian classic, *Pilgrim's Progress,* John Bunyan tells the story of a man who has a great burden on his back—a burden that threatens to sink him lower than the grave. The man sets off on a journey in search of a way to rid himself of the great burden that weighs him down. Christian, as the man's name becomes after he encounters Evangelist, in the course of his journey comes upon a cross on a hill. Only after Christian runs up the hill with the burden on his back and sees One hanging on a tree does the burden fall from his back and roll down the hill into an empty tomb, where it is seen no more.

Jesus is the One who came to give life and set people free. He is the great Liberator who extends God's grace to all, especially to the weak, oppressed, and marginalized. Through Jesus, the love and grace of God have been made manifest as in no other who has ever walked upon the earth. It is God's will that we have life and that we have it abundantly. This life has been revealed in Jesus Christ.

But in addition to taking the burdens from our backs, Jesus seeks to restore the human dignity that such burdens often steal from us. We are meant to feel that we are sons and

---

[2]Paul Tournier, *Guilt and Grace: A Psychological Study* (San Francisco: HarperSanFrancisco, 1982), pp. 210–211.

daughters of Abraham and beloved children of God, just as the woman in the story. And inasmuch as relieving burdens was the ministry Jesus felt called to perform, it should also be the ministry of the Church and all those who seek to follow him.

Just as the unnamed woman in Luke's Gospel was set free from the burden that held her down, we, too, can often find relief from the burdens of life that weigh us down because of our relationship with the Christ who calls out to us.—Randy Hammer

ILLUSTRATION

ABILITY TO SYMPATHIZE.   At the age of forty-six I suffered a ruptured disk. For eight long weeks I endured almost unbearable, unstoppable pain in my entire left leg. I prayed fervently for the burden to be relieved. Fortunately, I had the great love and care of my wife, family, and church members. Eight weeks to the day from the time the disk ruptured, God worked through a skilled Christian surgeon to provide me with instant relief from my burden of pain. Since that time I have been better able to sympathize with those who suffer extreme pain.—Randy Hammer

SERMON SUGGESTIONS

Topic: Going to the Father

TEXT: John 14:12

(1) "Going to the Father" was the full work of Christ. (2) It explains his life—and ours. (3) It sustains life. (4) It completes life.—Henry Drummond

Topic: The Conquest of Fear

TEXT: Rev. 1:17

(1) Jesus calls us to be unafraid of life. (2) We are to be unafraid of death. (3) We are to be unafraid of eternity.—George W. Truett

WORSHIP AIDS

CALL TO WORSHIP.   "Behold, I stand at the door and knock; if any man hear my voice and open the door, I will come into him, and sup with him, and he with me" (Rev. 3:20).

INVOCATION.   Kind Father, as we enter into worship, assure us again that we can never drift beyond your love and care. As we bow heads and hearts before you, speak tenderly to us words of encouragement. Grant on this very day, when we need you the most, your ever-present Spirit.

OFFERTORY SENTENCE.   "There is neither Jew nor Greek, slave nor free, male nor female, for you are all one in Christ Jesus" (Gal. 3:28 NIV).

OFFERTORY PRAYER.   Gracious God, to you who has rewarded our labors with the bounty of heaven, we acknowledge thankfully your favor. We now dedicate this portion of your gifts to the eternally satisfying ministries of the Spirit.

PRAYER.   Time and again, O Lord, you taught your disciples many things in parables. And "once upon a mountain," you gave us an old law in new dress: "Blessed are you poor, for yours is the kingdom of God; Blessed are you hungry now, for you will be filled; Woe to you who are rich, for your credit cards will expire; Woe to you who are full now, for you will be hungry." And the disciples, though slow, tried so hard to learn. But we—the TV and sound-byte generation—have short attention spans. We demand, at every turn, to be entertained, and history will not likely record that we were patient and attentive hearers of the things that last.

On this Teacher Recognition Sunday, forgive us our inner barriers to learning. Forgive us the Martha-like examples we set our children: "worried and distracted by many things, when one thing is needful." Forgive us the hard road that a quiet, gracious, and cumulative hearing of your Word has. Unplug us, if but a little, that we may listen. Unplug us, that we may be truly connected.—Peter Fribley

SERMON
Topic: You Can't Save Time in a Bottle
TEXT: Ps. 90:1–17; Gal. 4:4–5; Eph. 5:15–16

Time, as valuable as it is, cannot be kept. Time can never be replaced when it is gone. I wonder sometimes if Father Time—the mythical old man who supposedly controls time and keeps it in balance—ever laughs at the many ways mankind tries to save time. But who really is in charge of time? What does the Bible tell us about the elusive abstraction called time?

I. To begin, a foundational biblical concept is that eternity exists beyond and above time. Eternity stands before, during, and after time. The psalmist declared, "Lord, thou hast been our dwelling place in all generations. Before the mountains were brought forth, or ever thou hast formed the earth and the world, from everlasting to everlasting thou art God" (90:1–2). Eternity could not exist without being linked to the eternal nature of God. Before time was created, the great "I am"—God—existed. The primary difference between God and idols is that God's nature is eternal and the nature of idols is temporal. God is the same yesterday, today, and forevermore. Idols, on the other hand, come and go on the wings of fads of the times.

II. Not only does eternity exist beyond and above time, but compared with eternity, time is very brief. The psalmist says further, "For a thousand years in thy sight are but as yesterday when it is past, or as a watch in the night. Thou dost sweep men away; they are like a dream, like grass which is renewed in the morning; in the morning it flourishes and is renewed; in the evening it fades and withers" (90:4–6). The author of Psalm 90 was a man of mature experience. In his old age he gazes back upon his life and concludes how very fleeting it is in comparison to eternal life. It is like comparing a raindrop to the Atlantic Ocean. The brevity of this early existence, next to the timelessness of eternity, is similar to one snowflake lying among the vast snowdrifts of the Himalayan Mountains.

III. Indeed, our temporal life is short. Yet the Bible does not leave us hanging up this tree. Jesus Christ gave meaning to life by bringing the realm of eternity into the confines of time. Paul the apostle said with Christ "the . . . time has fully come" (Gal. 4:4). There are two types of time. *Chronos* is time that is measured by a clock. The Bible rarely presents this view of time. The biblical view is *kairos,* meaning a time of opportunity, fulfillment, or promise. In Christ all the promises of God have been fulfilled. With Jesus Christ, time and eternity crossed paths. The pre-existent Son of God in heaven left eternity and entered time in the form of an infant so that humanity could see the nature of God and be led to salvation.

IV. Let us ponder one more idea. Because time is a priceless gift from God, we ought to use it wisely. Again the psalmist tells us, "So teach us to number our days that we may get a heart of wisdom" (90:12). Could Paul, the writer of the letter to the Ephesians, have been reflecting on the psalmist's wisdom when he said, "Look carefully then how you walk, not as unwise men but as wise, making the most of the time, because the days are evil" (5:15–16). Each of us is called by God to be a good Christian steward of our time. Through Jesus Christ and his available power in your life, you have many opportunities to use time wisely. Whether you take advantage of God-given opportunities is your responsibility. God opens doors to serve him, because he is always active in history. God calls us to fulfill our part of the faith covenant with him.—Ron Blankenship

SUNDAY, SEPTEMBER 2, 2007
Lectionary Message

Topic: Courtesy Is Safety
TEXT: Luke 14:1, 7–14
Other Readings: Jer. 2:4–13; Ps. 81:1, 10–16; Heb. 13:1–8, 15–16

Have you seen the bumper sticker that reads, "Courtesy Is Safety"? It states a noble principle. It appeals for etiquette on the highway or in traffic. But have you ever driven for any distance behind that person? Do his deeds belie the statement? Jesus went to a feast one time and made a few remarks about etiquette. But in speaking about seating arrangements and invitation procedures, he hammered home some basic spiritual truths.

I. *The unexpected situation is to be handled with sympathetic understanding.* The lesson in etiquette was introduced by the appearance of a man with dropsy. Only suspicion greeted him. They had hoped to trap Jesus at the man's expense. Jesus expressed compassion for the man. They were at a loss to respond. And then Jesus noted their response in the clamoring for seats of honor.

II. *The choice of a seat by the guest is to be made with humility.* Jesus watched them elbowing and scheming for social ambition, asserting themselves, demanding their rights, despising others, exalting themselves. They were proud and cruel and snobbish and mean and nasty and selfish.

Jesus called for humility. The root word for *humility* refers to a meanness, a littleness, a shabbiness, a sneakiness, but faith takes it out of its mean surroundings and transforms it. Humility comes from self-knowledge; to face one's self may be a humiliating experience. Humility comes from setting life beside the life of Christ: when you compare yourself with him, you do not come off so well. Humility comes from the constant sense of our creatureliness; we are never more humble than when we are conscious of God's creation.

Humility can become a part of our own experience. It springs from gratitude, from reverence, from knowledge of sins forgiven. It is significant that Dante heard singing in paradise and understood the words of the hymn, "Blessed are the poor in spirit."

III. *The list of guests is to be made with graciousness.* Jesus saw the guests and reckoned with the problem the host had. The proposed list was probably quite long, and space was limited. There were many who had not even been considered. Those present were friends, family, influential neighbors; those absent were the poor, the maimed, the lame, and the blind.

Jesus sensed the motive of the host. Basically, the guests were invited because they could return the invitation. Does one entertain because it is pleasant and profitable or because one is compassionate? Is it because one's own group is at the center or because God sees all mankind as one family?

Our own motives come into question. Some are gracious out of a sense of duty. Some are gracious out of self-interest. Some are gracious out of a feeling of superiority. Some are gracious because the love within overflows to those in need.

Reward? Let us not pretend that our motives are so lofty as to despise the concept. If our graciousness is not repaid here, then our lot is happier because our repayment will come later. You see, true etiquette is unselfishness. It is love. Love places the other at least on a par with self and, perhaps in genuine Christ-likeness, considers the other fellow better. That sort of courtesy is safety.—J. Estill Jones

SERMON SUGGESTIONS

Topic: A Christian View of Work

TEXT: Eccles. 9:10; 1 Cor. 3:9

(1) Work has always been a part of God's plan. (2) The Church has made unreal distinctions between sacred and secular work. (3) We are morally bound to quality labor, thus bringing honor to God.—Lawrence Vowan

Topic: The Sin of Overwork

TEXT: 1 Kings 20:40

(1) Work is no sin, but overwork is. (2) The work suffers, as does the worker. (3) There is a place for leisure. (4) Keep in perspective the importance of home, friendship, and worship. (5) Remember the supreme values for which Christ stood.—Robert McCracken

WORSHIP AIDS

CALL TO WORSHIP.   "We are God's fellow workers; you are God's field, God's building. By the grace God has given me, I laid a foundation as an expert builder, and someone else is building on it. But each one should be careful how he builds. For no one can lay any foundation other than the one already laid, which is Jesus Christ" (1 Cor. 3:9–11 NIV).

INVOCATION.   O Lord our God, grant as we gather to worship that we will be vividly aware of your presence. May we be conscious of your power and protection, and may we experience in our beings the wonder and grace of your peace.

OFFERTORY SENTENCE.   "Set your minds on things above, not on earthly things" (Col. 3:2 NIV).

OFFERTORY PRAYER.   Lord Jesus, in your Word you taught us that to whom much is given much is required. Grant that we, whose lot is cast in Christian heritage, may strive earnestly in prayer and giving to encourage the coming of your Kingdom reign among all the world's people.

PRAYER.   Our Father, you have gifted us with numerous abilities that enrich our lives and offer opportunity for service to you. For the ability to think clearly, to plan precisely, to enter joyfully into the full expression of life, we are truly thankful. We are thankful also for strong and healthy bodies with which to offer productive labor. On this Labor Day weekend, we express gratitude for the nobility of work, for the joy that comes in the accomplishment of good things. In your gracious wisdom you put into our hearts such a need. So today we express thanks for each place of employment in our city, for those who are employers and those who are employees. We thank you for a strong economy that encourages the productivity our city enjoys. We pray that you will encourage all of us to become pastors in the marketplace. May we see those with whom we work, or for whom we work, or who work for us as persons of worth and dignity. And may our words and actions express the clear witness of our loyalty to Jesus Christ. May our worship today—"the work of the people"—express such devotion to you that we will live each day for you and share the gracious good news of Christ's salvation to all who are in our sphere of influence.—Lee McGlone

SERMON
Topic: The Person God Uses
TEXT: Gen. 25:19–34

What kind of person does God use? The Bible surprises us here. God used Moses, who had a speech impediment. God used David, who was morally impure. God used Saul of Tarsus, who persecuted the Church. Tonight we look at a well-known character from the Old Testament—Jacob.

Jacob's personality becomes clear to us when we recall how he deceived his father, Isaac, in order to steal the birthright blessing from Esau. We see it again when he went to live in Paddan Aram with his uncle, Laban. Jacob made a deal with Laban: he would keep all the dark-colored lambs and the spotted or speckled goats; Laban would keep the rest. That seems fair enough. But Jacob devised a plan for breeding the sheep and goats so the number of colored sheep and spotted goats greatly increased while the others decreased. (You can read about it in Genesis 30.) Years later, when Jacob left, he had almost all the sheep and goats.

That's Jacob: mover and shaker, wheeler-dealer, and scoundrel. But yet he was one whom God used in his redemptive plan. Recall that Israel—the name by which the people of God were called—was his name. His sons formed the nucleus of the tribal coalition into which the nation was later formed. How can God use such a person?

I. *God uses all kinds of people.* Think of the different personalities God used in the Bible. God used the brashness and boldness of Jacob. In the New Testament, God used the low-key, behind-the-scenes approach of Andrew. God also used the more aggressive approach of Simon Peter. There was Barnabas the encourager on one hand and Paul the zealot on the other. During the medieval Reformation, God used monks who hoed their gardens and prayed in secret, as well as Martin Luther, who stood up and changed the world.

Since God uses all kinds of people, we can rest assured that God is able to use each of us. Let's dare to be bold today, that is, to live out lives of faith being the persons God has intended us to be. Let's not seek to erase our uniqueness in order to become the way others perceive that we should be. God didn't erase the characteristics of Jacob's personality in order to use him. He redirected them so they became the source of blessing and not the source of trouble. He used Jacob's boldness for his Kingdom. God will use us.

II. *God uses determined people.* Jacob was a determined person. He refused to give up. You need to look no further than his passionate pursuit of Rachel. He loved her at first sight, but her father, Laban, required seven years' labor for her. The time passed by, for it "seemed like only a few days because of his love for her." On the wedding day, he thought he married Rachel but discovered he had been tricked and was married to her older sister, Leah. Jacob and Rachel is what he wanted; Jacob and Leah is what he got. Later, Laban explained the propriety of it all. The custom was that the older daughter was to be married first. He could still marry Rachel, but he would have to work another seven years. And that he did. He labored fourteen years to earn the right to marry the woman he loved. That's tenacity.

One of the greatest problems we as Christians have is our lack of determination. We tend to give up too soon. Marriages end too early. Parents quit on their roles when the going gets tough. Church members hop from one congregation to another. Pastors become discouraged and move to another place of ministry. In each case, it can well be argued that in giving up too soon we end the chance for God to work. Copernicus worked thirty-six years on his theory of the universe before anyone would publish it. Wilma Rudolph, "the fastest woman in the world" and U.S. Olympic champion, had to overcome polio, pneumonia, scarlet fever, braces, and poverty. She could have given up at any time. Madame Curie worked through over ten thousand failed experiments before she isolated the radium atom.

God uses people who refuse to give up easily. How committed are we to a task? Will we stay at it until it is completed, or do we give up when the going gets tough?

III. *God uses teachable people.* Jacob was a work in progress. What you see early is not what you see later. In his younger days he gave in to the quest for "instant gratification." As he grew older and matured, he came to appreciate the need for "delayed gratification." In the early days he didn't care about his brother. Later, he bowed down seven times to express his honest and humble desire to reunite. Early, he didn't care about God. Later, he held onto God's angel and declared that he would not let go until God blessed him. He was a man who grew as he learned the greater lessons of life. He was a teachable character.

God can use a teachable character. What we know is not so important, but what we are willing to learn is essential. When Yogi Berra began as a New York Yankee baseball player in 1947, he was slow and small, and his throwing was wild. Once on a throw to second base he hit the pitcher in the chest; later, he became one of baseball's greatest players. He received three Most Valuable Player awards and set eighteen World Series records. Those who knew him best spoke of his secret: "He knew how to learn."

What kind of person does God use? God used a man with a speech impediment, a boy with a slingshot against a giant, a man to build the Church who wanted to destroy the Church. God used a scoundrel who became the namesake for his people. And God uses you—and me. Odd choices, for sure. Thanks be unto God.—Lee McGlone

SUNDAY, SEPTEMBER 9, 2007
Lectionary Message

Topic: Counting the Troops
TEXT: Luke 14:25–33
Other Readings: Jer. 8:1–11; Ps. 139:1–6, 13–18; Philem. 1–21

Perhaps we ought to title the sermon "Counting the Stones." Actually, we are more familiar with the concept of counting the stones in building the church. But a battle? We might have expected Jesus to use a more peaceful analogy for his work. Can you imagine a builder beginning to build a huge structure and discovering, after laying the foundation, that he could not finish it? I've seen buildings like that. Perhaps it is a bit more difficult even to imagine a general leading his troops against a force twice their size. What courageous fool would attempt that? What sort of strategy is that?

I. *Assessing the volunteers.* Volunteers are an unproved factor. With enthusiasm they enlist, but when the going gets rough they may cool it a bit. Great crowds were following Jesus. He was on his way to Jerusalem. Did they expect some triumphant entry into the capital city? They enjoyed his teaching, they admired his healings, and they were satisfied with his food. What kind of volunteers were they? Could he count on them?

"Are you willing to leave all others?" he asked—all persons, all causes, all investments? Father, mother, wife, husband, children, brothers, sisters, what are you volunteering for? Could they know? Can we know? Does he lay out a detailed road map for all of our lives? "Are you willing to come after me?" he asked, away from the comforts of home, the community, respectability, to the rigors of rejection, arrest, judgment, the cross? What are you volunteering for? Volunteers need to be assessed. Volunteers need to assess themselves.

II. *Adjudging the peril.* The parables concerned Jesus and his attitude. He was seeking followers, but he wanted committed followers. There was the possibility that he might be embarrassed by the attitude and action of the volunteers. We rarely think of Jesus' embarrassment at our failures. He dealt forthrightly with these volunteers. Don't count on my being more foolish than you, he said. He needed to know how many would go with him all the way. A builder must know about both the quantity and the quality of his materials, lest he be taunted at his inability to finish the task. There are those who will laugh at our feeble efforts. Jesus wants solid citizens—solid as rocks—in his building.

There is more than embarrassment involved here. It's a rough world. It was then. It still is. Jesus asked his prospective troops in the second parable, "Do you want me to compromise? Do you want me to face defeat?" There is danger in a king's leading his forces against vastly superior forces. A general must know about both the quantity and the quality of his materials, lest he lose the battle. A building—a battle—why, Jesus sounds serious. We had thought it a lark.

III. *Setting the standard.* Jesus concluded the parables with "so therefore . . . ," whoever does not renounce all that he has cannot be my disciple. It is as if he were saying to us, "If you want to follow, I want you to follow, but don't take following lightly." Jesus was on his way to Jerusalem to build the tower—to lead the troops. He was counting the troops, counting the stones. Can he "count" on us?—J. Estill Jones

SERMON SUGGESTIONS

Topic: Paradoxes of Prayer
TEXT: 1 Cor. 14:15
(1) God knows what we need before we ask, but we still need to ask. (2) God is almighty but is limited at times until we enable him to work through us. (3) God to whom we pray also prays: the Holy Spirit makes intercession for us.—Charles Seasholes

Topic: On Growing Old
TEXT: Ps. 37:25
(1) Growing old gracefully requires acceptance of the terms life imposes. (2) Our ability to accept these terms depends on our spiritual and intellectual maturity. (3) Faith is the foundation out of which adjustments are best made.—Houston Cole

WORSHIP AIDS

CALL TO WORSHIP.   "Come unto me, all ye that labor and are heavy laden, and I will give you rest. Take my yoke upon you, and learn of me; for I am meek and lowly in heart: and you shall find rest unto your souls" (Matt. 11:28–29 KJV).

INVOCATION.   Almighty God, giver and sustainer of life, remind us that our worship is a moment of time lived in eternity. Open our ears that we may hear you. Soften our hearts that we may receive your Truth. Reveal yourself to us here and now that we may learn to find you everywhere.

OFFERTORY SENTENCE.   "God is not unjust; he will not forget your work and the love you have shown him as you have helped his people and continue to help them" (Heb. 6:10 NIV).

OFFERTORY PRAYER.   Kind Father, as we bring our gifts before you, remind us that they are to be given cheerfully and with glad hearts. May we understand our stewardship as a way in which we participate in sharing your love with persons everywhere.

PRAYER.   Our gracious and loving Heavenly Father, we come to you this morning in the name of Jesus, our Lord and Savior. We come, not as strangers or foreigners but as your children. We thank you for your faithfulness. Thank you, Lord, for all you've done for us, but most of all we thank you for who and what you are. So help us, Lord, to put first things first. Help us to keep our priorities straight. Help us to seek first your Kingdom and righteousness and let the other things fall into their rightful places. Help us to make the right choices that will count for eternity. We pray for the needs of our people today. We reach out to you, and we know that you're already reaching out to us. We pray for many different kinds of physical needs and financial needs, and there are those with emotional needs. We pray for our community. We pray for our government officials and those in rulership over us. We pray for divine wisdom and the ability to lead justly and wisely. We pray for our president and those in our national government. We pray for a revival of godliness and righteousness and holiness in our country. We pray for your Word, as it is preached around the world this very day, and for those of our brothers and sisters in countries that don't enjoy the freedom that we have. We pray for our pastor as he preaches in the services this morning. We ask for your divine anointing on him and the words he speaks, and may we all have open and obedient hearts. We pray in the name of Jesus.—Paul Meeks

SERMON
Topic: Fears We Ought to Fear
Text: Eccles. 12:13

Fear is commonly regarded as an unmitigated evil. The fact is, however, that there are fears and fears. Not all fears are irrational, obsessive, and neurotic. And some are prompted, not by fancied but by genuine dangers. All the way through the Bible you will find exhortations to master the type of fear that cripples, that paralyzes, and with the exhortations you will find directions as to how that sort of fear may be mastered—chief among them being the repeated counsel of Jesus: "Have faith in God." All the way through the Bible you will find another type of fear that is spoken of and urged on you; it is neither irrational nor neurotic but instinctive and wholesome, not destructive but constructive. Here's one: "Stand in awe and sin not." Here's another: "You have no reason for pride, but rather for fear." And the conclusion of the whole matter: "Fear God and keep his commandments; for this is the whole duty of man."

I. So much is said about fear as an evil. More emphasis should be put on its useful—its valuable—function. The inventions, the discoveries that have enriched civilization time and time again, have been by-products of human fear. Fear of ignorance makes for knowledge. Fear of tyranny prompts the struggle for liberty. Fear of the consequences keeps countless men and women from wrongdoing, from immoral behavior. And so long as that normal, wholesome fear is alive in us, there is little likelihood that we will become the prey of another kind of fear: the fear of detection, the fear of being found out, which really is obsessive and can be self-destructive.

II. Now it's time to turn from the inner to the outer world. From the beginning of man's life on earth people have sought to run away from disagreeable facts, from frightening fears, from challenging duties. But like Adam and Eve, sooner or later we discover that we are fooling ourselves if we suppose that by closing our eyes—by inaction, evasion, pretense—we are settling anything or improving anything. This life of ours is a very risky business. Civilization is engaged in a race with catastrophe.

Take, for instance, the threat of nuclear war. Since we are going to have to live with it probably all our days, we had better bring it right out into the open. We had better recognize it for what it actually is. Yet here also, there are fears and fears. Neurotic fears about nuclear war incline people to panic, to hysteria. And then you begin to find them urging resort to provocative, to extreme, to suicidal policies. "Let's strike first," they say. As Jesus would put it, this is what comes of casting out devils by Beelzebub, the prince of devils.

However, wholesome fears about nuclear war make people alert, vigilant, eager to arrive at constructive solutions, willing to confer and negotiate, reluctant to surrender goodwill and trust, putting their confidence in Atoms for Peace, not war. And isn't it regrettable that all around the world more faith is placed in military might than in economic and technical assistance? The amount voted by governments for the latter is only a fraction of the total voted for the former.

III. There's one other fear we ought to fear: the fear of God. So much present-day thinking ignores the severer element in the teaching of the Bible and conceives of God as a kindly, indulgent, amiable, good-natured Being who will see to it that everything comes out all right for everybody in the end, irrespective of considerations of character and conduct. We need to be reminded of the solemn imperatives that sound and resound in the Bible:

"Stand in awe and fear not."
"You have reason, not for pride, but for fear."
"Fear God and keep His commandments."

And the very words of Jesus: "Do not fear those who kill the body but cannot kill the soul; rather fear Him who can destroy both body and soul in hell."

I want to say that there need not be anything hysterical, neurotic about this fear. If we dwell on it, the thought of God—his greatness, his goodness, his holiness—fills us with awe, and the awe deepens as we contrast our sinfulness with the divine purity. The reaction is essentially a moral reaction—checking triviality, frivolity, indecency. When did you last get down on your knees before God? This service would not be without consequence, if before the day is done, half of our number were to get down on their knees before God.—Robert J. McCracken

SUNDAY, SEPTEMBER 16, 2007
Lectionary Message

Topic: Lost and Found

TEXT: Luke 15:1–10

Other Readings: Jer. 4:11–12, 22–28; Ps. 14; 1 Tim. 1:12–17

You've seen the sign, haven't you? "Lost and Found"—that's the name of a department in a store or of a booth at the county fair or of an umbrella closet in an office building. You report a lost object and hope that someone finds it and restores it to you. Most of us have lost something, and perhaps have found it. When we did find it, we were happy. How practical Jesus was in his teaching. Here are two parables, followed by a third, that are also true to life: a lost sheep, a lost coin.

I. *Sinners, sheep, and coins—lost.* You must read the introduction to the parables in verses 1 and 2. Note the contrast in the context: tax collectors and sinners were all attracted to Jesus. Pharisees and scribes were complaining about the sort of persons who followed Jesus. The parables were addressed to both groups, perhaps especially to the Pharisees and scribes.

Now, if Jesus had found the tax collectors and sinners and if they had followed him, they were no longer lost. Right? And if the Pharisees and the scribes were not following Jesus ("we don't like the company he keeps"), they were lost and had not been found. Right?

A man had a hundred sheep, and one of them was lost. How does a sheep get lost? Does it wander away from the flock and the shepherd? Why worry about it? There are ninety-nine left. Isn't this the nature of sheep—to wander away and get lost?

A woman had ten pieces of silver, and one of them was lost. Perhaps they constituted her sole treasure. How does a silver coin get lost? Does it fall from its treasure trove into a crack, concealed from sight? Why worry about it? There are nine pieces left. Aren't you always losing things around the house?

II. *Sheep and coins—found.* Someone missed them. Shepherds have a personal relationship with sheep; some know them by name—one is missing. You lose a tenth of your treasure, and of course you miss it. Someone was looking. The shepherd left the flock in the wilderness and looked for one sheep. Imagine the rocks, the thickets, the streams he walked over and through, looking for one sheep. The woman swept the house until she found the one missing coin.

Now what happens? Something was lost, and now it's found. So what? Why, someone rejoiced. The shepherd rejoiced over the one found sheep—more than over the ninety-nine who were not lost. The woman rejoiced over the found piece of silver. They called in friends and neighbors to join in their joy. How personal it becomes. Persons rejoice when the lost are found. And then the parable becomes even more personal.

III. *Sinners—received.* Of course, God looks for sinners and tax collectors. God loves sinners and tax collectors. Does he love them more than Pharisees and scribes? Well, as much anyhow! And here the parable reflects a personal response.

Neither the sheep nor the coin was able to respond as a person to a loving God. When persons know they are lost, they may respond in repentance: "God didn't lose us. We lost ourselves. We are sorry, and we are returning to the flock—to the treasure trove." And when they repent there is rejoicing in heaven, perhaps more than over the Pharisees and scribes who did not repent.

Why did the Pharisees and scribes not repent? Repent of what? Did they know they were lost? Did they know they were sinners? It would almost seem as if God were on the side of sinners.—J. Estill Jones

SERMON SUGGESTIONS

Topic: Redemption for All

TEXT: John 3:16

(1) The reason: "for God so loved the world." (2) The ransom: "that he gave his only begotten Son." (3) The rescue: "that whosoever believeth in him should not perish." (4) The reward: "but have everlasting life."—Lawrence Vowan

Topic: The Lord God Omnipotent Reigneth

TEXT: Rev. 19:6

(1) The omnipotent reign of God declares the liberation of our lives: we are free from worry, fear, and self-contempt. (2) It also means the doom of sin: we fight on, for the battle is his, not ours. (3) It also means the comfort for our sorrows.—James S. Stewart

WORSHIP AIDS

CALL TO WORSHIP.   "If anyone loves me, he will obey my teaching. My Father will love him, and we will come to him and make our home with him" (John 14:23 NIV).

INVOCATION.   Creator God, as we gather in your name, we stand in awe at the works of your hands. As we view the world around us and, through discovery, learn more about it, we are all the more overwhelmed at your greatness. And the more we discover of the discernable, the more we anticipate our need of the eternal. Lord, meet us here today.

OFFERTORY SENTENCE.   "A generous man will himself be blessed, for he shares his food with the poor" (Prov. 22:9 NIV).

OFFERTORY PRAYER.   Gracious Father, give us such a vision of your glory that no sacrifice will seem too great. Strengthen us in our walk of faith that we may move from selfishness to generosity.

PRAYER.   Dear Father, we praise you for your good character. We praise you for your faithfulness, when so many of those around us do not seem to be so faithful. Your constant love surrounds us, even when we do not clearly sense it. We are confident in your complete provision for our needs, even when it is not yet obvious to us. Father, we pray for the many hurts that we have, some known only by you. For those in marriage near divorce, for those whose loved ones are very sick, for those whose emotions have been deeply wounded by those they dearly love, for those needing money and seeking employment where, we believe, you have called us, and for those who need to express deep emotions—let us be near you now. This morning touch our lives with your strong and powerful hand. Help us to see ourselves, your provision for us, and your everlasting love for us through your caring eyes and sensitive heart. Prepare our minds, wills, and emotions, as well as our spirits, for worship of you this morning. Look clearly into our hearts as we sing and speak praise to you. We pray to receive all that you have to give us this morning. May our lips and lives glorify you. Through Jesus Christ, our Lord—Larry Ellis

SERMON
Topic: The Courage of Thankful People
TEXT: Acts 28:15

The Paul who emerges from the book of the Acts is anything but a sheltered intellectual who devotes his life to theological argument. Although he never sets himself up as the model of courage, few, if any, in all Christian history have shown themselves more courageous. This, we have to say, was a man of extraordinary courage, whether we like him or not.

I. I believe that this little note by Luke at the end of Acts indicates that the source of this courage was the faith that he so brilliantly expounds in his epistles: "He thanked God and took courage." This faith of Paul's was not a set of abstract beliefs for which he was prepared to argue. On the contrary, it was a living contact with a real God to whom he could give thanks in a real world. Here he is on the last lap of his journey to Rome. What lay behind him? There was that dangerous and critical moment in Jerusalem when Paul had been the victim of a riot and was nearly beaten to death in the Temple area.

There followed a whole train of events—imprisonment, murder plots, and, finally, his famous appeal to Caesar. What he had been through was enough to test the courage of any man, and what lay ahead was not a couple of weeks' repose at the Roman Hilton. What lay ahead was at least house arrest, a grueling trial, and probably execution. It was enough to sink the spirits of the bravest believer. They were now getting very near Rome, and on the horizon he could see the Appian Forum—an important junction forty miles from the city. In spite of the excitement of the moment, he must have felt a chill in his heart as he approached the center of imperial power. It was then that he saw ahead on the dusty road a group running to meet them, shouting and waving a greeting. And in a moment he was surrounded by members of the church at Rome, who had walked forty miles at the news of his coming. Suddenly, he knew that he was not alone. Paul was surrounded by the invigorating and uplifting power we know as "the fellowship of the Holy Spirit." His spirits must have been soaring, as this group of Christians surprised the other patrons of the tavern by breaking into the spontaneous songs of thanksgiving that were, and still are, the soaring, strengthening music of the Christian Church. "When Paul saw them [and heard them] he gave thanks to God and took courage."

II. The habit of thanksgiving to God is often, at this time of the year, commended to us as a duty. And it is. We are accustomed to the idea that thanksgiving is an essential element in Christian worship. And it is. We know how our own faith can be stimulated when we join with other would-be disciples in songs of praise. We know from experience how a spirit of thanksgiving can prompt us to be more concerned with the needs of the homeless and the hungry in our own land. But have you ever thought about the connection between thanksgiving and courage? When Paul saw these fellow Christians who were surrounding him with their love, he was caught up by a tide of thanksgiving, which poured new courage into his heart just when he needed it most. This is the true "fellowship of the Spirit."

For the spirit of thanksgiving represents the joyful, carefree, trust in God that Jesus not only taught but lived right through to the garden of Gethsemane and the little hill where all his disciples "forsook him and fled." He gave thanks as he watched his timid disciples set out to confront the pagan world, and some of that spirit of thanksgiving began to flow into their hearts, giving them nerve to stand up to the world, the flesh, and the devil with a boldness that astonished all three.

III. Is he not telling us that the courage we long for—courage to deal with dangers, real or imaginary, that surround us, courage to dismiss the worries that cloud our faith—can be ours in proportion as we cultivate that thankful spirit? "When Paul saw them he gave thanks to God and took courage." We see one another here this morning and hear one another thanking God. In that fellowship of the Spirit then, don't we all take courage?—David H. C. Read

SUNDAY, SEPTEMBER 23, 2007
Lectionary Message

Topic: A Smart Man—Good or Bad

TEXT: Luke 16:1–13

Other Readings: Jer. 8:18–19:1; Ps. 79:1–9; 1 Tim. 2:1–7

"A choice set of rascals!" That's the best way to describe the actors in the parable. Perhaps Jesus was telling one of his more humorous stories. Don't take it too seriously. At least don't miss the point by bewailing the action of the dishonest steward: "I'm about to get fired" or "I'm too old to dig" or "I'm too proud to beg" or "I've got it—I'll cheat." The steward was a rascal. The tenants were rascals. The master was a rascal—a choice set!

I. *A pointed parable.* The immediately recognizable point: Get smart! Now Jesus did not commend the crook. The master does not represent God, nor does the steward represent the disciple. But the parable is clearly and pointedly addressed to "his disciples." The point of the parable may be read in verses 8b and 9. Think it through. Use what you have. Make the most of every opportunity: "Be wise as serpents and harmless as doves." The children of this world are wiser than the children of light. Develop your ingenuity. Material possessions should be used to cement the relationships of life. Make life easier for your friends.

The steward was smart, realistic, alert, and he had insight into human nature. Make friends with your money; the miser has no friends, only a fortune. Prepare for the future, but the preparation is not that of placing your money in the strongbox. A time is coming when your money will be a thing of the past. Get smart—good or bad. The steward was guilty of incompetence and dishonesty, but he was a smart operator.

II. *A strong challenge.* Give an account of your stewardship. Whether great or small, wealthy or poor, a man is a steward. Our gifts are gifts from God—a trust, not a possession. Jesus had a way of emphasizing little things: a cup of cold water, the jot of the law, the one talent. Our lives are made up of little things. It is not the size of the means but the nobility of the end, the intensity of the need. A lantern, of itself, is a small affair but not when it shines as signal in the North Church belfry arch for Paul Revere to ride.

He who is faithful in little will be faithful in much. A man's way of fulfilling a small task is the best proof of his fitness or unfitness to be entrusted with a bigger task. When you are young, be a faithful steward, and it will be easier when you are old. I suppose it depends on whose it is—whose you consider money to be. Jesus describes us as stewards under God. Houses, lands, money—all belong to another. Money even bears someone else's signature, someone else's picture. Said Jesus in a discussion on taxes, "Show me a coin. Whose picture is on it? Caesar's? Then it must belong to someone besides you. Be careful that you do not belong to it." The factor in stewardship is not how much a man has but how he uses what he has.

III. *A clear impossibility.* "No servant can serve two masters." Divided devotion is clearly impossible. Don't try it. Many people try it and fail miserably. They have one God on Sunday and another God on Monday—the Father of Jesus Christ when they sing and pray and mammon when they work and play. This is a terrible kind of schizophrenia. You cannot be a slave to both at once. Serving God can never be a part-time or spare-time job. A smart man—good or bad—sees this!—J. Estill Jones

SERMON SUGGESTIONS

Topic: Things You Can Get for Nothing

TEXT: Isa. 35:1

(1) The privilege of life. (2) The joy of love. (3) The gift of salvation.—John Brokhoff

Topic: Finding Peace of Mind

TEXT: Job 23:3

(1) By coming to terms with our own selves. (2) By coming to terms with others. (3) By coming to terms with God.—Joe Harding

WORSHIP AIDS

CALL TO WORSHIP.   "It is good for me to draw near to God: I have put my trust in the Lord God, that I may declare all thy works" (Ps. 73:28 KJV).

INVOCATION.   Father, we approach you in worship trembling, for we are sinners, yet in bold gladness, for we are your beloved children. May our time together mold us even closer to the image of your dear Son, Jesus. Strengthen us in our walk with you that we will be able servants in the days of this week.

OFFERTORY SENTENCE.   "Now that you have purified yourselves by obeying the truth so that you have sincere love for your brothers, love one another deeply, from the heart" (1 Pet. 1:22 NIV).

OFFERTORY PRAYER.   O God, give us today keen insight to see the work of Christ among us and around us. May we choose him, steadfastly follow him, and be good stewards of your gifts to us. We give these offerings in his name.

PRAYER.   Loving God, Creator, Redeemer, and Sustainer of everything, we thank you for the joy of all creation on this holy day. As we have come to worship you today, Lord, each of us comes with our own deep feelings and inner thoughts that sometimes only you know. So we bring these feelings and thoughts to you, seeking your comfort and wisdom, and also bringing them as one of the ways of acknowledging your participation in our lives. We know that we are all your children and that we find our meaning and reason for being within you. We pray for persons who are in situations of oppression and abuse. We ask that you give these persons strength to rise up in your name and to free themselves. We pray for persons who are ill and perhaps are in treatment. We pray for them, as their bodies fight whatever is invading their body. We pray for persons who have lost loved ones and ask that you help them to know your presence and give them comfort in their grief. We pray, Lord, for relationships where there is conflict between or among any persons, for we know that it is your will that peace be present. We ask that your healing grace be wherever there is conflict. So, Lord, we have come together today in your name. Free us from whatever binds us, so we may worship you in spirit and in truth. These things we ask in the name of Jesus Christ, our Lord.—Peggy Goochey

SERMON
Topic: The Irreparable Past
TEXT: Mark 14:4-42

It is upon two sentences of this passage that our attention is to be fixed today—sentences that, in themselves, are apparently contradictory but are pregnant with a lesson of the deepest practical import.

I. *The irreparable past.* The words of Christ are not like the words of other men: every sentence of Christ's is a deep principle of human life. The principle contained in "Sleep on now" is this: the past is irreparable, and after a certain moment waking will do no good. You may improve the future; the past is gone beyond recovery. As to all that is gone by, so far as the hope of altering it goes, you may sleep on and take your rest; there is no power on earth or heaven that can undo what has once been done.

Time flows through the hands of men—swift, never pausing 'til it has run itself out. Yesterday, for example, was such a day as never was before and never can be again. And now from the undone eternity, the bosom of whose waves is distinctly audible upon your soul, there comes the same voice again—a solemn, sad voice—but no longer the same word: "Watch." Other words altogether: "You may go to sleep." It is too late to wake; there is no science in earth or heaven to recall time that once has fled.

II. *The available future.* We pass on next to a few remarks on the other sentence in this passage, which bring before us for consideration of the future, which is still available. The moment was come for action: "Rise, let us be going."

A Christian is to be forever rousing himself to recognize the duties that lie before him. Wake to the opportunities that yet remain. Ten years of life—five years—one year (say you have only that)—will you sleep that away because you have already slept too long? Rise, be going; count your resources; learn what you are not fit for and give up wishing for it; learn what you can do, and do it with the energy of a man.

Under no circumstances, whether of pain, or grief, or disappointment, or irreparable mistake, can it be true that there is not something to be done, as well as something to be suffered. And thus it is that the spirit of Christianity draws over our life, not a leaden cloud of remorse and despondency but a sky—not perhaps of radiant hope but yet of most serene and chastened and manly hope. There is a past that is gone forever. But there is a future that is still our own.—Frederick W. Robertson

SUNDAY, SEPTEMBER 30, 2007
Lectionary Message

Topic: A Certain Beggar
TEXT: Luke 16:19–31
Other Readings: Jer. 32:1–3a, 6–15; Ps. 91:1–6, 14–16; 1 Tim. 6:6–19

The story is not introduced as a parable, but we treat it as such. It was not given as a detailed description of heaven or hell but as an illustration of two facts: (1) the situation may be reversed in the life to come; (2) the decisions made in this life are binding for the life to come. How about some questions?

I. How did the rich man get into hell? By being rich? He was, in fact, rich. He was well clothed and well fed. Food was eaten with the hands, and the hands were wiped clean on chunks of bread, and the bread was tossed to the dogs—or to Lazarus. Yet his wealth did not send him to hell.

By being immoral? No charge of immorality is lodged against the rich man. The man spent his life harmlessly enough, but he did nobody any good. He did not love. His immorality does not appear to have sent him to hell. By ignoring a man? A sermon on the text has been titled, "The Punishment of the Man Who Never Noticed." He may have given Lazarus bread crumbs from his table, but he never noticed him. Lazarus was hungry, and he was a harmless, helpless man. He wasn't mistreating anyone. And Lazarus was a handy man. The rich man might have found a ready opportunity to help somebody. This is the only charge lodged against the rich man.

II. What was hell like? The answer is mercifully brief. Two characteristics are clear: (1) It was torment. The contrast is sharp: Lazarus was taken up by angels, and the rich man was buried. He was tormented by the sight of Lazarus. How could that be? He was tormented by his memory of his better life on earth. If only he might have had a vision of the future, as did Scrooge! (2) It was separation. Hell was separation from both God and the good. A great gulf was fixed, but then the rich man had fixed a great gulf between himself and Lazarus on earth. Every time he had walked past Lazarus, he had widened the gulf. Every time Lazarus refused to be embittered, the gulf became wider.

III. Was there any hope for the rich man? There was none whatsoever. At death one's last chance for eternal life has faded. The rich man had "had it." All his opportunities had been exhausted in his flesh-and-blood existence. His destiny had been decided.

It was a sad illustration of "too little, too late." It was too late to call on Abraham. He should have done that years before. It was too late to notice Lazarus. Even here, he spoke of Lazarus as a servant: "Abraham, send Lazarus to me." It was too late to think about his five brothers. He should have thought about them earlier. It was too late to talk about the Resurrection. He had passed beyond the veil of the Resurrection.

The last shall be first—the first shall be last—had not Jesus laid down the principle? God's values reversed the social order. Lazarus was now on the right side of the gulf, and the rich man was begging. "A certain beggar . . ."—J. Estill Jones

SERMON SUGGESTIONS

Topic: The Prayer of Faith

TEXT: Ps. 4

(1) The prayer of requesting faith (v. 1). (2) The prayer of rebuking faith (vv. 2, 6). (3) The prayer of rejoicing faith (vv. 7–8).—Stephen Olford

Topic: What Kind of Church?

TEXT: Eph. 2:19–22

(1) Some churches are like mausoleums: places of death. (2) Others are like museums: places of old memories. (3) Some churches are like coliseums: places where spectators gather. (4) But the Church is to be more like an academy: a place for learning and equipping to live as mature believers.—Richard McClain

WORSHIP AIDS

CALL TO WORSHIP.   "O come, let us sing unto the Lord: let us make a joyful noise to the rock of our salvation. Let us come before his presence with thanksgiving, and make a joyful noise unto him with psalms" (Ps. 95:1–2 KJV).

INVOCATION.   Father of mercies, who has gathered us together in this fine church, grant that we may never swerve from the pure intentions you have placed in us. May we today honor you in spirit and in truth, that your name may be glorified and that our fellowship will be with all the saints in heaven and earth.

OFFERTORY SENTENCE.   "Verily, verily, I say unto you, he that believeth on me, the works that I do shall he do also; and greater works than these shall he do. And whatsoever ye shall ask in my name, that will I do, that the Father may be glorified in the Son" (John 14:12–13 KJV).

OFFERTORY PRAYER.   O Lord, receive our offerings as expressions of our devotion. Help us to love you even more, that we shall have in our hearts the interest of your Kingdom and your people everywhere.

PRAYER.   These are the prayers of the people, O God. Heal our hearts, we pray, with the balm of time, the gentle kindness of a neighbor or friend, the patience and understanding of another broken heart. Even on a day as beautiful as this one, we read the papers and hear the news, and our spirits are darkened with fear and despair about the fate of our world. Strengthen in us our hope for the future. Help us help one another to nurture the seeds of peace and justice that are planted in our hearts, and grant us the courage to sustain our quest for truth. Guide those who wield power in every corner of the globe that they might love mercy and walk humbly in the path of love. O God of every season, we are so grateful for *this* new season: for the bittersweet month of September, for the abundance of the sustaining harvest, for the promise of refreshment in crisping air, for the coming together of renewed community. As we join together this year, let us strive to be grateful gardeners—faithful planters of new hope—patient cultivators of the teachings of love. Grant that someday soon we will dance with joy as we reap what we have sown and carry our gifts out from this circle into all our lives, and into the world. So may it be.—Rosemary Lloyd

SERMON
Topic: Dancing in the Dark
TEXT: Acts 16:25–34

Newsweek carried the fascinating story of Karen Hartley. During a skiing trip she was stranded and alone due to an avalanche. As the darkness and cold of night descended, she wondered, "What am I to do?" What came to her was this: she was to dance to the music that kept coming in her head. She could have curled up in a fetal position and allowed the darkness and cold to end her life. Instead, she chose to dance all night, and in the coming day she was saved.

Paul and Silas were in the cold and dark Philippian jail. There, in an unexpected place and time, they experienced a radical moving of God's Spirit. They sang and prayed, keeping their hearts alive, and at midnight the doors came open. The result of the marvelous night was not only their freedom but the eternal salvation of a particular jailer and his family. The gospel truly reaches unexpected places.

I. *Darkness comes to all.* The mystics in the Middle Ages spoke of the "dark night of soul" and a "winter of discontent." James Weldon Johnson, in *God's Trombones,* spoke of a darkness "like a 1000 midnights in a Louisiana swamp." Martin Luther King Jr. preached of a midnight that comes at noon in the moral areas of our racial and spiritual lives. And let's not forget the sure darkness of Calvary's cross and the grief of our dear Savior. There is the death of our loved ones, the loss of jobs, the betrayal of friends, and the separations of families. We are, as the psalmist declares, all men and women, born of sorrow, acquainted with grief.

II. *But darkness doesn't have to take away the light within.* Note in the text that Paul and Silas were "praying songs and singing songs." Before someone says, "you don't sing prayers," take a look at the hymnal and the Bible. Our songs and our Scripture are mostly prayer. Look at these prayer songs from the psaltery. Psalm 4:6 sings out, "Lord, lift up your countenance upon us." Psalm 18:28 declares, "Lord, you light my lamp, you light my darkness." Psalm 27:1 is crystal clear: "The Lord is the light of my salvation, whom shall I fear?" The truth is unmistakable. Even in the darkest of our days, in the death of a loved one, the loss of friendship, a failure or disappointment, in whatever dark moment afflicts us we are assured of the gospel light. Faith wins.

III. *Authentic witness is often born in the darkness.* The theme of Christian conversion lies at the heart of this text. The jailer and his family receive the grace of God. He had been at the jail throughout the night, even during their singing and praying. But was he converted through their worship? Hardly! He slept through it! What brought him to repentance and faith was the fearlessness of these two missionaries. He woke up, saw them still there, and the spirit within him was energized. What is this? Why are they still here? Knowing that he would have run away, he questioned why they did not. The answer is simple. Why should they? They were already free—free in Christ Jesus. No loose shackles or open bars could make them more free than they were. When the jailer saw it, he declared in his heart: "I want what these two have."

What was the source of such a relaxed spirit for Paul and Silas? It didn't just happen. They carried that spirit with them into the jail. In fact, they carried that boldness everywhere they went. They simply were living out what already was within them. They, like Karen, sang what came into their heads. The lyrics of life and faith, born out of past experience, rose up like a ringing in the ears. Perhaps the saddest person of all is the one who has no stored-up reservoir of Christian experience upon which to draw when that dark night of the soul arrives. But how marvelously blessed are those who have it.

IV. *We have something to dance about.* Most of the time, I am not an outwardly emotional person. I cannot sing. I cannot dance. But in my heart there is a melody. And there is a dance. It is not a polka but a waltz. Here is our Christian witness. God leads and we follow in step. For, you see, we have something to dance about: the forgiveness of sin, the purposes in life for which we exist, and the certainty of God's promise that guides our way. We have the same resources that were available to Paul and Silas, and the same audience of an unbelieving world, and the same witness before that needy world.

As a church we reach out to our world in thousands of different ways each week. In Sunday worship we do so as the church "gathered." In a few moments, we will go out to home, business, school, and community, and there we will be no less "the church." We will instead become the church "scattered." And our goal is the same: to live out the joy of our faith. May I have this dance?—Lee McGlone

SUNDAY, OCTOBER 7, 2007
Lectionary Message

Topic: Making Room for Lament
Text: Lam. 1:1–6
Other Readings: Ps. 137; 2 Tim. 1:1–14; Luke 17:5–10

The lesson from the Hebrew Scriptures for today presents the opening lines of the book of Lamentations. I dare say the gold has not been worn away from the trim of the pages of Lamentations in our Bible. And yet, most people of faith perhaps identify more with its message than the positive gospel spin we often give to the life of faith in our preaching. Reading the words of Lamentations, along with the accompanying psalm, might allow worshipers to hear their voice in worship perhaps for the first time in years. For many people, worship has seemed like an attempt to "sing the Lord's song in a strange land," the strange land of joy and gladness.

Sometimes our truest prayers are those of praise and thanksgiving. Sometimes they are cries of lament. Sometimes lament is our home. There are those days when we need a place to cry in the presence of God and others. Lament has a prominent place in biblical worship. The Psalms are full of lament. To read Lamentations and Psalms like the 137th in worship brings honesty and integrity to worship.

There are things I believe we should do together in worship, whether we feel like doing them or not. We should gather together. We should offer praise. We should confess our sins. We should pray. We should listen for God's voice.

What we should not do is say, "Life is great. I feel good. No worries at all," when that is the farthest thing from the truth. When life is painful we must be honest enough to admit it before God. When life is tearing us apart, when our heart is breaking, when we are being crushed under the load we're trying to carry, when grief, depression, loneliness, and failure haunt our every waking moment—all this brokenness must be brought to God in worship and expressed in lament.

Have you ever heard or prayed in worship: "Lord, help us remove from our minds everything about our lives and focus just on you?" While it does point us to the real reason for worship—a focus on God and not ourselves—that prayer can separate worship from real life. The words of Welton Gaddy offer correction to that prayer:

> Asking people who have gathered for a service to set aside all of their concerns, anxieties, preoccupations, and cares in order to worship is as completely unnecessary as it is unrealistic. The worship of God does not require a case of temporary amnesia regarding the rest of life. Actually, God desires for all of life to be brought into worship as an offering.[1]

Even our pain.

We need to restore lament to a prominent place in worship. I would hope that such a restoration would make people feel more willing to come to worship during the dark seasons of their lives. How many of us go through dark periods, and the first thing we do is stop coming to worship for fear we must hide our pain and express joy that's not there at all.

Worship includes more than joyful praise; it also includes honest lament. We often feel like the woman who was asked, "How are you?" and she replied, "I'm somewhere between 'Thank You Jesus' and 'Lord Have Mercy.'" Praise and lament are mixed together.

The Psalms are full of lament, though we largely exclude them from our worship. It is Psalm 22 Jesus quoted from the cross: "My God, my God, why have you forsaken me? Why are you so far from helping me, so far away from the words of groaning?" But the lament of Psalm 22 turns back to praise at the end: "I will tell of thy name to my people, in the midst of the congregation I will praise thee." Praise opens the door of lament, and lament opens the door to praise.

One of St. Francis of Assisi's most famous poems is the hymn we sing: "All creatures of our God and King lift up your voice and with us sing, 'O praise ye! Alleluia!'" But do you know he wrote that hymn, not in the prime of his life but in 1255, a year before his death, in midwinter, nearly blind and enduring excruciating pain in his head and stomach?

There is a sixth stanza of the hymn not included in most hymn books. It goes like this:

And thou, our sister, gentle death, waiting to hush our latest breath,
Alleluia! Alleluia!
Thou leadest home the child of God, and Christ the Lord the way has trod.
O praise ye! O praise ye! Alleluia! Alleluia! Alleluia!

Most of our laments have been banished from our hymn books and worship. And they've gone secular in blues and folk music and country-western with tunes like "I'm So Lonesome I Could Cry." Church growth experts say that if you want to grow, eliminate prayers of confession and lament (too negative thinking) and ban all music in a minor key.

---

[1]Welton Gaddy, *The Gift of Worship* (Nashville, TN: Broadman Press, 1992), p. 97.

But if we can't bring our real selves to worship, what good is worship? Jesus said worship is to be done "in spirit and in truth," that is, in the Spirit of God and involving the whole truth about your life. Prayer is bringing your real self before God, not your pretend self. God doesn't want your life to stay a lament, but when a lament is all you have to sing, God wants to hear that honest cry.

And so we weep. We weep for fractured relationships and shattered lives; we weep for crack cocaine and poverty and injustice and children who don't get a fair chance in life. We weep for hatred and fear, cruelty and terrorism. True worship includes lamentation. The hope of honest lamentation is healing and joy. Paul told Timothy, "I remember you constantly in my prayers night and day. Recalling your tears, I long to see you so that I may be filled with joy." When we share our lament with others, our presence together can bring healing and joy. We can know that we are not alone.

May we open our hearts to God in honest worship. May the tears of lament flow freely. And in due season, may God turn our sorrow into joy, our cries of lament into hymns of joy.—W. Gregory Pope

SERMON SUGGESTIONS

Topic: Our Need for Community
TEXT: Acts 4:32
(1) We need a community in which we can trust. (2) One that will nurture our inner life. (3) One that will form the basis for ministry. (4) One that exemplifies the ideal Christian life.—Craig Biddle

Topic: The Hidden God
TEXT: Isa. 45:15
(1) God hides himself because of his perfect holiness. (2) God hides because of his respect for human personality and the freedom of human choice and will. (3) God hides so that out of our struggles we may grow to maturity.—Raymond Abba

WORSHIP AIDS
CALL TO WORSHIP.   "The cup of blessing which we bless, is it not the communion of the blood of Christ? The bread which we break, is it not the communion of the body of Christ? For we being many are one bread, and one body: for we are all partakers of that one bread" (1 Cor. 10:16–17 KJV).

INVOCATION.   Eternal Lord, as we gather in worship, we declare that it is you who made us and not we ourselves. In your infinite wisdom, you made one race—the human race—to populate the world. May on this day, by the power of the Holy Spirit, all your people every-where be bound to you in union so strong that no barriers shall separate us. For Christ's sake, and the Church, we pray.

OFFERTORY SENTENCE.   "The entire law is summed up in a single command: 'Love your neighbor as yourself'" (Gal. 5:14 NIV).

OFFERTORY PRAYER.   O Lord, open our eyes that we may see your goodness. Open our hearts that we may be grateful for your mercy. Open our lips that we may give you praise.

Open our hands that we may give these offerings according to your will, and may they be used for the building of your Kingdom.

PRAYER. Gracious God, we come together as Christians from all over the world to share in the bounty of your table. We gather to share the cup of life and the bread that provides strength for our journey. We gather speaking many languages and worshiping you in ways unique to our culture and heritage. But in our diversity, there is unity. And so we humbly offer to you our lives and our spirits, just as we are, knowing that you can use our brokenness to bring about healing and wholeness in your name. And so, on this World Wide Communion Sunday, we lift our prayers to you, knowing that you already hear the yearnings of our hearts. We lift prayers for our global neighbors, especially those persons living in fear or poverty, and for those who have lost hope. Give us the courage to recognize and name the pain of our global neighbors and to reach out where we can. In your mercy, Lord, hear our prayers. We lift prayers for those close to us, some of whom we name in our hearts: the sick, the addicted, the abused, the imprisoned, the depressed, and those grieving some loss in their life. May they be comforted and fed by the bread and cup of new life. In your mercy, Lord, hear our prayers. Pour out your spirit upon all the nations of the earth, and upon all whom you have named and claimed as your own in Christ's name. For all the blessings in our lives and for your promise to always be with us, we lift our prayers of praise and thanksgiving.— Susan Gregg-Schroeder

SERMON
Topic: A Universal Spirit
TEXT: Acts 5:27–39

World Communion Sunday reminds us of our global ties and the value of generosity toward others. The early Church was having a tough go of it. Having been energized by the universal Spirit on Pentecost, they were preaching a controversial Christian message everywhere anyone would listen. The Jewish authorities were not amused, so they had the disciples arrested and brought before the council for questioning. In the midst of the explosive deliberations, a big-spirited rabbi named Gamaliel stood up to offer some wise counsel about tolerance: "If this undertaking is of human origin, it will fail. But if it is of God, you will not be able to stop it." Fortunately for the apostles, the council took Gamaliel's advice and let them go. Gamaliel was a voice of moderation in an intolerant religious atmosphere. His instincts were inclusive and progressive.

I. There are two kinds of tolerance. There is a permissive attitude that says, "anything goes, nothing matters, live and let live." That wasn't Gamaliel. His was a tolerance of conviction. He was loyal to Israel's covenant. He believed in God; in fact, his attitude toward the disciples was rooted in his belief about God. This really is a pivotal point in the gospel story. It was a situation where all the apostles could have been put to death at once, and there might be no Christianity today. But God always seems to have some Gamaliel type around to preserve his cause.

II. What does this teach us about causes that appear to be lost but, in the end, are not? Do they win? When two men came after dark to buy Jesus' body, it looked, for practical purposes, as though they had bet on a lost cause. But that was before Easter! So God has Joseph of Arimathea and Nicodemus. The disciples were before the Sanhedrin, in danger of being annihilated before Christianity barely got started. But then there was Gamaliel. Conversely, some movements appear destined to win. Adolph Hitler's Germany was a formidable force in the world in the 1930s. With military might and an agenda intent on conquering the world, it looked for a while there as if it would happen. The extreme claims and actions of the Nazis came to nothing in the end of the war. Things come and go. Gamaliel knew that. Be patient. Wait and see. Things are not always what they appear to be. You have to "winter and summer" with some movements before you realize what they're really like. There are always things about which people were very sure once upon a time, that they aren't so sure about anymore. Sometimes, what people thought was the will of God, later seems to clearly not have been God's will.

III. Throughout history, God has worked in ways few of us understand. To his everlasting credit, Gamaliel seemed to recognize that, which is why he advised: Be careful here. God may be at work! I think that's what Gamaliel was saying: *God is big.* Too many people in our day have a God who is too small. Before I'm around people too long, I ask them about their doubts—things they're uncertain of. That's because anybody who can't answer those questions is already a fanatic. And that includes those who are intolerant of the intolerant.

Gamaliel sees to it that certain things don't get done, like destroying the disciples in Jerusalem. It fell to Peter to be the leader of the early Christian movement, but he couldn't have done it without Gamaliel's universal spirit. Thus we celebrate the ministry of Rabbi Gamaliel on World Communion Sunday, because on this Sunday we are reminded that Christ has called us to a table that is universal, that encompasses all the diversities of this world—a table that sees difference as a gift, not a burden. It's time to gather around the table. In the spirit of Gamaliel, I invite you.—Dan Ivins

SUNDAY, OCTOBER 14, 2007
Lectionary Message

Topic: An Old Professor's Prayer
TEXT: Jer. 29:4–7
Other Readings: Ps. 66:1–12; 2 Tim. 2:8–15; Luke 17:11–19

The invitation of this sermon is to surround your life in prayer—a specific prayer, in fact, an old professor's prayer. It is a prayer with which most of you are familiar; it is attributed to one of the great minds of this century—a former professor of Christian ethics at Union Theological Seminary in New York City, the late Reinhold Niebuhr.

Story has it that Dr. Niebuhr jotted down a few lines for a prayer he was to offer one Sunday during worship. After the service, someone asked to see a copy of the prayer, which Niebuhr had folded up and put away. Out of his pocket Reinhold Niebuhr drew the lines that have become perhaps the most familiar of all modern American prayers: "God, grant me the serenity to accept what cannot be changed, the courage to change what can be changed, and the wisdom to know the difference."

I. *God: The hope and power of the prayer.* Before we focus on those things we can and cannot change, let us not hurry past the first word of the prayer. For the first word is the hope and the power of the whole prayer. The first word is *God.* The road to acceptance and the pathway to change is difficult enough in itself, but it will be a most difficult journey if we forget the most important first word.

Many alcoholics are familiar with this prayer. It is introduced at many Alcoholics Anonymous meetings. Alcoholics are at those meetings because they need a Higher Power to help them accept the things they cannot change and to change the things that can be changed. They have realized that alcohol does not help you accept unwelcome circumstances, nor does it help change the circumstances.

We should all be as wise. God and God alone is our hope and power for acceptance of unwelcome circumstances and change for what can be changed. Never forget the first word. The first word is *God.*

II. *Accept the things I cannot change.* "God, grant me the serenity to accept what cannot be changed." There are some things about our lives that we must learn to accept because they are not going to change any time in the near future, if at all.

Our Scripture lesson from Jeremiah is a text about living in the midst of difficult circumstances that are not going to change for some time. The children of God are in exile, and God has sent word through the prophet Jeremiah that they will not be leaving Babylon for quite some time—seventy years to be exact. So Jeremiah wrote them a letter about living with the things that could not be changed.

When we have to live in the midst of things that cannot be changed, we feel as though we are living in exile. Perhaps we can remember better times, and we long for those times in the same way we would long for home if we were actually in exile. And so, these words from Jeremiah are words to us as well.

The first thing he says to them is to acknowledge and accept the fact that things are not going to be changing any time soon. Those words are hard to hear. We usually do pretty well if we can believe that difficult times are soon going to end. Most of the time the difficulty or pain does pass. But how do we live with the things that will not change?

Jeremiah says to accept the fact that they will not change. He warns them to stay away from those preachers who say if you will only pray harder and have more faith or start living right, the difficulty will pass. Do not listen to those who say only what you want to hear. Things are difficult, Jeremiah says, and they are going to remain that way for quite some time.

Accepting the fact that some things may not ever change means that we cannot spend our lives waiting for things to get better. The prophet tells them not to put their lives on hold: "Go ahead and build houses—you will be here for the full thirty-year mortgage. Plant a garden—you will still be here when those butterbeans are ready to pick. Let your sons and daughters marry and have children—if they don't do it now they will be too old when they leave, and you'll never have grandchildren."

In essence, Jeremiah is saying that if we do not learn to make peace with our captivity, our exile, our conditions of difficulty, we will never have peace at all. Accept your circumstances. They cannot be changed. But you can live faithfully within them.

We all, I suspect, have something we would change if we could but simply cannot. We can let that something paralyze us and control us and eat us alive, or we can accept it and get on with life as best we can and enjoy what we can enjoy.

There is hope even in exile, even in the midst of circumstances that will not be changing any time soon, if at all. That hope, Jeremiah says, is that God will be present with us and has in store for us a future and a hope. There is the word of truth about God that is always greater than the most desperate situations of our lives. This word of truth is an incredible, magnificent word of hope. It is the affirmation of our faith that proclaims that despite all the evidence to the contrary, this is God's world, and God's plan is to give us a future and a hope.

If we refuse to accept the facts, we will mostly fall into a false hope. But if we fail to hear God's word of truth for us, we will most likely fall into false despair. Jeremiah's word to us is that God has not forgotten us. God is always caring for us. God has a plan for us. And that plan is to give us a future and a hope.

Frederick Buechner said that in God's word, the worst thing that happens to us is never the last thing that happens to us. The truth is that nothing in this world will ever separate us from the love of God, which is ours in Christ Jesus our Lord.

III. *"Change the things that I can."* Though there are times when our circumstances cannot be changed, there are times when things can be changed.

Change can be frightening, can't it? But change is necessary to live life in this ever-changing world of ours. Over the next few years if the Church is going to survive, it must change its way of doing things without changing its message. May God grant us the wisdom and courage to do what needs to be done—to change those things that need to be changed and that can be changed.

There are also changes in our personal lives that can and need to be changed. In some cases, the condition of our health is something we do have the opportunity to change. Through a proper diet and exercise, many times we can change the condition of our health. Other times, our circumstances cannot change but our reaction to those circumstances can change. In most cases we have the ability to choose our response to the situations of our lives.

We can choose our response to almost any unwelcome circumstance. Now, I'm not talking about the kind of positive thinking that ignores the hard reality of our situation or the situation of others. I am not a proponent of unrestrained optimism, nor am I a proponent of close-minded pessimism. We can err, I think, at both extremes. I like to think of myself as an optimistic realist or a realistic optimist. With the hope of the gospel and the presence and power of God in our lives, we have reason to look beyond and above our circumstances.

In extreme cases, however, the conditions of life can be so burdensome, the pain and grief can be so devastating that the realities of life can send us into the depths of depression. Those times call for a Higher Power, as well as professional help, along with a strong, supportive community of faith where our friends can stand beside us and enable us to go on. Feeling weak and stressed out and needing help from others is not a sign of a weak faith. It is a sign of our humanity and a realization that we all, at some point, need the help and support of each other.

And outside of those extreme cases where grief devastates us or depression overwhelms us, we can pretty much choose our response to the conditions of our lives. But it is a choice we cannot always make on our own. Again, we must never forget the first word—*God.*

The idea of choosing our response to the conditions of our lives is not a promotion of individual self-sufficiency. It is not to say, "Be strong and take care of yourself." But rather, it is an acknowledgment that we need help from Something or Someone beyond ourselves and our resources to change those things that can be changed.

Sometimes the change involved is a change of attitude toward circumstances that cannot be changed. Sometimes the change is one of response to the things that occur in our lives. Sometimes the call is to change our circumstances, to change our way of life.

Change is also an integral part of the gospel. Jesus' first words of proclamation in the Gospel of Matthew are, "Repent—turn around, change—for the kingdom of heaven has come near." And repentance is not something we do just once. We spend our lives being continually re-formed and transformed into the person we are called to be, into the image of Christ. And it seems that Jesus is saying if you want to be a part of the Kingdom—what Clarence Jordan called "The God Movement"—if you want to be working with God in the world, it will involve continual change on our part.

Matthew quotes from Isaiah offering hope for newness of life, offering hope for repentance and change: "The people who sat in darkness have seen a great light, and for those who sat in the region and shadow of death light has dawned."

The move from darkness to light is a change from one way of life to another, from living in one realm to living in another—a realm of light and hope. For the One who has come with words of repentance and change is the same One who comes as light into our darkness. Light has dawned. There is a way out of our darkness. There is a way out of those ruts in which we find ourselves, knowing we need to change but lacking the courage and hope to do so. Behold, your light in Jesus Christ has come. He is your courage, and he is your hope.

Let us never forget that our hope for change is in Jesus Christ. Let us remember that this talk of serenity in accepting the things that cannot be changed and the courage to change the things that can be changed has been wisely placed in the form of a prayer. Our hope for a new and better self is found in a life of prayer—a life of deep, abiding companionship with God. "God, grant me the serenity to accept what cannot be changed, the courage to change what can be changed."

IV. *The wisdom to know the difference.* What are those things that I can change? And what are the things I need to learn to accept? How we wish to know the answers to those questions. How we need the wisdom to discern. Here once again we are reminded to never forget the first word of prayer. It is only with the help of God and the wisdom of friends that we can discern which things can be changed and which things we must accept. May God grant us the serenity of acceptance and the courage to change and the wisdom to know the difference.—W. Gregory Pope

SERMON SUGGESTIONS

Topic: Job's Sure Knowledge
TEXT: Job 19:25
(1) Job had cruel friends. (2) But he had one true friend: "I know my 'redeemer' lives." (3) His "real" property was taken away, but his "eternal" property was secure. (4) He was promised absolute certainty amid uncertain affairs.—Lawrence Vowan

Topic: Qualities of Leadership
TEXT: Neh. 2:18
(1) Nehemiah was touched deeply by real and felt needs. (2) He made the situation a matter of prayer and fasting. (3) He determined the work that was to be done. (4) He won the confidence of the people. (5) He was not discouraged by his detractors.—Ray Adams.

WORSHIP AIDS
CALL TO WORSHIP.   "But thanks be to God! He gives us the victory through our Lord Jesus Christ" (1 Cor. 15:57 NIV).

INVOCATION.   O Lord God, in whom we live and move and have our being, whose perfect face is hidden from us by our sin, whose mercy we often forget in the busyness of life, grant today your presence in this place. May we, in meekness and lowliness of heart, draw near to your throne and in you find our refuge and strength.

OFFERTORY SENTENCE.   "Every man shall give as he is able, according to the blessing of the Lord thy God which he hast given thee" (Deut. 16:17 KJV).

OFFERTORY PRAYER.   Father, as we offer these gifts, remind us that deeds are more persuasive testimony than words alone. May we know that these gifts are but part of the pledge of loyalty you require of us.

PRAYER.   Creator God, you have placed us in the company of others to look after one another and that we might not be lonely. With each day's setting sun, you seek to end the cares of the day and to close out accounts with sleep. With each day's rising sun, you breakfast us upon the food of second chances. But we blow it. Again and again we see a new day, but in the mirror we see an old face and old fears and old ways. Yet you have promised to those who submit to the pruning of your commanding word, the lasting fruit of your abiding presence—the ultimate, companionable answer to the loneliness of Adam and Eve and of all thy children.—Peter Fribley

SERMON
Topic: How to Be a Blessing
TEXT: Acts 20:35

There is something I do know about the principle of giving. It's found in the text: "It is more blessed to give than to receive." Now that's hard to comprehend. But it's the truth. I know it is because the Bible says it. But what do you do with it? How do you process it? How do you make sense of it? How does a believer possibly live by it?

I. First, the text assumes that a Christian is attracted to the idea of being a blessing. To be a blessing means that you make a positive and lasting difference in or a positive and lasting contribution to someone else's life by the power of God in you to the glory of God. Now, is that attractive to you? The text assumes that a Christian lives to be a blessing. Have you arrived at that point of spiritual maturity yet? Or are you still living at the level where your chief concern—your only concern—is to take care of yourself and your own?

Sometimes people in the church get confused about stewardship and fundraising. But there is a basic difference between the two. A good stewardship emphasis will raise funds, but a good stewardship emphasis doesn't stop with that. Fundraising is merely a matter of putting together enough money to pay the bills, balance the budget, fill up a thermometer on a United Way chart, or meet some other goal. But stewardship is spiritual. It has everything to do with the way we live out our relationship to the Lord Jesus Christ.

II. The second truth the text reveals is how a Christian becomes a blessing: it's through giving! Even the smallest of gifts can become the greatest blessings to others. We live in such a self-absorbed world that any selfless action on behalf of others stands in sharp contrast to what we are accustomed to seeing. Gifts move people. They bless people. They melt people.

They stop people in their tracks and make them ask, "Why? Why would you give up something for yourself just so you could give something to me?" Isn't that the kind of person you would like to be? Hold on to that desire.

III. Finally, the text reveals the source of blessing: we give out of what we have already received. Life is a gift. In fact, everything that makes life worthwhile is a gift. What's more, one day, we too were rescued by a miracle from God. That's why we, like the old captain, have every reason to look into the sky every day and give thanks. When we give, we keep alive and pass on to others the goodness and the grace of God, which we did not earn or deserve. When we give, we pass on his gifts to others and keep his blessings alive so that they might be blessed also. And when we learn to give like that, that is our finest hour to his highest glory!—Gary C. Redding

SUNDAY, OCTOBER 21, 2007
Lectionary Message

Topic: The Biblical Invitation
TEXT: Jer. 31:27–34
Other Readings: Ps. 119:97–104; 2 Tim. 3:14–4:5; Luke 18:1–8

It sits on more coffee tables that coffee does. It gathers more dust than the nightstand. And yet, if opened and read and allowed to speak, it can change the dirtiest and darkest of hearts. It's the B-I-B-L-E—the gift of Holy Scripture, the testimony of God's Word, written on our hearts for the purpose of teaching, reproofing, correcting, training us in righteousness, and equipping us for good works. What role does it play in your life?

A pastor tells of his first years of ministry in the hills of eastern Tennessee. His parishioners were people of humble origins and means, mostly uneducated, yet vibrant in their faith. One Sunday afternoon, he decided to go calling. As he entered the first house in the hollow, he was warmly welcomed. The young couple invited him to sit at the table, and there lay a beautiful, huge, family Bible. It was obviously well used and deeply treasured. When the pastor called on the next house, he was astonished to find a large, beautiful, family Bible that looked suspiciously like the one he had seen at the first house. As he made his way to the next house, he noticed a young boy hiding behind the trees in back of the houses and running ahead of him with that very same Bible under his arms.

What role does the Bible play in your life? What is this book we read week after week, upon which many seek to pattern their lives? Is it just a list of dos and don'ts—an answer book to every question we have? Is it just ancient history? Or does it bring a Word from God that speaks to the depths of our lives?

To be sure, there are laws and commands in the Bible that are to give shape to the way we live our lives. The psalmist speaks of how God's law revived his soul and enlightened his eyes. He speaks of how God's word serves as a lamp unto his feet and a light unto his path, and how much more God's commands are to be desired than much fine gold. "Sweeter than honey" is how he speaks of the laws and guidance of God.

But is there more to the Bible than laws and commands? Yes, there is more. There is a Story—one Grand Story—that the Bible seeks to tell. And we need to know the whole Story to understand any part of the Story. Eugene Peterson says, "It takes the whole Bible to read any part of the Bible." And it is a Story that has changed the course of history. It is a Story that has transformed lives and continues to transform lives today, young and old, educated, uneducated. Gregory the Great of the sixth century said, "Scripture is like a river, broad and deep, shallow enough here for the lamb to go wading, but deep enough there for the elephant to swim."

The great Protestant reformer Martin Luther said, "The Bible is alive, it speaks to me. It has feet, it runs after me. It has hands, it lays hold of me." What kind of book could do such a thing? How could a book do such a thing?

Karl Barth has given us a very helpful image of reading the Bible as if we were looking out a window. As we look out the window, we see everyone looking up into the sky, shading their eyes with their hands. The people are excited. Something is happening to them. Something has captured their hearts. The people outside the window see something about the window that's hidden by the roof. When we read the Bible correctly, says Barth, we will want to race outside and join them in what they are experiencing. We will want to experience more than what the window can show us. Rather than simply reading the words of Scripture and hearing the stories in order to draw truths from them, we will want to get involved in the Story and experience the God beyond the window, beyond the mere words of the Bible.

The Bible Story is marvelously exciting, full of everything you've ever seen on the movie screen, from murder to adultery, love and hatred, violence and rejection, obedience and idolatry. It's all there and more. Many of its stories aren't fit for children. But they do speak to our lives. You will find something in the Bible that relates to whatever you've experienced, and because it's in the Bible, that means God can work redemptively in whatever you're experiencing.

It is this book, more than any other, that shapes our identity as the people of God. In fact, Will Willimon says, "When the Bible is read from a viewpoint other than its attempt to engender a new people, it is misread." We return to this book over and over again to be reminded of who we are and what we are called to be and do in the world.

When we hear Scripture rightly, says John Burgess, it helps us remember who God really is and who we really are. Rather than giving us a truth to defend, the Bible issues us a challenge to live more faithfully. We need to know this Story. It is our livelihood. It is a record of God's dealings with God's people, and it is a living testament as to how God wants to deal with us today. Through it God speaks. The words of Scripture "breathe something divine," says John Calvin.

Through the divine breath, the Bible extends to us an invitation. It is an invitation to enter into its pages and become a believer in God, a follower of Jesus Christ, and a member of the people of God. The Bible is our entrance into the world of God, into the realm and kingdom of Christ where God is present in power and grace, redeeming our lives and redeeming the world. We continue coming back to these sixty-six books again and again because we believe that they are the very words of life.

The biblical invitation is to enter into covenant with God as a part of God's people and learn to see the world differently and live in the world differently. The Bible does not call us to remove ourselves from the world but to immerse ourselves in the world and work to transform it from within, with the love and mercy and justice and compassion of God.

We do not simply learn or study or use Scripture. We take it into our lives in such a way that it comes forth from our lives as acts of life, cups of cold water, plates of pancakes and sausage—acts of mission, healing, and evangelism throughout the world.

By entering into covenant with God through the biblical Story, we make the Story our own. We come to live out of that Story. We embrace the Story. We make the journey with Abraham, departing to a land we know not. We travel with Israel through the wilderness into the Promised Land. We allow ourselves to be formed and shaped as God's people. We go with Israel into exile where our lives and our faith are uprooted, and we learn to live differently in a strange land. And then we are led out of exile and learn to begin life anew. God's Messiah then comes for us to save us, and as the redeemed people of God, we become shaped into the Church.

The biblical invitation is to covenant—of God's promises to Israel and the Church made and fulfilled—that then runs throughout the pages of Scripture, from Noah after the flood to Abraham and his descendants, Israel. Israel would repeatedly be unfaithful to the covenant. And God would always call them back, until finally God decided upon a new covenant, a new way of relating to us—the way of suffering love, the way of the cross of Jesus.

The biblical invitation is to enter into covenant with God and God's people through Jesus Christ, God's new covenant with the world. We live in that covenant as we live in the pages of the Bible, making the biblical Story our own, drawing us into the presence of God, transforming our lives.—W. Gregory Pope

SERMON SUGGESTIONS

Topic: Glimpses of God
TEXT: Rom. 15
(1) Ours is a God of patience (v. 5). (2) Ours is a God of comfort (v. 5). (3) Ours is a God of hope (v. 13). (3) Ours is a God of peace (v. 33).—Perry Webb

Topic: Survival of the Word
TEXT: 2 Tim. 2:9
(1) The Word of God has successfully withstood every attempt to destroy it. (2) Enemies have tried to keep it out of the hands of people. (3) Intellectual assaults have been levied—and withstood. (4) Heaven and earth will pass away, but not God's Word.—Frank Pollard

WORSHIP AIDS
CALL TO WORSHIP.   "Wait on the Lord: be of good courage, and he shall strengthen thine heart: wait, I say, on the Lord" (Ps. 27:14 KJV).

INVOCATION.   Father, we come to worship with glad hearts. We thank you for your Word that is truth. We thank you for the living Word, Jesus Christ, who dwells among us. Grant that today we shall so experience your nearness that your thoughts may be our thoughts and your ways our ways.

OFFERTORY SENTENCE.   "Give, and it will be given to you. A good measure, pressed down, shaken together and running over, will be poured into your lap" (Luke 6:38 NIV).

OFFERTORY PRAYER.   Gracious Lord, open our eyes that we may see the beauty of the world as your gift. Grant us the desire and wisdom to do our part in bringing your light to the dark places. For this purpose we do now dedicate these offerings.

PRAYER.   O God, Thou hast found us and not we thee. At times we but dimly discern thee; the dismal mists of earth obscure thy glory. Yet in other and more blessed moments, thou dost rise upon our souls, and we know thee as the Light of all our seeing, the Life of all that is not dead with us, the Bringer of health and cure, the Revealer of peace and truth. We will not doubt our better moments, for in them thou dost speak to us. We rejoice that thou hast created us in thine image. Thy love has stirred us into being, has endowed us with spiritual substance. In the intellect, whose thoughts wander through eternity; in the conscience that bears witness to thy eternal righteousness; in the affections that make life sweet, and reach forth to thee, O Lover of Mankind—in these, we are made heirs to the riches of thy grace. And when we wandered from thee into the far country and there wasted our substance, thou didst not forsake us. Thy love followed after us and would not let us go and compelled us to return.

We praise thee that in the advent of thy dear Son, all that thou art hast become visible to faith. His passion has become our deliverance, his wounds our healing, his cross our redemption, his death our life. Make us one with him in faith and penitence, that as he died, so we may die unto sin, that as he rose again triumphant over wrong and shame and despair, so we may rise with him into newness of life.—Samuel McComb

SERMON
Topic: Can We Cast Our Burden Upon the Lord?
Text: Ps. 55:2; Gal. 6:2, 5

I want to bring three texts to your notice this morning: (1) "Cast thy burden upon the Lord and He shall sustain thee," (2) "Bear ye one another's burdens," and (3) "Every man shall bear his own burden."

I. Are they all true? Can they all be true? The last most certainly contains truth, though in my view not the whole of the truth. Can we look at that one first? Every man shall bear his own burden! In this text we catch a haunting glimpse of life's essential loneliness. Some burdens you cannot accept once and for all. You have to accept them again every day. And there falls upon the spirit an awareness: "This is a grief, and I must bear it." "Every man shall bear his own burden."

II. But thank God that is not all the truth. Many of us—I, for one—can speak from experiences for which we thank God that our dear ones share our burdens. Real love, of course, desires to share the burden of the beloved. "Every man shall bear his own burden"—true in a sense, but he could never bear the entire burden.

III. Now we are ready to draw near to the words of the Introit again. Says the psalmist: "Cast thy burden upon the Lord." We hardly need to "cast" it, for love always desires to share the burden of the beloved. But let us be very honest: I used the word *share,* not *bear.* Many of us are carrying heavy burdens, and at times the loneliness of it all will fall upon us with a stab of terror. But in fellowship with others, we shall find the load lifted a little. "Cast thy burden upon the Lord; He shall sustain thee."—Leslie Weatherhead

SUNDAY, OCTOBER 28, 2007
Lectionary Message

Topic: Dare to Be a Sinner

TEXT: Luke 18:9–14

Other Readings: Joel 2:23–32; Ps. 65; 2 Tim. 4:6–8, 16–18

In this well-known parable of self-righteousness and humble confession, it is difficult to tell "the good guy" from "the bad guy." The Pharisee was "the good guy," meticulously keeping the Law of Moses. The tax collector was "the bad guy," rounding up the money for the Romans and keeping what he could for himself. And yet, in this parable, as he often does, Jesus turns cultural presumptions inside out. By the time the credits roll, the Pharisee leaves worship as "the bad guy," and the tax collector departs as "the good guy." Or is it as simple as that? This short parable confronts us with our own attitudes in worship and prayer and dares us to be sinners. Confession is a necessary activity in honest worship and prayer.

In that ancient paradigm for worship, we see Isaiah and his proper response to a vision of God's holy grandeur. What did Isaiah say? "Woe is me! I am undone! I am a man of unclean lips and I live in the midst of an unclean people." Worship includes not only praise but also confession, sorrow over our sins. Encountering God face-to-face makes it difficult not to come face-to-face with ourselves. To come before the holiness of God is to be reminded of our unholiness.

In general, we are not too excited about confession. We do not want to admit our sins or failures. We tend to be perfectly willing to talk about the pain inflicted upon us, but we are less than enthusiastic when it comes to talking about the pain we have inflicted. Confession is crucial because sin is not private, nor is it only individual. Our sins affect others. And we participate in sin with others—corporate, systemic, institutional sin of which we are often unaware. From racism to economic oppression to excluding others in the Church or from the Church, it is important for us to acknowledge together in worship the sin in which we all participate.

When we gather for worship, we confess the sins of the Church and the world of which we are a part. The great fault of the Pharisee's prayer is not just his self-righteousness but the separation his prayer espouses. We must make sure that our confession does not result in a self-congratulatory humility, separating ourselves from the self-righteous. We must be careful not to pray, "God, I thank you I am not like this Pharisee." There is self-righteousness in us all. There is also the capacity for humble confession within us all. So it is best to confess our sins together.

Corporate prayers of confession remind us that we are not the only sinner in need of forgiveness. It puts us all on the same level. Corporate confession might say something we would hesitate to say if left to confess in silence. Confessing sins is sometimes the hardest work of worship. Culture conditions us to disguise our weaknesses, cover our faults, reject guilt, and remain silent about our sins. So when we do the hard work of confession, we are forced to confront the dark side of our nature with stark honesty and ponder the consequences of our sins realistically. Nobody likes to do that. But all of us need the experience.

Will Willimon says that in confession we are forced into honesty about our sin. Many of us come dressed in our Sunday best, all washed and scrubbed, smiling and friendly, but we are not as pure as we like to think we are. We admit that here, right now, at the very beginning, our hymns, our praying, our preaching are not some escape from reality. Confession keeps us tied to the truthful reality about our life together. You're not going to believe this, but some people say the Church is full of hypocrites. Well, confession allows us to admit that we are a gathering of sinners in the hopes of avoiding hypocrisy.

The Prayer of Confession is a willingness to be known, to lay oneself open before God, to come "Just as I am, without one plea." If Scott Peck is right in his book *People of the Lie* that evil arises in the refusal to acknowledge our own sins, then the Prayer of Confession in worship keeps evil from growing within us and keeps us from hiding behind the good. So we pray each week, "Forgive us our trespasses." We need that confession as individuals, as a congregation, as a nation and global community.

The tax collector's prayer is a plea for mercy: *God, be merciful to me, a sinner.* He comes as someone inferior to someone who is superior. There is humility to his words as he comes before a Holy God with his plea for mercy and forgiveness. And to make a "plea" means that there is no obligation on the part of the one being asked to grant mercy. He is saying, "Lord, I know I don't deserve it. I know I'm not worthy of it. But Lord, I need your mercy. I need your forgiveness."

Oscar Wilde, a very popular literary figure of his day, back in the nineteenth century, was caught in an act of public humiliation. And as he was carted off to prison, his reputation torn, he made a very flippant comment, saying, "God will forgive me; that's God's business." And forgiveness *is* God's business; else we would all be doomed. But we do not confess our sins with the attitude that God owes us forgiveness—that God is *supposed* to forgive us. The forgiveness of God is an undeserved gift of grace and mercy. The tax collector knew that. And you can tell it in his plea: *O God, have mercy on me.* That is how we should come confessing to God our sin. Confession is an acknowledgment of our sin; we are taking personal responsibility, making a plea for God's mercy, knowing full well we are undeserving of it. It is with a broken spirit and repentant heart that we offer our confession to God.

Confession is not for the purpose of beating us into a sense of guilt. We confess our sins in the security that we are loved and that God will not let us go. Confession of sin is never an end in itself. We confess our sin in order to confront our guilt and be met with God's forgiving grace in Jesus Christ. In the words of Robert Benson, "Confession is not only about the stupid stuff we did yesterday, it is also about the magnificent stuff God did while we were yet sinners."[2]

The guilt of confession apart from the grace of forgiveness is absolutely deadly. Because of God's great love we can be honest with God, with one another, and with ourselves. We have no need to hide our sin. For we have a high priest who is able to sympathize with our weakness, one with whom we can boldly come before the throne of grace to receive mercy and find grace to help in time of need. As far as the East is from the West, so far God has removed our transgressions from us. Such an encounter with grace through confession and pardon has the power to create a transformation within us.

If there is no forgiveness, then worship cannot continue. But there is forgiveness, and worship can continue. Life can go on. We can bask in the delight of God's love. We can live in

---

[2]Robert Benson, *Living Prayer* (New York: Putnam, 1998), p. 27.

the joy of sins forgiven and relationship restored. We can give thanks for the immeasurable, never-giving-up-no-matter-what love of God.—W. Gregory Pope

SERMON SUGGESTIONS

Topic: The Reformation Continues

TEXT: Luke 18:14

(1) As we live under the control of God who created us. (2) As we recognize our radical alienation from God, that is, our sin. (3) As we accept God's grace that removes the alienation. (4) In the text, the publican addresses God, confesses his sin, and is justified through God's grace.—Charles P. Price

Topic: Justification by Faith

TEXT: Luke 16:1–9

(1) Faith alone makes us good and makes us friends of God. (2) Good works are to be done out of free love, without seeking gain. (3) It is God alone, not saints, who receives us and bestows the rewards of eternity.—Martin Luther

WORSHIP AIDS

CALL TO WORSHIP.   "Grace and peace to you from God our Father and the Lord Jesus Christ" (Phil. 1:2 NIV).

INVOCATION.   Father of all, as we enter worship we are reminded that we know you through others who came before us. Their faithfulness and love prepared the way. May we too be faithful and loving, that those who come after us will know you. And may we celebrate your presence in this place. Lord, meet us here.

OFFERTORY SENTENCE.   "Everyone who has been given much, much will be demanded; and from the one who been entrusted with much, much more will be asked" (Luke 12:48 NIV).

OFFERTORY PRAYER.   Lord God, we give thanks that through tithes and offerings we may participate in the eternal work of your Kingdom. We dedicate our gifts as an opportunity to illuminate the future and to glorify your present work among us. May these gifts bring blessing to the One who is the light of the world.

PRAYER.   Lord Jesus Christ, we acknowledge you as the Son of God, the Savior of sinners, and the head of the Church. Triune God, we thank you that in your all-wise providence you have so directed history that the Protestant Reformation occurred. We rejoice as we celebrate it today. Holy Spirit, fill our hearts and enable us to learn from the Bible—the Word of God. Humble us so that we may understand the insufficiency of our own works and the total sufficiency of Jesus' work for our salvation. And encourage us to use the way of prayer that has been opened to us through Jesus' finished work. Quicken and strengthen faith in human hearts and unite your people around the truth of the gospel. Grant that the truths that we rediscovered at the time of the Protestant Reformation may find lodging in many hearts even today. Hear us, for Jesus' sake.—Joel Nederhood

SERMON
Topic: Seeing Clearly
TEXT: Ps. 34:1–8; Mark 10:46–52

The story from Mark's Gospel today is a story about a person who is described as being blind, and yet he sees extremely well. Bartimaeus, we are told, is a blind beggar. Yet when he hears that Jesus is coming by, he calls out, "Jesus, Son of David, have mercy on me!" ("Son of David" is a messianic title.) Bartimaeus, who is blind, can see who Jesus is before he ever sees him with his eyesight. He has great insight into the personal Jesus.

I. Bartimaeus can see what life is all about. And what life is all about in all four Gospels is that we are called to give life to those around us; we are called to give life away. He can see clearly things of the spirit. He knows what Jesus is about, and he knows what following Jesus means, and he chooses those things.

There is wonderful imagery in the story, when Bartimaeus is called by Jesus. We are told that he springs up and throws off his cloak. He is anxious to be about giving life to others because now he has received it himself, so he wants others to see as well. He is a man who may be blind but has no spiritual blind spots, no spiritual floaters. But what Bartimaeus demonstrates for us is that when we focus on Jesus, we can see clearly. When we see clearly, we will follow Jesus. It's a two-step process: focusing on him first and thus seeing all of life clearly, and then following him; in following him, we help others to see clearly as well.

II. This is Reformation Sunday. Those of us in the Protestant tradition tend, on this Sunday, to look back to Luther, or Calvin, or Wesley—our forbearers in the faith. We hope that from looking at their lives and their messages, we can learn for our lives. On this day, Mark helps us reform our lives by refocusing, by inviting us, and calling us to do what Bartimaeus did—to see Jesus, to see him clearly, and then to follow him. In that we will have clarity about our own lives, and we will be living clearer lives for others to follow as well. One of the things that amazes me is the style in which we live our lives in our culture. There are so many people living in compact areas with others. We have families living in small single-family dwellings. We have multiple-family dwellings that are inhabited by more and more people. And yet, in spite of all of that being together, there is such intense loneliness in our culture.

III. I am convinced that part of the problem is we do not take the time to see others and to understand others and to try and help others. Most often our vision is a very limited vision of seeing what those others can do for us, instead of what we can do for them. That always leads to loneliness. It is Bartimaeus' witness to us that if we can focus our life on Christ, we can see, and in seeing, we can see the need of others. Then we can relate to them and can overcome our loneliness; we can find community.

My friends, what is it in your personal life that you can't see today? What is it in our community life that escapes our vision? What is it in our national life that we cannot see, or in our global life? Whatever it is, this is a day to rejoice and to celebrate. This is a day to give thanks to God because of the witness of Bartimaeus. When we cry out to Jesus, "Help me to see," he is the one who can help us see clearly.—Jim Standiford

SUNDAY, NOVEMBER 4, 2007
Lectionary Message

Topic: Through the Eye of a Needle

TEXT: Luke 19:1–10

Other Readings: Hab. 1:1–4, 2:1–4; Ps. 119:137–144; 2 Thess. 1:1–4, 11–12

I. *What's up with Zacchaeus?* I will never forget the last time Jesus came to town. It was early in the day, and there was already a large crowd following him. We knew of Jesus' teaching and healing, so many of us dropped what we were doing and joined the crowd. As we moved along, I looked up, and there he was. But what was *he* doing here? What was the most despised man in town—Zacchaeus, the tax collector—doing here?

In our day, the Roman government contracted with local businessmen to collect taxes. These "chief tax collectors" were required to pay the Romans in advance. Then they would employ others to collect the taxes from the rest of us and make a handsome profit in the process. The system was often abused, and we assumed that any Jew who stooped to collecting taxes for Rome was dishonest, and we hated him for adding to our oppression.

Maybe that will help you understand why we were so surprised and disgruntled to see Zacchaeus that day. What did he want with Jesus? He couldn't collect taxes from him. Jesus was from Nazareth. What was up with him?

II. *Desperate men do desperate things.* What happened next was bizarre. All of a sudden Zacchaeus started running, right toward a tree. At first I thought he was going to steal some fruit. I wouldn't put that past a tax man, but the tree was a sycamore-fig, and only the poorest of the poor ate fruit from those trees. Zacchaeus would never stoop to that. No, he actually started climbing the tree. The branches were low, and it was easy to climb. But what was he doing?

As it turns out, he perched up there to get Jesus' attention, and what a sight he was. Picture the richest man in your town sitting up in a tree in a designer suit. We laughed at the sight of him and wondered what he was so desperate about—what made him shed all of his pretenses and dignity to climb a tree to get to Jesus.

We didn't have long to wait. Soon enough, Jesus, in the middle of this big crowd, was right underneath the tree where Zacchaeus was perched. We expected Jesus to blast Zacchaeus for working for Rome and for cheating us out of extra taxes. We just knew that was about to be done. We leaned forward in anticipation.

That wasn't what happened at all. Jesus paused under the tree, and very calmly, as if he conversed with tax collectors in trees every day, said, "Zacchaeus, hurry and come down, for I must stay at your house today." In a flash, Zacchaeus dropped out of that tree, and they started talking like long-lost friends.

We were outraged. Didn't Jesus realize Zacchaeus was unclean and that eating with him would make Jesus unclean, too? Why eat with him instead of with us law-abiding, righteous folks? It wasn't right.

As we were grumbling, Zacchaeus turned to Jesus and said, "Half of my possessions I will give to the poor; and if I have defrauded anyone of anything, I will repay them four times." We couldn't believe it. Did Zacchaeus hit his head in the tree? Was he putting on a show for Jesus? His offer of restitution went far beyond what the law required. To say we were suspicious was an understatement, but Jesus believed him. Jesus turned to us and said, "Today salvation has come to this house, because he, too, is a son of Abraham. For the Son of Man came to seek out and save the lost."

Well, that certainly quieted us down quickly. Who were we to question Jesus' judgment of a man? One-by-one we turned away. It was a lot like that day when the religious leaders gathered to stone the woman caught in adultery. Jesus said, "Let the one who is not guilty cast the first stone." One-by-one they realized they had no right to hurl anything at her. That's what we realized that day, too: we were all children of Abraham and all in need of grace, even—or especially—those of us who grumbled.

III. *Other lessons learned.* Another lesson we learned that day was how easy it is to maintain our prejudices and to think that people never change. Haven't you ever said, "Some people never change"? After all, Jesus said it was easier for a camel to go through the eye of a needle than for a rich man to enter the kingdom of heaven. But we saw it that day. The Kingdom of God was at work, and we saw Zacchaeus transformed before our eyes. If Jesus could work in his life, the possibilities were endless. It gave us a new perspective and a new hope.

We also learned that saving the lost has multiple meanings. Yes, Zacchaeus' eternity had changed, but he had been made whole in this life, too. There were social and economic dimensions (he became more fair and shared his wealth); we were a little less oppressed.

What about you? You live in uncertain times, just as we did. If you are like Zacchaeus, desperately searching for God, know this: God has already been searching for you, and your search can be over. No matter what you have done, Jesus is ready to walk beside you.

And the rest of us—we who follow God willingly but are prone to grumbling—remember that the Kingdom of God is among us. Let us open our eyes—we who have eyes to see and often do not see—and let us see and be willing to align ourselves with the work of God in the world. There is no telling what other miracles God may be about.—Tracy Hartman

SERMON SUGGESTIONS

Topic: I Am a Millionaire
TEXT: 1 Cor. 3:21–23
(1) The ministry to which we have been called is a gift to us. (2) The world for which Christ died is a gift to us. (3) Life itself is a gift of unmeasured worth.—Perry F. Webb

Topic: Do You Want to Be Rich?
TEXT: Acts 20:35
(1) Try giving yourself away. (2) Spend life for that which will live beyond it. (3) Invest yourself in mercy and justice. (4) Give yourself to the wisdom and work of Jesus Christ.—Everett Palmer

WORSHIP AIDS
CALL TO WORSHIP. "How lovely is your dwelling place, O Lord Almighty! My soul yearns, even faints, for the courts of the Lord; my heart and my flesh cry out for the living God" (Ps. 84:1–2 NIV).

INVOCATION. Lord, you have taught us that the love of money is the root of all evil. Teach us now to love that which money cannot buy: opportunity and not security, participation in the world and not withdrawal from it, usefulness and not prestige. Help us to manage our earthly affairs in the spirit of our Savior, Jesus.

OFFERTORY SENTENCE.   "But just as you excel in everything—in faith, in speech, in knowledge, in complete earnestness and in your love for us—see that you also excel in this grace of giving" (1 Cor. 8:7 NIV).

OFFERTORY PRAYER.   We praise you, O Lord, for the unmeasured gifts of your grace—the countless blessings that come from your generous heart. Accept these gifts we bring as expressions of our gratitude.

PRAYER.   We come into this sanctuary, God, to praise you, to talk to you, and to listen to you. It is a place to be still sometimes and know that you are God. Here we can leave for a little while the tragic images of war and terror, and the constant appearances of those who come and go in positions of responsibility for the governance of our country. Here we look for that ephemeral rainbow of light—our only decoration, the little prism in the window. We watch the closely moving changes of our seasons, seen as murals with our lovely windows forming their frames. We have respite from the ever-thronging traffic and from the machines, the motors, the keyboards that our lives require us to care for. In this sanctuary we listen to the voices of our choir and of our congregation, who share the feelings so many of us have in times of grief, in periods of anxiety, and in episodes of great joy. We are with each other. And we truly understand that where two or three are gathered together in your name, here you are in the midst of us. We are grateful that in this place our ministers, who know your ways, can give us new perspectives, new insights to help us to live with the wisdom, and the courage we so much need.—Marnie Wengren

SERMON
Topic: The Church—God's Giving People
TEXT: Phil. 4:10–19; Matt. 22:15–22

Here in the last chapter of Philippians we find the apostle Paul writing a thank-you note, almost as an addendum to this letter. They have once more taken up an offering to send to Paul. In this offering Paul sensed their love and devotion, not merely to him but to Christ. Why should we, as Christians, bring tithes and offerings to the church? This morning I wish to review some basic principles of Christian giving that are inseparable from being a follower of Jesus Christ.

I. The tithe is the Lord's. Throughout the Bible, from the offerings to Cain and Abel to the prophetic accusations of Malachi that God's people have robbed God, from Jesus' affirmation that the tithe is something we should do—and more—to the letters of Paul, the note sounded is consistent and firm: the tithe belongs to the Lord.

Are you aware that the New Testament says five times as much about money as it does about prayer and six times as much as about eternal life? Tithing is God's way of protecting us from the demon-god of materialism. If you wish a prescription for disaster for your personal and spiritual life, then become materialistic.

II. Tithing is God's way of spreading the gospel of Jesus Christ throughout the world. When God's people bring God's money to God's house, then God's work flourishes. What we are doing here is not the same as the Rotary Club or any other civic organization. We are about God's business—the business of sharing the good news of Jesus Christ here and around the world. This does not mean that Christians do not use these other organizations as a part of their Christian witness. They do, and do so well. However, with all their good and worthy programs, none of these has as its main tenet the spreading of the gospel of Jesus Christ. None of these other organizations are focused on bringing persons to a loving relationship with Jesus Christ.

III. Tithing is a first-level matter of our faith relationship with Jesus Christ. The more we cling to possessions, the less room we have to open our hearts to the love of God. If we are unwilling to return 10 percent of our income to God and trust that God will enable us to live on the remaining 90 percent, then how in the world can we trust God with our eternal destiny? Until you tithe, until you get this matter of ownership settled (it all belongs to God), then you will never have the joy, the peace, and the personal satisfaction that comes from full obedience to the call of Christ.

IV. No one can outgive God. The Philippian church knew the joy of giving to support the spread of the gospel. Why did they do this so well and, seemingly, so often? Because they knew that when they gave, they received so much more than they had ever imagined.

We are confused with our image of God. God is too small for many of us. We do not think that God can take care of us—or else we just do not want to do what God has commanded, in which case we should take a hard look at our commitment to Jesus Christ from the bottom to the top.—Robert U. Ferguson

SUNDAY, NOVEMBER 11, 2007
Lectionary Message

What Do You *Really* Want to Know?

TEXT: Luke 20:27–38

Other Readings: Hag. 2:1–9; Ps. 145:1–5, 17–21; 2 Thess. 2:1–5, 13–17

I. *Wondering about heaven.* What are your questions about heaven? Do you wonder whether heaven will really have streets of gold and pearly mansions, or whether angels really sport feathery wings? Do you wonder whom you will see there and how you will relate to people you love in eternity? Children sometimes ask if a favorite pet will be waiting for them on the other side. Adults sometimes eagerly await a joyful reunion with a parent, a beloved spouse, or even a child who has gone on before.

On the surface, today's Gospel lesson seems to answer the basic question about marriage in heaven. In response to the Sadducees' overly exaggerated question about which man a woman who had been married eight times would be married to in heaven, Jesus responds that in the resurrection, we will not be married at all. For folks who have been happily married, this perhaps comes as a disappointment. For others who have spent time in less-than-ideal marriages, this may be a huge relief.

However, Jesus' answer addresses much more than marriage issues. An understanding of the world in Jesus' day will help us understand how he knew what the Sadducees *really* wanted to know.

II. *A deeper look.* In Jesus' day, as in ours, there were good religious people who had a hard time agreeing on much of anything. The Sadducees and Pharisees were two such groups. The Sadducees were wealthy men, members of the priesthood. They rejected the authority of oral tradition, accepted the Law of Moses, and denied a belief in angels and in the resurrection. They disagreed with the Pharisees on nearly all of these issues. The Sadducees' question about marriage in the next life was more about the reality of a bodily resurrection than it was about marital relations in eternity. They had a theological debate going with the Pharisees that they wanted Jesus to settle.

First, Jesus dealt with their presenting questions about marriage in the afterlife. When we read his response, we must remember that in the first-century world, marriage was viewed primarily as an arrangement between a man who had a "right" to a wife and a woman who had a "right" to male support. Jesus makes it clear that there will be no need for such arrangements in heaven.

Then Jesus deals with the larger issue of the resurrection from the dead. Again Jesus makes it clear that he believes in the resurrection (he calls those who have gone on "children of the resurrection"). He then reminds the Sadducees, who did not believe in the resurrection but did believe in the Law of Moses, that Moses believed in the resurrection as well. He called on one they viewed as an authority to support his position. By declaring the God he encountered in the burning bush to be "The God of Abraham, the God of Isaac, and the God of Jacob," Moses was saying, in essence, that these pioneers of the faith were very much alive in God. They had been resurrected. Finally, Jesus seals his argument by saying God is the God of the living, not the dead, for to God all of them are indeed alive.

III. *What do we really want to know?* I imagine that most of us are somewhat like the Sadducees. We may believe in our heads that there is an afterlife, but we honestly can't imagine what it will really be like. This is true of much in our lives now. When we are young, we look forward to starting school, but we can't imagine what that will really be like. As we move toward adulthood, we anticipate falling in love and getting married, but we can't really know what that is like until we experience it. A child is not yet able to grasp the complexities or the pleasures of adulthood. As we get older, we know that one day we will die and transition into the next life, but the unknown and the finality of that move can make it hard for us to even want to imagine what that may be like.

As humans, we are not yet able to grasp the complexities or the pleasures of the resurrection and the life beyond. Sometimes all we can do is recognize the mystery of the unknown and the limitations of our own understandings. The apostle Paul says it this way: "When I was a child, I spoke as a child, I reasoned as a child; when I became an adult, I put an end to childish ways. For now we see in a mirror dimly, but then we will see face to face. Now I know only in part; then I will know fully, even as I have been fully known" (1 Cor. 13:11–12).

The God who created human life, complete with marriage, has provided life after death for those who respond to God's love. It is a gift, albeit one that I am not permitted to open yet. For now, that's all I *really* need to know.—Tracy Hartman

SERMON SUGGESTIONS

Topic: The Kingdom Message
TEXT: Mark 1:14–15
(1) Delivered in confidence and authority. (2) Announces the in-breaking of God's rule. (3) Calls sinners to repentance.—Lawrence Vowan

Topic: Always in Debt
TEXT: Rom. 1:14–15
(1) We fear debt. (2) We seek independence and freedom. (3) We can never be out of debt. (4) A strange joy comes in acknowledging our debt.—Gerald Kennedy

WORSHIP AIDS

CALL TO WORSHIP.   "Give ear to my words, O Lord, consider my singing. Listen to my cry for help, my King and my God, for to you I pray. In the morning, O Lord, you hear my voice; in the morning I lay my requests before you and wait in expectation" (Ps. 5:1–3 NIV).

INVOCATION.   Father of all, we are grateful for the beautiful world you created, for the singing birds, the radiant flowers, the blue sky, the soft breeze; we too are thankful for the dark night that gives way to the light of day; for the good earth, which produces such bounty—wheat, corn, beans—that our bodies may be fed. Help us now to share this treasure with all who are in need.

OFFERTORY SENTENCE.   "The earth is the Lord's, and the fullness thereof; the world, and they that dwell therein" (Ps. 24:1 KJV).

OFFERTORY PRAYER.   Lord, you have given us the privilege of life and filled us with many gifts. Help us now to magnify eternal values and to express by our lives and our tithes the living Christ who guides our way.

PRAYER.   O Lord, you have been our dwelling place in all generations. No matter how many idols we have sought to fashion, you remain our God—the only god worthy of the name. So we bring our prayer, asking that our devotion will be deepened today, that our commitment will be more genuine. Help us not only to say that we believe but also to live what we believe, to know from experience what it means to call you "Lord." In our joys and in our sorrows, we seek thy presence. In youth and in old age we believe that you come to us and give meaning to whatever life may offer.

As we worship this morning, we give thanks for the good news—the gospel of Jesus Christ—for the belief that while we were yet sinners, Christ died for us. We have so much for which we are grateful, and yet there are some at worship today who cannot respond to the good news. Their spiritual sensitivities are clouded by the trouble and the pain of their lives. You know, O God, who we are; we are those overcome by bad news; we are those who feel left out, perhaps those betrayed by a friend. We are those who cannot drop the burden that we feel for a loved one, those who seek healing for a great loss. We are those who understand that the disease in our body threatens life itself. And so for all of these and others as well, we lift our hearts in prayer. Let them hear the good news of thy love; let them see the light of thy presence. Bring the gospel to life, we pray, in all our shadowy valleys of death. In the name of Christ.—Charles F. Hoffman

SERMON

Topic: Three Philosophies of Life
TEXT: Luke 10:25–37; Acts 20:35

As we study the parable of the Good Samaritan that was read from Luke, we see something of the benevolent spirit. But we also see there two other approaches to life. Indeed, we can find in the parable of the Good Samaritan three philosophies of life—three philosophies that were as real and prevalent in Jesus' day as they are today.

I. The first philosophy of life we see here is "what's yours is mine." This is the philosophy of the robbers who beat and stripped the unfortunate traveler. It is the philosophy we see every day in the morning paper and on the evening news. With little regard for human life and the personal property of others, those who hold the philosophy that what's yours is mine, break and enter, rob and steal, take by force, sometimes injuring and killing in the process. For these people, the eighth commandment means nothing.

II. A second philosophy of life we see in this parable is "what's mine is mine, and I'm going to keep it." This is the philosophy we see in the priest and Levite who saw the man beaten and bleeding alongside the road but who passed by on the other side. Not only did they not want to get involved and soil their clothes, they had no desire to give what the unfortunate traveler needed. Many folks fall into this what's-mine-is-mine mind-set today. They work hard, they earn their money, and they keep it, never even considering giving a portion of it to charity.

III. Thank God there is a third philosophy of life: "what's mine is yours." This is the philosophy we see epitomized in the Good Samaritan. The Samaritan was moved with pity or compassion for his fellow human being. This, Jesus said, is the kind of neighbor all of us should strive to be—the kind of neighbor who is ready to give, to share, to sacrifice. "Go and do likewise," Jesus says.

The practice of giving is the natural way of the world. Giving is an eternal law of the universe. God gives; the earth gives its produce; the sun gives warmth; the clouds give rain; the trees give shade, shelter, fruit, beauty, and oxygen; the animals of the field give us meat, milk, and cheese. The whole world survives on the principle of giving. How can we not give in return? It is through giving that we can make a difference in the world.

Three philosophies of life: (1) what's yours is mine, and I want it, (2) what's mine is mine, and I'm going to keep it, and (3) what's mine is yours, for I'm willing to share it. What will your philosophy be? Before you answer, remember the words of Jesus: "It is more blessed to give than to receive."—Randy Hammer

SUNDAY, NOVEMBER 18, 2007
Lectionary Message

Topic: Not Yet
TEXT: Luke 21:5–19
Other Readings: Isa. 65:17–25; (responsive reading): Isa. 12; 2 Thess. 3:6–13

Are these the last days? Since the time of Jesus, people have been asking this question. The new millennium brought a rash of predictions about when the end of the world would occur, and the interest continues. What do we make of these texts that deal with the end of time? What is their message for today?

I. *Message to the first readers.* To understand what this passage means for us, we must understand its meaning for the original readers. The Gospel of Luke was written around 80–85 A.D. By then, almost fifty years had passed since Jesus had been crucified and resurrected, and eyewitnesses were passing away. Controversy was arising about who Jesus was, his purpose in coming, and who the early Church should be. Luke was writing primarily to Gentiles to address these issues.

Today's passage occurs late in Jesus' ministry, between Palm Sunday and the Last Supper on Thursday. Tensions were high, and the religious authorities were after Jesus. In this context, Jesus announces that the Temple will be destroyed. Immediately, the crowd asks the questions that we still ask today: When will this be? and What signs should we look for? Jesus said nothing about a sign, but the hearers assumed that there must be one, probably because Old Testament prophets had identified signs signaling the destruction or deliverance of Jerusalem. But instead of answering their questions, Jesus issued three warnings: do not be led astray; do not follow false prophets; and do not be terrified.

Jesus' first warning—not to be led astray—encompassed being led into sin, being taught false teachings, and being deceived about end-time events. Concern over deception about the end of time led to his warning not to follow false prophets. Then Jesus warned listeners not to be terrified by the inevitable wars.

The difficulty in today's text is sorting out what parts of the passage refer to readers' present situation and what parts refer to the end of time. Scholars believe that verses 5–11 refer to the destruction of the Temple in 70 A.D., after Jesus had died but before Luke wrote this Gospel. Verses 12–19 refer to the disciples' immediate future—events that would occur after Jesus died but before the destruction of the Temple. Almost all of the events predicted in these verses occurred in the book of Acts.

Verses 12–19 serve as both a warning of coming trials and an exhortation to prepare to endure them faithfully. In his letter to the churches, James encourages early Christians to face trials with joy, knowing that "the testing of your faith produces endurance." Further, he adds, "Let endurance have its full effect, so that you may be mature and complete, lacking in nothing." In the Gospel, Luke concludes with one last lesson on how to save one's life. Those who seek to save their lives will lose them, but saving one's life comes from losing it for Jesus' sake. Such discipleship will require endurance, but the result is that one gains life.

II. *Message for today's readers.* But what do these verses mean for us today? Jesus' words about the future command a special fascination for those in every generation who seek signs of the end times. In times of great danger, stress, and hardship, it is natural for persons and communities of faith to turn to God and to the future for hope and the promise of deliverance. But for those who have the power to relieve suffering and oppression, as most Americans do, idle preoccupation with the prophecies of the end times can be a perversion of the gospel. We all need to distinguish biblical teachings and sound biblical interpretation from the sensational claims carried by the media and current-day false prophets. Jesus did not call his disciples— or us—to *be* prophets but to disregard the false prophets and not to be led astray.

For some in every generation, religion is simply a form of escape into the fantasy of futurism. Although they may look for that in these texts, today's Gospel reading does not offer a way of predicting the end of the world. Rather, Jesus offers the spiritual resources to cope with adversity and hardship. Following Jesus always exposes the faithful to opposition from the authorities. But every generation has also had its courageous and prophetic visionaries who devoted themselves to Jesus' call to create community, oppose injustice, work for peace, and make a place for the excluded.

III. *Application.* These verses allow us to examine two visions of what it means to follow Jesus. One is focused on prophecies of the future and makes little-to-no difference in how one lives in the here-and-now. The other calls for such a commitment of life that those who dare to embrace it may find themselves among the persecuted.

In the book of Revelation, we read about the perfect world that is to come—a land where there is joy and delight, where there will be no suffering and weeping. That day is coming, but we do not know when or where. For now, dangers and hardships for the faithful are real indeed. Truth is tested and faith is confirmed, not in idle speculation but in the crucible of adversity. Those who wish to find a more vibrant religious experience, therefore, should look not for signs of the future but for signals that it is time to live by Jesus' call for obedience right here, right now. Every generation is called back to the teachings of Jesus by the examples of those who have suffered persecution and hardship. These disciples dared to strive to live out Jesus' call for a community that transcends social barriers, that cares for its least privileged, and that confronts abuses of power and wealth. May it be so for us, even as we wait. In the meantime, "Do not be terrified."—Tracy Hartman

SERMON SUGGESTIONS

Topic: A Lesson in Thanksgiving

TEXT: Luke 17:11–19

(1) Noble thanksgiving is expressed by the example of the single leper, a Samaritan, who returned to give thanks to Jesus. (2) The other nine perhaps had good reasons for not returning, echoing our modern responses. (3) Only the one who returned received the healing of his soul: "Go your way, your faith has made you whole."—Jerry Hayner

Topic: A Call to Celebration

TEXT: Num. 10:10

(1) We have a heritage of growth to celebrate. (2) A heritage of outreach to celebrate. (3) A heritage of sacrificial service to celebrate. (4) A heritage of challenge to celebrate.—Hoover Rupert

WORSHIP AIDS

CALL TO WORSHIP. "Enter into his gates with thanksgiving, and into his courts with praise: be thankful unto him, and bless his name. For the Lord is good; his mercy is everlasting; and his truth endureth to all generations" (Ps. 100:4–5 KJV).

INVOCATION. Father, we are grateful for the Thanksgiving season. Today we recognize the bounty of your favor so lavishly given. May every day and every season and each of your gifts to us be occasions for such gratitude throughout the year. Even as your mercies are new each morning, may our praise raise to you each day and hour.

OFFERTORY SENTENCE. "Thanks be unto God for his unspeakable gift" (2 Cor. 9:15).

OFFERTORY PRAYER. O Lord, we truly give thanks this day for your gifts to us and are reminded that every good and perfect gift comes from above. Receive these gifts, make them holy, and use them according to your will to encourage the ministries of your Kingdom.

PRAYER. Eternal God, we come in prayer to you this day with a sense of thanksgiving for all the gifts that we have received from your hand. We thank you for the gift of life, for love, for work, play, hopes and dreams, and tasks to be done. We thank you for the sacrifices and ideals we have inherited from our forefathers and foremothers, who made the way that we might live and exist in this particular time in our history as a nation.

We confess today that too often we come to you only with our problems. So this day we pause to say thanks. We thank you for accepting us when we are unacceptable. We thank you for hope when we have lost our dreams, for your presence when we feel abandoned. Thank you for all of the wonder, mystery, and beauty in our world, for the touch of friends when the burdens of life get heavy, for moments of silence in a busy world. We thank you for your hand of assurance when life crashes in upon us, for the joy of helping others when they are in need, for the assurance that you have made a place for each of us when we feel inadequate.

We thank you for the gift of life when we feel defeated, for the struggles of life when we become too complacent. We thank you for your peace in times of fear, for forgiveness when we fail and sin, and for your love when we feel unloved. We thank you for the freedom we have in this country. But above all, Father, we are grateful for the sense of your sustaining power that has come through your grace that continuously blesses us. Through Jesus Christ, who loves us and gave himself for us, we pray.—William Powell Tuck

SERMON
Topic: Thanksgiving
TEXT: Matt. 6:25

"Therefore I tell you, do not worry about your life" (Matt. 6:25). If only it was that easy. Just consider how indigenous worrying is to the human condition. Even as children we worry about everything from losing our homework to missing the bus; some children worry about whether they can make it home safely; others worry about whether their parents will ever stop arguing.

As young adults, we worry about finding the right job or the right mate and about having friendships that are mutually supportive and satisfying. In midlife, we worry about our children and about finding the right place to settle; we worry about whether or not our marriages will last, whether our jobs are secure. Later in life, we worry about our adult children, our grandchildren, our health, and where we will spend our last years.

I. Regardless of our age, education, gender, race, or economic state, worrying is a normal exercise for the human psyche. It is no accident that this passage from Matthew's Gospel is the one presented for the day we call Thanksgiving. Have you noticed that we are more apt to speak to God of what we need and what we are anxious about than we are to say thank you for the people, places, and things we enjoy?

Gratitude is an acquired state of heart and mind. Life and breath are gifts. We are here on earth for only a few moments when we think in terms of eternity. Life is fragile. To spend our short and precious time here pining for what could have been or should have been is to squander our appreciation for what is. I daresay many of us have had experiences of loss, illness, or betrayal when we've felt bereft, like men and women out of God's mind, left teetering in a world where chaos rules—at least for a season. And in those times, it is hard to summon up gratitude for what remains, though that is what heroes and heroines—people of faith—do.

II. What Jesus is telling us in this Gospel passage is that as our faith and trust in his love increase, our anxiety decreases. As we are more and more able to seek God first, everything else in life arrives at its rightful place. It is difficult to be grateful for what we have, for what is right around us, when we are sad, angry, or devastated about what we don't have. Jesus is reminding us in this passage that if God cares for the birds of the air and the lilies of the filed, ensuring that they have what is necessary for their well-being, how much more will God supply what we need for ours—we, who are made in God's image; we, who are known to God by name; we, for whom God sent Christ into the world?

III. When we are anxious about what we will eat or drink or wear, we miss out on so much of the sheer enjoyment for which Christians are made. We need these things. There's no doubt about that, and life is frightening without them, yet we are told that God already knows we need these things.

Jesus invites us to let go of the fear and anxiety and to rest in the assurance that God is with us and for us. When we seek God's Kingdom first, God is with us, even when we feel most alone, most without.

Let me end with God's words to the prophet Isaiah: "Fear not, for I have redeemed you. I have called you by name. You are mine. When you pass through the waters, I will be with you, and when you walk through the rivers, they will not overwhelm you. When you walk through fire, you shall not be burned, and the flame shall not consume you. You are precious in my eyes, and honored and loved."—Ann Stevenson

SUNDAY, NOVEMBER 25, 2007
Lectionary Message
Topic: What Kind of King? (Christ the King Sunday)
Text: Jer. 23:1–6
Other Readings: (responsive reading): Col. 1:11–20; Luke 23:33–43

I. *What does "king" make you think of?* What do you think of when you hear the words *king* or *royalty?* Americans have never been under the rule of a king or queen, so our experience is limited. Some of us may think of Disney characters or fairytale kings or queens. These rulers are often wicked characters that need to be overthrown. Others may think of the British royals. In our day, these kings and queens, princes and princesses serve largely as figureheads rather than as rulers with any real power. We follow the royals for entertainment and for soap opera value, not for the leadership they provide. Today, on Christ the King Sunday, it is hard for us to get an accurate picture of what Christ-as-King means.

The people of Israel had clear ideas of what they expected in a king. Early in their history, God was the King of Israel. At first, the patriarchs (Abraham through Moses) led Israel. After the people became too numerous to be led by one person, judges or charismatic warlords were appointed to lead the people. But these judges were often unfaithful to Yahweh, and the people asked for a king. Even though God warned them against rejecting God's kingship in favor of an earthly king, the people insisted. They wanted a visible political ruler who would provide military protection and help Israel look like other nations. But just as God predicted, the kings soon ceased to follow Yahweh, and eventually other countries defeated both the Northern and Southern kingdoms. Israel ceased to exist as a nation and, once again, the people found themselves oppressed by unfriendly foreigners.

II. *Jesus as the King?* By the time of Jesus, many faithful Jews were tired of oppression by the Romans. They were anxious for a messiah who would once again be the political ruler who would re-establish Israel as a nation and free the people from the domination of others. Once again, they were clear about the kind of king they wanted. They may have recalled the words of Jeremiah in 23:5: "The days are surely coming, says the Lord, when I will raise up for David a righteous Branch, and he shall reign as king and deal wisely, and shall execute justice and righteousness in the land." Although these words were originally written during an earlier (though no less tumultuous) time in Jewish history, Jews in Jesus' day would have certainly resonated with this promise as well.

The Israelites who were looking for this kind of king found themselves sorely disappointed. For in today's Gospel passage, we find the King of the Jews being put to death at the hands of the Romans who continued to oppress Israel. Instead of Jesus wearing a royal robe, we find the soldiers casting lots for his simple clothing. Mockingly they cried, "If you are King of the Jews, save yourself." One of the criminals beside him joined in, saying, "Are you not the Messiah? Save yourself and us!" What kind of king was this?

III. *Christ the King.* What kind of king indeed? Obviously, Jesus did not intend to be a political leader. So what can we expect of Christ the King? Surely, he is not a fairytale ruler or an evil king who needs to be overthrown. And surely, he is more than a benevolent figurehead without any real power at all. So what kind of king is he?

The apostle Paul describes Christ the King this way:

He is the image of the invisible God, the firstborn of all creation; for in him all things in heaven and on earth were created, things visible and invisible, whether thrones or dominions or rulers or powers—all things have been created through him and for him. He himself is before all things, and in him all things hold together. He is the head of the body, the church; he is the beginning, the firstborn from the dead, so that he might come to have first place in everything. For in him all the fullness of God was pleased to dwell, and through him God was pleased to reconcile to himself all things, whether on earth or in heaven, by making peace through the blood of his cross.

Paul helps us to gain a much more comprehensive picture of kingship. In this passage, we see a king who has power and dominion far beyond the earthly realm. We see Christ as Creator, with God, of the universe, redeemer of humanity, and head (or king) of his body—the Church. Yet we also see a king who lived his earthly life in humble service, one who came not to impress the rich and powerful but one who came to heal, to restore, and to redeem, one who was willing to give his very life for the people he loved, one who was willing to forgive the thief on the cross beside him and welcome him into paradise.

It seems, then, that only one question remains: What kinds of subjects are worthy to serve this servant-ruler of the universe? What, indeed, can Christ the King expect from us?—Tracy Hartman

SERMON SUGGESTIONS

Topic: God's Provisions

TEXT: Phil. 4:19

(1) God's provisions are sure: "My God will supply . . ." (2) They are sufficient: "all your needs." (3) They derive from God's grace: "according to his riches in glory."—Brian Harbour

Topic: The Right Book

TEXT: Ps. 12:6

(1) The Bible has the right questions. (2) The Bible has the right answers. (3) The Bible gives us the right vision.—Gerald Kennedy

WORSHIP AIDS

CALL TO WORSHIP.   "Whatsoever things are true, whatsoever things are honest, whatsoever things are just, whatsoever things are pure, whatsoever things are lovely, whatsoever things are of good report; if there be any virtue, and if there be any praise, think of these things" (Phil. 4:8 KJV).

INVOCATION.   Kind, divine Father, you have left us your Holy Word to be a lamp unto our feet, a light unto our path. From your Word may we this day learn, as guided by the Spirit, what is your will, and may we frame our lives in obedience to it. All to your honor and glory.

OFFERTORY SENTENCE.   "Upon the first day of the week let every one of you lay by him in store, as God hath prospered him" (1 Cor. 16:2 KJV).

OFFERTORY PRAYER.   Father, may we today see clearly your providential hand at work in all the experiences of our lives. Encourage us now to have such boldness of character and clarity of faith that we shall offer these gifts with unselfish joy.

PRAYER.   Our Father, in the eternal scheme of things it seems that you are always the giver and we are the takers. All we have to offer in return is our thanks and ourselves. It is therefore entirely appropriate that our prayer during this special season of thanksgiving be dedicated to that purpose. We thank you, Father, not only for the common blessings but for the special blessings—special blessings so soon forgotten. We thank you for the faint sparks of peace that on occasion shine around the world. We thank you for those times when we cried out in desperation and found you were there, for those moments of crisis when we were sure we would perish without your sustaining power and found it readily available. We thank you for those special blessings that surprise us or confound us but always, undeniably, rescue us. And we thank you for the greatest blessings; in the words of Paul, "Thanks be to God for his unspeakable gift," for your Son, our Lord, without whom both life in the flesh and life in the spirit would be impossible. Help us to celebrate this season in the spirit of those first celebrants huddled on the shore of a strange new land, who found that the abundance of this earth could be shared with people of other cultures and customs who knew that whatever else separates us, we have in common our dependence upon your Spirit. Since we are all takers, Lord, help us not to be among those who take for granted but those who take with gratitude. We ask this all in the name of Christ.—Robert Morley

SERMON
Topic: One Last Time
TEXT: Luke 9:51–56

To encounter Jesus is to meet the most fascinating person who has ever lived. I believe Jesus is the most completely authentic, the most completely real human being ever to have drawn breath on this planet. There is clarity about this man. He's open and honest. He's a truth teller. His purposes are never nebulous. Jesus pushes the edges of the envelope and takes us further than we ever thought it was possible to go.

I. The Gospel according to Luke includes more episodes from Jesus' final journey to Jerusalem than any of the other Gospels. Included in Luke are some of the most beloved of Jesus' parables, along with some of his most difficult sayings. Once Jesus has "set his face towards Jerusalem," an underlying urgency permeates his teachings, which compel even the passing listener to wake up and pay close attention.

And as Jesus grows in his understanding that his time is drawing near, he focuses on transmitting his core message to the disciples closest to him. He tells them some hard things like, "Occasions for stumbling are bound to come, but woe to anyone by whom they come! It would be better for you if a millstone were hung around your neck and you were thrown into the sea than for you to cause one of these little ones to stumble. Be on your guard!"

The disciples, who are beginning to understand the challenge Jesus presents to live by a "kingdom ethic in which they would be repeatedly called upon to confront and forgive one another, beg Jesus with a mixture of fear and desperation, Increase our faith!" It's a legitimate request. When the disciples understand the size of the task, they want what they feel they don't have.

II. But we all want what we don't have. And Jesus must tell his disciples that more faith is not what they really need. "They need to understand that faith enables God to work in a person's life in ways that defy ordinary human experience. Even with a grain, a speck of faith, they can live by his teachings on discipleship."

To "know who you have believed" makes everything new. And because Jesus knows so completely who he is, he helps us to know ourselves. He knows every human being wants to be "about something." He knows no one is satisfied with simply putting in time and surviving 'til Friday. He knows we *want* more because we've been created to *be* more. It's in our bones. And so Jesus continues to teach his disciples about how to live.

III. I believe every human being is a gift from God. Look at yourself. Look at your life! You are so incredibly precious to God! When God looks at you, God sees God's very own child. God's grace is a gift, waiting to be received by people like us—people who have so little faith sometimes that we can barely see the tiny seeds of it in our outstretched hands. Isn't it amazing that the One who knows us best, the One who knows everything about us, is the One who loves us most?—Dean Elliott Wolfe

SUNDAY, DECEMBER 2, 2007

Lectionary Message

Topic: The Dream of a Peace-Loving Man

TEXT: Isa. 2:1–5

Other Readings: Ps. 122; Rom. 13:11–14; Matt. 24:36–44

In those years just before and during World War II, I remember hearing my parents and other adults talking a lot about lasting peace. When the fighting in Europe and the Pacific was at its worst, they would declare that such was the price you had to pay to obtain peace. All I knew was that newsreels and radio news told of war horrors that frightened a young boy and caused him to wish for the day when people everywhere would learn to live in peace. I still remember feeling relief when the news came that victory had come in Europe, followed soon by victory in the Pacific. It was, for those of us who had lived most of our lives in a war-dominated period, a feeling of new beginnings, when everything would be better and, above all, peaceful.

The dreams that dominated that period of my life were not new dreams. They are likely as old as history itself. How many times has some visionary surveyed the present chaos in which life is lived, where war is ravaging the land, and dreamed of peace? We know that the Bible records visionaries who dreamed such a dream. The prophet Micah tells us of such a dream of vision (4:1–3). Such was the case with Isaiah, that prince of prophets, as recorded in the passage for today. He certainly lived in a dangerous world where war seemed imminent. Little Judah was overshadowed by large empire-hungry powers that hung like a dark cloud on the northern horizon. At any moment the overwhelming forces of invaders could sweep through the land like a devastating tsunami. Momentary peace fostered a false sense of security among the people, and the prophet knew that what passed as peace was in danger of being destroyed with the coming of the next dawn. Prosperity had dulled the senses of the multitudes and caused them to think that they were secure in their little cocoon. In the midst of the unstableness of his times, Isaiah had a vision—a dream of a day when nations and people would live at peace with one another, a time when wars would be no more and the instruments of war would be put to use enhancing the peace and meeting the daily needs of the people. For him it was no futuristic vision for some other time in history or beyond history. He dreamed of a permanent peace for his people in his time.

In our present world, with its endless conflicts, incidents of terrorism, and nuclear threats, we might do well to take a long look at Isaiah's vision for a peaceful world. What pathway did he indicate as the way that ensures a world at peace?

I. The pathway to peace must begin with a return to the Lord. Isaiah speaks of the Lord's house being established and people inviting each other to go to where God is that he may teach them his ways so they can walk in his paths (vv. 2–3). Returning to the Lord has always been seen as the pathway to righteous reform that leads to lasting peace. Such has been the call of prophets and seers throughout history. Especially has that call been sounded by Jesus, the Prince of Peace.

When God's ways, God's path, and God's laws are ignored and replaced with man's wisdom, man's decisions, and man's ideals, peace is shattered. Some strong and charismatic leader can quickly take a nation down a pathway to ruin or set a nation on a road that destroys peace. We have witnessed that too often in our own times. It is only when men and nations return to the Lord that there is any hope for peace among individuals that can lead to peace in communities, followed by peace in nations, and, finally, peace among nations. In our fragmented and fragile world, is it not time that we heard and answered the call to return to the Lord?

II. The pathway to peace will lead to building the future on a foundation of faith that is rooted in God (v. 3). Isaiah saw the day when people and nations would willingly walk the pathways of God. This would be no forced walk, but a walk of faith in the trust that God would accomplish his high and lasting purpose of peace. Only Godlike faith will suffice as an indestructible basis for peace. Godlike faith is so designed that it believes in others, even when others do not believe. It seeks the highest in others, even when the highest is not easy to discover. It works to resolve hard differences, even when to do so is a danger to the cause, as well as personally. Godlike faith turns the other cheek, walks the second mile, and gives what is necessary to win the trust and faith of the adversary without compromising integrity and truth. Isaiah understood that only such a foundation of faith would secure God's kind of lasting peace. He knew what we must not forget—that faith in God leads to faith in ourselves and fosters faith in others. In our world where trust is so often a missing commodity, is it not time that we began to build the future on the solid foundation of faith, exemplified by walking the pathways of God?

III. Following God's pathway to peace, as envisioned by Isaiah, will lead to turning all the weapons of war into productive instruments for peaceful use (v. 4). Such will not happen unless and until men and women of peace truly turn to God and build solid, peaceful foundations on the bedrock of faith in him. Through the ages all other approaches to peace have been tried and have failed. Throughout history men have followed the gods of war, building ever more powerful weapons of destruction and death, declaring that such is the way to ensure lasting peace. This method has failed. Negotiators of every stripe have sat around tables to hammer out peace treaties designed by the wisdom of man. Such treaties have not lasted. Highly hailed documents of peace and arms agreements have been ignored multiple times.

Is it not time that we listen closely to the dream of the visionary prophet? Is not all that we are called to do as followers of Christ designed to make peace everywhere and at every level of human relationships a reality? Is it not time for each of us to truly come unto the Lord, build our lives on the solid foundation of Godlike faith so that we can live at peace with ourselves, our families, our neighbors, and the world? Is it not time for us to beat our personal swords into plowshares and our spears into pruning hooks? Is it not time for us to commit ourselves to the presence and power of the Lord, who will change our lifestyle from one that sows the seeds of dissent and war to one that fosters grace and peace? Is it not time that we grasp the vision of a long-ago peace-loving visionary and make it our own?—Henry Fields

SERMON SUGGESTIONS

Topic: Advent Lecture—The Power of God to the Greeks

TEXT: Rom. 1:14–17

Four characteristics marked Greek life and religion: (1) Restlessness in life, in spirit, and in quest of numerous religious philosophies. (2) Worldliness, declaring the world in its fallen state "good." (3) Superficial devotion to beauty, as opposed to the true beauty of the cross of Christ. (4) Worship of humanity, yet neglect of the baser human inclinations.

Conclusion: they had no sense of sin and no remedy for it. No prescription for this human malady exists except in the Redeemer's blood.—Frederick W. Robertson

Topic: Advent Has Three Tenses

TEXT: Heb. 1:1–2; Matt. 28:20; Rom. 8:21

(1) Advent past: a remembrance of the historical Jesus. (2) Advent present: the immediate encounter with the living Christ. (3) Advent future: the assurance of final victory brought by the work of God.—Graham W. Hardy

WORSHIP AIDS

CALL TO WORSHIP. "And we declare unto you glad tidings, how that the promise which was made unto the fathers, God hath fulfilled the same unto us their children" (Acts 13:32–33 KJV).

INVOCATION. Eternal Father, who in your providence made all the ages a preparation for the Kingdom of your son, may our worship today make ready our hearts to receive you in fullness of power, spirit, and persuasion. Prepare us for the brightness of your glory and the fullness of your blessing.

OFFERTORY SENTENCE. "Every good and perfect gift is from above, coming down from the Father of the heavenly lights, who does not change like shifting shadows" (James 1:17 NIV).

OFFERTORY PRAYER. Father, just as you gave us the gift of your Son, stir within us such love toward others that we will gladly share what you have entrusted to us for the relief of the world's sorrow and the coming of your Kingdom.

PRAYER. Eternal Father, as we come into this Christmas season, may we make room within our hearts once again for your Son to find lodging. Open our eyes that we might see you coming in the ordinary, unexpected places of life all around us. Help us to open our ears that we may hear again the singing of angels, that we might hear the glad good news once more. Open our hearts and mouths that we might proclaim the gospel to all persons. Open our minds that we might have the insight of the Wise Men, who came searching for the Christ child centuries ago, as they followed the star. Open our spirits that we might sense your Spirit in the midst of all our rushing and busyness.

Open us to life in our dark moments, encouragement in our fears, hope in our despair, and peace in our turmoil. Open us to experience in our confusion the forgiveness of our sins. Open us to experience the tenderness of your Spirit. In this Christmas season may we open our hearts and minds and total being that we shall sense your coming as we have never sensed it before. We pray through Jesus Christ our Lord, whose birth we celebrate in this Advent season.—William Powell Tuck

SERMON

Topic: To the Lords of This World

TEXT: Isa. 45:5–6

There is one aspect of being a Christian that can trouble even the most convinced and the most active. What I am thinking of this morning is a theological question that lurks in the mind of, I would guess, everyone here. The question is, Do I really believe that God is in charge of the destiny of this world?

I. The temptation is to detach our religious beliefs from the world of international politics. We isolate our religious beliefs from the struggle, almost as if the Lord God reigns in his churches but has abdicated his authority and control of human history to the lords of this world. Here we are as active Christians now in the season of Advent. It is a time for refreshing our faith in the God who comes to judge us and to save us—the God whose Son was born to blaze the way home for the whole human family.

II. So we come to the text and the question with which I began: "I am the Lord, there is no other; there is no god beside me. I will strengthen you though you have not known me." To whom are these words spoken? The answer may surprise you. They were not addressed to the oppressed and disconsolate Hebrews languishing as captives in Babylon but to none other than a prince of this world who was consolidating the most powerful empire the Middle East had ever known. "Thus says the Lord to Cyrus his anointed, Cyrus whom he has taken by the hand to subdue nations before him and undo the might of kings."

The name Cyrus II of Persia is not as familiar as Alexander the Great, but in his day he was as famous and as feared. It was Cyrus who made possible the survival of this people of God, giving them not only permission to return but the right to rebuild the walls and reconstruct the Temple of the Lord. What a nerve this prophet had to speak of the mighty Cyrus as an instrument through whom the Word of the living God, the Lord of lords and King of kings, would spread across the world, "that they may know" from the rising and the setting sun the great revelation: "I am the Lord, there is no other."

III. There are two amazing facts that emerge from this prophecy. One is that it did indeed happen. Because the Hebrews were allowed to return and rebuild their Temple, the religion of the one true God not only survived, but through the birth of the Savior Christ and the spiritual power of the Church was literally carried to the ends of the earth. The other amazing fact that emerges from this text is that the instrument used by God for this religious revolution was himself an unbeliever. The word to Cyrus says it twice: "I have called you by name, and given you your title though you have not known me. . . . I will strengthen you though you have not known me."

IV. What drew me back to this passage in the Bible was to hear what it says to us about the sovereignty of God, in a time when we are more than ever impressed by the power of the lords of this world to control our destiny. Nothing has changed except that the lords of this world have raised the stakes. Human pretensions to take over the destiny of the human race have added some new stories to the towers of Babel in the attempt to be our own god.

So the Advent invitation goes out to the lords of this world, not only to the worshippers in our churches. Our task is to surround them with our prayers, that they may be the instruments of the purposes of God. As we have learned from the story of Cyrus, all can be his instruments—believers and unbelievers. It remains true. There is One who says to the whole human family, "I am the Lord, there is no other." And the promise rings out to all men and women of goodwill. "I will strengthen you. Be still, all the lords of this world, believers and unbelievers. In my will is your peace."—David H. C. Read

SUNDAY, DECEMBER 9, 2007
Lectionary Message
Topic: The Character of a Leader of Peace

TEXT: Isa. 11:1–10

Other Readings: Ps. 71:1–7, 18–19; Rom. 15:4–13; Matt. 3:1–12

We have seen them rise to world prominence many times in recent years—those leaders in countries around the world who gain the confidence of the people by promising to bring peace to war-torn lands, yet who never deliver on their promises. In most instances the result of following such leaders is a situation that is worse than what existed prior to the leader's rise to power. Isaiah had seen such happen in his time. Kings came to the throne of nations with promises of peace, only to lead their nations deeper into chaos. During his lifetime he had witnessed the efforts of leaders of peace, as well as leaders of war and chaos in his own small country. With wisdom that comes only from God, he saw that a leader who would promote true peace must have a character molded by unshakable high moral and ethical qualities. Viewing the situation in which he lived, he understood that someone must take the high road that leads to lasting peace and make it happen. Then, as now, peace does not just "come about." Peace is the product of preparation, prayer, patience, and performance by strong leadership that cherishes peace and looks beyond itself for strength to achieve peace.

The figure that stands out in Isaiah's oracle is not just an ideal to hope for; it is a character—the living embodiment of the qualities that are to be expected of anyone worthy to govern with truth and righteousness. What are the characteristics of one who would lead to peace and then lead in peace? Isaiah gives several characteristics that a leader of peace must possess.

I. First, the prophet declares that a leader of peace must have wisdom and possess understanding. No one in any area of leadership can accomplish his or her purpose without wisdom and understanding. Wisdom has been loosely defined as mental power acting upon the fullest knowledge possessed so that the most effective way of action can be accomplished. Understanding is basically possessing knowledge and good sense. In short, it doesn't take a genius to be a good leader, but it does require someone who has knowledge of the situation faced and the courage to use that knowledge and good sense for the highest good of everybody. We have seen leaders in our own country who would not be classified as rocket scientists. Yet these leaders have had an understanding of the situations faced by our nation, and possessing the good sense or wisdom to act on what they understood, they have brought us through difficult and chaotic times. Isaiah was right in his assessment that wisdom and understanding are bedrock characteristics of any leader who seeks peace.

II. Second, a leader of peace must give good counsel and have the personal might to make peace happen. Too often the prophet had seen leaders give false counsel when people were listening for truth. He had seen promising kings buckle under pressure and fail to stand firm for what would make peace a reality. That is no ancient story. It is as new as the most recent sunrise. A cursory survey will indicate that in every area of life leaders have failed to be truthful and exert personal moral conviction that wades through the chaos to the goal of peace. We have seen it in the religious strife of our times. We have seen it in political arenas. We have seen it in economic settings. We have witnessed it in family life and in personal struggles. Pressures come on strongly when the status quo is challenged. It is much easier to retire into the peace of what is momentarily popular than it is to stand against the tide that would destroy real and lasting peace. It is much easier to say what folks want to hear than it is to tell them what they need to hear. Only a leader who tells the truth in all circumstances and exerts personal might through unbending conviction, no matter the cost to himself, will suffice as a leader to peace.

III. Third, a leader of peace must possess knowledge of God and God's revealed truth. By this, Isaiah meant more than the fact that God simply exists and that tipping your hat to him occasionally is all that is needed for the leader of peace. He is talking about an intimate knowledge of God—a knowledge that comes from constant communion with him, a knowledge that is the result of a close personal relationship.

I have a friend whom I have known for over forty years. Through all those years we have kept in touch and talked with one another on a weekly basis. Our relationship has grown through the years so that I can predict his actions in certain situations, as he can mine. I know before he speaks what his thoughts are going to be on certain subjects. Though we live in separate parts of the country and see each other on rare occasions, I have a knowledge of him that has, at times, allowed me to speak and act for him, as he has for me. I think that the prophet is speaking of a relationship of that nature, yet with more intensity, when he declares that a leader of peace must have knowledge of God. Such a leader will understand what God's peace is all about. He will know what Jesus meant when he said, "My peace I give unto you." And he will bend his efforts to implement God's kind of peace in the world. Why will he do this? He will do this because he will possess a wholesome fear of God. Isaiah's use of the word *fear* means a reverence for God that is above all other reverence. It is not a fear that paralyzes but a reverence that encourages action in God's name and on God's behalf. Such a leader will stand tall among his peers and subjects. Did such a leader emerge in Isaiah's time? Sorrowfully, the answer is no. Yet in the fullness of time, Jesus came. He is the embodiment of what a leader of peace is. He set the standard to be followed by all who seek to bring peace in disturbed and chaotic times. Following him will indeed bring peace to the troubled heart, the troubled family, the troubled world. Our problem is that we have not followed him as he leads to peace. We have chosen to set our own course, choose our own means, and use our enforcing weapons to create a climate of peace in the world. Yet peace has not come. It will remain a stranger until we choose first the Kingdom of God and his right ways of doing life with one another at every level, from the least to the greatest. Then under leaders who lead in God's ways we will indeed build peace in our world.—Henry Fields

SERMON SUGGESTIONS

Topic: Advent Lecture—The Power of God to the Romans
TEXT: Rom. 1:14–16
(1) In its public life, Rome existed to display a copy on earth of the law of the numerous divine hierarchies. (2) In its private life, it celebrated virtue lived out as courage and duty to the public good. (3) The decline of Roman life came as a result of the corruption of moral character,

which was not protected by the finest of Roman intentions and philosophies. It was necessary that the full Truth should come into the world, even Jesus the Christ.—Frederick W. Robertson

Topic: Unto You Is Born This Day a Savior
TEXT: Luke 2:1–14

(1) "For to you": the Christmas story happened for each person individually and for all people collectively. (2) "Born this day": Christ's birth signals the day of life—all of life in all its fullness. (3) "A Savior": the Savior brings salvation to all because we all need a savior.—Karl Barth

WORSHIP AIDS

CALL TO WORSHIP.   "Send forth your light and your truth, let them guide me; let them bring me to your holy mountain, to the place where you dwell" (Ps. 43:3 NIV).

INVOCATION.   Our Father, help us in this season to remember how you pointed us to the coming of our Savior, the Lord Jesus Christ. Let us be mindful that you did not leave us alone, that you did not condemn us to darkness but instead that you provided the way to light and life. Lead on, O King Eternal.

OFFERTORY SENTENCE.   "As every man hath received the gift, even so minister the same one to another, as good stewards of the manifold grace of God" (1 Pet. 4:10 KJV).

OFFERTORY PRAYER.   Lord, may we find our giving to be a joyful experience. Help us to remember that our gifts are made in the name—and for the sake—of Jesus, our Savior. Grant us the wisdom of men of old who saw a star, worshipped a child as the newborn King, and made offerings at his feet.

PRAYER.   Lord, we pray today that nothing may keep us from receiving Christ's joy in this season. Remove from us any thought, motive, wrong intention, or superficial desire that could make these holy days like all other days. May we in this Advent season share the wisdom of Jesus so that we may become one with him. And on that great and glorious day when he comes again to reign in eternal glory, grant that we shall be prepared to receive his coming. As we wait, give to us great faith and patience, and encourage us each day to watch. Let not the greed of this season overtake us and spoil the joy promised to all who seek him. May the bright light of the glory of the gospel dispel the darkness that so mightily enters our world. Grant in these days that we will find the joy of the season, even as we discover once again the reign of Christ in us.—Lee McGlone

SERMON
Topic: Why Jesus Came
TEXT: Matt. 1:21

The textual story reminds us that Jesus was not just another child born into this world and that his name was not a tag chosen at random or in haste. The name "Jesus" identified him as Savior, and it readily helps us to know why he came among us: "call his name Jesus, for he will save his people from their sins."

I. The text holds two terms that are problematic for some people today: *save* and *sins.* Salvation was neither an abstract notion nor a strange concern to the people of Jesus' day, but some in our time view both salvation and sin as mere notions, and they speak about these themes in different ways, sometimes with unashamed blandness, unsympathetic tolerance, or even enmity.

II. Those to whom Jesus came knew this. The national literature was filled with stories about sin and forgiveness, about how God had delivered his people now and again, and about how he had saved them from sorrowful conditions and rescued them from hazards and horrors because of his covenant with the patriarchs. *Sin* and *salvation* were not strange words to informed Hebrews. As Jesus ministered to his people, they began to understand the meaning of salvation at deeper levels of their lives. They found that, along with a deepened sense of accountability, they also experienced a new power to obey. In place of a sense of estrangement, they realized a sense of acceptance that the ritual claim for oneness with God was now a real communion with him.

III. As he dealt with his people, Jesus made them face up to their sins of vanity. Then as now, vanity was a central sin because it is how pride most readily grows in the human spirit. The Hebrews needed to be saved from their blinding pride over being God's chosen people. Salvation from vanity always happens when we get and hold a right view of self in relation to God and others. And only the truth about ourselves can lead to such a freedom.

As he dealt with his people, Jesus made them face up to their sins of violence. Violence is the selfish use of power to gain advantage over someone else for personal reasons. Violence is often an extreme action taken to overcome someone. Salvation from the attitude that spawns violence is a need in our time as well. Aggressively violent persons and groups keep our newscasts filled with sad news, as they use violent means to gain their ends.

As he dealt with his people, Jesus called attention to sins of vice, with the intent to free all who wanted release from the disposition to practice what is unworthy and harmful to themselves. The New Testament carries several lists of self-injuring practices, and any serious look at those lists should warn us about the penalties we pay and the losses we suffer when we defy God-given rules and try to live without divine guidance. Those who give themselves to vices later look up out of a ruined life and wish for salvation and another chance at life. Jesus came to save us from our vices, bring us to virtue, and help us to obey the counsel of godliness.

IV. Jesus came to save us from our sins, but we must let him do so. Sin deteriorates relations, undermines health, dulls the mind, misdirects energies, destroys community, and ruins character. Jesus came to save us, setting us free to become what God's grace can make us. As this truth is proclaimed, the power of the gospel becomes known and experienced.—James Earl Massey

SUNDAY, DECEMBER 16, 2007
Lectionary Message

Topic: When Peace Finally Comes

TEXT: Isa. 35:1–10; Matt. 11:2–11

Other Readings: (responsive reading): Luke 1:47–55; James 5:7–10

None of us travels far down the road of life without experiencing the wrenching pains that destroy our peace. When the heated winds of adversity begin to blow against our settled lives, we long for a time and place when such disturbance will no longer invade our journey. Yet it seems that constant invaders come to disturb, if not destroy, our joy and peace. Someone who is the rock of our life suddenly is diagnosed with an incurable illness, and life for us turns into a desert. A marriage fails, and the hot desert winds blow ferociously against life, burning away our joy and hope. A child with great talent and promise chooses to waste a promising future on trivial pursuits, and the shadow of a desert windstorm blots out our fond dreams for the child's future. Economic circumstances, once secure, suddenly crumble through no fault of our own, and life becomes frighteningly miserable. In a multitude of ways our peace is challenged and vanishes like the morning mist before the power of the absorbing sun.

It is then that we, like many others from the misty pages of history, begin to ask for some word, some glimpse of a place and time when the sorrows, sicknesses, and losses of life will be no more, and we will live in joy and peace. Our prayer is for the hastening of such a day. Our prayer is that God will send someone to show us where to find the gate to the road that will lead us to such a state and place. Into the darkness of life we cry, "Is there any word of hope and help, anyone who can lead us to a land that is fairer than day, where peace and joy abound?"

I. Words attributed to Isaiah, couched in magnificent poetical form, come to our rescue. Chapter 35—the salvation chapter—tells of God's redemption from all that takes away the peace and joy in which he intends his people to live. Seeing life as a journey rather than a settled state, the prophet turns the eyes of his hearers to a new vision of the road they are traveling. His people had always been on a journey following the leadership of God. Their travels had taken them through every experience imaginable. Exile had turned their hearts and dreams toward their beloved Zion. Yet that city of their dreams was miles away across a trackless desert. How would they ever reach home and peace and joy again? How would they overcome the evil that gripped them and gain a new beginning?

In majestic words the prophet turns thoughts from a world of brutal cruelty to an earth where peace is a reality, where beauty is restored, where wounds are forever healed, sorrows lifted, and joy is complete. His certainty that God will do this for his faithful followers is like a clarion call to the ages. He understood that his God would raise up a leader who would make these mighty hopes become reality. He knew that the power of God would make a desert of evil into a place of beauty and plenty and peace. That is the meaning of the beautiful imagery of his poem. God has heard the cry of his people. He has not abandoned them, nor will he suffer them to languish in misery forever. He will come to them and redeem them and turn their howling deserts into lush, peaceful fields and gardens and streams.

II. I am sure that skepticism met this declaration, even as it likely does today. For many, the long history of human suffering is so burned into their minds and hearts that they likely see this prophetic dream as a fantasy, not a reality. Yet in the fullness of time, when the world was gripped in misery, God sent the needed leader to prove the reality of the ancient promise. Jesus came and moved among people of all walks of life, declaring that the Kingdom of God is at hand. In vivid words and powerful deeds he told of what was happening in their very midst as proof that the long road leads to home and joy and peace.

No more positive picture of this is found than that which occurred when John sent his disciples to ask if Jesus was the promised one who would lead to God's Kingdom, or if he should look for another (Matt. 11:2). In answer, Jesus declares that the Kingdom dreamed of by Isaiah and hoped for throughout the long, silent, waiting generations has come. The dream has become reality! God has sent the Prince of Peace, who is even now busy building the foundation of the new Kingdom, where peace will forever stand. "Tell John how the blind gain sight, the lame are made to walk, those who have leprosy are cured, the deaf are made to hear, the dead are raised and the good news is preached to the poor." In other words, tell John that all the factors that destroy peace are being defeated. All the events in human living that create chaos are being managed and removed from life. All the elements that disturb hope and joy are meeting the only One who can master their power over human hearts and souls. Tell John that a highway across the desert, that highway Isaiah envisioned, is here. It has been opened, for Christ has "opened a new and living way" (Heb. 10:20). Tell John and the waiting world, tell every person of every generation that those who commit themselves to that new and living way will find that the world is indeed transformed and all things are new. Tell everyone everywhere that "if any man be in Christ, he is a new creature" (2 Cor. 5:17). Tell everyone everywhere that when we walk with the Lord the eyes of faith are open, ears once deaf to the voice of God are quick to hear, feet once shuffling in reluctance are made swift and sure, as they travel the highway that leads to home and God.

As in Isaiah's time, as in Jesus' time, life is still dangerous and filled with the things that destroy peace. But every one of us can be safe in God's hands and abide in the gladness of a living faith. The life, the love, the victory of Jesus Christ have brought peace to the world. He has truly transformed the prophet's dream into an eternal fact. It is left to us to believe and accept that truth and then, transformed by his grace and power and love, live in his peace, now and evermore.—Henry Fields

SERMON SUGGESTIONS

Topic: Advent Lectures: The Power of God to the Barbarians

TEXT: Rom. 1:14; Acts 28:1–7

The Barbarians (a contemptuous term) were understood as any religion that was not Roman or Greek. Note in this text: (1) Their virtues "showed us no little kindness." (2) Their inclination was to retribution: "this man is no doubt a murderer and by vengeance should not live." (3) Their conception of Deity was this: "when the snake fell off his hand, they believed he was a god."

Conclusion: the coming of Christ was not to proclaim a mystery but a Father who loves all people.—Frederick W. Robertson

Topic: Thanks Be unto God

TEXT: 2 Cor. 9:15

(1) The gift of God in Christ is an unspeakable gift: God in human flesh transcends our understanding. (2) It declares the mercy granted to us in Jesus Christ: it is joy to the world. (3) It declares God's eternal triumph: all other gifts decay, but this gift lasts forever.—Walter A. Maier

WORSHIP AIDS

CALL TO WORSHIP.   "Lo, the star which they saw in the east, went before them, till it came and stood over where the young child was. When they saw the star, they rejoiced with exceeding great joy" (Matt. 2:9–10 KJV).

INVOCATION.   Dear Lord Jesus Christ, you who are the light of the world, shine to all who walk in darkness and who dwell in the valley of the shadow that they may have the light of life. May your Word be to us a lamp unto our feet and a light unto our path. May today your name be praised.

OFFERTORY SENTENCE.   "If you then, though you are evil, know how to give good gifts to your children, how much more will your Father in heaven give the Holy Spirit to those who ask him" (Luke 11:13 NIV).

OFFERTORY PRAYER.   Our Father in heaven, we praise you as the giver of all good gifts. In gratitude we bring our offerings on this day of joyous worship. Take these gifts, refine them in the mint of your divine purpose, and use them to the end that your Kingdom may come on earth, as it is in heaven.

PRAYER.   Father of our Lord Jesus Christ, we come to you, the faithful One who stands with us in and through all things. We rejoice this Advent season in the sure and steadfast hope that is ours through the coming of Jesus the Lord and to the surety of his second coming as the hope of glory. In these difficult days give strength to our feeble hands and make firm our unsure knees. To the fearful among us, declare boldly, "Fear not. I am with you." Grant to us your mercy, O Lord, and make us your people. As we draw closer each week to our Savior's birth, keep us whole in mind and body. Enable us to walk each day in holiness and purity. May our lives express such devotion to the faith that has claimed us that there is no wavering testimony about us but instead that our witness of love will be clearly understood. May we be clothed in the Lord Jesus Christ and filled with the Holy Spirit. Help us to stand watchful and ready until your dear Son is revealed in the fullness of his glory. And may we rejoice in his Presence, known to us today and forever, world without end.—Lee McGlone

SERMON
Topic: The Greatest Christmas Pageant Ever!
TEXT: Luke 2:1–20

There are lots of lessons to be learned from that wonderful story—not new lessons but lessons that have been a part of Christmas all along, lessons that were first taught in the first and greatest Christmas pageant ever, played out in the night skies over and outside Bethlehem, in the dark fields of shepherds and sheep, in a lonely stable out back of a crowded inn and in the courts of a king in a faraway land—old lessons that we've somehow forgotten or lost across the years. Let me remind you of a few of them again.

I. The first is this: the first time you hear, see, or experience something is always the best, most magical and memorable time. So ask God to show you something for the first time every Christmas. There was a first time, you know. It was that night when the real mother of Jesus gave birth to a baby who would cause the blind to see, the deaf to hear, the lame to leap, the dumb to speak, and the dead to live again.

Some time ago, there was also a first time for you—a time no doubt lost and forgotten now, locked up and shut off with so many of your other most precious and priceless childhood memories, way back in the darkened labyrinths of your mind. Can you recall the wonder and the awe that stirred in your heart and mind the first time you heard it? Probably not. Here's an idea. Why not read the Christmas story from a different translation or two this year? Why not learn some new Christmas music this year? Why not do something this Christmas you've never done before?

II. That's the second lesson I want you to recall: be open to letting something completely new take place. Some of us are so concerned about preserving tradition, not changing things, making certain that everything is done just the way everything has always been done that I doubt we'd ever have been chosen as part of the original cast of Christmas. You see, if there's one thing the birth of Jesus tells us, it's that God doesn't always color inside the lines. He's not locked into doing things the way they've always been done because he's not convinced that the way things always have been done is the only or best way to continue to do them. It's a lesson lots of us could stand to learn. For as long as we remain closed to doing something new, God will never be able to make us new or accomplish anything new through us.

III. The final lesson I want to remind you that's taught in the Christmas story is this: there are people who've never heard the story—people who don't know how much God loves them and how far he's willing to go to get through to them! The irony is, they're the very ones the story—the gesture of love—is intended to reach. "Come and behold Him," we've sung, and our actions have echoed our invitation. It's funny, I know, but those who go all year without paying any attention to him suddenly see him at this season of the year. People who're accustomed to using his name only in vain pause at Christmas to use it in praise. All of a sudden, he's everywhere. He is Emmanuel. He is with us. He is here!

It's the best story ever told, I tell you! And the best part of it is that it's true—every word of it is true. Hey, ya'll! Unto you a child is born! Things are going to start getting better now!—Gary C. Redding

SUNDAY, DECEMBER 23, 2007

Lectionary Message

Topic: The Coming of the Prince of Peace

TEXT: Isa. 7:10–16; Matt. 1:18–25

Other Readings: Ps. 80:1–7, 17–19; Rom. 1:1–7

What would it be like to suddenly be informed that you were to be the fulfillment of an ancient prophecy? Granted, it would be a prophecy stated for the time of the prophet speaking, but long years later God sees fit to make that prophecy of a peace leader come true through you. How would you handle such knowledge? How would you bear up under such awesome responsibility?

This morning, come with me for a while to a room in a cave in Bethlehem, where a peasant couple has just witnessed the birth of their first child. Accompanied by the noises of the surrounding animals, the sweet smell of fresh hay, the flicker of a small oil lamp, the miracle of birth has taken place. Picture the young mother, perhaps no more than fourteen or fifteen, resting beside the rough rock feeding trough that had been chiseled out of the sandstone that serves as the cradle of the newborn child. Look in the close shadows and see the young man, a first-time father, standing protectively over his new family with a look of wonder on his face. What do they think of this event, this strange and mysterious event that has caused ambivalence in him and apprehension in her?

Look at Mary—a devout Jew, she had heard the mighty prophecy of Isaiah. She knew that the longing for a messiah was a strong hope that dwelt just below the surface of every Jewish heart. She had heard the sermons preached about this young woman who would bear a son who would fulfill that heart-longing. But she never saw herself as the young woman of Isaiah's vision—that is, not until that fateful day when God's angel brought the news that he had chosen her as the vessel whereby he would come to live with the people he had created in love, to experience life in all its aspects with them that he might love them completely and lead them eternally. What a burden for one so young! Those months of waiting for the child's birth had been hard. Her husband had nearly dropped her during the engagement period when he discovered that she was pregnant. Who could blame him? Then there were the whispers and the looks as folks started counting the months, the feeling of isolation as friends and then some family members withdrew from her because of their belief that she had grossly sinned. After that was the long journey to Bethlehem, the crude shelter of the cattle stall, the birth itself, with no one except her husband to assist in her deepest hour of need. How could she bear all that and still believe that it was all of God? If you were a woman in her circumstances, how would you feel? How would you hold up? How would events affect your faith? Yet that night, in that stable, through that young woman God came to earth as never before.

Look at the young man, known to us as Joseph. His life with Mary had to be hard, not because of her but because of all the factors with which he was suddenly forced to deal. Only God's intervention kept him from walking away from one he loved, one he anticipated marrying, one with whom he desired to raise a family. Now he is called upon to raise a child she claims is the product of God's Spirit and her yielding. That would be hard for any man to handle.

It takes a good and noble man to accept such mystery and agree to raise the child as his very own. What an example he sets for all men of every age—belief in the power of God, acceptance of unfathomable mystery, caring for and standing with a young woman in spite of every argument to walk away. That is what can happen when men listen for God to speak and are willing to follow his instructions, even through the unbelievable. Look at the baby; reach down and pick him up in your arms. Think of who you are holding close to your heart. This baby is none other than God incarnate, God with us, the Wonderful Counselor, the Prince of Peace! And here he is in your arms. Feel the gentleness of his breath against your cheek. Brush the straw from his downy hair, and count his fingers and toes. Listen to his shrieks of hunger. Observe his baby anger as he waves his tiny arms and kicks spastically with his churning legs. This is God among us, God so weak he can't turn over by himself, God so freshly born that he cannot communicate in understandable ways with us, God so baby frail that we wonder why he chose this means of joining our human tribe. Yet here he is, resting in your arms, the God who once said, "Let's make a covenant. I'll do my part and you do yours and we will work life together." He kept his part, and we didn't keep ours, so this same God said, "O.K., I'll just give you all the rules you will ever need for living together on earth and in my care. I'll even write them in rocks so you won't lose them."

But we soon forgot the rules and lost the rocks and left God behind. So this same God, whose love is boundless, beckoned us again to come to him that he might simplify the old covenant by reducing it to two commandments: "Love me and love your neighbor." But we didn't even know how to do that. So this God you are holding in your arms said, "Forget the old covenant. Put it on hold. I have something new in mind. It is harder for me but easier for you. You won't have to come to me anymore, I will come to you. I will come in a way that you will understand. I will come as a baby, entering your world like every person does. I will become bone of your bone and flesh of your flesh.[1] I will experience what you experience, feel what you feel, and struggle as you struggle. I will do this for the simple reason that from the beginning when I first created you I have loved each of you as if you were the only one to love, and I will do whatever is necessary to make you understand how much that love covers. Throughout my stay on earth with you, I will show you how to love one another, how to live by high principles for building a noble life together, how to keep covenant with me. I will extend forgiveness to you in person, give grace unending and sacrifice life itself that you may know the depth and power of my love."

So it was that on that night of nights, God himself came down the stairway of the stars, entered our world through the miracle of human birth, and nestled in the humility of a manger. The Word that night did become flesh to dwell among us. The echo of the prophet's words sound with fresh insight for the waiting world. Through the channel of a village maiden, Emanuel—God—came to be with us, with you and me, to love us and lead us and save us. "Glory to God in the highest and peace on earth, good will among men" (Luke 2:14).—Henry Fields

SERMON SUGGESTIONS

Topic: The Principle of the Spiritual Harvest

TEXT: Gal. 6:7–8

(1) The principle is clear: "God is not mocked; what we sow we shall also reap." (2) The principle is applied in that if we sow to the flesh we will, from the flesh, reap corruption, whether it be in pampering our unruly human appetites or in investing life in an invisible harvest. (3) But those who sow to the Spirit shall reap eternal life.

Conclusion: don't give up. Doing good—sowing to the Spirit—is its own reward.—Frederick W. Robertson

Topic: Five Joys of Christmas

TEXT: Luke 2:10–11

(1) The joy of seeing. (2) Of hearing. (3) Of fulfillment. (4) Of forgiveness. (5) Of eternal life.—John Rilling

WORSHIP AIDS

CALL TO WORSHIP.   "Behold, I bring you good tidings of great joy, which shall be to all the people. For unto you is born this day in the city of David a Savior, which is Christ the Lord. Glory to God in the highest, and on earth peace, good will toward men" (Luke 2:10–11 KJV).

INVOCATION.   Gracious Father, our hearts are hushed by the mystery and wonder of the birth of the Christ Child. As we enter worship, open our hearts to the wisdom of that Child, so that once again the high and noble truth of the incarnation will be born among us. May we today open wide the doors of our hearts, and homes, to receive him.

---

[1]Barbara Brown Taylor, *Mixed Blessings* (Boston: Cowley Publications, 1986), p. 50.

OFFERTORY SENTENCE.   "For God so loved the world, that he gave his only begotten Son, that whosoever believeth in him should not perish, but have everlasting life" (John 3:16 KJV).

OFFERTORY PRAYER.   Precious Lord Jesus, whose birthday has become a season of benevolence and giving, refresh within us the joy of sharing in your ministry to the world. Receive these gifts and bless them. We make them with gratitude in our hearts and make them in response to your unspeakable gift to us.

PRAYER.   Loving God, as we come this last Sunday before Christmas, once again we pray that our minds may turn to the celebration of the coming of your Son into the world. Help us to make room for the Christ within our hearts. We thank you for this season and for its beauty. May we learn to use this time to pause and to think about you and your love. As we reflect on your greatness, may it remind us of our own impurity, cause us to confess our sins, seek release from our guilt, and find the peace that comes from your presence.

In this Christmas season may we once again be excited about the wonder of it. May we become as children as we reflect upon our need of you and on the great gift that you have given us, through Jesus Christ our Lord. May he come into our lives in this Christmas with a sense of newness and freshness, as we pray in the power of his strong name.—William Powell Tuck

SERMON
Topic: Miracle of Miracles
TEXT: Heb. 2:1–4

We have often heard extolled the greatest miracle to be the conception and birth of a child. How much mightier the miracle when it is God's *own* child, conceived by the Holy Spirit, born of a virgin—a child meant to be brother to all and Savior of everyone! So it is that we come professing him to be the miracle of miracles—born a child, yes, an *ordinary* child in appearance and needs, yet born in an extraordinary way at an extraordinary time under extraordinary conditions. For this child is the divine Son of God, as well as the human infant carried in Mary's womb. He is not only the miracle of miracles but the One who works an even greater miracle in the salvation of the sinful by his own atoning sacrifice and his ultimate conquest of death.

I. We must focus on Bethlehem, the City of David, that tiny walled town within walking distance of Jerusalem. No palace nursery awaited the infant of God. There was only a stable closeted in a wind-carved cave. It housed a straw-filled feeding box. Perhaps there was a fire radiating its warmth. It is certain there were animals there. Mary gave birth to Jesus before the wondering, gaping eyes of the stable's four-legged residents, and the sleepy, roosting hens who probably could not keep awake. The miracle of miracles—God with us—happened in the simplicity of a homely setting.

If what went on inside the stable was commonplace, it was not at all commonplace *outside.* Shepherds heard more than one angel, but the whole choir of heaven sang of God's miraculous wonder, born that night in Bethlehem's stable. These herdsmen rushed to see it and discovered the angel had not misinformed them. He said to the terrified herders in the middle of that springlike night, "I am bringing you good news of great joy for all the people: to you is born this day in the city of David a Savior, who is the Messiah, the Lord" (Luke 2:11). They, who kept lambs for the Temple sacrifices, found the Lord Christ, the Lamb of God, just as the angel said, snuggling warm and sweetly in a manger—this Lamb that one day would atone for the sins of the world.

But that was not all that was going on outside the stable nursery. The heavens were illumined by the shining of stars, and one was so bright that it attracted the attention of stargazers hundreds of miles away. The Magi were set to wandering the pathways of the Middle East following that brilliant, leading star. That was no customary event. They were tracing the star's path to the miracle of miracles.

II. It was a night the world has not forgotten. Even in non-Christian lands, Christmas is observed. To be sure, it is often only a *commercial* event. They string lights, erect ornamented trees, and sell non-Christians on the idea that gift giving is important—or at least gift *buying*! They are unaware, perhaps, that behind this miracle of miracles, which began the whole idea of giving gifts in the first place, is a greater concept. God gave the most splendid gift of all in the giving of his Son. Wise Men later gave gifts also—gold and frankincense and myrrh—but it was the giving of Jesus Christ to the world to redeem us that is the notable gift, the miracle of miracles, the unsurpassed Christmas gift.

III. So this night we share in the miracle of miracles all over again. It can be more a miracle to you than just *another* pleasant Christmas. It is all in your perspective. It can be a holiday or a holy night, whichever you choose. This Christmas, see the gift of God as that costly gift that cost God everything he had—his Son, his life, his prestige—for he died a criminal's horrible death. When you see it as the gift beyond all gifts, it is no longer merely a legend, a pretty story, a reason to decorate or go on a buying spree, but the very inspiration for life itself. It is God's gift to *you.* Birth, then, as wonderful as it is, is not the greatest miracle, nor is conception, as grand as that is. But God loving us enough to send a Savior—that is the Miracle of Miracles.—Richard Andersen

SUNDAY, DECEMBER 30, 2007
Lectionary Message

Topic: The Prince of Peace in a Hostile World

Text: Matt. 2:13–23

Other Readings: Isa. 63:7–9; Ps. 148; Heb. 2:10–18

Last week we rejoiced in the coming of Emmanuel. We marveled that the Creator God of all the universes, the sustainer of worlds without end, would stoop to meet us as one of us. We pondered how God would enter humanity as we all enter humanity—choosing a village maiden as the channel for that entry and a carpenter-farmer to partner with her in the rearing of this God-child.

Now the first excitement of the event is past. Eastern astrologers and mystics have identified this child as the longed-for world King. The news is out, at least to those in the court of the reigning king of Judea, who is a brutal Eastern potentate. What seemed like such wonderful news of a world redeemer quickly turns into a vicious, heartbreaking story, for although the Prince of Peace has come to the world, the world was—and yet remains—a hostile foe to peace and goodwill among men. This week we walk through the first installment of the aftermath of Christ, God's only Son, coming to dwell among us.

I. First, rather than see him receive a joyous welcome throughout the land, power people resented his arrival and plotted to rid the world of his presence. Matthew tells of Herod's underhanded method to discover the identity of Christ (Matt. 2:7, 8). His desire for information from the Wise Men was not so he could worship Christ but so he might find him and destroy him.

History is replete with countless rulers who see Christ as a threat to their position, not as one who can, if allowed, enhance their position. Herod was, in reality, the first among many who saw Christ as a threat to be removed, not an ally. Kings and rulers are not alone in their view of Christ as a threat to their desires and plans. Countless common folks have and still do see Christ as a burden-bringer rather than a burden-lifter, a hindrance to full life rather than the giver of meaningful, lasting, and full life. Their voices join the chorus of rejection rather than acceptance of Emmanuel, God with us.

II. No matter the ruler's or man's attempt to remove Christ from life, such is not allowed in God's plan to dwell among us as one of us. Matthew tells of loyal, staunch Joseph, who, dreaming and obeying the dream, moves quickly to protect his young family, slipping away in the night to Egypt, there to live in one of the many Jewish communities. Joseph becomes the instrument for saving the life of the God-child whose time had not yet come to die. God always seems to move in his quiet, powerful way to preserve his presence with us. This he does against the most ominous foes. Roman might was unable to annihilate him in the primitive Church. Other hordes could not drive him into oblivion. Communist power could not erase him from society. Once he has come, he remains, even if just below the surface, hidden no deeper than the human heart. Times without number some Joseph or groups of Josephs have risked life-and-limb to protect the presence of Emmanuel: early believers, hiding in limestone caves, protecting the good news they had found; medieval monks voluntarily removed from society, guarding libraries of discovered truth; persecuted Christians in a godless Soviet Union and a communist China, keeping the faith in Emmanuel and being guided by his ever-present Spirit. All have confounded evil rulers bent on the destruction and presence of the Prince of Peace in the world. Brutal effort has followed brutal effort, as Herods through the ages have slaughtered the innocents (Matt. 2:16), thinking such brutality would eliminate Christ and intimidate to silence any who would proclaim him. Such strategy has failed, and Christ still prevails. Sometimes he resides quietly in some Nazareth, as he did when the primary enemy, Herod, was gone (Matt. 2:19–23). There he waits until the time has come for him to move powerfully to the forefront again. Christian history records those quiet Nazareth years over and over again, only to be followed by revival fires that bring majestic change to the world. The hostile world and the Prince of Peace seem ever to be at odds.

III. If Christ is the Prince of Peace, and peace among men is still absent, how does Christ's peace become a reality in our world? First, we must realize that Christ's peace is not the kind of peace the world seeks. The world wants cessation of war—the sheathing of the sword and the mothballing of guns. The world wants laws enforcing peace, powers enforcing the laws (good or bad), and the removal of anyone who resists this method of ensuring peace. The world through the ages has thought that power can force and enforce peace, no matter the attitude and spirit of human beings. Over and over this legalistic, power-enforced method has failed. The *Pax Romana* of Jesus' day was not the kind of peace Jesus came to earth to give.

Second, the peace of God—the kind of peace that Jesus offers—begins within the individual and works outward. It does not begin outside and work its way inward through force. Jesus offers a gift to be received, not a law to obey. It comes through our individual invitation for the Prince of Peace to enter our warring and sinful hearts and lives and take control. When he comes, he rearranges the furniture, casting out what is broken and useless, cleaning what has been tarnished by misuse, and installing new what is needed to complete the furnishings we will need to live at peace within. Once we are inwardly at peace through his abiding Spirit, we learn to live peacefully in our tumultuous world. Like an oasis in a desert, we then become a source of lasting refreshment for strugglers about us, as we help them find their inward peace in a warring world. Thus "the kingdom of this world becomes the kingdom of our God and of His Christ where he shall reign forever and ever."[2]—Henry Fields

SERMON SUGGESTIONS

Topic: Faith in Hard Times
Text: Eccles. 11:1–6
(1) Demands bold action in the face of uncertainty. (2) Calls for a determined faith that will not give up. (3) Requires diligence when hope seems to fade.—Lawrence Vowan

Topic: Eternal Life
Text: John 3:16
(1) Eternal life is in Christ. (2) It is a life of serving God. (3) It is a life of goodness. (4) It is a life of worship.—John Brokhoff

WORSHIP AIDS

CALL TO WORSHIP.   "How good it is to sing praises to our God, how pleasant and fitting to praise him" (Ps. 147:1 NIV).

INVOCATION.   Holy Father, as we enter to worship on the last day of the year, make us aware of the frailty of our days. Since we cannot know what a day may bring or the events of another year ahead, make us truly aware that the present hour is for serving you. May we wake to the claims of your will and yield today to your eternal purposes. Consecrate with your Presence the way our feet should go.

OFFERTORY SENTENCE.   "For if the willingness is there, the gift is acceptable according to what one has, not according to what he does not have" (2 Cor. 8:12 NIV).

OFFERTORY PRAYER.   Father, grant that we as followers of Christ will bring forth fruit consistent with our profession of faith. May these gifts of tithes and offerings be so used that others will hear the gospel story of your redeeming love.

PRAYER.   Creator God, we come to you this morning as travelers, as a people on a journey—a journey of faith. Like those Israelites so long ago, we are often led into the

---

[2]From Handel's "The Messiah."

desert—into a personal wilderness. But you have promised, O God, to show us the road through the wilderness. The journey is at times accompanied by feelings of weariness, disappointment, loneliness, and personal emptiness. But in recognizing our own shortcomings, we also become aware of your constant presence. Enable us to share the joy of your love with others. Enable us also to be aware and to reach out in love where there is illness, where there is fear, where there is hurt, where there is suffering. We rededicate ourselves this morning to you, O God, and to your call to move through the wilderness. For in the journey we will find out who we are meant to be. In the journey we will discover our identity. In our pain we will find joy. In our challenge we will find change. And in our dying, we will find new life.—Susan Gregg-Schroeder

SERMON
Topic: Sorry We Missed Your Birthday
TEXT: Isa. 40:1–5, 42:18–20

"All flesh shall see it together." But it didn't happen that way, did it? That first Christmas came and went, and only a handful of people knew about it. We sometimes forget that in our sense of Advent ecstasy. After all, here were all these stories of people who did see, people whose lives were changed, presumably forever—a mere handful of people, perhaps fifteen or twenty, out of hundreds of thousands in the world. All those people in Bethlehem, so crowded that there was no room in the inn for the Savior to be born there. And, apparently, none of the rest of them knew a thing about it. The Savior of the world was born in a stable behind the local hostelry, and they didn't even hear about it. Sort of eases our guilt about Christmas, doesn't it? I mean, here we are, celebrating the birthday of the Prince of Peace, and many of us didn't give it a real thought, did we? "All flesh shall see it together." But not this Christmas, any more than the first Christmas.

I. I often feel that that's what this Sunday, the Sunday after Christmas, does for a lot of worshippers. It gives you a chance to make a confession—to say, "Lord, I missed it again; I meant to watch for it and be ready this year, but you know how busy I've been"—and then to feel his presence and his peace fall like a mantle over you, silencing your noisy heart and restoring you to a sense of what life is all about. It is, after all, only human to get in this bind and let Christmas go by without having truly received it, without having seen the baby in the manger again.

II. I am consoled that though we were not converted and time was not stopped forever in its tracks, we came away again with a glimpse of what God and life are all about. For I have found that revelation—the burning bush and the Damascus Road experience aside—usually comes in glimpses. It is like those persistent drop-drop-droppings of water in a limestone cave that eventually leave such a deposit of their visits that a stalactite is formed and then a stalagmite and, eventually, a column to stand for all eternity. One day, perhaps when we least expect it, the column forms and ceases to be transparent, and we know in all our being that God is here, that he has never been away, that the One who was in the beginning before all things were made was also born in a cattle stall in Bethlehem and was put to death on a cross on a hillside near Jerusalem and is now stalking our lives from the future, whence he shall rapture us and carry us away to what has always been our home, even when we didn't know it.

III. Perhaps Christmas is that way for us, even when we have missed it, when we were too busy to celebrate it or to see the mystery of it. It leaves its small deposit, its gentle reminder that life is interlaced with holiness, that the kitchen table is real, not because we scrub it but because it is held somehow, inexplicably, in the mind of God. I hope so. And I hope that if you didn't have a merry Christmas, you will still have it, recalling the glimpses along the way.—John Killinger

CONGREGATIONAL MUSIC RELATED TO THE LECTIONARY

BY PAUL A. RICHARDSON

The hymns have been chosen for their relation to the Scripture readings for each service. They are not merely compatible with the theme of the pericope but reflect the particular language, imagery, or content of the passage. Several choices are provided for some readings; others have no readily accessible companion in the hymnic literature. Sometimes the scriptural link, though evident, is not that of traditional usage (for example, "Joy to the World," typically sung at Christmas, is a paraphrase of Psalm 98). The use of a familiar text in a different context can prompt new awareness of both Scripture and hymn.

Because hymn texts have often been altered, even in their first lines, the author's surname or the source is provided as an aid to location. No judgments are made as to authenticity of attributions, nor are preferences expressed for particular translations. The texts are listed in alphabetical order within each grouping.

Seven hymns are identified in connection with three or more distinct passages. Learning and repeating these in their multiple relationships offers a way to expand a congregation's enduring repertory for worship. These hymns are:

"Christ, from Whom All Blessings Flow" (Wesley)
"Christ Is Risen, Christ Is Living" (Martínez)
"Christ, You Are the Fulness" (Polman)
"Come Down, O Love Divine" (Bianco of Siena)
"O Day of Peace That Dimly Shines" (Daw)
"Of the Father's Love Begotten" (Prudentius)
"Sing Praise to God Who Reigns Above" (Schütz)

If a hymn is widely published, no source is cited. For those found in only one of the hymnals listed here, that book is indicated using the following abbreviations:

BH *The Baptist Hymnal* (Nashville: Convention Press, 1991).
CH *Chalice Hymnal* (St. Louis: Chalice Press, 1995).
HWB *Hymnal: A Worship Book* (Elgin, IL: Brethren Press, 1992).
NCH *The New Century Hymnal* (Cleveland: The Pilgrim Press, 1995).
PH *The Presbyterian Hymnal* (Louisville: Westminster/John Knox Press, 1990).
RS *RitualSong: A Hymnal and Service Book for Roman Catholics* (Chicago: GIA, 1996).

UMH *The United Methodist Hymnal: Book of United Methodist Worship* (Nashville: The United Methodist Publishing House, 1989).

WC *The Worshiping Church* (Carol Stream, IL: Hope Publishing, 1990).

Particular mention must be made of *Hymns for the Gospels* (Chicago: GIA, 2001)—an anthology of texts chosen specifically for use with the Gospel readings for most Sundays in the three-year lectionary. Because of its focus and function, this collection is cited with the abbreviation HG for every relevant text, even if it also appears in one or more of the hymnals.

Hymns identified with the Psalm readings are closely related to the corresponding text, in keeping with the design of the Revised Common Lectionary, which intends that the Psalm itself be a response to the first lesson. Because numerous recently published resources, including many hymnals, provide brief responses for use with the reading or chanting of the Psalms, none of these is cited here. Rather, all hymns listed in connection with the Psalms are metrical versions; that is, they are in traditional multi-stanza hymn form. Many of these come from *The Presbyterian Hymnal.* A more extensive collection of stanzaic Psalm settings is found in the Christian Reformed Church's *Psalter Hymnal* (Grand Rapids, MI: CRC Publications, 1987), which contains metrical versions of all 150 Psalms.

Those who would use hymns not found in their own congregational hymnal are reminded of the obligation, both legal and ethical, to observe the copyright law. Each of the collections cited provides clear information about copyright owners and agents.

Three services make available a wide range of this material without great cost or complex paperwork:

1. Christian Copyright License International (17201 NE Sacramento Street, Portland, OR 97230; www.ccli.com)
2. LicenSing: Copyright-cleared Music for Churches (Logos Productions, 6160 Carmen Avenue East, Inver Grove Heights, MN 55076–4422; www.joinhands.com)
3. OneLicense.net, found on the Web at that address

Though all three are useful, the last is particularly so with the literature covered here, as it provides access to materials from GIA and Oxford University Press.

January 7 (Baptism of the Lord)

Isaiah 43:1–7 "How Firm a Foundation" ("K")

Psalm 29 "The God of Heaven Thunders" (Perry) PH; "Worship the Lord in the Beauty of Holiness" (Monsell)

Acts 8:14–17 (Although no hymns treat this specific passage, many relate to the coming of the Holy Spirit. See the listings for May 27 [Pentecost] and the weeks following.)

Luke 3:15–17, 21–22 "Christ, Your Footprints through the Desert" (Stuempfle) HG; "Mark How the Lamb of God's Self-Offering" (Daw) NCH; "Songs of Thankfulness and Praise" (Wordsworth); "What Ruler Wades through Murky Streams" (Troeger) NCH; "When Jesus Came to Jordan" (Green) HG

January 14
Isaiah 62:1–5 [none]
Psalm 36:5–10 "Come, Thou Fount of Every Blessing" (Robinson); "Thy Mercy and Thy Truth, O Lord" (*The Psalter,* 1912) PH
1 Corinthians 12:1–11 "Christ, from Whom All Blessings Flow" (Wesley); "Come, Holy Ghost/Spirit, Our Souls Inspire" (Maurus); "Come to Us, Creative Spirit" (Mowbray) WC; "Forward Through the Ages" (Hosmer); "Many Are the Lightbeams from the One Light" (Cyprian of Carthange); "Spirit, Working in Creation" (Richards) WC
John 2:1–11 "As Man and Woman We Were Made" (Wren) UMH; "Come, Join in Cana's Feast" (Stuempfle) HG; "God, in the Planning and Purpose of Life" (Bell and Maule) RS; "Jesus, Come, for We Invite You" (Idle) WC; "Songs of Thankfulness and Praise" (Wordsworth)

January 21
Nehemiah 8:1–3, 5–6, 8–10 "Stand up and Bless the Lord" (Montgomery)
Psalm 19 "God's Law Is Perfect and Gives Life" (Webber) PH [verses 7–14]; "Nature with Open Volume Stands" (Watts); "O/Let's Sing unto the Lord" (Carlos Rosas); "The Heavens Above Declare God's Praise" (Webber) PH [verses 1–6]
1 Corinthians 12:12–31a "Christ, from Whom All Blessings Flow" (Wesley); "God of Change and Glory" (Carmines) NCH; "In Christ There Is No East or West" (Oxenham)
Luke 4:14–21 "Arise, Your Light Is Come" (Duck) [based on Isaiah 60 and 61]; "Live into Hope of Captives Freed" (Huber) PH; "O for a Thousand Tongues to Sing" (Wesley) [see UMH for relevant stanza]; "The Kingdom of God Is Justice and Joy" (Rees) WC; "A Year of God's Favor" (Dufner) HG

January 28
Jeremiah 1:4–10 [none]
Psalm 71:1–6 [none]
1 Corinthians 13:1–13 "Gracious Spirit, Holy Ghost" (Wordsworth) PH; "Not for Tongues of Heaven's Angels" (Dudley-Smith); "Though I May Speak with Bravest Fire" (Hopson); "Where Charity and Love Prevail" (anonymous Latin)
Luke 4:21–30 "God Has Spoken by His/the Prophets" (Briggs) HG

February 4
Isaiah 6:1–8, 9–13 "God Himself Is with Us" (Tersteegen); "Holy God, We Praise Your Name" (Franz); "Holy, Holy, Holy, Lord God Almighty" (Heber); "I, the Lord of Sea and Sky" (Schutte); "My God, How Wonderful Thou Art/You Are (Faber); "Thuma Mina [Send Me], Lord" (South African) [verse 8]
Psalm 138 "I Will Give Thanks with My Whole Heart" (Webber) PH
1 Corinthians 15:1–11 Christ Is Risen, Christ Is Living" (Martínez); "This Is the Threefold Truth" (Green)
Luke 5:1–11 "Lord, You Have Come to the Lakeshore" (Gabaraín); "When Jesus Walked Beside the Shore" (Stuempfle) HG

February 11
Jeremiah 17:5-10 [see Psalm 1]
Psalm 1 "How Blest Are They/The One Is Blest Who, Fearing God" (Gower); "Like a Tree Beside the Waters" (Martin) NCH
1 Corinthians 15:12-20 "Christ Is Risen, Christ Is Living" (Martínez); "Christ the Lord Is Risen Today" (Wesley); "Sing with All the Saints in Glory" (Irons) UMH
Luke 6:17-26 "Blessed Are the Poor in Spirit" (Edwards) NCH; "Your Ways Are Not Our Own" (Bayler) HG

February 18
Isaiah 55:10-13 "Isaiah the Prophet Has Written of Old" (Patterson); "Seek the Lord Who Now Is Present" (Green) UMH; "You Shall Go out with Joy" (Rubin) TWC
Psalm 92:1-4, 12-15 "It Is Good to Sing Your Praises" (*The Psalter*, 1912) TWC
1 Corinthians 15:51-58 "Abide with Me; Fast Falls the Eventide" (Lyte); "Alleluia! Alleluia! Give Thanks to the Risen Lord" (Fishel); "Christ Has Arisen" (anonymous Swahili) HWB; "Christ High-Ascended" (Dudley-Smith) TWC; "Christ Is Risen, Christ Is Living" (Martinez); "Christ the Lord Is Risen Today" (Wesley); "In the Bulb There Is a Flower" (Sleeth); "Jesus Lives, and So Shall I" (Gellert) TWC; "My Lord, What a Morning" (African American spiritual); "O, When Shall I See Jesus" (Leland) TWC; "Rejoice, the Lord Is King" (Wesley); "Steal Away to Jesus" (African American spiritual); "The Strife Is O'er" (anonymous Latin); "These Are the Facts as We Have Received Them" (Saward); "Thine/Yours Is the Glory" (Budry)
Luke 6:39-49 "Deliver Us, O Lord of Truth" (Stuempfle) HG; "My Hope Is Built on Nothing Less" (Mote); "We Would Be Building" (Deitz) NCH

February 25
Deuteronomy 26:1-11 "As Men/Those/Saints of Old Their Firstfruits Brought" (Christierson); "For the Fruit of All Creation" (Green); "God, Whose Farm Is All Creation" (Arlott) HWB; "Great God, We Sing That Mighty Hand" (Doddridge); "We Give Thee but Thine Own" (How)
Psalm 91:1-2, 9-16 "Be Not Dismayed, Whate'er Betide" (Martin); "Safe in the Shadow of the Lord" (Dudley-Smith) WC; "Sing Praise to God, Who Reigns Above" (Schütz); "Within Your Shelter, Loving God" (Dunn) PH
Romans 10:8b-13 "Here, O Lord, Your Servants Gather" (Yamaguchi); "Immortal Love, For Ever Full" (Whittier)
Luke 4:1-13 "Forty Days and Forty Nights" (Smyttan); "From the River to the Desert" (Dunstan) HG; "Jesus, Tempted in the Desert" (Stuempfle) RS; "Lord, Who Throughout These Forty Days" (Hernaman); "O Love, How Deep, How Broad, How High" (anonymous Latin)

March 4
Genesis 15:1-12, 17-18 "The God of Abraham Praise" (Dayyan)
Psalm 27 "God Is My Strong Salvation" (Montgomery)
Philippians 3:17-4:1 [none]
Luke 13:31-35 "O Jesus Christ, May Grateful Hymns Be Rising" (Webster); "Welcome, All You Noble Saints" (Stamps) HG

March 11

Isaiah 55:1–9 "All You Who Are Thirsty" (Connolly) RS; "Come, All of You" (anonymous Laotian); "Seek the Lord Who Now Is Present" (Green)

Psalm 68:1–8 "God Is My Great Desire" (Dudley-Smith) WC; "O God, You Are My God" (Webber) PH; "O Lord, You Are My God" (Dunn) PH

1 Corinthians 10:1–13 [none]

Luke 13:1–9 "Come to Tend God's Garden" (Dalles) NCH; "Sovereign Maker of All Things" (Daw) HG

March 18

Joshua 5:9–12 [none]

Psalm 32 "How Blest Are the People Possessing True Peace" (Wollett) WC; "How Blest Are Those Whose Great Sin" (Anderson) PH

2 Corinthians 5:16–21 "God, You Spin the Whirling Planets" (Huber); "Love Divine, All Loves Excelling" (Wesley); "My Song Is Love Unknown" (Crossman); "O Come and Dwell in Me" (Wesley) UMH; "The First Day of Creation" (Troeger) CH; "This Is a Day of New Beginnings" (Wren); "Walk on, O People of God" (Gabaraín); "We Know That Christ Is Raised and Dies No More" (Geyer)

Luke 15:1–3, 11b–32 "A Woman and a Coin" (Vajda) CH; "Far, Far Away from My Loving Father" (anonymous) HWB; "Far from Home We Run Rebellious" (Stuempfle) HG [verses 11b–32]; "Our Father, We Have Wandered" (Nichols) RS; "Shepherd, Do You Tramp the Hills?" (Stuempfle) HG [verses 1–3]

March 25

Isaiah 43:16–21 "This Is a Day of New Beginnings" (Wren)

Psalm 126 "Let Us Hope When Hope Seems Hopeless" (Beebe) NCH; "When God Delivered Israel" (Saward) PH

Philippians 3:4b–14 "All That I Counted as Gain" (Joncas) RS; "Ask Ye What Great Thing I Know" (Schwedler); "Be Thou My Vision" (anonymous Irish); "Before the Cross of Jesus" (Blanchard); "When I Survey the Wondrous Cross" (Watts)

John 12:1–8 "Said Judas to Mary, 'Now What Will You Do?'" (Carter) HG

PALM SUNDAY
April 1

Luke 19:28–40 "All Glory, Laud, and Honor" (Theodulph of Orleans); "Filled with Excitement, All the Happy Throng" (Ruíz); "Hosanna, Loud Hosanna" (Threlfall); "Rejoice, O Zion's Daughter" (Stuempfle) HG; "Ride on, Ride on in Majesty" (Milman)

Psalm 118:1–2, 19–29 "Open Now Thy Gates of Beauty" (Schmolck); "This Is the Day the Lord Hath Made" (Watts)

PASSION SUNDAY

Isaiah 50:4–9a [none]

Psalm 31:9–16 "God of Our Life, Through All the Circling Years" (Kerr); "God of the Ages" (Clarkson) WC; "In You, Lord, Have I Put My Trust" (Reissner) PH

Philippians 2:5–11 "A Hymn of Glory Let Us Sing" (Bede); "All Hail the Power of Jesus' Name" (Perronet and Rippon); "All Praise to Thee, for Thou, O King Divine" (Tucker); "At the Name of Jesus" (Noel); "Creator of the Stars of Night" (anonymous Latin); "Lord of All Nations, Grant Me Grace" (Spannaus) RS

Luke 22:14–23:56 "A Purple Robe, a Crown of Thorns" (Dudley-Smith); "Bread of the World, in Mercy Broken" (Heber); "For the Bread Which You Have Broken" (Benson); "Great God, Your Love Has Called Us Here" (Wren); "Jesus, Remember Me" (Taizé); "Jesus Took the Bread, Daily Gift of God" (Duck) NCH; "Kneeling in the Garden Grass" (Troeger) RS; "Lone He Prays Within the Garden" (Stuempfle) HG; "Now to Your Table Spread" (Murray); "There Is a Fountain Filled with Blood" (Cowper); " 'Tis Midnight; and on Olive's Brow" (Tappan)

April 8

Isaiah 65:17–25 "O Day of Peace That Dimly Shines" (Daw)

Psalm 118:1–2; 14–24 "Come, Let Us with Our Lord Arise" (Wesley) WC [also relates to the Gospel]; "Open Now Thy Gates of Beauty" (Schmolck); "This Is the Day the Lord Hath Made" (Watts)

Acts 10:34–43 [none]

or

1 Corinthians 15:19–26 "Christ Jesus Lay in Death's Strong Bands" (Luther); "Christ the Lord Is Risen Today" (Wesley); "Come, Ye/You Faithful, Raise the Strain" (John of Damascus); "Jesus Christ Is Risen Today" (anonymous); "Sing with All the Saints in Glory" (Irons)

John 20:1–18 "I Come to the Garden Alone" (Miles); "O Mary, Don't You Weep" (African American spiritual) UMH; "The Sun Was Bright That Easter Dawn" (Stuempfle) HG; "Woman, Weeping in the Garden" (Damon) CH

April 15

Acts 5:27–32 [none]

Psalm 118:14–29 "Open Now Thy Gates of Beauty" (Schmolck); "This Is the Day the Lord Hath Made" (Watts)

Revelation 1:4–8 "Christ the Lord Is Risen Today" (Wesley); "Jesus Christ Is Risen Today" (anonymous); "Jesus Shall Reign Where'er the Sun" (Watts) [based on Psalm 72]; "Lo, He/Jesus Comes with Clouds Descending" (Wesley)

John 20:19–31 "Breathe on Me, Breath of God" (Hatch); "Chosen and Sent by the Father" (Clarkson) HG; "O Breath of Life, Come Sweeping Through Us" (Head); "O Sons and Daughters, Let Us Sing" (Tisserand); "Show Me Your Hands, Your Feet, Your Side" (Dunstan) HG; "These Things Did Thomas Count as Real" (Troeger); "Thine/Yours Is the Glory, Risen Conquering Son" (Budry); "We Walk by Faith and Not by Sight" (Alford)

April 22

Acts 9:1–6, 7–20 [none]

Psalm 30 "Come Sing to God, O Living Saints" (Anderson) PH

Revelation 5:11–14 "All Hail the Power of Jesus' Name" (Perronet and Rippon); "Blessing and Honor and Glory and Power" (Bonar); "Fairest Lord Jesus" (anonymous German); "See the Morning Sun Ascending" (Parkin) UMH; "Ten Thousand Times Ten Thousand" (Alford); "This Is the Feast of Victory for Our God" (Arthur); "What Wondrous Love Is This, O My Soul" (anonymous); "Ye/You Servants of God, Your Master Proclaim" (Wesley); "Ye Watchers and Ye Holy Ones" (Riley)

John 21:1–19 "More Love to Thee, O Christ" (Prentiss); "O Risen Christ, You Search Our Hearts" (Stuempfle) HG; "The Empty-Handed Fishermen" (Leach) HG

April 29

Acts 9:36–43 [none]

Psalm 23 "My Shepherd Will Supply My Need" (Watts); "The King of Love My Shepherd Is" (Baker); "The Lord's My Shepherd, All My Need" (Webber); "The Lord's My Shepherd, I'll Not Want" (Huber); "The Lord's My Shepherd, I'll Not Want" (Scottish Psalter)

Revelation 7:9–17 "Behold the Host, All Robed in Light" (Brorson) NCH; "Christ the Lord Is Risen Again" (Weisse); "Crown Him with Many Crowns" (Bridges and Thring); "For All the Saints Who from Their Labors Rest" (How); "Here from All Nations, All Tongues, and All Peoples" (Idle) WC; "John Saw the Number" [Alabaré] (anonymous Latin American) CH; "Lift High the Cross" (Kitchin and Newbolt); "O What Their Joy and Their Glory Must Be" (Abelard); "Ye/You Servants of God, Your Master Proclaim" (Wesley); "Ye Watchers and Ye Holy Ones" (Riley)

John 10:22–30 "Savior, Like a Shepherd, Lead Us" (Thrupp); "You, Lord, Are Both Lamb and Shepherd" (Dunstan) HG

May 6

Acts 11:1–18 "Spirit of the Living God, Fall Fresh on Me" (Iverson); (See also other hymns on the Holy Spirit listed for May 27 [Pentecost] and the weeks following.)

Psalm 148 "All Creatures of Our God and King" (Francis of Assisi); "Creating God, Your Fingers Trace" (Rowthorn); "God Created Heaven and Earth" (anonymous Taiwanese); "Let the Whole Creation Cry" (Brooks); "Praise the Lord! Ye Heavens Adore Him" (anonymous English); "Stars and Planets Flung in Orbit" (Stuempfle) NCH

Revelation 21:1–6 "Be Still, My Soul" (Schlegel); "Come, We That Love the Lord" (Watts); "For the Healing of the Nations" (Kaan); "Here, O My/Our Lord, I/We See Thee/You Face to Face" (Bonar); "I Want to Be Ready" (African American spiritual); "In Heaven Above" (Laurinus); "Jerusalem, My Happy Home" (anonymous English); "O Holy City, Seen of John" (Bowie); "O Lord, You Gave Your Servant John" (Patterson); "O What Their Joy and Their Glory Must Be" (Abelard)

John 13:31–35 "Lord, Help Us Walk Your Servant Way" (Stuempfle) HG; "Love Is His Word" (Connaughton) RS; "We Are One in the Spirit" (Scholtes); "Where Charity and Love Prevail" (anonymous Latin)

May 13

Acts 16:9–15 [none]

Psalm 67 "God of Mercy, God of Grace" (Lyte) PH; "Let All the World in Every Corner Sing" (Herbert)

Revelation 21:10, 22–22:5 "I Want to Walk as a Child of the Light" (Thomerson); "O Holy City, Seen of John" (Bowie); "O Lord, You Gave Your Servant John" (Patterson)

John 14:23–29 "Come Down, O Love Divine" (Bianco of Siena); "May God's Love Be Fixed Above You" (Dalles) HG

May 20
Acts 16:16–34 "And Could It Be That I Should Gain" (Wesley)
Psalm 97 "Earth's Scattered Isles and Contoured Hills" (Rowthorn) PH; "Sing Praise to God Who Reigns Above" (Schſtz)
Revelation 22:12–14, 16–17, 20–21 "Come, Ye/You Thankful People, Come" (Alford); "O Morning Star, How Fair and Bright" (Nicolai); "Of the Father's Love Begotten" (Prudentius); "The King Shall Come When Morning Dawns" (Brownlie); "Welcome, All You Noble Saints of Old" (Stamps) RS
John 17:20–26 "At That First Eucharist Before You Died" (Turton) RS; "Eternal Christ, Who, Kneeling" (Reid) HG

May 27
Acts 2:1–21 "Filled with the Spirit's Power" (Peacey); "Like the Murmur of the Dove's Song" (Daw); "O Breath of Life, Come Sweeping Through Us" (Head); "O Church of God, United" (Morley) UMH; "O Holy Dove of God Descending" (Leech); "O Spirit of the Living God" (Tweedy); "On Pentecost They Gathered" (Huber); "When God the Spirit Came" (Dudley-Smith) RS; "Wind Who Makes All Winds That Blow" (Troeger)

or

Genesis 11:1–9 [none]
Psalm 104:24–34, 35b "Bless the Lord, My Soul and Being" (Anderson) PH; "Many and Great, O God, Are Thy Ways" (Renville); "O Worship the King, All Glorious Above" (Grant)
Romans 8:14–17 "For Your Gift of God the Spirit" (Clarkson); "Praise the God Who Changes Places" (Wren) RS
John 14:8–17, 25–27 "God Is Unique and One" (Kaan) HG; "Holy Spirit, Truth Divine" (Longfellow); "Love Divine, All Loves Excelling" (Wesley) [verses 25–27]; "Blessed Jesus, at Your Word" (Clausnitzer); "Come Down, O Love Divine" (Bianco of Siena); "May God's Love Be Fixed Above You" (Dalles) HG

June 3
Proverbs 8:1–4, 22–31 "Source and Sovereign, Rock and Cloud" (Troeger); "Who Comes from God as Word and Breath" (Michaels) CH
Psalm 8 "How Great Our God's Majestic Name" (Dudley-Smith) BH; "Lord, Our Lord, Thy Glorious Name" (*The Psalter*, 1912); "O How Glorious, Full of Wonder" (Beach) NCH; "O Lord, Our God, How Excellent" (Anderson) PH
Romans 5:1–5 "Come Down, O Love Divine" (Bianco of Siena); "Come, Holy Ghost, Our Souls Inspire" (Maurus); "Come, Holy Spirit, Heavenly Dove" (Watts); "Creator God, Creating Still" (Huber)
John 16:12–15 "Holy Spirit, Truth Divine" (Longfellow); "Let Your Spirit Teach Me, Lord" (Clarkson) HG

June 10
1 Kings 17:8–16, 17–24 "Though Falsely Some Revile or Hate Me" (Ni) NCH
Psalm 146 "I'll Praise My Maker While I've Breath" (Watts)
Galatians 1:11–24 [none]
Luke 7:11–17 "The Ranks of Death with Trophy Grim" (Stuempfle) HG; "Your Hands, O Lord, in Days of Old" (Plumptre) RS

June 17
1 Kings 21:1–10, 11–14, 15–21a [none]
Psalm 5:1–8 "As Morning Dawns, Lord Hear Our Cry" (Anderson) PH
Galatians 2:15–21 "Alas, and Did My Savior Bleed" (Watts); "Alleluia, Alleluia, Give Thanks to the Risen Lord" (Fishel)
Luke 7:36–8:3 "Said Judas to Mary 'Now What Will You Do?'" (Carter) HG; "Two Fishermen, Who Lived Along the Sea of Galilee" (Toolan) WC; "When Jesus Came Preaching the Kingdom of God" (Green) RS

June 24
1 Kings 19:1–4, 5–7, 8–15a "As Water to the Thirsty" (Dudley-Smith) WC; "Dear Lord and Father of Mankind" [many variants] (Whittier) [also relates to the Gospel]; "Though Falsely Some Revile or Hate Me" (Ni) NCH
Psalm 42 "As Deer Long for the Streams" (Webber) PH [verses 1–7]; "As Pants/Longs the Hart for Cooling Streams" (New Version)
Galatians 3:23–29 "Baptized in Water" (Saward); "Blest Be the Tie That Binds" (Fawcett); "Christ, from Whom All Blessings Flow" (Wesley); "In Christ There Is No East or West" (Oxenham); "One Bread, One Body" (Foley) UMH; "Pan de Vida" [Bread of Life] (Hurd and Moriarty) RS; "When Minds and Bodies Meet as One" (Wren) NCH
Luke 8:26–39 "Silence, Frenzied, Unclean Spirit" (Troeger) HG [Though based on Mark 1:23–27 and parallels, there are connections to this passage.]

July 1
2 Kings 2:1–2, 6–14 "Swing Low, Sweet Chariot" (African American spiritual)
Psalm 77:1–2, 11–20 "How Long, O Lord, Will You Forget" (Woollett) WC [based on Psalm 13]
Galatians 5:1, 13–25 "As Sons of the Day and Daughters of Light" (Idle) WC; "Lord of All Hopefulness" (Struther); "Of All the Spirit's Gifts to Me" (Green); "Spirit of God, Descend upon My Heart" (Croly)
Luke 9:51–62 "O Christ, Who Called the Twelve" (Stuempfle) HG; "O Jesus, I Have Promised" (Bode)

July 8
2 Kings 5:1–14 "God of the Prophets, Bless the Prophet's Sons/Heirs" (Wortman)
Psalm 30 "Come Sing to God, O Living Saints" (Anderson) PH; "Wake, My Soul, with All Things Living" (Canitz) NCH
Galatians 6:1–6, 7–16 "Ask Ye What Great Thing I Know" (Schwedler); "Called as Partners in Christ's Service" (Huber) [verses 1–6]; "In the Cross of Christ I Glory" (Bowring); "Lord,

Make Us Servants of Your Peace" (Quinn); "Lord, Whose Love in Humble Service" (Bayly); "When I Survey the Wondrous Cross" (Watts)

Luke 10:1–11, 16–20 "Let Us Talents and Tongues Employ" (Kaan); "Lord, You Give the Great Commission" (Rowthorn); "Not Alone, but Two by Two" (Daw) HG

July 15

Amos 7:7–17 "Let Justice Flow Like Streams" (Huber) NCH

Psalm 82 [none]

Colossians 1:1–14 [none]

Luke 10:25–37 "Jesu, Jesu, Fill Us with Your Love" (Colvin); "They Asked, 'Who's My Neighbor?'" (Wesson); "We Praise You with Our Minds, O Lord" (McElrath); "We Sing Your Praise, O Christ" (Stuempfle) HG

July 22

Amos 8:1–12 "Make a Gift of Your Holy Word" (Imakoma) NCH

Psalm 52 [none]

Colossians 1:15–28 "Christ Beside Me, Christ Before Me" (Quinn) WC; "Christ Is Risen, Christ Is Living" (Mart,nez); "Christ, You Are the Fulness" (Polman); "God of Creation, All-Powerful, All-Wise" (Clarkson) WC; "O Christ, the Great Foundation" (Lew) NCH; "Of the Father's Love Begotten" (Prudentius); "We Are Pilgrims on a Journey" [many variants] (Gillard); "When Peace, Like a River, Attendeth My Soul" (Spafford)

Luke 10:38–42 "Lord, Grant Us Grace to Know the Time" (Stuempfle) HG; "When Jesus Came Preaching the Kingdom of God" (Green) RS

July 29

Hosea 1:2–10 [none]

Psalm 85 [none]

Colossians 2:6–15, 16–19 "Baptized in Water" (Saward); "Great Work Has God Begun in You" (Birkland) NCH

Luke 11:1–13 "Forgive Our Sins, as We Forgive" (Herklots); "Let All Who Pray the Prayer Christ Taught" (Troeger) PH; "Lord, Teach Us How to Pray" (Stuempfle) HG; "Lord, Teach Us How to Pray Aright" (Montgomery); "Renew Your Church, Her Ministries Restore" (Cober)

August 5

Hosea 11:1–11 "Like a Mother Who Has Borne Us" (Bechtel) NCH

Psalm 107:1–9, 43 "Jesus, Thou Joy of Loving Hearts" (Bernard of Clairvaux); "Now Thank We All Our God" (Rinkart)

Colossians 3:1–11 "Christ, You Are the Fulness" (Polman)

Luke 12:13–21 "Lord, Whose Then Shall They Be?" (Stuempfle) HG

August 12

Isaiah 1:1, 10–20 "Come, Let Us Reason Together" (Medema)

Psalm 50:1–8, 22–23 "Golden Breaks the Dawn" (Chao)

Hebrews 11:1–3, 8–16 "Faith, While Trees Are Still in Blossom" (Frostenson); "For the Faithful Who Have Answered" (Dunstan) NCH; "Forward Through the Ages" (Hosmer); "How Clear Is Our Vocation, Lord" (Green); "Rejoice in God's Saints" (Green)
Luke 12:32–40 "God Whose Giving Knows No Ending" (Edwards) HG

August 19
Isaiah 5:1–7 [none]
Psalm 80:1–2, 8–19 "O Hear Our Cry, O Lord" (Anderson) PH
Hebrews 11:29–12:2 "For All the Saints Who from Their Labors Rest" (How); "Guide My Feet" (African American spiritual); "I Sing a Song of the Saints of God" (Scott); "I Want to Walk as a Child of the Light" (Thomerson); "The Head That Once Was Crowned with Thorns" (Kelly); "They Did Not Build in Vain" (Luff) NCH
Luke 12:49–56 "Thou/God/Christ, Whose Purpose Is to Kindle" (Trueblood) HG

August 26
Jeremiah 1:4–10 [none]
Psalm 71:1–6 [none]
Hebrews 12:18–29 "Come, We That Love the Lord" (Watts)
Luke 13:10–17 "By Peter's House in Village Fair" (Albright) HWB; "O Christ, the Healer, We Have Come" (Green) HG; "This Is the Day When Light Was First Created" (Kaan) RS

September 2
Jeremiah 2:4–13 [none]
Psalm 81:1, 10–16 [none]
Hebrews 13:1–8, 15–16 "For the Beauty of the Earth" (Pierpoint) [The connection is made by using the original refrain: "Christ, our God, to thee we raise/ this our sacrifice of praise."]; "Jesus Savior, Lo, to Thee I Fly" [Saranam] (anonymous Pakastani); "Jesus, Thou Joy of Loving Hearts" (Bernard of Clairvaux); "O Jesus, I Have Promised" (Bode); "Your Love, O God, Has Called Us Here" (Schulz-Widmar)
Luke 14:1, 7–14 "Christ, the One Who Tells the Tale" (Leach) HG; "God of the Ages" (Clarkson) WC

September 9
Jeremiah 18:1–11 "Have Thine Own Way, Lord" (Pollard)
Psalm 139:1–6, 13–18 "Search Me, O God" (Orr); "You Are Before Me, Lord" (Pitt-Watson) PH
Philemon 1–21 [none]
Luke 14:25–33 "For God Risk Everything" (Troeger) HG; "Take up Thy Cross and Follow Me" (McKinney); "Take up Thy/Your Cross, the Savior Said" (Everest)

September 16
Jeremiah 4:11–12, 22–28 [none]
Psalm 14 [none]
1 Timothy 1:12–17 "Immortal, Invisible, God Only Wise" (Smith)

Luke 15:1–10 "I Will Sing the Wondrous Story" (Rowley); "Our Father, We Have Wandered" (Nichols) RS; "Savior, Like a Shepherd Lead Us" (Thrupp); "Shepherd, Do You Tramp the Hills" (Stuempfle) HG

September 23
Jeremiah 8:18–9:1 "There Is a Balm in Gilead" (African American spiritual)
Psalm 79:1–9 [none]
1 Timothy 2:1–7 "God of Our Fathers/the Ages, Whose Almighty Hand" (Roberts); "Lift Every Voice and Sing" (Johnson); "O Beautiful, for Spacious Skies" (Bates); "O God of Every Nation" (Reid)
Luke 16:1–13 "Lord of All Good, We Bring Our Gifts to You" (Bayly) WC

September 30
Jeremiah 32:1–3a, 6–15 [none]
Psalm 91:1–6, 14–16 "Be Not Dismayed, Whate'er Betide" (Martin); "Safe in the Shadow of the Lord" (Dudley-Smith) WC; "Sing Praise to God, Who Reigns Above" (Schütz); "Within Your Shelter, Loving God" (Dunn) PH
1 Timothy 6:6–19 "All My Hope on God Is Founded" (Neander); "Fight the Good Fight with All Thy Might" (Monsell); "He Is King of Kings" (African American spiritual)
Luke 16:19–31 "Through All the World, a Hungry Christ" (Murray) NCH; "Thou/God/Christ, Whose Purpose Is to Kindle" (Trueblood) HG

October 7
Lamentations 1:1–6 [none]
Psalm 137 "By the Babylonian Rivers" (Bash) PH; "I Love Thy Kingdom, Lord" (Dwight)
2 Timothy 1:1–14 "I Know Not Why God's Wondrous Grace to Me He Hath Made Known" (Whittle); "Like a Mother Who Has Borne Us" (Bechtel) NCH
Luke 17:5–10 "Faith, While Trees Are Still in Blossom" (Frostenson); "Let Us Plead for Faith Alone" (Wesley) UMH; "When Our Confidence Is Shaken" (Green) HG

October 14
Jeremiah 29:1, 4–7 "All Who Love and Serve Your City" (Routley); "O Jesus Christ, May Grateful Hymns Be Rising" (Webster)
Psalm 66:1–12 "Let All the World in Every Corner Sing" (Herbert)
2 Timothy 2:8–15 "Come to Me, All You Weary" (Young) RS; "How Clear Is Our Vocation, Lord" (Green); "Keep in Mind That Jesus Christ Has Died for Us" (Deiss) RS; "O God, Our Faithful God" (Heerman); "We Hold the Death of the Lord Deep in Our Hearts" (Haas) RS
Luke 17:11–19 "An Outcast Among Outcasts" (Leach) NCH; "Banned and Banished by Their Neighbors" (Stuempfle) HG

October 21
Jeremiah 31:27–34 "Deep Within I Will Plant My Law" (Haas) RS; "O God, Who Gives Us Life and Breath" (Daw) HWB
Psalm 119:97–104 [none]

2 Timothy 3:14–4:5 "Powerful in Making Us Wise to Salvation" (Idle) WC
Luke 18:1–8 "Eternal Spirit of the Living Christ" (Christierson) HG

October 28
Joel 2:23–32 "Fear Not, Rejoice and Be Glad" (Wright) WC; "Return, My People, Israel" (Martin) NCH
Psalm 65 "Mountains Are All Aglow" (Lim) UMH; "Praise Is Your Right, O God, in Zion" (Wiersma) PH; "Sing to the Lord of Harvest" (Monsell); "To Bless the Earth God Sends Us" (*The Psalter*, 1912)
2 Timothy 4:6–8, 16–18 "Awake, My Soul, Stretch Every Nerve" (Doddridge); "Fight the Good Fight with All Thy Might" (Monsell)
Luke 18:9–14 "Here Master/O Savior in This Quiet Place" (Green); "In a Lowly Manger Born" (Yuki) HG

November 4
Habakkuk 1:1–4, 2:1–4 [none]
Psalm 119:137–144 [none]
2 Thessalonians 1:1–4, 11–12 [none]
Luke 19:1–10 "When Jesus Passed Through Jericho" (Stuempfle) HG

November 11
Haggai 2:1–9 [none]
Psalm 145:1–5, 17–21 "O Lord, You Are My God and King" (*The Psalter*, 1912) PH [verses 1–13]; "Your Faithfulness, O Lord, Is Sure" (Patterson) PH [verses 13–23]
2 Thessalonians 2:1–5, 13–17 [none]
Luke 20:27–38 "In the Bulb There Is a Flower" (Sleeth) HG

November 18
Isaiah 65:17–25 "O Day of Peace That Dimly Shines" (Daw)
Isaiah 12 "Surely It Is God Who Saves Me" (Daw); "With Joy Draw Water" (McKinstry) NCH
2 Thessalonians 3:6–13 [none]
Luke 21:5–19 "Here from All Nations" (Idle) HG

November 25
Jeremiah 23:1–6 [none]
Luke 1:68–79 "Blessed Be the God of Israel" (Quinn) BH; "Blessed Be the God of Israel" (Perry); "Now Bless the God of Israel" (Duck), NCH
Colossians 1:11–20 "Christ Is Risen, Christ Is Living" (Martínez); "Christ, You Art the Fulness" (Polman); "O Christ, the Great Foundation" (Lew) NCH; "Of the Father's Love Begotten" (Prudentius); "We Are Pilgrims on a Journey" [many variants] (Gillard); "When Peace, Like a River, Attendeth My Soul" (Spafford)
Luke 23:33–43 "A Purple Robe, A Crown of Thorns" (Dudley-Smith); "Jesus, Remember Me" (Taizé); "Lord, You Give the Great Commission" (Rowthorn); "Son of God, by God Forsaken" (Stuempfle) HG

December 2
Isaiah 2:1–5 "Behold a Broken World, We Pray" (Dudley-Smith) UMH; "Christ Is the World's True Light" (Briggs); "God Is Working His Purpose Out" (Ainger) [also relates to the Epistle]; "O Day of Peace That Dimly Shines" (Daw); "O God of Every Nation" (Reid); "Wake, Awake, for Night Is Flying" (Nicolai) [also relates to the Epistle and the Gospel]
Psalm 122 "With Joy I Heard My Friends Exclaim" (*The Psalter,* 1912)
Romans 13:11–14 "Awake, O Sleeper, Rise from Death" (Tucker)
Matthew 24:36–44 "Waken, O Sleeper" (Forster) HG

December 9
Isaiah 11:1–10 "Let Our Gladness Have No End" (anonymous German) HWB; "Lo, How a Rose E'er Blooming" (anonymous German); "Lord, Today We Have Seen Your Glory" (Balhoff) RS; "To a Virgin, Meek and Mild" (Boe and Overby); "O Come, O Come, Emmanuel" (anonymous Latin); "O Day of Peace That Dimly Shines" (Daw); "O Morning Star, How Fair and Bright" (Nicolai) [also relates to the Epistle]; "Who Would Think That What Was Needed" (Bell and Maule) NCH
Psalm 72:1–7, 18–19 "Hail to the Lord's Anointed" (Montgomery); "Jesus Shall Reign Where'er the Sun" (Watts)
Romans 15:4–13 "Help Us Accept Each Other" (Kaan); "Hope of the World, Thou Christ of Great Compassion" (Harkness)
Matthew 3:1–12 "Comfort, Comfort Ye/You My People" (Olearius); "On Jordan's Bank the Baptist's Cry" (Coffin); "When John Baptized by Jordan's River" (Dudley-Smith) RS; "Wild and Lone the Prophet's Voice" (Daw) HG

December 16
Isaiah 35:1–10 "Awake! Awake, and Greet the New Morn" (Haugen) [also relates to the reading from Matthew]; "Strengthen All the Weary Hands" (McMane) NCH; "The Desert Shall Rejoice" (Grindal) PH; "When the King Shall Come Again" (Idle) WC
Luke 1:47–55 "For Ages Women Hoped and Prayed" (Huber); "My Soul Gives Glory to My God" (Winter); "Tell Out, My Soul, the Greatness of the Lord" (Dudley-Smith)
James 5:7–10 [none]
Matthew 11:2–11 "Are You the Coming One" (Stuempfle) HG

December 23
Isaiah 7:10–16 "O Come, O Come Emmanuel" (anonymous Latin); "To a Virgin Meek and Mild" (Boe and Overby)
Psalm 80:1–7, 17–19 "O Hear Our Cry, O Lord" (Anderson) PH
Romans 1:1–7 "God of the Prophets, Bless the Prophet's Sons/Heirs" (Wortman)
Matthew 1:18–25 "Hark, the Herald Angels Sing" (Wesley); "Joseph Dearest, Joseph Mine" (anonymous German); "Of the Father's Love Begotten" (Prudentius); "The First Noel the Angel Did Say" (anonymous English); "The Hands That First Held Mary's Child" (Troeger) HG

December 30
Isaiah 63:7–9 [none]
Psalm 148 "All Creatures of Our God and King" (Francis of Assisi); "Creating God, Your Fingers Trace" (Rowthorn); "God Created Heaven and Earth" (anonymous Taiwanese); "Let the

Whole Creation Cry" (Brooks); "Praise the Lord! Ye Heavens Adore Him" (anonymous English); "Stars and Planets Flung in Orbit" (Stuempfle) NCH

Hebrews 2:10–18 "My Faith Looks up to Thee" (Palmer); "O God, We Bear the Imprint of Your Face" (Murray)

Matthew 2:13–23 "In Bethlehem a Newborn Boy" (Herklots); "O Sleep, Dear Holy Baby" (anonymous Spanish); "Our Savior's Infant Cries Were Heard" (Troeger) HG

SECTION IV

RESOURCES FOR COMMUNION SERVICES

SERMON SUGGESTIONS

The Lord's Supper: A Healing

TEXT: 1 Cor. 11:23–34

As a young boy, I paid close attention to the worship of my dad. I thought some of his worship habits were unusual. He wouldn't pray in public, like other men of the church did. While others sang the hymns of faith, he would sit quietly and read the hymns. But he would never sing. And most unusual was this: when we came to the Lord's Supper services, he would never participate. Later I discovered that his reason for not receiving communion was based on the verses we just read. Somehow, even as a boy, I knew that Dad had missed what was intended. And I hurt for him.

The church in ancient Corinth was a troubled congregation in many ways, especially when it came to worship. When we seek for patterns for public worship, we'll do well to avoid the Corinthian patterns. Paul wrote to them and said, "This is how *not* to do it." As they gathered for communion, they were fractured and broken—a sick congregation. They didn't truly love God or one another. They needed to be healed. Paul believed that sitting at the table together, with the right spirit, mends our brokenness. Here we sense that the gospel of Christ, so obviously sufficient to forgive our sins, is also sufficient to heal our wounds. The prophet of old raised the question: "Is there a balm in Gilead? Is there a place of healing?" The life of Jesus Christ, the Scripture we read, and the Lord's Supper we celebrate—all say yes. There is a healing—a healing for the fractured spirit, the hurting soul, for a lost world—for each of us.

It's a healing that begins as we look inside ourselves. One part of his clear instruction involved abuses at the Lord's Supper. For some, it has become an occasion for hilarity, not reverence. These caustic words follow: "Whoever eats the bread or drinks the cup 'unworthily' is guilty of profaning the Lord. And because of your insincere motives and divisive loyalties, some among you are sick, and others have died." Notice he doesn't say that if you live such a fragmented and dysfunctional life, you may become sick; he said you already *are* sick.

I came across an article recently in one of the journals of psychology that caught my attention. The author said that a full 80 percent of the physical maladies that place patients in our hospitals are there with illnesses rooted in the emotional stresses with which we live. The call to wholeness declared by the Bible begins within us. Abraham Lincoln—our nation's president during that most divisive and deadly war in our history, the War Between the States—spoke of the greatest civil war that was raging inside his own heart. This fractured, wounded, and grieving heart needs to be healed. Perhaps you have one.

Two terms here need to be defined. The first is *unworthily.* We come to the table unworthily if we come selfishly (without regard for others) and flippantly (as if there is nothing here of great consequence). The other term is *examine ourselves*—an expression used to describe the testing of metals to ensure their quality. As used here, it is to probe deeply into our innermost selves and to come to grips with that which truly claims us. Such introspection yields an open heart, a willing spirit, and honesty with God and ourselves. As we come to the Lord's table, we are called to search deeply, to come to grips with our sins, to confess, repent, and get right with God and with our fellow man. And it's not just a good thing to do; the Bible says it's a healthy thing to do.

This healing also looks around us. That is, a healthy person is one who lives in vital community with others in God's family. Paul's challenge to the Corinthian Christians included this: "You're not rightly discerning, you're not making good decisions about the Lord's body." The commentators are in disagreement as to what this means. Is it the Lord's physical body they weren't making good decisions about? Or is it how one views the bread of the Supper, which Jesus called his body? Or can it be that Paul refers to the Church, which is called the body of Christ? This last answer makes sense to me, since the matter at hand was the Church's inability to get along and to make good decisions.

At the heart of the charge lay the Church's failure to exercise love at the Lord's table. It was a place where one could indulge. At the love feast, of which the Lord's Supper had become a part, some were guilty of gluttony—so much so that by the time the poorest of the people arrived (the ones for whom the feast was established), the food was gone, and the poor went away hungry. Others drank so much that they became drunk. Paul said, "This ought not to be." They tended to forget the basis of their gatheredness—that love was the cornerstone of their community. They were to love God with all their hearts and to love their neighbors as themselves. The second commandment really wasn't intended to be different from the first; it actually grows out of the first. How can a person truly love God and then, in turn, not love those whom God loves. In their contrivance of worship and ministry, they showed no love for God or for neighbor. When you "come together," wait for each other. Here is a kind of high and noble living that lives in relationship.

This healing also looks above us. The discussion begins with these words: "For I received from the Lord what I also passed on to you, that on the night of his betrayal, he took bread and blessed it and broke it and said, 'my body for you.' And he took the cup, poured it, blessed it and said, 'my blood, for you. My body, my blood, my love . . . for you.'"

Let's not miss the clear intention that something of eternal consequence is declared here, something forever valid, something everlastingly secure. God took the initiative and came to us so he could draw us to himself. God came and did for us, through Jesus Christ, what we could never do for ourselves. Augustine, in the third century, said it powerfully: "The soul was made by God and it cannot rest until it rests with God." God's marvelous work of redemption draws us to that place where our disrupted, malfunctioning, discontent ways find help and hope.

One of my favorite movies is the Sally Field classic, *Places in the Heart.* It's set in rural Texas during the hard days of the Great Depression. The movie begins in church, with the congregation singing "Blessed Assurance, Jesus Is Mine." The scene changes. The local sheriff, a dear and loving family man, is accidentally shot and killed by a black teenager. The teen is lynched by the townsmen, dragged behind a truck, and hung from a tree. Hatred fills the air. The sheriff's widow is left alone on a poor farm to raise two children.

But along comes a drifter—a black man, who becomes the helper around the farm, a share-cropper; he works hard to make that summer's crop a success so the farm's mortgage can be paid to the bank. The hard work pays off, and the farm is saved. All seems well until the local Klan arrives and beats the black sharecropper and drives him away from the farm. Again despair rises. A sense of disequilibrium rises up. You can't help but ask, "What happens next?"

The final scene is back at church again, and the congregation is singing "Blessed Assurance, Jesus is Mine." The pastor rises to read the Scripture just before the Lord's Supper: "If I speak in the tongues of man and of angels, and have not love, I am like a noisy gong or a clanging symbol." As the pastor continues to read 1 Corinthians 13, and the choir sings "I Come to the Garden Alone," communion is passed. As the bread and cup are passed through the congregation, the first surprise is when you see the black sharecropper eating and drinking. He's supposed to be out of the picture. Then others of the characters receive communion. There is a married couple, whose marriage has been rocked by infidelity, now sitting hand-in-hand, eating together. The Klansmen are there, eating alongside the black sharecropper. The widow shares the meal with her children. Then, with great surprise, she turns and offers communion to her husband—the sheriff—who had died when the movie began. Then, surprise upon surprise, he turns and shares communion with the black teenager who accidentally shot and killed him. They exchange the age-old words of grace: "The peace of God."

You know, I can see my dad there, and my mother, and brothers and sisters, and my dear Brenda and our children, and our extended families—and yes, all those who gather as the body of Christ. And I can envision us singing in the holy reverence of hushed tones: "The love of God, the love of God, can you see from that tree the love of God? There for you, there for me; he bleeds for you, he pleads for you; He gave all for you. Hear Him call to you who are weary, come to me."

As we come to the Lord's table today, we are aware of the living presence of our Lord, who meets us here. Perhaps you hear him say, "Good health to you!"—Lee McGlone

Topic: Holy Communion: Past, Present, and Future
TEXT: 1 Cor. 11:23–26

These are precious words for Christian believers. Unfortunately, we've heard them so often that sometimes our minds are on automatic pilot, and we don't really think about what we're hearing. So I challenge you today, before we actually come to the Lord's table, to really listen with your mind and with your heart. God wants to be known. God invites us into the divine presence.

I. *The past.* We know that the celebration of the Lord's Supper takes us back to events past. The disciples who had left all to follow Jesus shared a Passover meal with him under solemn and foreboding circumstances. They heard strange words from him that were impossible to understand at the time. "This is my body which is broken for you" (1 Cor. 11:24). "This cup is the new covenant in my blood" (1 Cor. 11:25). We look back at a series of events that happened in the past. The words are still awesome and mysterious, and, if we are honest, we acknowledge that they're still hard to understand. But through the lenses of Holy Scripture and generations of faith and interpretation, we do have some understanding. And we dare to affirm that Jesus Christ did something that broke the power of sin and evil in our lives.

This concept of "vicarious atonement" is not unique to Christianity. Medieval Jews, who often lived with persecution and suffering, loved to tell the story at Rosh Hashanah of "the ten holy rabbis" who were martyred by the Romans when they refused to renounce their faith and render homage to Caesar. It was said that the beauty of their holiness covered the unfaith of their people and saved them from destruction. In Jesus Christ we believe that God has been personally present, that God has personally intervened to absorb the hatred and the betrayal and the pain that mark our lives and to resolve the contradiction between God's own holiness, which must judge and eliminate evil, and God's infinite love and mercy, which cannot let us go.

The Scriptures say that Christ "once for all" entered the Holy of Holies (Heb. 10:10) and took upon himself the consequences of our sin. It is this unique past event that usually is front and center in our celebration of Holy Communion. That was so for Paul. He handed on to his flock what he had also received (1 Cor. 11:23). And it's so for us. But there's more.

II. *The present.* We might say that it's a beautiful concept contained in the Christian doctrine of atonement: God intervenes in our sinful world to take the suffering and the destruction upon God's self. But is it real? Where is God when the terrorists strike and horrified survivors are surrounded by the stench of death and paralyzed by the fear of "more to come?" Our best answer is this: God is there in the rubble, weeping with us, lending us strength and compassion to begin digging out, and, eventually, giving us courage to believe in a better future. Yes, there is one sense in which Christ's holy suffering was unique—and "once for all."

It is no accident that one name for the service of the Lord's table is Holy Communion. Our present togetherness in this place reminds us that we are all in this human condition together, with all its joys and all its suffering. We are all alike—broken children of God, standing before our Creator, as beggars for God's grace. The heroic patriot and the vengeful terrorist differ only by degree. When we come to this table in sincere repentance, we are together grateful for God's unmerited favor, and we together begin to believe in God's forgiveness and transforming power. We *together* begin to live toward God's future.

III. *The future.* The words stand out as we take the bread and the cup: "do this in remembrance of me" (1 Cor. 11:24, 25); that is, we are invited to ponder what Christ has done for us in the past. But Paul adds these further words to his account: "For as often as you eat this bread and drink the cup, you proclaim the Lord's death until he comes" (1 Cor. 11:26). When we come to the Lord's table, we dare to believe that things will be different, in this wounded world, as well as in the age to come. We dare to pray: "Your kingdom come, your will be done, on earth as it is in heaven" (Matt. 6:10). We dare to believe the vision of the prophet Micah, that in days to come the citizens of many nations shall learn from the Lord and trust the Lord for their security. And "they shall all sit under their own vines and under their own fig trees, and no one shall make them afraid" (Mic. 4:4). We dare to look the last enemy—death—in the eye and with Paul proclaim: "Death has been swallowed up in victory. Where, O death, is your victory? Where, O death, is your sting?" (1 Cor. 15:54–55).

When we have to make hard choices, when we must suffer the worst, we know that God is at our side. Because God bears with us, there is a different and better future ahead. Coming together at the Lord's table strengthens our faith in that future and clarifies our vision of it. As we believe in it, we begin to live it, and we become God's collaborators in bringing it about. All these insights, and more, are implicated in the simple words of institution of the Lord's Supper and in the simple acts of breaking bread and taking a cup. God calls us to be mindful as we celebrate Holy Communion.—David L. Wheeler

Topic: Communion Meditation

TEXT: 1 Pet. 1:17–23

How do we live as exiles in a strange land? This letter from Peter was written to the exiles—strangers in this world—in Asia Minor. Peter knew that to acknowledge and worship God as revealed in Jesus Christ was to make you, in many ways, a stranger in this world. When the Christian faith was spreading out across the face of Asia, the acceptance of God's love in Jesus Christ made you different from your neighbors. You did not want to participate in the patriotic gatherings that proclaimed the emperor "god." You were not welcome in the Jewish communities. You no longer wanted to support the worship of the Greek or Roman gods and goddesses. You were part of a very small minority with very little significance. You were different from those around you.

We have not been strangers in our culture for a very long time. But now we are beginning to feel like we are being pushed out. We are being made to feel like we are not wanted. We complain about lots of the decisions by the culture—decisions saying to us that we, as Christians, are not welcome. And the response to our criticism is that it doesn't really matter because nobody really takes it all seriously. But the reality is that the alliance between Christianity and culture is over. We have to learn how to live for God in a strange land.

But we can't live in this culture as orphans. The glorious good news of the grace made visible in Jesus Christ is the life-transforming discovery that we are children of God. We are not slaves made for sport for the gods. We are children of God. We call God our Father. We are loved by God the way parents love their children.

When we hear the good news of God's love in Jesus Christ, we are rescued from the empty ways of life that are promoted by the world. No wonder we get tired and bored with life. No wonder there are drug and alcohol problems. We are told that it is all sound and fury, signifying nothing. All the prizes turn out to be brass rings that turn our fingers green. There are three billion of us. But Jesus says that God is Abba. God is Father. God is Daddy. God loves us the way a parent loves us. God cares what we do. What we do has consequences. Life is now our participation in the family of God. God loves us and desires for us to become the best child we can become, part of the best family—the people of God—we can become. Love has expectations and discipline. We are God's children, who are invited to use our talents and time in the work of God's Kingdom.

Peter tells us that since we now call God "Father," we had better mind our P's and Q's. We need to live in awe, reverence, fear, and respect. Because God is our Father, what we do is important to God. Peter warns us not to expect that God will let us get by with less just because we are his children. We may think we can get special treatment from our earthly parents if they coach our team or teach us in school. But Peter says that God's expectations for his children are not lowered because he claims us as his own.

We are ransomed, rescued, liberated from the futility and emptiness of the world by the claim that God is our Father. God loves us. We matter. We matter enough that God is going to push us to become the best he created us to be. He loves us that much. He loves us enough to expect the best. How can we know he loves us that much? By the sacrifice that is displayed on this table. We are rescued from the meaninglessness of the world by the love made visible on this table. Because of the sacrifice on this table, we can indeed believe that God loves us the way a parent loves a child, and we can live in the hope and joy of that love. Come now to the joyful feast of the people of God.—Rick Brand

COMMUNION PRAYER.   We do praise you, O God, for all your goodness to us and to all peoples. As we draw near to you, O Father, we come with the assurance that you are already turned toward us in the eternity of your love. As on this occasion, we recall through word and sacrament your mighty deed for our salvation, we rejoice.

Help us to come with such integrity—loving you with all our mind, heart, and strength—that we worship you in spirit and in reality. In the name of the Father, Son, and Holy Spirit.—John Thompson

COMMUNION PRAYER.   We praise you, O God, for word and sacrament by which we live and move and have our being. We pray for all those we have named and for all others among us who are suffering, that we may experience the healing of your grace. As we walk in the valley of the shadow of death, lead us through to the Light of the Eternal Dawn. We pray for healing for the brokenness in our community, in our state, in our nation, in the fractures between nations, in the ethnic differences that divide the human family.

In the peace and quiet of this place, let us not forget the anguish of those victims of the senseless violence in this country and around the world, the anxiety of the oppressed in countries where the powerful exploit the weak, and the desperateness of those suffering the ravage of floods. We pray for all those who courageously persist in ways of peace. As the Divine Host, you prepare a table for us, even in the presence of our enemies: our doubts, our fears, our anxieties. In your love you are calling us each by name, affirming: "My daughter"—"My son." In your gracious hospitality you hand to us a cup of grace that is not only full but running over. In your house there is bread enough and to spare. Praise be to you, Father, Son, and Holy Spirit.—John Thompson

COMMUNION PRAYER.   O Thou, who comes to us offering the bread of life, we thank thee. Receiving this bread opens our eyes to the beauty of the world, opens our ears to songs of praise, and opens our hearts to the love that sustains thy people. We welcome this bread, for it increases our understandings of thy purposes, thy directions for our lives, and the meanings of each day. O give us the bread of life—bread that helps us understand the curious events of our years, politicians' promises, nations' maneuvers. Help us to penetrate the fogs that hide the road to peace and justice. Grant us wisdom to escape the frenzy of the moment and view our time from the perception of the living bread. O living bread feed us. Feed us, that we may leave this place increased in understanding, strengthened in purpose, and growing in the grace of our Lord Jesus Christ.—E. Rod Barr

RESOURCES FOR FUNERALS AND BEREAVEMENT

SERMON SUGGESTIONS

Topic: The Heart of Faith
Funeral Sermon for Josh Houston
TEXT: Ps. 27:1, 4; Rom. 8:28–38; 2 Cor. 4:13–5:1

I'm not sure I know how faith is nurtured in the soul. I just know how very real faith is when it rises up and is lived out profoundly in the life of a young man like Josh Houston. Josh had a heart of faith. At times faith is a great mystery. On Wednesday night, at our prayer meeting, one of the dearest ladies of our church leaned across the pew and said to me, "I don't understand this, pastor. Explain it to us." I can't do that. There is no explanation, no satisfactory answer that will remove the pain. What we can do is what Josh himself did. We can measure today by the calendar of eternity, not eternity by the calendar of today. Josh's heart was a heart of faith.

The psalmist wrote long ago with enthusiasm: "The Lord is my light and my salvation; whom shall I fear? The Lord is the stronghold of my life; of whom shall I be afraid?" The certainty with which the psalmist wrote those words is the same certainty with which Josh lived. And live he did. He lived with gusto. Josh was a lover of life, a lover of people; he had a smile as big as the world. I will never forget that it was only a year ago that he brought me a unique poster. It was a hand-drawn colored picture of Mike the Tiger, wearing an LSU apron, cooking a razorback over an open fire. The caption read: "Today's special: Roasted Razorback." Josh was a special young man.

One of the most significant texts in the Bible is Romans 8:28: "In all things, God works to bring about good for those who love him, those called according to his purpose." Notice the verse doesn't say that everything is good, or even that everything is God's will. What it declares is that "in all things," regardless of how bad they may be, God works to bring good from it. I suspect Josh believed that promise more than any of us. A year and a half ago, during one of the hard times for Josh, he said to me, when I asked him about his fear: "I'm not afraid; I'm just ready to go home to be with God."

I'm impressed with this third text that was read: "I believe, therefore I speak. I speak because I know that the one who raised the Lord Jesus Christ from the dead will also raise us . . . therefore we don't lose heart. Though outwardly we are wasting away, yet inwardly we are being renewed day by day." This is the message of every Christian; certainly, it is Josh's message to us. This earthly body will someday come to nothing. But there is another building, this one made in the heavens, which is eternal. This we proclaim! This Josh proclaimed: "I believe, therefore I speak." Josh was the preacher among us. He lived out his calling. He was preacher extraordinaire. By life and by death, he showed us the way.

I whispered to Josh on the night he died, "Josh, God holds you in his hands." He whispered back, "I know that!" Josh, we know that, too. And so, with everlasting faith in God our Savior, we entrust you, and ourselves, to the eternal home. We miss you. But we will see you again, there in that great day when all God's people join together around the throne. We shall live together in that world, where there is no ending.—Lee McGlone

Topic: Blessed Forever
Funeral Sermon for Marj Mullens
TEXT: Ps. 23:1–6; John 14:1–4; Rev. 21:1–6

Our first memories of Monroe, Louisiana, include Marj and John Mullens. The first voice I heard was from John. The first meal we ate was with them. In fact, it was a conversation with Marj that helped us make the decision to come to Parkview Baptist Church so many years ago. Over the years, we have enjoyed deep moments of worship and warm times of conversation. Such good memories make our hearts glad.

The Mullens family has been greatly blessed. It was a wonderful occasion just yesterday to sit with John and his children and to reminisce. Those years are blessed memories—even that of a golf swing that drove the ball only a foot or two. I suggest that we cherish the memories. I say we must talk often about the joys of life with Marj as wife, mother, grandmother, and friend. Marj was a lady who loved a lot—and was loved a lot.

Recent years have been difficult for Marj and John. We've watched her handle a difficult disease and maintain faith. She's taught us a great deal about grace and suffering and about how those two are often closely intertwined. For those who knew her well, there's no surprise here. The Jesus she loved and served had also known grace and suffering. Following the Crucified One was strength enough for her. Her life reflected that which is said of Christians in the Bible—those who are "afflicted in every way, but not crushed, perplexed but not despairing, struck down but not destroyed. This outer body is wasting away but the inner being is renewed day by day." How does this happen? We are "always carrying within us the death of Jesus—so that the life of Jesus will be real to us" (2 Cor. 4).

Marj's relation to Jesus was real to her. She once remarked to me, "I really think we need to speak more often of Jesus, the person Jesus. The word *Christ* is simply not personal enough." Honestly, that's not a distinction I had thought about. Today I say, "Thank you, Marj, for letting Jesus be alive in you. We're better people because of you." It is Marj's commitment that makes the biblical texts we read so important and so natural. I suspect we turn to these passages at times of death about as often as any in the Bible.

Psalm 23—the shepherd psalm—declares the deep, throbbing notes of assurance. The hand of God leads us, as the shepherd guides the sheep. Needs are provided for—abundantly. The table overflows with grace gifts, so that we sing, "Bread of heaven, feed me till I want no more." And when the walk of faith takes us through the valley of the shadow, whether the shadow of death or that of a difficult, disquieting portion of life, we fear no evil. And in the end, we dwell in the Lord's house forever!

John 14—this is a portion of Jesus' farewell discourse. "Let not your hearts be troubled, neither let them be afraid." How welcome are these words when our sad heart aches 'til it nearly breaks. Yet intermingled with the sadness is a holy gladness—the absolute assurance that life in faith does not end and that death does not win. God wins. God's gives the victory.

Revelations 21—John the seer was exiled on the island called Patmos. Surrounded by sea, he was separated from friends, family, and calling. But then, he had a vision. He saw a new heaven and a new earth, and there was no more sea. There was nothing to separate him from life again. God was there, and God's people were there. In that place there would be no more pain, sorrow, tears, suffering, or death. The former things had all passed away. Everything was new. Here is the promise on which we stand today.

I opened yesterday my C. S. Lewis file, for I knew Marj had read Lewis. They were, I think, kindred spirits. I found this poem. I'm not sure Lewis wrote it; it is anonymous, but it sounds like him.

> If everything is lost, thanks be to God.
> If I must see it go, watch it go,
> Watch it fade away, die,
> Thanks be to God that He is all I have.
> And if I have Him not, I have nothing at all,
> Nothing at all, only a farewell to the wind.
> Farewell to the gray sky.
> Goodbye. God be with you October evenings.
> If all is lost, thanks be to God.
> For He is He, and I am I.

Thanks, Marj, for being you—for us! Now to God's strong hands and into our eternal home, we let you go. At another day, we will gather with you again—and with all of God's faithful—heart touching heart, life touching life, hand-in-hand around the Great Throne of our Father above. Dear God, give us grace for the living of our days!—Lee McGlone

Topic: A Lasting Legacy
Funeral Service for Tom Scott
TEXT: Ps. 23; 2 Cor. 4:16–5:1

Longfellow wrote of a person's legacy:

> The lives of great men all remind us
> We can make our lives sublime,
> And, departing, leave behind us
> footprints on the sands of time.

Mr. Tom Scott left his footprints on the sands of our time. And he did so for each of us in unique ways. We gather as family, as friends, as church friends, as coworkers, business part-ners, and community leaders—and as fellow pilgrims who travel the self-same paths of life toward death. Together we mourn the loss of one so dear. Yet intermingled with the sadness within is the high note of gladness. Mr. Tom Scott lived a life full of accomplishment—a noble life that evinced the highest of moral values. His legacy will carry on. All this we celebrate. But most of all, we celebrate the assurance of eternal life that comes through faith.

Today we come to celebrate his life, to remember a man who touched us all deeply. Our memories are personal and unique, and they offer us help in dealing with our grief. Let's use our memories, for they are a resource for great living. In these brief few moments, I want to share with you, in a personal way, the Tom Scott I have come to know. Here are some of the footprints he has left in my life.

Mr. Tom Scott was a great churchman. It has been a great joy to serve as pastor. These two, Tom and Mayme, came to Parkview in April of 1948, at the time when the church was a young and aspiring congregation, in an area of town that was also young and aspiring. These two loved this church, supported it in every way, and stood by it in times of joy and sorrow. I think I can honestly say that I have never known a church member who loved his church more than Mr. Tom. In church life, many things are unsure. But one thing I could count on each week was Mr. Tom's presence. He was always there, in his place, in his pew, in his Sunday school class; he was there with words of encouragement and praise. This past Sunday was a sad one for me as I looked back—and he wasn't there.

Mr. Tom Scott had about him an uncanny evaluation of the human spirit. He believed in people, in our ability to rise high and to accomplish great things. He believed that there was more in people than naturally came out and that with encouragement, education, and hard work, we could be the best we could be.

You could see it in his bright eyes and in his broad smile, as he sat and watched our children's choirs perform or listen to the personal testimonies of teenagers who are growing in their faith. Nothing pleased him more than to watch young people in the process of becoming. He was glad to be a part of their lives, whether they were youngsters at the Louisiana Baptist Children's Home, whom he deeply loved, or college students taking their first steps into academia; he was glad to be a part of helping many of them succeed. We came to know that we mattered to him.

Mr. Tom Scott was a man of integrity. I recall many years ago my father lamenting the cultural shifts he had seen over his lifetime. He believed the day of honesty and integrity in business was a relic from a heartier past. "There was a time," my father said, "when a man's word was his bond, when deals were sealed with nothing more than a handshake, when a man's word was more important than the contract into which the deal was written. But those days are gone forever." I wish my father had lived long enough to have known Tom Scott. Perhaps he would have seen that such nobleness still exists and is still honored.

His integrity made him a man of influence. When he spoke, people listened. We listened because he had something to say. I watched him years ago in church committee meetings when things were not always clear, when matters of different opinions were on the table. He would listen, weigh options, determine priorities—and then he would speak. And when he spoke, everyone said, "That's right. What a great idea. Why didn't we think of that?" His influence was weighed by his honesty, and integrity carried the day.

Mr. Tom Scott was a man of unlimited optimism. I'm not sure that the phrase, "We can't do that," was ever in his vocabulary. If so, I never heard it. His vocabulary was always, "yes we can," and "no problem," and "absolutely." With his clear word of intention, we went to work and solved the problem. His optimism encouraged our own. On Sunday, one week ago, he came to me after morning worship and said, "You know, Lee, that was a great service of worship. I'm so proud of our choir, and those young people and children, and you preached a great sermon. You know, I'm more proud of Parkview now than ever in my life." A pastor appreciates such remarks. I thanked him for what he said and then asked, "Mr. Tom, how are you feeling?" "Never felt better in my life," he said. He was the eternal optimist.

Mr. Tom Scott was a man of faith. Look at this. He was a great churchman, with a high view of the human spirit, unmeasured integrity, and unlimited optimism. Where did those noble characteristics come from? They came from the source of everything good and eternal. They came from God. Before Mr. Scott was anything else, he was first a man of faith.

You who knew Tom best know that he never got over Mayme's death. He cared for her during her illness with such tenderness. After she died in April, almost two years ago, his life was never quite the same. He was never quite able to cope without her. When you are married sixty-three years, it's not an easy thing simply to "get over." But here is the good news. The hurt of grief is now ended. Tom and Mayme are together. The poet, Frederic Knowles, said this: "The lordliest of all things!—Life lends us only feet, Death gives us wings."

Mr. Tom, we will miss you. Please know that we love you and mourn your separation from us. But we know with abounding assurance that we will gather again in the far country— and there will never know separation again.—Lee McGlone

FUNERAL SERVICE INVOCATION.   Our Father who is in heaven and on earth, enshrined in the majesty of Creation yet ever present in the lives of your people, to you we come this hour to give honor and praise. Grant now the presence of your Holy Spirit that we may hear the quiet and gentle voice of eternity. Truly our days are as grass, nourished and healthy in the morning but by day's end tired and worn. Yet our hearts hold dreams that time cannot quench. Upon the promise of your eternal Word, we take our stand. May your holy name be forever praised! Great is thy faithfulness, O Lord God. Through the name of Jesus, the Son of God, we pray.—Lee McGlone

FUNERAL SERVICE BENEDICTION.   Father, let now the grace that has guided our lives to this point be forever our hope and shield. Grant your continued blessings to this dear family, and hold them close to your side. Give to us all, loving Father, what you will, when you will, in whatever measure pleases you, and in all things have your way with us.

Now unto him who is able to keep us from falling, and to present us as faultless before the presence of his glory with exceeding joy—to the only wise God, our Savior, be glory and majesty, dominion and power, now and forever. In Jesus' name we pray.—Lee McGlone

FUNERAL PRAYER.   As the Good Shepherd, you call us each by name. You know us altogether. You are sensitive to our deepest need, even when we are not. Minister to the depths of our spirits the comfort that only you can give. Still the anxieties of our minds and hearts with the holy hush of your loving presence. Yours is the strong hand of the father, clasping the trembling hand of a son or daughter. You are the mother, stroking our feverish brow with the soothing hands of love. You are the comfort that the world cannot give and the world cannot take away. Kindle the fires of faith that we may trust you in life or in death. May we receive your grace mighty to save, a cup that is not only full but running over. May we embrace one another in the love that seeks not its own but only the good of the other, as the Master did—as our beloved did. Renew a right spirit within us that in thought, word, and deed we may glorify you in all things.—John Thompson

FUNERAL PRAYER.   O God, we draw near to you with the assurance that you are already turned toward us in the eternity of your love. We thank you for the light of your presence, shining through the shadows of this hour. We praise you that even in sorrow we can give thanks. As in this time we sense our weakness, we are grateful for the strength of your everlasting arms. For your Word, which is as a well of living water springing up into everlasting life, we give you thanks. As we drink deeply of its meaning, may it be as an oasis for our spirits in a dry and thirsty land.

We praise you for your love that nothing in this world or in the world to come can separate us. Help us to realize that this crisis we call death can teach us so much of life. May we be faithful to the stewardship of sorrow. May we deepen down into him who is our life. May we listen for "deep speaking unto deep." As we are sensitive to the Eternal in the temporal, may we have courage to live, not as those without hope but as those with a living hope. O you, who are the God of all comfort, tenderly strengthen and encourage these, your children, of this home and family. With the comfort you give them, may they comfort others in their time of need. And grant to all of us that assurance that "life is ever Lord of death and love can never lose its own."—John Thompson

LENTEN AND EASTER PREACHING

SERMON SUGGESTIONS

Topic: A Word on Behalf of Sin

TEXT: Matt. 1:21; Rom. 5:6–11

The apostle Paul does not hesitate to speak about the reality of sin. In the fifth chapter of Romans, Paul states, "God commands his love toward us—that while we were sinners, Christ died for us" (Rom. 5:8). Here Paul contrasts human love with God's love. He draws a distinction between the amazing love of God and the unworthiness of the sinner.

I. He uses four expressions to describe the sinfulness of men and women.

(a) *Missing the mark.* Jesus was confronted by some religious leaders in his day who attempted to make rules and regulations about life exact and formalized. All people had to do was to abide by the rule book. If they did, their relationship with God would be all right. But that approach got difficult very early, because those who drew up the rule book began to add footnotes to their regulations and then footnotes to the footnotes. But then there are those who want to be on the other end of the moral scale and say, "Well, just let me make my own decisions. I will decide. My conscience will determine what is right and wrong for me." I am very troubled by those who want to say, "I will let my conscience be my guide," because the history of the world is filled with pages stained by blood based on individual decisions about right and wrong.

(b) *Weakness.* Paul uses "weakness" or "powerlessness" (v. 6) as images for sin. Some people reveal the weakness of their own character when they cry out, "I am not responsible for the sins of society." In our society today, some of us almost always want to say, "Not me." We point to somebody else for the blame. We blame heredity, environment, illness, circumstances, or emotions.

(c) *Ungodly.* Paul notes that we are also ungodly as sinners. Sin is what separates us from ourselves, from God, and our fellow human beings. Sin is the fragmentation that destroys relationships. Sin, in its widest sense, is not just our individual sin; it is our sense of sinfulness—our "god-almightiness." This is our way of saying, "I want to take control of my life, without any sense of needing God. I am totally in control. I am the master of my fate, the captain of my soul. I do not need others or God." Sin is the reality that leads, the Scriptures declare, to death. Sin, in all its seriousness, creates death within our authentic self, death in our relationships with other people, and, most profoundly, separates us from God. The Scriptures are very clear about the darkness of sin. "The wages of sin is death" (Rom. 6:23). Sin threatens our sense of life's meaning, and our self-centeredness results in death. Death is the consequence of a meaningless life that has lost its sense of direction and purpose.

(d) *Enemies.* Paul states, "When we were God's enemies" (v. 10), we had rebelled against God. We chose to turn our back on God and go our own way. God doesn't will that, but God permits it. He gives us freedom to do his will or to violate it. For example, he gives me the freedom to abuse my body or to make it stronger. He gives me the freedom to try to learn to do good or to do evil. He gives me the freedom to try to live a moral life or to live an immoral life. God does not force me to conform. When I violate the moral and spiritual laws that are built into the universe, into my life, and into relationships, I often can get hurt. Or I may hurt other people. Though we may receive forgiveness, and hopefully we will, that does not remove all the consequences that may have resulted from some sinful act. God forgives us, but sometimes the consequences of our sinfulness may go on for a long time.

II. Let us now turn the page and look at Paul's description of the amazing love of God in contrast to our sinfulness. In verse 8 Paul writes that God commends, recommends, demonstrates, or proves God's love to us. *Proves* is a word of logic and is not too satisfying to me. *Commends* addresses the heart.

(a) *Holy love.* A great gulf separates us from God because of God's holiness. God is wholly and holy "other." When Moses saw the burning bush and experienced God's presence, he was commanded to take off his shoes because he was in the presence of the holy God. Isaiah saw the holiness of God in the Temple in a great vision. God is righteous; we are sinners.

(b) *Undeserved love.* Paul notes in our text that a person might be willing to die for a just person but not for an unworthy person or undeserving individual (v. 7). But God's love was extended to us, even while we were sinners. A person might have hated God, but God still loves that person. Even while I am rebelling against God, God loves me. We may not be deserving of God's love; nevertheless, God loves us anyway.

(c) *Sacrificial love.* Paul states that "Christ died for us" (v. 8). This is a sacrificial death on a cross. Christ died for us while we were sinners. God did not say we had to be good before he would love us. God loves bad children or bad adults. It's not that he likes for us to do bad things (to sin) but that he loves us, even while we are bad; he laid down his life for us. If sin is not considered serious business, we make a mockery of the cross. Whatever else we may want to say about the cross, it stands in the center of the universe as the great symbol of God taking sin seriously. The cross stands as God's love, which reaches from eternity into time to touch your life and mine and offers us forgiveness for our sin and a new beginning. Forgiveness is serious business, and so is sinfulness. But God's love is a great love.

III. *Proof of God's love*—the sacrificial death of Christ. What Paul states in verse 8 is "proof" of God's love for us. "God demonstrates [proves] his own love toward us, in that while we were sinners, Christ died for us." Twice Paul uses the phrase "much more" (vv. 9–10) to affirm that the center of our religion is a new kind of life that we have experienced in the sacrifice of Christ. We are now "in Christ" or "in the love of God." We are reconciled to God by the death of Christ. God's forgiveness allows us to become the authentic persons he has created us to be. His redemption restores us with the quality of life that we were created to have. He reveals to us what we can be through the power of his redeeming love.

Sin has created a sense of brokenness within us between God, ourselves, and others. But God, in his forgiveness, offers us an opportunity to build a new bridge, to restore our broken relationship with him, to help in the restoration of our relationships with others, and to help pull our broken self together. God brings us back together again.

This morning before you leave this building, I hope you will silently make a confession of your sins—those unacknowledged ones, those that you often dare not bring into focus. Seek this morning to find forgiveness and experience the grace of God. This salvation is free, but you must be willing to accept it and walk in the environment and companionship with Christ.—William Powell Tuck

Topic: Can We Make the Most of a Second Chance?
TEXT: Luke 13:1–9

Luke points this week to a barren fig tree. We find the tree planted in the lushest of garden spots. The gardener treats it with a special tender care. But alas, after three years, nothing! The owner expresses disappointment—and then he gives up. "Get rid of it!" the owner commands. "It squanders time. It dissipates resources. Dump it!"

Do you recall the gardener's reply? It goes something like this: "O chief, please, not so fast. Let's give the tree another year. Maybe I've failed to do everything necessary to nourish it. In any case, let's give it another shot, another chance, and if next year it continues to fail, then maybe we'll get rid of it."

Luke's point is clear. He compares those of us in the churches to that barren fig tree. Luke shows us that through the creative love of God, we are set here on this earth as brothers and sisters—a glorious human family—and yet, in the one body—the Church—charged with illustrating this solidarity, we still find ourselves frequently the most dysfunctional of families. Luke knows we confuse worship of the holy God with religious ritual, failing the ethical dimensions emerging from our loyalty to this God of Jesus Christ. In short, Luke tells us that our perfectly located fig tree blossoms, with leaves here and there, can be beautiful. But Luke knows it can also be barren of fruit. The garden might be better off without it. "Get it out! Remove it! Find something new!" Do you sympathize with the owner? Do you share his frustration with the fig tree, his exasperation with the Christian Church?

But there is that other character in our story: the gardener. And it is with him I would like to identify. His tool is not the axe but the trowel. I want to do some digging, some loosening of the soil; I want to apply some fertilizer—no axes, no chain saws—just loam and peat.

I. The first leaf from my gardener's catalog is this: I hope our worship, music, education, outreach, and pastoral care—that smorgasbord of church activities listed in the bulletin— roots itself in the grace and power of the living God. I hope that through whatever we do here, we can find that Presence. I hope those groping for courage to face the worst, assurance to buttress trust, comfort to transform sorrow, forgiveness to begin again will all be touched and embraced in this place and among us, as we open ourselves to and share the love and grace of God mediated through our Lord and Savior, Jesus Christ.

II. A second leaf from my catalog reads like this: we are a people who live toward and, even more important, from a vision. We remember our future. We live out of our hope. We remember the wonderful promise in the book of Revelation where John of Patmos sees a new city—a city where the caprice of nature, the stupidity of nations, and people's own unsettled selves resolve into a harmony radiant in friendship and solidarity. We recall the prophet Isaiah envisioning the lion and the lamb dwelling together. We remember the apostle Paul describing the barrier-breaking Christ uniting what he considered our human polarities of Jew and Greek, free and slave, male and female. We want to incarnate that vision in our life here. Jesus, the universal and barrier-breaking Christ, is in charge of this house.

III. Which leads us to the next leaf in my catalog. We live also to see this vision blossom in God's world. And that, friends, calls us to the ministry of justice and peace. You know what that means. If our purpose includes striving for justice, then who holds power? How it is accumulated, sustained, used, and abused is a subject for our analysis and action. If, as Christians, we find ourselves invited to follow One who tilts toward the poor, the maimed, those who find themselves socially crippled, we will be advocates and discover ourselves joining the struggle against a complacent, resistant, well-heeled political or economic status quo. Ours is a contract with the God of the prophets and the Christ to confront poverty—to feed the hungry, house the stranger, clothe the naked, care for the sick and imprisoned, and do it, not only as an act of charity but, even more persistently, do it as an act of justice, seeking to alleviate the root causes of poverty.

IV. The last leaf in my catalog says this: this church needs people who love it. We need people who see this house, its congregation, its location, not as ends in themselves but as vessels to pass on the treasure of the gospel to new generations, to the curious and the spiritually hungry; to exercise leverage on behalf of the suffering and the bound; to serve as a haven for those threatened elsewhere or on the verge of falling apart; a fresh oasis for those thirsting, as the Gospel of John says, for "living water." God grant it may be so.—James W. Crawford

Topic: Lessons from the Narrow Places of Life
TEXT: Num. 22:21–35

The story in the book of Numbers about Balaam and his ass is one of those difficult passages in the Old Testament. For some folks, it is clear evidence that the Scriptures are an ancient relic and have absolutely no meaning for us today. For others, it is a clear sign of the miraculous within the Scriptures. How do we deal with a passage that has an animal talking? Let me suggest the following lessons.

I. The first is this: Balaam represents one who felt that he could live his life in total independence. He felt that his self-reliance was sufficient. He felt that he did not need to rely just on God's word. How like Balaam many of us are today. We go through life thinking that our self-reliance and our independence can take us through every situation.

Too often we attempt to set our own will, purpose, and way against God. To these people, it doesn't make any difference what God might want or what guidance other individuals might want to give us. They alone make the decision. When we try to live life this way, we often find that it collapses around us, because we are not open to the power and presence of God's direction. We have made ourselves the only source of guidance.

II. Notice that Balaam met God in unexpected places. Balaam thought he already had a message from God. After all, he had his vision. He had his dream, and he was traveling to deliver that message to the king of Moab. But he met God unexpectedly in a narrow place of life. How often God encounters us in unexpected places! Moses was attending sheep on a mountainside, when suddenly a bush began to burn, and the very presence of God confronted him. Jacob was fleeing from his brother to save his life when he encountered God in a wilderness place. Isaiah went to the Temple grieving because of the loss of his beloved king, and there in that experience of worship, he met God. Jeremiah was on a casual walk when he saw an almond tree blooming, and from that ordinary experience he had a vision of God. While Paul was traveling on the road to Damascus to persecute and put to death the early Christians, he met the very Christ whom he was seeking to defeat, and his life was changed! Down through history people have encountered God in all kinds of places.

III. But notice also that the Word of God came in judgment. Balaam met the angel of God. The word *angel* is translated from the Hebrew word for "adversary." God confronted him as his adversary because he came in judgment. Balaam was going to Balak with the wrong message. We are not certain how the message had become distorted. It is uncertain whether he was going there to misrepresent what God had told him to say. Was he going there to curse the people of Israel and not to bless them? Had he assumed that his message was God's message? That has become the curse of too many preachers. We turn our opinion into God's word. Too many believe that whatever they think and whatever their opinion is, automatically is God's opinion. Is that what had happened to Balaam? We do not know for certain, but he is confronted by the angel of God. God told him to go and deliver only what he had told him to say. God confronted him in judgment.

Before you and I can sense the power of God, he first comes in judgment into our lives. He comes in judgment to change us and to direct us to open our lives so our sinfulness can be transformed by his power. He calls us to be more like what he has created us to be. God comes into our lives to bring love and grace and redemption. But if our lives are constantly filled with hatred and sin of all kinds, he cannot communicate his love and grace. He first comes in judgment. The holiness of God cannot stand in the presence of sin.

IV. Notice finally that Balaam is met by the presence of God. In the Old Testament the expression "the angel of the Lord" does not refer to God's helpers. This is a reference to the presence of God himself. When Balaam is confronted by the "angel of the Lord," it means he experienced God himself; Jehovah God confronted him and challenged him.

Sometimes in the narrow places of life, we shall experience the presence of God. The angel of God will come and minister to us. He may come in the narrow place of grief, illness, pain, or suffering. He may come in the narrow place of rejection, ridicule, loneliness, and depression. He may come as the very angel of God to minister to your need and lift you up. God may come to you speaking through a friend, a telephone call, a note, or a letter. He may come to you in many places and ways and communicate his presence to you as power, grace, and love. In the narrow places of life, God is there. Let him open your eyes.—William Powell Tuck

Topic: Peace with God
Text: Rom. 5:1–11

I. Paul begins with the grim, dismal, depressing waste of sin. There is the harsh waste of the evil around us from which there does not look like there is an escape. Everybody has lost his righteousness, and everybody has lost the power to recapture it. Many devices and tricks are tried, and many, many attempts to escape are made, but the struggle is ineffective. The spiritual landscape revealed in the early part of this letter is black and gloomy. In this horrible bondage, every one of us is a prisoner.

No way out. No way out—until God comes and makes a new way, until God does a new thing, until God acts in a way that leads us into a new way of living. God's love met our deep necessity, and across the waste a path appears, which brightens more and more, even into a perfect day. In the new and radical act of God's love, in this Jesus Christ, God has placed before us the gift that permits the prisoners of despair to become the children of eternal hope. Through the sacrifice of God in the power of the cross, everybody can recover their crown. In the death whose mysteries of light, no one can fully explore the springs of a new life. So completely and so fundamentally does this divine act of God's love in Jesus Christ meet our need that we may not only leave the imprisoning desert, we can also drop our bonds and our chains. The gift is not only freedom—the change in our status from being bound to being free—but it is also the gift of strength, courage, and provision.

II. God in Jesus Christ gives those in bondage freedom and endows them with new life and new gifts of joy, peace, hope, love. And that brings us up to this word *therefore.* "Therefore, seeing we are justified by faith, let us have peace with God through our Lord Jesus Christ." It is not an assertion that we already have it. It is an assertion that it is already there if we will receive it. An amnesty is offered. Receive it.

But can we see the great possibility and refuse to translate it into glad experience? That seems to be the strange suggestion held out by Paul. Peace with God is offered—a peace that is deeper and beyond the limits of our logic and our reason but that is wider and broader than our strife with life; yet it is rejected. The old hymn ends, "The peace of God it is not peace, but strife sown in the sod, but brethren pray but for one thing, the glorious peace of God." And yet people will not receive it.

III. Our Wednesday night Lenten study talked about this deep necessity to come to the place where you can let go of your pain, your grief, your loss. There was talk about accepting the forgiveness of God, giving our burden of sorrows to Christ. And then there was the honest confession that we often cannot leave them there. We keep picking them back up. We dump them out and then race to the bottom of the hill to catch them again.

Here is the God-given appointed place where the heavy-laden pilgrim is invited to lay down the burden of the past and find rest and peace. There is no peace until we let go and let God. That is why our Christian story is the old, old story. Peace with God is only to be found at the place where we cast our burdens upon the Lord and trust in him for all our strength. And we are to tell that over and over again. And it is not just a one-time decision. Each day must be brought and given to the Crucified.—Rick Brand

Topic: Recognizing the Risen Lord
Text: John 20:14

In Bible stories about Jesus' Resurrection, we find again and again that friends of Jesus who met him after he rose from the dead didn't recognize him at first. Why didn't they recognize him? Maybe Jesus looked somewhat different. Then again, maybe his friend didn't expect to see him again. It may also be that Jesus didn't want them to recognize him right away.

It was possible to see the Risen Lord without recognizing him. It's also possible to recognize the Risen Lord without seeing him. That's vital for us, because we can't see him. So how does Jesus make himself known to us? A good way to answer that is by learning from people who had the opposite experience—people who could see Jesus but couldn't recognize him.

I. One person who saw Jesus but didn't recognize him was Mary Magdalene. Mary was devastated by Jesus' death. Mary was the first person to meet the Risen Lord Jesus, but even when she saw two angels and Christ himself standing there, she still didn't know what was happening. Mary was so busy looking for a dead corpse that she didn't recognize the living Christ. It wasn't the sight of Jesus but the voice of Jesus speaking her name that finally made her recognize him.

If you think Jesus is nothing but memories from the past, you can miss out on the joy of the living Lord here in the present. Sometimes religion can be like an embalmed corpse. Jesus is not just someone who lived long ago. He lives right now. But the Lord is near, even when you don't recognize him. You may not recognize him or expect him to be there, but he is. What does it take to recognize that Christ is near? Perhaps not the sight of his face but the sound of his voice calling your name: "Mary!"

II. Others also met Jesus on the first Easter but didn't recognize him. Two people were walking to Emmaus, a village about seven miles from Jerusalem. "As they talked and discussed these things with each other, Jesus himself came up and walked along with them; but they were kept from recognizing him" (Luke 24:14–16). Jesus asked what they were discussing. They told him how the miracles and teachings of Jesus had raised their hopes that he was the Savior God had promised and then how their hopes had been crushed by Jesus' death. They also said his tomb had been found empty and there were rumors that Jesus was alive, but there was no proof, and nobody had actually seen Jesus. So they remained gloomy.

"And Jesus explained to them what was said about himself in all the scriptures." He sat down to eat with them, took the bread, and said the blessing; then he broke the bread and gave it to them. Then their eyes were opened and they recognized him, but he disappeared from their sight. They said to each other, "Wasn't it like a fire burning in us when he talked to us on the road and explained the scriptures to us?" (Luke 24:25–32, TEV). As he explained to them what the Bible said about himself, they sensed a fire being lit inside them, and they didn't want it to stop. So, too, when you read the Bible or hear someone explain how the Bible reveals the suffering Savior and his victory over death, you are hearing the voice of Christ himself, even if you don't realize it.

Notice also that the Emmaus travelers recognized Christ in the breaking of the bread. Did they see the nail marks on his hands, as he took the bread and broke it? Whether they saw the nail marks or not, they suddenly recognized their Lord in the breaking of the bread. And today, in any true church, whenever bread is broken in Holy Communion, the bread is given to us by the nail-scarred hands of Jesus himself, and we can recognize that he is among us. If the biblical words of Christ are burning in your heart and the bread of Holy Communion is in your mouth, then Christ is with you. Recognize him and rejoice!

III. Here's another story that occurred sometime after the first Easter. By this time Jesus' apostles knew he was alive. But they still weren't sure what to do or where to go. Early in the morning, Jesus stood on the shore, but the disciples did not realize that it was Jesus. He called out to them, "Friends, have you any fish?" "No," they answered. He said, "Throw your net on the right side of the boat and you will find some." When they did, they were unable to haul the net in because of the large number of fish.

What made the disciples so sure it was Jesus? It was the fact that after accomplishing nothing on their own, they suddenly got amazing blessings simply by doing what the stranger on the shore told them to do. If the disciples had not done what Jesus said, they would not have caught those fish, and they would not have recognized that Jesus was with them.

Does Jesus seem like only a distant stranger to you? Stop doing everything your own way. Do things differently. Take your directions from Jesus. The Lord will multiply blessings for you, and like those disciples, you will recognize that the Risen Lord is with you. Whatever form Christ's blessing takes, when you experience it you recognize the Risen Lord at work.

Great things happen when you listen to Jesus and respond with obedience. He blesses you, warms and nourishes you, and commissions you to fish for people, not just for fish.

We've seen that it's possible to see without believing, but we've also seen that it's equally possible to believe without seeing. If you sense the Lord calling you personally by name, if he sets your heart afire with the Bible and reveals himself in the Lord's Supper, if he challenges you to do something different and then blesses you, then you don't need to see him to recognize the Risen Lord.—David Feddes

Topic: An Unfulfilled Dream
TEXT: Gen. 11:31–32

Someone has said, "Dreams are the stuff futures are made of." A little boy looks at baseball cards, buys them and trades them, all the while dreaming that someday he will be a big leaguer. A young lady browses through *Bride Magazine,* dreaming about a special day that will be all her own. We sing along with the radio, hang posters of movie stars on the walls, ponder ideas about family and career, and imagine what it takes to be happy. These are our dreams. And they are good—and necessary.

I. Today's text is the story of a man who had a dream. The man is Terah, the father of Abraham. It's a part of the Abraham story often missed. "Terah took Abram his son and Lot his grandson and Sarai, his daughter in law, and they set out from Ur of the Chaldeans to go into the land of Canaan." Now Ur wasn't just any old place in the world. It was centered in perhaps the most fertile land in the known world. A portion of it is modern-day Iraq. The greater portion of the earth's population at the time was located there. It was the center of civilization and the heart of the Chaldean religion. It was the kind of place people wanted to go to, not get away from. And besides all that, it was home for Terah and his family. But a dream arose in his heart (based on what, we do not know)—a dream that carried him away from all that had become familiar and comfortable and toward an open and available future. He was a man of faith.

Dreams like that determine our future. We are made by what we seek. We are changed by what we desire. It's the dream, once it gets into us, that directs us, motivates us, pushes and drives us, and keeps us going. When Martin Luther King Jr. preached his famous "I Have a Dream" sermon, his heart was filled with the possibilities for the future, and his dream caught fire in the heart of the American culture, and to this day that dream has not faded.

II. Dreams can be lost when we settle for less. What happened to Terah that his dream wasn't fulfilled? There is no clear word of assurance, but one word in the text helps us understand. "He came to Haran and he *settled* there." He settled there. He found something he liked and decided to stay there. There is nothing wrong with that, except that in doing so he lost his dream. "Settling down" implies a closed life; the days of adventure and excitement were over.

"Settling," in terms of religious faith, is not seen in the Scripture as a good thing. Believers are more pioneers than settlers. We are on-the-move people, facing each new day with some new agenda. The believer's motto is "leave the past, greet tomorrow, scorn danger, take a risk, live it to the fullest or lose it. There is more out there in the future yet unclaimed than we know today." Reality says, however, that most of us are right along with Terah. We've had dreams but, alas, they were for our youth. Now as adults we've found satisfaction in the kind of persons we've become, and we don't want to go any further. Maybe that's what happened to Terah.

"Settling" brings some sorrow. Not only did he settle there. He died there. He wanted to go to Canaan, but he "settled" in Haran. And in the end, he died there. David longed to build a Temple for his people, to place it there on the high hill, calling out to the weary as a place of rest, for the wounded as a place for recovery, for the half-hearted as a place for courage to be restored. But God said to David, "You will not build the Temple. You've shed too much innocent blood, taken too many innocent lives." His dream died. In 2 Timothy 4:10, Paul wrote that, "Demas, in love with the world, has deserted me." An old fable tells of a nightingale that traded away its feathers to a peddler for worms. One feather for one worm. It doesn't sound so bad, except that the nightingale finally traded away so many of its feathers that it could not fly. If our dreams can be thought of as feathers on which we fly, can we afford to trade them away?

Losing dreams can happen to people, to families, to churches. There are lots of things that we can do without. But we cannot do without our dreams. Visioning for the future is the motivation that hurls us past every obstacle along the way.

III. But God's dreams never die. Let's take our eyes off Terah and look at God. God was at work in the whole affair. The dream was fulfilled in his son. Jesus lived for a dream he called the Kingdom of God. He saw it as a hidden treasure, a lost sheep, a lost coin, and a lost son. He spoke of the tiny seed, the little leaven, and the coming of the Kingdom that is already in you. Think of how it happens for us. What of those strange imperatives that rise up within, which propel us onward? Where did they come from? What of the strange twist in our situations, the unexpected maneuver in our souls? What of the sorrow and the hurt? Can it be that God is moving among us and toward a dream that perhaps we can't even now recognize? The promise of Romans 8:28 is lived out within us over and again: "In all things God works for good."

The crowds thought God's dream was over at the Crucifixion, but Good Friday was only the beginning. God's great work—the Resurrection, the Church, now alive for twenty centuries, touching and blessing the lives of countless millions of lives and guiding history—was just beginning. And we are a part of it.

God comes to us in strange angles. We may not be sure of where God is going, but we can be absolutely sure of God's guiding hand. And so we're to live by faith and not by sight. In doing so, we are to live together honorably, to serve faithfully, to love unconditionally, to yield before Christ unapologetically—and in the end, we allow God to do the rest! And that's how God's dream is fulfilled in us.—Lee McGlone

EVANGELISM AND WORLD MISSIONS

Resources to Encourage Evangelism: A Four-Sermon Series

BY JOHN L. HIIGEL

Many pastors would say that their church members, in theory at least, would like for their friends to know the Lord, to be saved, to experience the sure-footedness, security, and well-being that can come from being a Christian. They would also say that, in practice, too few of their members actually tell their friends about Jesus. Moreover, truth be told, their members find the subject of evangelism troubling and distasteful, even though they love the Lord. Why is this?

One reason is that so many of them have noticed how uncomfortable their friends or acquaintances become when the subject of Jesus or Christian life comes up in conversation. Some Christians come to dread bringing up the subject of our life with God for fear it might introduce tension into the conversation or even into the whole relationship with their friend. A second reason is that, both for our members and for those outside, evangelism may have an unpleasant reputation. To many in our society, evangelism means being a jerk, sticking your nose in where it doesn't belong, and being pushy and opinionated.

Then there is the problem that our friends appear to be doing just fine in their lives, so it does not seem particularly urgent to help them know the Lord. This lack of urgency comes, in part, from an inadequate view of God's holiness and greatness, as well as from a superficial view of our friends' actual inner condition. An additional obstacle is that some of our members may have their guard up toward any "evangelism emphasis" because of a scarcity of lasting results from the previous ones.

The proposal here is for a sermon series that chips away at these obstacles and clarifies what we are trying to do when we do evangelism. The first sermon considers that response of discomfort we see on our friends' faces when the subject of Jesus or Christian life comes up. By observing what I call the "exaggerated case"—the wild Gerasene demoniac in Luke 8— we see dramatically what then happens again more subtly in the "normal people" of the town and what is likely happening in the minds of our own friends. All react to Jesus out of fear, hoping he will leave them alone, when in fact Jesus comes to bring them peace and well-being. Jesus does not give up on such people. Rather, his command to the healed man is to stay and live among his home folks and tell them what God has done for him.

The other three sermons in this series come from Paul's first letter to the Thessalonians. Here we observe a successful case of leading some people to Christ. We have indications from the letter that, despite daunting obstacles, Paul's evangelistic work in Thessalonica was remarkably effective. In succession, these sermons ask what the marks of successful evangelism were, what Paul's approach was that worked so well, and what it was about Paul's ministry that it produced such lasting results in the lives of the converted.

I remember vividly the testimony of one of my old chums from high school who was explaining at a class reunion how he had become a Christian. He said, "I found my way into this group of people at a church, and they *loved me* to Christ." Those church people had lived out something like Paul's approach in Thessalonica—the loving approach, the long-term loving approach. Such an approach has wonderful appeal for church members, because it so clearly contrasts with the syndrome of impersonal, insensitive pushiness. Another point of great benefit emerges from these chapters as well. Paul's letter will help our members appreciate more fully that it is God who goes ahead of us, God who is doing evangelism, God whose work enables us to be fruitful.

Topic: Afraid of Jesus
TEXT: Luke 8:26–39

I recommend beginning this sermon with an anecdote out of your own personal experience. Tell about an actual conversation you have had. The object is to help the congregation identify with you about that moment that happens when talking either with people we associate with frequently or with a casual acquaintance (the person cutting our hair or the one in the plane seat next to ours). We're chatting away about normal things when, either by our design or by happenstance, it comes out that we are Christian. We have all seen that brief flash of panic on the faces of individuals we are talking to. They freeze for just a moment, squint, or do a kind of double-take, and look slightly sick. It all takes place quickly. And then they gather their wits and shift into their mode for handling religious people.

Many of us are startled by that reaction and become uncomfortable ourselves, so we find that both of us in the conversation start talking faster and beating a retreat to safer topics. To our frustration, our discomfort with a friend's discomfort can effectively deter us from ever moving forward with sharing our faith, whether right then or later on. Thinking about Jesus, talking to him, and serving him may be the most natural thing in the world to us, but that reaction we come to expect from the non-Christian makes us afraid to bring Jesus into our conversations. What is going on in our friend's double-take and retreat, and how can we get beyond it?

I. *The exaggerated case.* The story in Luke shows, at an exaggerated level, what is going on in miniature in the normal friend who is startled to run into Jesus through conversation with us. Do our friends have problems in their lives? This man trumps them. Do they feel alarm in encountering Jesus? This man expresses outright terror.

The most obvious point about the man who meets Jesus in Luke 8 is that he is demon-possessed. (As a matter of strategy in the sermon, it is probably not advisable here to spend time discussing the nature of demon possession or whether it is a demon rather than the man who cries out.) His life is utterly out of control, and he has become a fearsome nuisance to those he knows. The parallel story in Mark's Gospel speaks of unsuccessful attempts to chain the man down and of his utter incapacity to function among normal people. He lives in terrible loneliness and distress. Something evil and destructive has gotten hold of him so that he has lost all his relationships and has become only marginally human. He is captive, body and soul.

So this man encounters Jesus. We notice two things immediately. First, Jesus spots what is controlling and ruining him and orders it to cease. Jesus "had commanded the unclean spirit to come out of the man" (v. 29), which is to say that Jesus went straight to the core of the man's problem and was already intervening to fix it. The other thing we see—and here is the surprise—is that as the man is approached by the one person who could relieve his horrible burden, instead of greeting Jesus with open arms and relief, he starts screaming in terror, "I beg you not to torment me!" The guy's life is a wreck, and he desperately needs release from the demons that own him. Clearly, he will be vastly better off if Jesus can do his transforming work on him, and yet he is screaming at Jesus to leave him alone.

II. *Normal people.* Normal people's slavery to what is dehumanizing and isolating and evil in their lives is more miniature. The bondage that harms their lives and damages their relationships with others is more moderate. But they would clearly be better off if they could be set free. Just as with "Legion," when Jesus encounters a person, he goes straight for the person's needs and problems and seeks to relieve them. Normal people don't scream, "What do you want with me, Jesus, Son of the Most High God? I beg you not to torture me!" But in a more moderate and subtle way, that is likely how they are responding. We who are familiar with Jesus know that he comes not to torment but to heal and restore, to forgive and set free, to bring balance, richness, meaning, and fullness to life. He comes with all power and authority and with his capacity to overturn and disrupt—characteristics that *would* terrify us if he were not also the author of love. But people *need* for him to come with all that power and authority if he is to tackle the forces that get hold of their lives.

In one sense, normal people's instinctive fear of Jesus is right on target. Jesus does throw things into upheaval as he draws near. Our man "Legion" is, of course, utterly changed, clothed and in his right mind, now able to live peaceably with others, whole and fully human. It is a massive upheaval for good.

But his is not the only life that Jesus has disrupted. We have a sea full of dead pigs. These pigs were presumably significant to the economy of the town and countryside from which all the normal people pour out in fury and fear. Jesus provokes fear because his priorities are right, and the people's are not. Jesus sees that this one human "discard" is more valuable than the temporary financial stability of the town, but for the people of the town, his intervention for that man is enormously disruptive and costly.

Who are possessed by fear at the end of the story? Who are unable to rejoice at the healing of this man, who had been so troubled and so difficult? Who have isolated themselves from human compassion and from God for fear of being tormented? The normal people! The evidence that Jesus has come to bring relief and joy to hurting people is right before their eyes: the formerly desperate man sitting at Jesus' feet, clothed and in his right mind. Yet they are "afraid," and they ask Jesus to leave.

III. *Declare what God has done.* It is striking, then, that Jesus insists that the man go "home and declare how much God has done for you." Home is the city (v. 27), the same city from which these fearful "normal people" have come who are sending Jesus away (v. 34). This is significant in two ways. First, we see that, despite their fear—despite that expression of discomfort we observe on our friends' faces—Jesus wants fearful people to be told about

God's goodness. As the newly healed man tells what God has done, his words will be reinforced by the change his home folk can see in his life. That flash of fear on people's faces that their defenses may soon be penetrated can become an incentive rather than a disincentive to share our faith. However fine our friends' lives may appear to be in general, we are saddened to glimpse their fear, and we realize they need Jesus, who can remove their fear and bring deep well-being. Second, Jesus' command tells us what to say. "Tell people how much God has done for you." Our testimony to God's mercy in our own lives can be what he uses to lower people's defenses, ease their fears, and open their hearts.

Topic: A Successful Case
TEXT: 1 Thess. 1:1–2:2

First Thessalonians, perhaps the oldest surviving Christian document, is exciting because of the wonderful insight it gives us into some early Christians' endeavors to lead people to Christ. We see from the letter and from Acts 17 that the visit to Thessalonica by Paul and his companions was necessarily short, because persecution by locals forced them to leave early. Nevertheless, we find that they were able to establish a community of new believers who remained steadfast and vital Christians. This letter is Paul's enthusiastic response to the first news he has received about their progress since he was forced out of town. He is overjoyed that "our visit to you was not in vain." Part of the strategy of the rest of this sermon series, beginning with this sermon's introduction, is to draw your congregation into the drama of that successful visit. Invite them to imagine a congregation in which, after Paul has left, no one in the whole church has known the Lord for more than a few months, yet they soon become well known for their faith in Christ throughout their region and beyond. What does it take to get people off to such a great start?

Our purpose in this sermon is to see what counted, for Paul, as evidence that his evangelistic work among these people had been a success. What are we trying to do when we share our faith? Knowing how to proceed depends on having a clear view of the goal. If our goal is to get people to say the right salvation prayer or to agree to a series of propositions about sin and salvation and Christ, we will adopt one strategy. If our goal is an enduring change in people's lives—real, heartfelt, lasting love relationships with God—we will adopt a different strategy. Paul's goal was the latter, and he can now say that goal has been met.

I. *They have turned.* Paul uses a vivid expression to describe the Thessalonians in verse 9: they have "turned." Their lives were headed in one direction, but now they have turned and are headed in another direction altogether. They have turned from idols to serve the living, true God and to wait for God's Son from heaven. The fact that they have turned reveals that Paul was seeking far more than what people often settle for as "evangelism." How many in our day have come forward at a meeting or "prayed the prayer" without a real turn happening in their lives? They may have responded with sincerity in a moment of emotion and conviction, fully intending to change, but it only ends up being a momentary deviation from the general course of their lives lived independently of God.

In verses 9 and 10, Paul sees the turn these Thessalonians have made in their actions (they are now serving the living and true God) and in their new frame of mind (Christ is on their minds as they await his return). Verse 1:3 reinforces the point. Something new now drives them, namely the three-fold characteristic of the Christian heart: faith, hope, and love. Again, what emerges from their Christian hearts now is action. TNIV and NIV capture this, translating the genitives of origin, "your work produced by faith, your labor prompted by love, and your endurance inspired by hope." In Paul's view, then, the success of his evangelistic visit is displayed by the turn in their lives. (Our term *conversion* expresses this idea of turning.) Old motivations have been replaced by faith, hope, and love (ideas worth lingering over in the sermon), and a sustained energy of action is the result.

II. *The Word rings out from them.* Perhaps the most satisfying evidence for Paul that his visit to the Thessalonians had not been a failure was that these new believers had become evangelists themselves. Their work of faith and labor of love has taken the particular form of telling others the good news. They have not merely followed the example of Paul and his cohort, but they themselves have become examples to everyone else. They seem as eager as Paul does to lead others to Christ, and they are gaining a wide reputation for their combination of personal faith and words of witness (vv. 7–8). This is especially impressive because it has come about while these people were under persecution (v. 6). The passage, incidentally, puts aside the notion that evangelism is something only for apostle-types and super-mature Christians to do. These are all novice Christians.

Notice what their reputation is not. It is not that they have made pests of themselves in Achaia and Macedonia. They have not become known for their pushiness or aggressiveness. What has become known is the Lord's message, confirmed by their genuine faith. Evangelism does not have to have a bad reputation. These are people who received the Word in the joy of the Holy Spirit, and they are passing it on in that spirit. Presumably, because they consciously imitate Paul (v. 6), their message has come in power, and in the Holy Spirit, and with full conviction. This leads to the third point.

III. *God is making it happen.* Here is the most reassuring part of the first chapter. God preceded Paul and his companions to Thessalonica and empowered their ministry. God similarly empowers the testimony of these new converts.

A key insight comes from Paul's use of the Greek word *eisodos.* When preaching, I am generally sparing in referring to Greek terms, but this one is genuinely helpful. The word comes twice in the text, first in 1:9, where NRSV says "people of those regions report about us what kind of *welcome* we had among you," and second is in 2:1, where it reads, "our *coming* to you was not in vain." The word *eisodos* appears today in any shop in Greece where one door is the entrance (*eisodos*) and the other is the exit (*exodos*—a word people will find familiar). Paul is saying we had "entrance" to you, entrance to your hearts. God gave us an opening into your hearts and lives. People all around report how open you were to us and to our message (1:9). God prepared an entrance into your hearts, and we did not miss it (2:1). So says Paul. What we today are looking for as we grow in desire to share our faith is those openings into people's hearts that God has gone before us to create.

The whole first chapter is a thanksgiving to God. God is the source of these new believers' faith, hope, and love (v. 3). God has chosen them and loved them (v. 4). God's Holy Spirit empowered the preaching of the word in their midst (v. 5) and inspired them with joy (v. 6). God has shown himself in their story more than ever to be the living and true God (v. 9).

Why are the Thessalonians the "successful case" of evangelism? Paul credits it to the work of God, in which he and his companions were merely cooperating and fulfilling an opportunity.

The sermon could conclude with a dual invitation, first, to turn fully to God as the Thessalonians have, and second, to become people sensitive and eager to spot those openings God has prepared in the lives of our friends to hear God's word from us. God grant our members courage so that those openings—those entrances to people's hearts—may not be in vain.

Topic: The Loving Approach
TEXT: 1 Thess. 2:1–12

In the previous message, we will have noted that for some, both outside the church and within it, evangelism has acquired a bad name because of the way it has been done. Here we want to offer a way of evangelism that avoids this syndrome. In introducing the sermon, it might be helpful to point out some less ideal approaches to evangelism, perhaps using a bit of caricature and humor, in order to set up a presentation of the loving approach modeled by Paul.

What starts out as a desire to care about people sometimes descends into something less loving. Some approach evangelism as a *moral watchdog.* They develop an acutely sensitive nose for sin and nastiness in others. They are interested, not so much in inviting people to freedom and joy as in imposing a set of scruples. Others approach evangelism as a *warrior,* not, alas, doing battle against the devil and the powers of evil but against the evangelism "target." Speaking of God descends into winning arguments and a contest of wills. If the person being evangelized ever becomes a Christian, it will have to be because he admits he is wrong and our warrior is right. Others approach it as a *salesperson.* The gospel becomes a commodity to sell, and it is to be brought to people's attention any way possible as often as possible, using guile and manipulation if necessary to force the subject into view, hoping that in a moment of weakness or restlessness they will buy into our gospel. Still others do evangelism in ill-considered bursts as *guilt downloaders.* We're having another evangelism emphasis, and I'd better do it to somebody soon so I won't feel guilty for never doing it. No wonder evangelism has a bad name. What all these approaches have in common is the scarcity of actual love shown toward the person who is hearing.

I. *Our conduct was pure, upright, blameless.* Paul says what he *did not* do in order to affirm what he *did* do. What he and his companions *did not* do was manipulate people. Verse 3 focuses on purity of *motives,* verse 5 on nonmanipulative *words,* and verse 10 on blameless, upright *actions.* In verse 7, which continues this theme of integrity, the NRSV ("we might have made demands as apostles") probably best captures the idea of burden: we could have thrown our weight around—we could have pulled rank—but we did not. So Paul, the effective evangelist, used no flattery, no deception, no power games, no putting on airs to be impressive, no slipping in under people's radar and then springing the gospel on them. The helpful cross reference here is 2 Corinthians 2:17: "We are not peddlers of God's word like so many, but in Christ we speak as persons of sincerity." You may have an anecdote or two about manipulative methods you have seen people try.

Eliminating the slick salesman image will bring relief to many in our congregations. If what we are being asked to do is be real in the presence of our friends, *that* we can do. This way we are free to be caught in the act of struggling to live out our faith rather than trying to put on some sort of smudge-free, plastic perfection for public consumption. We are not seeking praise from people; we are living to please God, who tests our hearts (vv. 4, 6). Rebecca Manley Pippert's experience, narrated in her classic book *Out of the Saltshaker and into the World,* was that it was only when her friend saw her honestly struggle and fail that there was the first flicker of actual interest in her words about Jesus.

II. *We loved you so much.* Paul's model for sharing faith in Christ, which was evidently picked up by the Thessalonians for their own evangelism (1:6), was to love people. Verse 2:8 is the centerpiece. It begins, "So deeply do we care for you [we loved you so much]," and ends "you have become so dear to us." There is a bit of the Golden Rule in this. We would all rather be loved than manipulated, so that is how we treat people whom we want to know Jesus.

Paul says, "Because we loved you so much, we were delighted to share with you not only the gospel of God, but our lives as well." Sharing our lives means sharing our life story with words, and it also means sharing ourselves in caring actions. For Paul, that meant working hard not to be a financial burden to them (v. 9). For others it might mean helping fix their friends' car or watching their kids so they can go out. Our members know instinctively how to love their friends, and it is remarkable how all that is forgotten in some attempts at evangelism. Even a big-event evangelist like Billy Graham depends mostly on people who have already built a loving friendship with people they have brought with them to the rally.

Paul's images for loving are worth drawing out. In verse 7, he pictures a nursing mother with her tender infant. We were gentle among you, says Paul. Think of a mother so eager to meet the needs of her baby that she weeps when she can't. Who is more attentive than she is? Who listens more carefully? She pours herself into knowing and understanding her child and is sometimes the only one who can decipher its utterances. In turn, she adjusts her vocabulary to what the child can understand. Then we have the image of the father involved in long-term nurture of his son or daughter (vv. 11–12), urging, encouraging, pleading with his young one to live a life worthy of God. These parental images highlight sustained, heart-felt, dedicated love, not seniority or authority over the person being loved.

III. *We had courage in our God to declare the gospel.* We have to press on to this point. Paul says we loved you so much that we shared the gospel of God (v. 8). We had courage in our God to declare to you the gospel (v. 2). At the right time, with sensitivity, our members must have the courage to *speak* the gospel. Verse 8 is not, "We loved you so much that, though we never actually told you the gospel, we shared our lives *instead*!"

To reinforce the point made in the first sermon, what God would have us do is to tell people what he has done for us. That will take the form of personal anecdotes of times when we saw God most clearly at work in our lives. But it will also include telling the New Testament's message of what God has done for us.

Paul is aware of how scary it may be for some Christians to share the good news. He speaks in verse 2 of his own temptation to be intimidated into silence but says, "We received courage *in* our God to speak the gospel *of* God." As God has provided the opening into people's hearts and has given us much love for these people, he can also give us the needed courage to speak up. God is never more with us than at that moment, however clumsy or inadequate we may feel. We may picture him standing beside us, encouraging and helping. Courage *in* God to speak *of* God: this is our empowerment from him. Along with Paul (v. 4), our members can say—they really can!—"we have been approved by God to be entrusted with the message of the gospel, and so we *speak.*"

Topic: The Drama of Follow-Through
TEXT: 1 Thess. 2:13–3:13

Drama is a useful image for what is happening in today's text. Among the fine arts are forms that freeze a moment in time: painting, sculpture, or photography. But there are also art forms that unfold through time: music, dance, theater, and film. The Germans have a colorful term for what is needed in order to appreciate the longest such art forms, such as long operas or symphonies or movies. They say you need *Sitzfleisch* (sittin' flesh)—a well-padded rear end. Evangelism takes plenty of *Sitzfleisch* (pronounced zits-flysh). Evangelism is a long drama, not a moment in time. Despite our "instant society" in which we expect everything to be accomplished and resolved quickly, we have to abandon the pray-the-salvation-prayer-and-it's-finished mentality in favor of long-term caring that attends carefully to the drama of follow-through.

I. *The drama up to the moment of decision.* Here we remind the congregation about the drama that led up to a decision for Christ, first in the story here about the Thessalonians and then in their own stories. In Thessalonica, it was a drama God was involved in before Paul and his friends arrived. There was plenty of drama in the evangelists' story, as they were coming to Thessalonica (Acts 16–17; 1 Thess. 2:2) and then in the dramatic opening of the Thessalonians' hearts so that they turned to God (1:9–2:1). In today's text, Paul recounts it again in 2:13. But the drama does not end with their decision to turn to God. People in our own congregation will be able, likewise, to remember the drama of their having come to faith, whether it was eventful or gradual. It was not a moment-in-time thing, even if their story involved a dramatic event of decision. That moment had a context in their life story, and God will have been leading up to that moment for some time. Thanks be to God for that time of decision. Then what? It is like a marriage. The event of wedding day is the culmination of a decision to enter into a permanent relationship. But at that point, the drama is only beginning, and everyone knows that just because a marriage begins is no guarantee that it will last. Or it is like a birth. There is plenty of drama in the lead-up and day of birth, but the drama of the new life is just starting, and attentive care is needed, especially at first, because of the child's great vulnerability.

II. *The new believer's vulnerability.* The letter points clearly to hindrances faced by the Thessalonians. They encountered fierce persecution from their compatriots, which Paul says is the common experience of new Christians (2:14–15; the point of these verses is not to make a slam at Jews but to say that converts experience persecution from their own group—the people among whom they used to circulate easily). Also see 3:3–4. The drama of establishing the Thessalonians firmly in Christ is portrayed as a spiritual battle, with Satan hindering them from being with the people who could most effectively nurture them in faith (2:17–18) and with the Tempter trying to trip them up (3:5). So, far from being over, the drama intensifies when a person begins to follow Christ. We may see this three-fold dilemma of the Thessalonians' as a warning regarding new converts we care about: pressure from their previous associates who are nonbelievers; insufficient interaction with mature Christians, and general temptation to disobey God can all imperil new believers. Each of the three dangers may be worth illustrating. New believers are vulnerable and need our support.

III. *The evangelist's zeal for follow-through.* Precisely because the drama intensifies for the new convert, Paul's zeal for follow-through intensifies as well. We highlight here the strong language in 2:17, Paul's feeling "orphaned" from them as he was forced out of town by persecution—in person, but not in heart—and his great eagerness to see them again face-to-face. When he could no longer bear the lack of news about them (3:1, 5), he sent his last companion, Timothy, to strengthen them and to bring him a report. The exceedingly intense language continues in 3:7–10, where he says, "We *live* if you continue to stand firm in the Lord," and he tells them of his earnest prayer night and day. The passage ends with more prayer, as he beseeches God that he might be able to come himself to build them up and prays that they would increase in steadfastness and Christ-like love (3:11–13). (That Paul depends so much on prayer, not just on his preaching skill, suggests that we must do the same!) Paul's loving approach extends well beyond their conversion, and he can only point to them as a successful case of evangelism many months after their initial decision to follow Jesus. You may have anecdotes about people this zealous in their follow-through. I remember the testimony of the great Christian leader, John Stott, who said that the man who led him to Christ wrote to him weekly for years thereafter to encourage him.

We may point finally to the evangelist's joy. Having said, "We live," if these loved ones remain firm in their faith, he expresses overflowing joy, both in the anticipation (2:19–20) and in the receiving (3:6, 9) of the good news about their progress. The letter's whole first three chapters are an extended expression of thanks and joy. Perhaps Paul's testimony of personal joy from doing evangelism is the richest incentive to our members to make Jesus known.

RESOURCES FOR PREACHING EXPOSITORY SERMONS

BY WILLIAM E. HULL

Topic: The Secret of Significant Living
TEXT: Mark 10:45

By the time Jesus was born, the ancient world had developed three basic routes to self-realization that endure under various labels to this day. Let us identify and evaluate each of them in a quest to discover the secret of significant living.

I. *Know thyself!* To gain self-understanding was the oldest wisdom of Greek philosophy. Viewed historically, this maxim represents the first great break with traditionalism and social conformity. It signals the emergence of the individual from the crowd. Socrates was accused, condemned, and executed for being anti-Athenian because he dared to think for himself so radically that he was seen to be undermining all external authority by daring to challenge public values and views. At the bedrock of this approach is the conviction that "the unexamined life is not worth living."

We may celebrate the many virtues of this emphasis. It has sundered the shackles of coercive dogmatism. It has enlarged our sense of inwardness, as described particularly by poets and mystics. And yet, for all its values, there are pitfalls in this approach as a comprehensive way of life. It fosters an individualism that can isolate from community. A preoccupation with subjectivity may also blind one to social injustice, cut the nerve of commitment to the common good, and smother courageous public action. The problem, finally, is that a preoccupation with self-knowledge is too self-centered. What if I truly know myself but don't like what I find? In Romans 7, Paul probed his own depths and found that apart from Christ, he felt "wretched" (v. 24).

II. *Control thyself!* Out of antiquity came another route to human satisfaction. In light of their view of reality, the Stoics urged persons to search for order within both their personal and their collective lives. That required discipline and self-control—the harnessing of the emotions by the mind. Here is a lifestyle shaped by the dictates of duty, by the exercise of the will, by the formation of character.

We can easily see the many virtues of this approach today. It encourages decent, law-abiding citizenship. It fosters the faithful discharge of duty. And yet here, too, dangers lurk. The achievement of order is but a small step from enforced conformity. At bottom, we have here a religion of the will. But what if the will is fractured? Order comes from obeying a rational will, but what if our will becomes irrational and does not obey its own best resolves?

Again in Romans 7, Paul discovered a cleft in his will between noble intentions and their implementation (v. 19).

III. *Enjoy thyself!* The last great alternative in the ancient world was advocated by Epicurus. Sensing the insecurity of skepticism at one extreme and idealism at the other, he sought to root reality in the incontestability of immediate experience. We can know only what we feel. This did not mean that life would always be euphoric; rather, the memory could build up a fund of pleasures on which to draw in times of misfortune. Today we have rediscovered the need for a playful, carefree, festive lifestyle, and yet, how easily this answer becomes a problem. The "Playboy Philosophy" began as an explicit form of Epicureanism, but it soon degenerated into shallow self-gratification. For many, sexual activity is not a deeply shared intimacy but a compulsive exploitation. Ironically, spectator sports have now become not just a game or even an entertainment but an obsession.

Why is it that all three of these answers, each of them profoundly useful as a contribution to human fulfillment, are yet so fatally flawed? Let us step back and look at them together: all are concerned with dimensions of selfhood: *self*-knowledge, *self*-control, *self*-gratification. All three are *self*-centered searches for fulfillment. But what if the self is flawed at its core? The efforts to know, to control, and to enjoy are all fine: it is the self that is our problem.

IV. *Give thyself!* To this problem of a wayward self, Jesus gave history's most decisive answer. To Jesus, the secret of significant living was not self-knowledge, self-control, or self-gratification. It was self-denial. His startling new way: Give thyself! This revolutionary alternative did not contradict any of the three great options just surveyed. Yet his way of service went beyond all three. It solved the problem of the self by insisting that we give it away. The other three routes, taken alone or together, end in failure because they seek knowledge and order and enjoyment only for the self. The radical difference with Jesus was that he sought all of these, not to keep for himself but to give away to others in a life of service (Mark 10:45). Jesus gave others the best he had to offer: his love, his forgiveness, his understanding of God. And what he gave was costly, for it was his very selfhood, not some surplus that he would never miss.

Ultimately, each of us will be either a getter or a giver, a seeker serving self or a sharer serving others. And the difference is as decisive as life and death. Because he "emptied" himself, God "exalted" him, and he will do the same for us. The paradoxical "therefore" of Philippians 2:9 on which the passage pivots lies at the heart of the gospel. It is the "good news" of how to live a fulfilling life.

Topic: Let Them Grow Together
Text: Matt. 13:24–30

What we call the Parable of the Wheat and the Tares (Matt. 13:24–30) is a little story that Jesus told about what to do with some weeds that threatened to ruin a crop. He did not tell such tales to entertain his hearers but as a way to communicate with them in a context of controversy. We begin, as did Jesus, with a story that is not easily understood or forgotten.

I. *The story.* The plot seems simple enough: a farmer sowed his field. But no sooner had this work been done than an adversary slipped in under cover of darkness while others slept and sowed bad seed among the good (v. 25). We are left with the sober realization that even our best efforts can be undermined by spite and jealousy when least expected. In order to grasp the cunning of this dark deed, we need to identify the kind of bad seed that was scattered on top of the good. The problem is that it cannot be distinguished from wheat in the blade but only in the ear, after it has ripened enough to make a head, which becomes poisonous from hosting a fungus. If harvested and ground together with the wheat, the flour is ruined and the whole crop lost.

With this clarification we are able to grasp the dilemma that confronts the farmer once his crop is discovered to be corrupted. The field hands wanted to pull up the wretched weeds (v. 28). But the owner realized that the buried roots of the wheat and the weeds had become so entangled with each other that to yank out one would uproot the other as well. Concerned for a maximum yield from all their efforts, he wisely decided, "Let them both grow together until the harvest" (v. 30). Then everything could be reaped and the separation take place in such a way that the weeds would be bundled up and dried for fuel while the wheat would be gathered into the barn (v. 30). To be sure, this approach required more time and patience on the part of everyone, but the results would be well worth the wait.

II. *The setting.* Why would Jesus tell such an earthy story and liken it to the grandest theme of his gospel: "the kingdom of heaven" (v. 24)? For one thing, his parable warned against the dangers of a premature separation between good and evil that the Judaism of his day was attempting on every hand. The Pharisees practiced a rigid code of conduct that built a wall of exclusion between them and those less observant of religious law. The Essenes relocated to a desolate wilderness so that they would not be defiled by what they considered a corrupt priesthood in Jerusalem. The Zealots were agitating for a decisive break with Rome, even if it meant all-out war with a fight to the finish. Because of this apartheid mentality, many expected that a primary role of the Messiah would be to gather a purified remnant of the righteous, but here was Jesus consorting with publicans and sinners, harlots and centurions—letting bad weeds infest good wheat!

Closer to home, John the Baptist had prepared for the ministry of Jesus by picturing the coming Messiah with a winnowing fork in his hand that would separate the wheat from the chaff so that the latter could be burned "with unquenchable fire" (Matt. 3:12). Closest to home, a terrible weed was growing within the innermost disciple band. Judas seemed to have Zealot sympathies, which would have put him at the opposite extreme from a Roman collaborator like Levi. Surely, the innermost core of followers needed to be purged of its poisons if the movement was to have any integrity. After love's last appeal was rejected in the Upper Room (Matt. 26:20–25), Judas finally excluded himself from the twelve by an act of betrayal in which none of the others joined him.

III. *The meaning.* In light of these challenges to his ministry from without and within, what new insights did Jesus seek to plant in the minds and hearts of his hearers by telling this little story? Let us look at four.

First, inclusivism is a hard sell, and its foes abound on every hand. Jesus sought to sow the seeds of the Kingdom on a field as wide as the world (v. 38), to universalize the grace of God by making it available to every person, regardless of race, gender, ideology, or nationality. But the custodians of the status quo felt so threatened by outsiders that they restricted their legacy to one small group, arbitrarily limited by ancestry, willing to embrace a common culture. To this day, most people prefer sameness to otherness.

Second, in this Kingdom under siege, it is hard to tell friend from foe, for weeds may come disguised as wheat. Because authenticity cannot be determined until their fruits are known

(Matt. 7:16–20), it is always dangerous to attempt premature separation, which is precisely why it is so difficult to be a zealous reformer.

Third, the presence of so much ambiguity calls for the practice of patience to give people and ideas a chance to prove themselves. In such cases, we may need to buy time and put up with what is bad for the sake of a greater good. Our options do not always involve a clear-cut choice between black and white. Sometimes, like wheat and bearded darnel, both sides seem to be a tattle-tale gray.

Fourth, none of this means that Jesus encouraged an easy relativism that was indifferent to moral reality. Both the story—and even more the interpretation of it—come to a climax at harvest time, when there will be an absolute separation between the wheat and the weeds, with the former destined for the barn and the latter for the fire. This is but a vivid way of saying, "Judge not" (Matt. 7:1) but let God do the judging (Rom. 12:19).

IV. *The application.* These insights may be given the widest possible application because, as the interpretation of our story explains, "the field is the world" (v. 38). I have selected three areas in which the truths of our text are especially relevant for today: the individual, the nation, and the Church.

(a) *The individual.* One of the greatest threats to human survival today is a creeping fundamentalism in the culture of every major world religion that would absolutize its understanding of good and evil to the point of justifying violence in the name of the sacred. Whether it be the ultra-Orthodox Jew, or the Protestant and Catholic Christians, or the Shiite and Sunni Muslims, they are all united with the field hands of old in saying, "Let's pull up and destroy the bad weeds we don't like in order to protect the good wheat that we have." And it sounds so sensible, even "godly," until we realize how many weeds of bigotry, prejudice, and hatred are sown by such misguided zealotry.

(b) *The nation.* The recent presidential campaign permitted the mass media to engage in a year-long orgy of divisiveness on the theory that everybody loves a good fight. The political gurus urged their candidates to disparage their opponents so relentlessly that whoever was elected would be discredited before taking office. But is it wise to divide our country up into a party of wheat and a party of weeds? The wisdom of our story is, "Let them grow together," even if each side considers itself wheat and the other side weeds! The two-party system has served our nation well throughout its history. The majority party in office needs the critical scrutiny and informed dissent of the minority party to protect it from the intoxication with power that is the Achilles' heel of every politician.

(c) *The Church.* You doubtless know that every major denomination in America has been engaged in outright civil war over the past generation. At the root of the conflict is an unwillingness to tolerate some of the sharp differences that characterize contemporary life. Nowhere is there a greater tendency to divide all of life into wheat and weeds than in a church with an authoritarian mind-set. To be sure, there are plenty of weeds in every church. To throw them out only denies them the opportunity to hear and see a witness that might one day change their lives.

Do these applications, and the story on which they are built, imply that we are to be moral pacifists who fail to oppose evil until the weeds overwhelm us? No, "Let both grow together" (v. 30) is the imperative of our text. We are not to give up sowing good seed and let bad seed take the field. Rather, we are to be busy growing an ever-stronger faith that can more than hold its own, even in a weed-choked field. Further, doing this "together" rather than in isolation points us to the life of dialogue in creative coexistence with those who differ.

After all, people are more than plants, and in the give-and-take of honest sharing, change can occur. But what about the weeds that never seem to change? God will know best what to do with them.

Topic: Surprised by God
TEXT: Exod. 3:1–6

What an unpromising time and place to have a life-changing experience! Moses was already advanced in age; he was eighty years old and fixed in his habits. Once he had rested in Egypt's fairest gardens, but now he trudged about in the sand and sage of the wilderness. Banished to the back side of nowhere, he lived a dead-end existence if ever there was one. But in this most unlikely setting, the life of Moses was suddenly transformed. Here a forgotten and forlorn has-been found a future that would turn a lonely shepherd into his people's Savior. Let us try to get inside his experience so intimately that we will be able to make it a part of our experience in the days ahead.

I. *Mystery.* It all began with a blaze that caught the corner of his eye: an ordinary scrub brush was burning with a flame that did not seem to die. Unknown to Moses, an angel of the Lord was lurking in the flickering tongue of fire (v. 2), but he would not discover that secret unless he paused to look more closely (v. 3). So why did Moses turn aside? It was merely to investigate why the bush was not yet consumed: Was it because "there is a place in my soul that burns like a flame, and isn't burned up?"

In any case, it was not until "the Lord saw that he had turned aside to see" (v. 4) that God addressed Moses. The particularity of "Moses, Moses!" (v. 4) meant that this call was for him and him alone. With a now-or-never urgency it was God's way of saying, "I need you for a special assignment, and you will not fulfill your intended destiny unless you accept it." In this exclusive encounter we see the limits of generic religion, that is, religion-in-general. It is only when we hear God call us by name that we grasp the mystery of the burning bush. God has a mission for each of us to fulfill. We can be agents of the Almighty in the great task of setting his people free from bondage.

II. *Majesty.* Once Moses realized that he had been singled out and called by name, this was not the time to say, "I will try to find somebody to help you." Instead he replied, "Here I am," which meant, "You wanted me and now you have me. I am at your disposal." Now that God had Moses' undivided attention, he needed to prepare him to receive his marching orders. The great danger in any religious assignment is overconfidence. Many persons who suppose that God is on their side soon come to believe that they can do anything! From the outset it was crucial to cleanse Moses from any presumption that he could do the Lord's work in his own strength.

And so, in that barren wasteland, God disclosed his mystery in terms of majesty. The voice that called his name had seemed to invite him to come closer, but now it bade him stand back and keep his distance (v. 5). Moses was being treated to his own personal Theophany— a private audience with the Sovereign of the universe who remembered his name and came seeking his assistance—yet he must take nothing for granted or assume that God was at his beck and call. To underscore the nature of their relationship, God instructed Moses to slip off his sandals and stand barefooted before him as a little child, vulnerable even to the soles of his feet. Make no mistake: this miserable mountainside, devoid of any trappings of religion, was nothing less than "holy ground" (v. 5). If Horeb could become "holy ground," it meant that majesty was willing to squander its prerogatives on ordinary people, that the most obscure corner of life could be set ablaze with divine glory!

III. *Memory.* Standing as a barefoot volunteer in sand that had suddenly become a sanctuary, "Moses hid his face, for he was afraid to look at God" (v. 6). Humbled by the holiness that surrounded him, it was time, not to look but to listen, to wait quietly for God to disclose his will on his own terms. If this act of submissiveness contained an element of human passivity, it was a passivity that invited divine activity. As the old song puts it, "Have Thine own way, Lord! . . . while I am waiting, yielded and still."

We might suppose that God would respond to this touching display of humility on the part of Moses by bolstering his self-esteem with a word of encouragement, but instead he offered him a brief history lesson: "I am the God of your father, the God of Abraham, the God of Isaac, and the God of Jacob" (v. 6). It was God's way of saying that this was not the first time his people had needed a courageous leader to help them make a new beginning. He had guided Abraham all the way from Mesopotamia to Palestine. He had spared Isaac from the knife of sacrifice. He had brought Jacob back from Babylon and prepared him to face Esau.

But more: this tour of memories would remind Moses of promises made to the patriarchs that had not yet been fulfilled. There was still an inheritance to be claimed, a homeland to be settled, a reward to be received (Heb. 11:8; 13–16, 26). Here God activated the memory of Moses, not as the nostalgic recollection of a hallowed past but as the gathering of "so great a cloud of witnesses" to surround him every step of the way (Heb. 12:1). And this precious companionship is made available to us, as it was to Moses, because ours is a God, not of the dead but of the living! Heaven is not a celestial mausoleum where God gathers his people as a collection of corpses turned to dust.

May I invite you this morning to the back side of nowhere in quest of holy ground. If you are willing to turn aside, to take off your shoes, and to hide your face, then what becomes of the flame lit by God? In the case of Moses, did the bush finally burn up and the fire go out? Or did that flame kindle the heart of Moses until it finally blazed forth to set his people free? Are you willing to become part of an incendiary fellowship?

Topic: The Struggle for a Global Faith
Text: Gal. 5:1–6

We tend to take an idealistic view of the New Testament Church as an idyllic fellowship free of conflict—a model of harmony because of the love that the first Christians had for one another. In actuality, an explosive conflict raged at the heart of apostolic Christianity. That painful struggle not only defined the essential nature of our faith but it permanently determined the relationship between Christianity and Judaism.

We are timid about digging into this problem because the conflict was originally framed around the issue of circumcision, which, to us, has no religious significance at all. But before you dismiss the subject out of hand, remember that circumcision was the most explosive issue in Paul's pivotal letter to the Galatians. Moreover, it was the central controversy prompting the Jerusalem conference of Acts 15, the watershed event of the apostolic era. Are we free to ignore so important an issue just because it seems to be dated and irrelevant in our day?

I. *The problem.* The New Testament period was a time of escalating tensions between Judaism and its enemies. The Jewish leadership of that day practiced the politics of polarization, which soon erupted in a fight to the finish against the mighty Roman Empire. In this struggle for survival, the Jews had no flag around which to rally, thus they made circumcision the symbol of their embattled identity. The fanaticism with which circumcision was championed is not unlike the way in which some among us today have made a crusade out of exhibiting the Ten Commandments on public property.

Paul himself had been born and raised as a good Jew, "circumcised on the eighth day" (Phil. 3:5). He was willing for Timothy to be circumcised to facilitate his missionary work with Jews in their synagogues (Acts 16:3). But Paul adamantly refused to require it of Titus, a Greek who would work primarily with Gentiles (Gal. 2:3). This does not mean that Paul simply abandoned a practice clearly taught in his Hebrew Bible. Rather, he had learned from the martyr Stephen that the Abrahamic covenant of circumcision (Acts 7:8) failed to circumcise the heart and ears of the people, causing them to resist the Holy Spirit and brutally reject God's messengers (Acts 7:51–53). Far from ignoring circumcision, Paul internalized its meaning so that his Christianity would become a religion of the spirit rather than of the flesh (Col. 2:11–13).

II. *The solution.* Paul's insistence on eliminating circumcision from his gospel to the Gentiles was bound to result in open conflict (Gal. 2:4–5). Put as simply as possible, it raised the issue of what one had to embrace from Judaism in order to become a Christian. The solution seemed so fair and simple: Gentiles did not have to become Jews in order to become Christians, nor did Jews have to become Gentiles in order to become Christians. It seemed like a win-win approach for both sides. But this solution soon came apart, precisely because of its success. A small but fanatical group called Judaizers refused to accept the "two-spheres" strategy but instead insisted that every Christian must obey the ancestral customs of the Jews. By insisting on their understanding of the purity of the Church, the Judaizers were disrupting the unity of the Church.

As political and cultural tensions rapidly mounted in Palestine, the Judaizers increased their agitation by insisting that circumcision was essential to salvation (Acts 15:1). When this led to "no small dissension and debate" (Acts 15:2), it was decided to convene a summit in the Holy City, which we call the Jerusalem Conference. As the debate unfolded, both Peter and James sided with Paul, emphasizing that salvation was only "through the grace of the Lord Jesus," and therefore Jewish legalistic requirements should not be imposed on "the Gentiles who turn to God" (Acts 15:11, 19).

With all the key leaders in agreement, it might seem that the matter had finally been settled, but such was not the case. The next time Paul came back to Jerusalem, he found a powder keg of political extremism ready to explode. To his heartbreak, the issue was finally settled, not by apostolic summitry but by Roman armies that brutally crushed a suicidal uprising of Jews formed by the same kind of religious absolutism that had tried to wreck Paul's ministry.

III. *The lessons.* The first thing we learn from this titanic struggle is that Christianity is not an otherworldly, escapist religion. Because of its rootedness in the real world, cultural pressures on the faith can become enormous. Particularly potent is the combination of patriotism and piety that seeks to make the Church an agent of some group's political agenda. Religious people take seriously their earthly citizenship, as well as their ethnic identity, and they desire to be loyal to their inherited traditions. In our country it has resulted in a strong tradition of exclusivism, with its frequently violent expressions of hostility to anything foreign. Sad to say, religion has often been in the forefront of strident efforts to sanctify sameness and demonize differences.

Second, in light of this enormous cultural diversity, it is not only legitimate but often necessary to have multiple strategies for evangelization. In the New Testament, this required one approach to Jews and another to Gentiles, whereas today it may require different approaches to the first world and the third world, or to the older generation and the younger generation, or to liberals and conservatives. Just as in the first century, we still have bitter "culture wars." The remarkable thing is that, no matter how diverse we become, the spirit of Christ has a universal appeal to all groups, regardless of their nationality, gender, political persuasion, or ideological preference.

Third, when we seek to resolve the tension between the particularity of our religious customs and the universality of our Risen Lord, doctrinaire extremists can wreak havoc and subvert the worldwide outreach of the Christian faith, regardless of the solutions we devise. In troubled times of fear, an inflexible fundamentalism often triumphs for a season and inflicts terrible wounds on the faith. The book of Acts embraced a wide spectrum of opinion that included Stephen on the far left, Paul on the near left, Barnabas in the center, Peter on the near right, and James on the far right. But this tolerance did not extend to the Judaizers who, by their legalistic mind-set, were splitting the Church and hindering its world mission.

Fourth, even when an irreconcilable impasse is reached, that does not mean that we throw up our hands in despair. Rather, our only choice is not between the two sides in whatever culture war is raging. We can always follow the example of Jesus himself, whose choice was that "the will of the Lord be done" (Acts 21:12–14). Christianity stands or falls, not on our ability to solve all the problems presented to us by our diverse backgrounds but on the credibility of Christ himself to redeem those of every background. Only God is the providential Lord of history who can use even our disagreements to accomplish his will.

IV. *The applications.* Now that you have heard the sermon, let me return to the question with which we began: Why preach on such a hard and heavy subject at this time? The first reason is that this is precisely the struggle that brought Christianity to the Gentiles, and that, my friends, is who we are! If the Judaizers had won, if customs such as circumcision had been made prerequisite to salvation, then Christianity would have become little more than a minor reforming sect with Judaism.

Another reason is that just now our church is deeply engaged in global missions in Sri Lanka and Ecuador. Why should we invest so much time and effort and money to help those in such different cultures? The answer is that we have something utterly crucial to offer every person in the world. Ours is a global rather than a national faith.

A final reason for the urgency of this message is that today almost all American denominations are divided by a variety of cultural cleavages such as conservatives versus liberals, Democrats versus Republicans, pro-choice versus pro-life. So serious are our denominational disagreements that we can no longer deny their existence. Our long-held consensus about what it means to be Baptist has been shattered, thus each church must consider afresh how best to do its work.

In approaching that decision, does this history lesson from Holy Scripture provide any insight for our guidance? The deepest truth of its message is unmistakable. When faced with conflict, do not commit your Christianity to one side in the latest culture wars but to the spirit of Christ, who is Lord of all cultures. Go with those who are trying to reach all peoples across every barrier. Avoid the polarizers, who often win for a day, and embrace the reconcilers, who are often vindicated only by the long march of history. When the curtain fell on the earliest chapter of Church history in the book of Acts, the Judaizers seemed to be firmly in control, while Paul was imprisoned in Rome. But today the Judaizers are in the dust-bin of history, while Paul, as well as Peter and James, are honored for their courageous stand in advocating a worldwide faith. Unfortunately, such a faith does not come without a struggle, which may be personally costly, but it is worth whatever price must be paid. Without it, we Gentiles would not even be here today!

Topic: Our Thirst for God
Text: John 19:28–29

What is the thirstiest you have ever been? The body's need for water is rivaled only by its need for air. Unless we breathe and drink on a regular basis, we will soon die. Terrible as physical thirst may be, even worse are those compulsive cravings that drive us to the brink of losing self-control. Think of the thirst for alcohol, or the thirst for fame and fortune, or the insatiable thirst for power. Our thirsts can become so uncontrollable that they consign us to the torments of hell where, like Dives in Jesus' parable, we plead for someone "to dip the end of his finger in water and cool my tongue, for I am in anguish in this flame" (Luke 16:25). So we ask, What does Jesus know about our thirsts, and what can he do about them?

I. *The human thirst of Jesus.* In his humanity, Jesus experienced the thirst common to us all. When he met a Samaritan woman, he reminded her that they were both thirsty. At the Feast of Tabernacles, when the entire nation was pleading for winter rains to water the thirsty earth in preparation for a new farming season, he spoke to a universal need with the invitation, "If anyone thirst, let him come to me and drink" (John 7:37). Jesus experienced not only the ordinary thirsts of daily life but the extreme thirst associated with the horrors of crucifixion. When at the end of his ordeal, Jesus said, "I thirst," he was expressing a far greater need for something to drink than we shall ever know. Here in this briefest word from the cross, we learn the costliness of the incarnation. Think of it! The one who had created oceans, rivers, lakes, and streams was desperate for a single drop, which he could not have without the help of his executioners.

II. *The holy thirst of Jesus.* Think now about those deeper thirsts that cannot be satisfied by any earthly drink. We are not left to wonder about the hidden thirsts of his heart because our tiny text is surrounded by three explanations of what Jesus was thirsting for most as his life came to an end: (1) Jesus knew "that all was now finished," that his job was completed. (2) The divine plan for his life involved "fulfilling scripture." (3) What he wanted most to declare was that he had now reached the consummation of his mission; he had now done what he set out to do, despite the fact that he seemed to be utterly defeated (v. 30). This three-fold commentary in the context helps the reader understand that the deepest thirst of Jesus was not to drink a little sour wine from a sponge but to do the will of God, as anticipated in Scripture and accomplished by his death.

The imagery in our fifth word from the cross is simple and clear. At the moment when the most basic human desire for self-preservation made its deepest claim on Jesus, when his flesh was racked with pain, he instead allowed his physical thirst to be overridden by a spiritual thirst to fulfill his Father's mission. Yes, Jesus was thirsty for something to drink, but, most of all, he was thirsty for God.

III. *Jesus and our thirsts.* His victory becomes our opportunity. Because he thirsted for God on our behalf, we may now claim the promises of Scriptures as never before. As the Beatitudes put it, "Blessed are those who hunger and thirst for righteousness, for they shall be satisfied" (Matt. 5:6). The last book of the Bible promises, "To the thirsty I will give water without price from the fountain of the water of life" (Rev. 21:6). Jesus himself promised, "Whoever believes in me shall never thirst" (John 6:35).

The thirst of Jesus was not satisfied until he had emptied the cup that the Father had given him to drink. And every day, we have to ask ourselves, "Am I really *that* thirsty?"

MESSAGES FOR ADVENT AND CHRISTMAS

SERMON SUGGESTIONS

Topic: What Will Christmas Bring?

TEXT: Isa. 2:1–5

What will Christmas bring? What do we expect this year at this gala celebration? Of course, our children, our grandchildren, and our nieces and nephews harbor dazzling dreams of a great Christmas cornucopia.

I. But even as we surrender to this commercial holiday season, there exists side-by-side with it another promise of what Christmas may bring. It resides in those magnificent words of Isaiah we read just a moment ago—words, you will recall, drawing an image of many peoples gathering at the base of God's holy mountain, beating swords into plowshares, spears into pruning hooks—an image of nations flowing together, no longer lifting weapons against one another, people transformed from a culture of war to a community of peace.

The Old Testament narrates the sordid and bloody history of Israel and Judah, their diverse peoples being smashed and crushed amid the intrigues of international politics, their existence always under the threat of the insatiable appetites of marauding tyrants. When Isaiah speaks of the nations and people beating swords into plowshares and spears into pruning hooks, he speaks from the military graveyards of those who died in the conflicts over blood and earth. He anticipates this vast conglomerate of peoples from across the world being transformed from the human race to the human family—nation no longer targeting weapon against nation, no one studying war anymore.

II. Is that great promise of Isaiah's something we can hope for? Is this Advent hope of peace something Christmas might bring for us? What can we expect this Christmas? We see Isaiah's radiant vision of peoples gathered in mutuality and support stumbling on nothing less than human sin.

Now why these observations? As we come to this holy table this morning, we are reminded of that unholy and sinful tangle of interest brutalizing not only the nations and peoples of Isaiah's time but the people and nations slaughtering one another in genocidal conflict in our own time. This table, with its elements of bread and wine, under this cross, demonstrates for all time how self-interest and injustice can brutalize this world. This cross shows us how national and religious interests frequently conspire to wreak havoc on innocence and vulnerability. Jesus' death is the story of the world as it is. Jesus was crucified to keep the peace. The cross of Christ is, in a sense, bad news about human life. It shows us life as pathos, the human condition as tragedy.

III. Now hear this: our God is not one who sits up there in the sky somewhere, unaffected and out of reach of our troubled and clouded condition. Our God submits to the sinful circumstances of a world, and in that very submission our God shows us the way to a peace

273

that is literally—*literally*—beyond our understanding. It is the peace promised at Advent; it is the peace Christmas promises.

So, my friends, I invite you to this holy table on this first Sunday in Advent. Here we encounter and participate in the deepest mystery of our faith: on the one hand, ours is a world where bodies are broken and blood is spilled. On the other hand—praise be to God— we are grateful for, we share, and we commit ourselves to the way of the cross, the way of this table. For here, in truth, we discover the true way of peace that Christmas brings.—James W. Crawford

Topic: Advent Discoveries
TEXT: John 1:35–51

The Advent season is a holy time when we prepare ourselves for the birth of the Son of God. But we are not preparing for the first Christmas because the first Christmas happened nearly two thousand years ago. Every year, the Advent season is a time of preparing ourselves for the second Christmas. Whereas in the first Christmas God's Son was born into this world, the second Christmas shows us that God's Son is being reborn in us, in the manger of our hearts, in the Bethlehem of our very lives and experiences.

I. Therefore, in the Advent season we allow ourselves to discover the reality of Christ's presence in our lives, the meaning of our Christian faith in relation to everything, and the scope and power of the Kingdom of God in this world. It is our hope that as we continue to discover these new beginnings, our lives will also be transformed in accordance to God's will.

For Christ's followers, the Advent season couldn't have come at a better time. The message of Advent arrives with much conviction, relevance, and power. Our waiting for Christ's coming becomes an avenue whereby we discover the truth about ourselves, about God, about the world around us, and about our relationship with others. There is always a new day coming, a new hope in the offing; always a new reality is setting, a new challenge is beginning, a new life is in the making, every time Christ is born in the lives and experiences of his people.

This was the greatest discovery made by Andrew and Peter, Philip and Nathaniel in our morning Scripture. According to John, the Gospel writer, they were the first disciples to follow Jesus. Of the four, Andrew's story comes out with distinction, as it mirrors the process by which many of us have come to know Christ. It first began with a discovery of who Christ was (*personal faith*). Then that discovery was affirmed by an invitation to a closer and deeper relationship (*discipleship*). Shortly after that, there was a sharing of that newly found discovery to another person (*evangelism*). Andrew and his companion discovered in Jesus something that made them leave their previous acquaintances and lifestyle. They followed Jesus almost immediately, without any reservation.

II. Second, belief leads to discipleship. Andrew asked Jesus where he was staying, as it was nearing evening time, to which Jesus replied, "Come and you will see." Jesus' answer goes beyond the physical invitation to come inside the house. Jesus' answer, "Come and you will see," was actually an invitation extended to all who have discovered a new relationship with him. "Come and you will see" means that those who have taken the first step of faith, like Andrew, are welcome to explore the vastness of God's Kingdom awaiting them. It is an invitation given to us by the Son of God himself to come to know him in the most intimate of ways in our prayer time, service, fellowship, and worship. It is an invitation to share his passion and convictions as if our own and truly to become one with him, not only as his disciples but as his sisters and brothers in the family of God.

III. Third, as personal faith leads to discipleship, discipleship results in evangelism. The Scripture tells us that it did not take a long time for Andrew to look for his brother Simon, known later as Peter, and with much enthusiasm told Simon of the good news that had taken over his life. He had met the Messiah! An interesting psychology almost always happens when one becomes the recipient of good news. The good news cannot be kept to one's self. This understanding probably led a Christian missiologist to define *evangelism* as "a beggar telling another beggar where to find bread." The Advent season creates the awe-inspiring possibility for human hearts to be greatly moved by a direct action from God. If it happened to Andrew and the rest of the disciples, it could happen to us.

Last, the Advent season reminds us that the God who had spoken in and through Jesus Christ has penetrated our erstwhile thick and stubborn human-made defenses, rendering us vulnerable and, ultimately, defeated by his redeeming love and abundant grace. This, perhaps, is the greatest discovery we will make this Advent season.—Kenneth Y. Kho

Topic: Is There Anything I Can Do?
TEXT: Phil. 1:3–11; Luke 3:1–6

You hear it from well-mannered guests: "Is there anything I can do?" It is the polite question to ask the hostess. That question is asked more rarely after the meal. At other times people will ask, "Is there anything I can do?" when someone is in trouble or is in sorrow or sickness. There are just times when it is the right thing to do. It is good manners and a sign of thoughtfulness to ask, "Is there anything I can do?"

I. There was a time two thousand years ago when it was the most commonly asked question of serious-minded people. "Is there anything I can do to prepare the way for the Messiah?" In those days it was believed that the Messiah would not come until everything was ready. Not until the forces of evil had been defeated. Not until this world was put into shape, tidied up. Then the Messiah would come—and the Kingdom. That is the difference between the Jewish expectation and the Christian understanding of the Messiah. The Jews believed that the world must first be put into shape, and then the Messiah would come. We as Christians believe he came before the world was ready. Luke used Isaiah's prophecy to speak of the prophet who would come before the Messiah: the voice of one crying in the wilderness, prepare the way of the Lord, make his paths straight. Every valley shall be lifted up, and every mountain and hill made low; the crooked made straight and the rough places a plain. And all flesh shall see it together. That was Isaiah, writing four hundred years before Jesus, saying that one day a prophet is going to come out of the desert, whose vocation is to prepare the people for the coming of the Messiah.

This scene gives us a wonderful picture of social life in the first century in Palestine. There were the poor, and there were the rich. The rich, in order to get ready for the Messiah, were to have compassion for the poor, to feed them and to clothe them. The powerful were to stop using their power for personal gain. A common practice among tax collectors, since their fee was taken right off the top of the taxes they collected, was to tax as high as they could and as often as they could, in order to get more money. Lack of compassion for the poor. Misuse of power for personal gain. "Is there anything we can do to prepare for the Messiah?"

Yes. You can stop doing those things.

II. "Is there anything else?" Yes. Look at the Epistle lesson for this morning. Paul writes, "My prayer is that your love may abound." That's for beginners. That's where he starts—that your love may abound, that it may grow and grow.

"Is there anything I can do?" Yes. You can get rid of all in your life that is phony, trivial, cheap, and unworthy of a child of God. Just get rid of it and know only what is excellent. Exercise some discernment. What a wonderful word, *discernment*. It means making choices on the basis of having some standards in your life. We live in an age in which just about everything is permissible, everything is tolerated, all in the name of freedom. But because everything is tolerated doesn't mean that everything is of equal value. Paul is telling the Christians to use discernment in life. Hold on only to that which is the highest, only that which is worthy of you, only that which is excellent. You have a choice.

III. These two lessons are given to us in the season of Advent to suggest how we can prepare for his coming into our lives. Christmas proclaims that he came before we had everything ready. But it also says that only those who expected him saw him. It's the same today. Those who don't expect a Messiah won't see one. He's here. Christ is here. He has already come. But they don't even look for him. Look at the Christmas story. Only two kinds of people saw him in that story: wise men, who saw the signs and had open minds, and shepherds, who heard the announcement and had open hearts. Even at the Second Coming, according to the revelation of John, he comes to those who are ready. Behold, I stand at the door and knock; if anyone hears my voice and opens the door, I will come in to him and eat with him, and he with me.

Eleanor Roosevelt kept up a backbreaking schedule of public appearances with organizations she believed in, mostly civil rights and humanitarian organizations. She got the reputation in her later years of being a "do-gooder"—a term people used pejoratively when they spoke of her. But she kept it up. Even when she became frail in the last years of her life and didn't feel like keeping these appointments, she always did. She came to one meeting and was greeted by a man at the curb. She said, "You'll have to help me out, my head is heavy." He helped her out. Then she said, "You'll have to keep me steady now as I walk." He held her arm, and they walked toward the crowd. A little African American girl came out of the crowd with an armful of flowers and presented them to Mrs. Roosevelt. She turned to the man who helped her, and said, "You see I had to come. I was expected."—Mark Trotter

Topic: Here We Go Again
TEXT: Jer. 33:14–16; Luke 21:25–36

The whole chapter of Luke 21 is the record of Jesus' prediction of the destruction of the Temple and the city of Jerusalem. The church he wrote to was in Asia Minor, what we today call Turkey. The Gospel is written to Luke's church to give them reassurance that, although Jerusalem has been destroyed, God is still in charge. Other worldly powers will fall. Then the Son of Man will come, and there will be a new heaven and a new earth, and the kingdoms of this world will become the Kingdoms of our Lord, and God's will shall be done on earth, just as it is in heaven.

I. But I remind you, the Son of Man did not come, nor did any of these signs come, nor did Rome fall (not for another four hundred years), and the end of history has not come, not even yet. Yet some people still read these prophesies as if they were describing our time right now, as if nobody else had really understood them until now. I tell you there are very few certainties in this life, but one of them is this. Every single prediction of the end of the world has been wrong, which I would think would prompt people to have some reticence about making future predictions. But it doesn't even slow them down. The title of this sermon is "Here We Go Again," because this has happened so often. It has happened in every generation, because every generation has earthquakes. Every generation has comets. Every age's empires will fall. Why do they keep predicting?

The answer is important. To be a human being is to expect that life is going to be better than it is now. That is why the most human characteristic is "hope." That is what it means to be human. To be human means to be a hopeful being. Hope is the expectation that things are going to get better.

II. There are two great stories in Jewish history. The first is the Exodus. The second is the Exile. Both are stories of "not having." The Exodus says that life is a journey from where we are to where we want to be. It is a journey filled with many dangers, snares, and toils. At the end of our journey, there is a Promised Land—a life the way we want it to be, a life flowing with milk and honey.

The other image is that of the Exile. In the Bible, it is also called the Babylonian Captivity. The Exile is when life arranges itself so that we are in captivity, bondage, alienated from the life we used to have. We used to have a good life, but then it was taken away from us. Now we live in lonely exile here. There isn't a person in this world who hasn't already, or someday will, experience a good life and then lose it and not be able to recapture it. There isn't a person in this world who doesn't know that someday, somehow, in some event or in some person, something will happen to lead them to a promised land or end the exile and take them back to the life that they used to have. Hope is the most universal of human characteristics, because incompleteness and isolation and deprivation and alienation are universal human experiences. Some people mourn that life has never been the way it should be. Other people mourn that life is no longer as good as it used to be. One is an exodus to a Promised Land, and the other is an exile from that Promised Land.

III. But there is a different way to read these texts. This different way is the way that speaks to people of faith. The Church has arranged the seasons of the year so that the biblical stories will inform our story. The Christian year begins this Sunday with Advent, as a description of the human condition. The lessons are the literature of Israel's waiting and longing for a Messiah.

Christmas announces that the one who is to come and save us has come. "For unto us a child is given." Only he did not bring the Kingdom in its fullness; he brought it as a seed. That is what he taught us. He said the Kingdom is here as a seed, and it will grow. The Kingdom is here for those who have eyes to see. The Kingdom is here as a new promise (a new *covenant* is the word he used). He said, "I give you my body and blood as a new covenant, a new promise." The promise is that he will always be with us.

IV. Our text concludes with the counsel, "When these things come to pass, stand up and lift up your heads, for your redemption is drawing near." That's been the experience of Christians for all these years. Whether they are in exodus or in exile, we are not alone. Jesus told his disciples, "Nobody knows the hour or the day. So watch." Then he told parables of watching to illustrate for us what it looks like to watch. In every one of them people continue to live their daily lives, building houses, investing in the market, raising children, planting gardens, thinking of others, getting outside themselves, all the while, watching and waiting for the Son of God to appear.—Mark Trotter

Topic: The Covenant Name
TEXT: Mal. 1:11–14; Matt. 1:18–21

What's in a name? Names are unique and individual. To share our names means sharing who we are; thus, sharing becomes a pathway to intimacy. In the Old Testament, knowing God's name meant knowing God. The name identified God's essential character. It was a name never to be taken casually, not even spoken, yet it was around the name that the covenant between God and Israel was framed.

I. *It is a name to be honored.* The conversation in the text began as a stern rebuke: "You have dishonored my name, says the Lord" (1:6). The people asked how. "When you say, 'This talk wearies me,' and when you turn your noses up at me ['when you sniff at me'] . . . cursed be the cheat who declares a healthy male of the flock, but who gives a blemished animal" (v. 14).

The name of God—the authority of God—is the basis of faith on which we stand and before which we bow. We are called many names: Christians, Church, body of Christ, Temple of the Holy Spirit, the Way, the Bride, and the People of God. Each declares the unique relationship we have rooted in the covenant name. Herein is our identity.

II. *It is a name to be shared.* The missional nature of God is then declared: "My name is great among all the nations" (1:11, 14). The love of God—and the rule of God—is universal. No person or place is beyond the scope of God's care. And thus our calling is also missional and universal. Central to the life of our church is its missional enterprise. For twenty centuries faithful believers have maintained the integrity of the gospel's proclamation. Now it is our turn.

III. *It is a name made personal in Jesus Christ.* Here is the heart of the Advent and Christmas celebrations: "You shall call his name Jesus, for he will save his people from their sin" (Matt. 1:21). John's Gospel declared further, "The Word became flesh and dwelt among us full of grace and truth. . . . He came to his own but his own received him not, but to those who did receive him, who believed in his name, he gave them the right to become children of God" (John 1:14f). Today, we are baptized in his name. We live in his name. We are persecuted for his name's sake. We preach, teach, and give a cup of water in Jesus' name. We receive a child in his name.

Many noble personalities have graced the pages of history as great teachers but none so powerfully as Jesus. Every human sphere of achievement has been enriched by the baby born in Bethlehem, whose name was called Jesus. Even the calendar is marked by his birth: A.D., *annos domini,* "in the year of our lord."

"All hail the power of Jesus' name, let angels prostrate fall, bring forth the royal diadem, and crown him Lord of all." Bless his Holy Name.—Lee McGlone

SECTION X

CHILDREN'S SERMONS

January 7: New Things
TEXT: Isa. 42:9
Objects: Dirty pennies, paper towels (one moistened), jar of vinegar mixed with salt, bowl

Today, we are going to see if we can get these old, dirty pennies clean. First let me try this. I'm going to yell at the pennies and see if they will come clean. [*Put them in your hand and yell at the pennies.*] "Be clean, pennies!" Did it work? [*Let the children respond.*] Now let's try a wet paper towel. Would [child's name] like to try and clean the pennies? [*Let a child try to rub the pennies clean. Though they may remove some dirt, the pennies still won't shine.*] Let's try one more thing. I brought a jar of vinegar mixed with salt. Let's put the pennies in the jar and shake them around. [*Place the pennies in a bowl. Then take them out of the bowl and wipe them with a paper towel.*] Yes, we did get the old, dirty pennies to look new again!

God can do new things with us. [*Open Bible.*] Isaiah 42:9 says, "See the former things have come to pass, and new things I now declare; before they spring forth, I tell you of them." God can and will do new things by God's Spirit working through each of us. Just the way we used vinegar and salt to clean the pennies, God can work in us as we help others. We can share the story of Jesus when we visit the sick, make cards for shut-ins, or just enjoy time with our friends. As we do these things and many others, God's love and power working through us can make a difference in the lives of other people. It can make them new.[1]—Marcia Thompson

January 14: We're Easily Impressed
TEXT: Col. 3:1–2
Object: Modeling clay or Play-Doh

I have taken some Play-Doh and smoothed it out on this piece of plastic. Now, I'm going to take this screwdriver and write my name in the clay. See this. There is my name. Now, what I have done with this clay is called "making an impression." An impression is made on things that are open to being changed. Our minds and lives are like this clay. Impressions are made in our lives in a similar way. For instance, our pronunciation of certain words is impressed by where we grow up. We naturally listen to the way words are spoken around us, and we form words in the same way. When we go on vacation to a distant city and the residents hear us speak, they may smile and say, "You're not from around here are you?"

We are impressed by many things besides the way others speak. We are impressed by patience, anger, racism, and good and bad ideas. Everyone around us makes a lasting

---

[1]Marcia Thompson, *Help, I'm Leading a Children's Sermon* (Macon, GA: Smyth and Helwys, 2003), p. 14.

impression on our personalities and behavior. We are to be impressed by people who try to live for Jesus. When we are around people, we learn to pray for those in need and witness to the lost. Those with special lives have an impact on us by their obedience to God.

God's word tells us we are to seek to be impressed by the things of God. We are to turn away from earthly things and seek heavenly things. Listen to these verses. [*Read Col. 3:1–2.*] We are impressed by the things that we allow to gain our attention. In turn, the way we live impresses others. Therefore, we are to focus our attention on heavenly things and be impressed by the truth and ways of God.—Ken Cox

January 21: God Cares for You

TEXT: Eccles. 3:11
Object: Bird feeder

Hello boys and girls. I'm holding a bird feeder, used to provide food for winter birds. In many parts of our country, the winters are cold, and snow or ice cover the ground. In these conditions, birds cannot find food on the ground. That's why it is important that we feed those in our yard.

The Bible tells us that God cares for the birds. He provides food in the form of grains, berries, and insects. Birds find water from lakes and streams. If God provides for birds, we are more important than any other living creature. I know our Heavenly Father cares for us.

Can someone tell me how God cares for you? [*Wait for a response.*] God provides families to take care of boys and girls. Now a family may be a single-parent mom or dad, two parents, grandparents, or a people in a foster home. You live in a home that has heat to keep you warm in winter, food to nourish your body. If you are sick, your family seeks medical care. Yes, one way God takes care of us is by providing people in our lives who love us.

During this week, think about the ways God takes care of you. Thank him for your family. Ecclesiastes 3:11 says, "He has made everything beautiful in its time."

PRAYER.   Dear God, thank you for caring for these boys and girls. Help us to realize that every good and perfect gift is from you.

SONG.   As children return to their seats, ask the pianist to play "All Things Bright and Beautiful."

TAKE AWAY.   Place a bird feeder near a window of your home. Keep a count of the different types of birds that come to your feeder. Make a photograph and share with your Sunday school teacher.—Carolyn Tomlin

January 28: Don't Be Double-Minded

TEXT: James 4:8
Objects: Double-headed cartoons (drawing of Janus, for example)

I have some strange pictures for you to look at. These are pretend pictures, cartoons. These drawing are not real animals or people. I am using these sketches of imaginary things to help us understand a truth of the Bible. Here is a two-headed wolf. Here is a double-headed bald man.

One bald head is frowning; the other bald head is sticking his tongue out at the other. Here is a two-headed pig. One head is on both ends of the pig. It doesn't look like that pig could make much headway. One end of the pig is headed east, and the other end is trying to walk west.

There are other ways to picture double-mindedness. In Roman mythology there was a character by the name of Janus. Janus was depicted with two faces on one head, looking in opposite directions. One way to symbolize drama or acting is through a head with two faces. On one side of the "drama" face there is a frown, and on the other side there is an expression of laughter or joy. These silly pictures do remind me of a Bible verse. Listen to this verse. [*Read James 4:8.*]

The verse speaks about people who are not fully committed to Jesus Christ as Lord. They are called "double-minded." On one hand these double-minded folks were attempting to be obedient to God. Another part of their behavior indicated they were trying to fit into the world that practiced evil. Double-minded folks asked for something from God but didn't really believe that they would get an answer. This lack of faith would have them pulling in various directions, like our two-headed pig.

The Lord Jesus died on the cross for our sins to show the extent of his great love for us. Jesus left heaven to live in a sin-filled world so he could bring salvation to all that believe in him. The total commitment of his life for our good calls for a commitment on our part. The Lord advises us to be totally committed to and trusting in him. When we are trusting in him, he proves himself to be completely trustworthy. One sad part of being double-minded is the frustration of trying to live in two separate worlds, pleasing two separate masters. Someone who can't make up her mind never has a sense of contentment and peace. However, when we fully accept Jesus' purpose for our lives, we discover a life of simple pleasures and joy. The more we focus on living for Jesus, the happier our lives become.

So, don't be a two-headed pig. Be single-minded. Accept Jesus as your savior, live for him, and pray to him with simple, trusting faith. Your focused life will please God and bring joy to every life you touch.—Ken Cox

February 4: The Measure of Greatness
TEXT: Heb. 10:22
Objects: Peanuts in the shell

Hello boys and girls. During the month of February, we honor black Americans who contributed many ideas and inventions to make our world a better place. Of course, we should honor these people throughout the year. One man who comes to mind is George Washington Carver. Born a slave in the 1800s, the boy worked hard and studied. He became recognized all over the world for making life better for others. He realized that many people in the South grew peanuts on their farms. Carver took this simple peanut [*hold up a handful of peanuts*] and, through experiments, created many products that we use daily. Did you know that the peanut butter you eat was developed by Mr. Carver?

God blessed Mr. Carver, and he spent his life helping others. Yes, Carver was awarded many honors and awards during his lifetime. Do you ever wonder what God has planned for your life? How can you know what God wants you to do?

Listen as I read Hebrews 10:22: "Let us draw near to God with a sincere heart in full assurance of faith."

PRAYER.   Dear God, thank you for these precious boys and girls. Help all children here to use their talents to achieve great things for you. Guide them to know the direction their life should take as they serve you.

SONG.   As the children return to their seats, ask a soloist to sing, "I Am Thine, O Lord."

TAKE AWAY.   Choose a famous black American, and write a report on this person. How did this person make a contribution to our world?—Carolyn Tomlin

February 11: Be Separate from Evil
TEXT: 2 Cor. 6:17
Object: A lava lamp

Motion lamps like this were invented in England in 1963 and became popular in the United States shortly thereafter. It is called a lava lamp because there is a tiny light in the base that lights up the room and heats up the components. The colored heavier material is not lava from a volcano but seems to flow and move like molten rock. The "magma" is paraffin wax that forms various designs in the mixture of water and propylene glycol. Lava lamps can be purchased at most garage sales.

The lamp fluids don't mix; they stay separated. The wax and propylene glycol create interesting shapes as they shift and stay apart. When a lava lamp is on, it is fun to watch the flowing materials move about in globs, blobs, and bizarre shapes. A lava lamp can teach us about evil and righteousness. God has warned his children that good and evil don't mix. Evil is opposed to God's righteousness and attacks what is good, seeking to destroy what is pleasing to God.

In God there is no evil at all. The Lord is righteousness and truth and has nothing to do with deeds of darkness. I wish it were the same for humans or that we were like the components of a lava lamp, moving in the same area but not mixing. When humans experiment with evil, they are infected with the darkness of the deeds they commit. The evil enters their lives and takes up residence like a disease. That is why we must always resist temptation. Once we succumb to the devil's invitation to lie, steal, or curse, the purity of our lives is infected.

We may make the mistake that we can be with evil people and be stronger than they are. Most of the time, we can't. When we are with people who practice evil deeds, we begin to do the same rotten things. Evil is present in our world, and in many cases we can't eradicate it. All we can do is separate ourselves from it. God has given a very simple instruction about evil. We are to stay away from it. Listen to this verse. [*Read 2 Cor. 6:17.*] Remember, we are fooling ourselves if we think we can experiment with evil and not be harmed. The only safe practice is to keep our distance from all evil deeds.—Ken Cox

February 18: A Key to Our Heart
TEXT: Exod. 20:6
Object: Set of car keys

Hello boys and girls. I'm holding a set of car keys. To start a car or automobile, you must have a key. Without a key, the engine will not start. If we are to live a good life, what do we need?

[*Wait for a response.*] Do we need a lot of money? What about a big expensive home? What about a lot of clothes? No, these are thing we may want, but we don't need these things to live a good life. What boys and girls need more than anything else in this world is to have a personal relationship with Jesus Christ. When we accept Jesus as our Savior, and he comes into our lives and forgives us of our sins, he is really all we need. Other things become secondary.

Exodus 20:6 tells us, "For I, the Lord your God . . . show love to thousands who love me and keep my commandments." Aren't we glad that Jesus promises to love us? And you know something? He never forgets that promise.

PRAYER.   Dear Heavenly Father, thank you for loving us. Help us to realize that you fulfill all our needs.

SONG.   Lead the children in singing "I'd Rather Have Jesus" before returning to their seats.

TAKE AWAY.   Write a short note to a grandparent or other relative who has encouraged or supported you. Tell that person how much you love him or her.—Carolyn Tomlin

February 25: Thoughts Are Our Software
TEXT: Heb. 3:1
Object: Laptop computer

This is a laptop computer. The computer that you have at home or use at school may be larger and look different from this one. However, this handy laptop computer can do all the tasks a larger desktop model can do. There are two important parts to a computer. First, there is the "hardware." The hardware is the tangible—mechanical or electronic parts; hardware includes the screen, mouse, and processing chips. We can see and touch the hardware. Second, there is the computer's "software." The software of a computer is the programs that operate the hardware—the instructions that direct the computer. Someone who develops software is called a programmer. I want to talk to you about the software of the computer.

There is an old adage about computer software and input. The saying is, "Garbage in, garbage out." That means if the software is crummy the output, like the images that appear on the screen, will be crummy, too. No matter how advanced the hardware is, if the program or input is faulty, the output will be bad as well. The same thing is true about humans. Our minds are like the software that controls our bodies and lives. Our minds can be trained by the best schools. We can read a library full of books and earn multiple degrees, but, if we allow evil thoughts to exist in our minds, our actions and lives will be evil, too. It is not the capability of the brain that makes the person helpful and beneficial to society. It is the thoughts and choices of the individual that determine the goodness or evil of their lives.

There are many things in our minds. There are purposes or goals that we set. There are prejudices—wrong ideas that we assume about other people. There are also good things that can be in our thinking. For instance, we can be taught to love and care for others. We may read about those who are compassionate and caring and decide to do the same. These thoughts, either good or bad, are the center of our minds and will determine how we live.

As believers in the Lord Jesus Christ, we are called to allow God's truth to control our lives. To accomplish this, we must fix our thoughts on our Savior. Listen to this verse. [*Read Heb.*

3:1.] When we focus our minds on Jesus and love the Lord with all our hearts, our actions will be transformed by our right thinking. God wants to be the programmer of our minds. When the Lord is in control of our thoughts, we are a blessing to the world, and we are a blessing to ourselves, too. When we love God with our thoughts, we can be filled with joy.—Ken Cox

March 4: Don't Be a Windbag
TEXT: Prov. 27:2
Object: A balloon

I'm going to blow this balloon up to demonstrate what bragging is like. When the balloon is fully inflated, it is huge. However, when I take my fingers off the end, it deflates quickly, revealing that the content of the balloon was only wind. Someone who brags is called a windbag. A braggart is just like this deflated balloon. The boastful person would like to be prominent in life but feels empty and small.

What is bragging? Bragging is constantly exaggerating our possessions, physical traits, or personal assets. For instance we could boast and say, "I get a big allowance. I have five dollars in my pocket and I can spend it however I want." This is said when the braggart knows that none of his friends have any money. Or boasting could be, "I have a new dog at home that my dad got just for me." A boaster will say this, even though none of his friends are fortunate enough to have pets.

Bragging is something people do when they are insecure. They talk about themselves to make others think they are big, when they feel really small inside. Some boastful persons are fearful, and their words are a way to reduce their fright. Sadly, most of the people they are trying to impress can see they are like a balloon, puffed up on the inside. Listen to this verse. [*Read Prov. 27:2.*]

We all want to impress others and gain their affection. We fear being left out or forgotten. So we all exaggerate a little. The Lord wants us to be courageous enough to be ourselves. God created each of us for a very different purpose. In the Lord's Kingdom there is a need of many different abilities and desires. When we try to be like someone else or inflate our abilities, we may miss the very special reason God has given us life. We should live to please God. When we know in our hearts we are doing our best to please God and that he is aware of why we do what we do, we can be confident. The more we brag, the less confident we become. The more we live for Jesus, the more secure we are in our own hearts.—Ken Cox

March 11: God Controls the Wind
TEXT: Mark 4:41
Objects: Toy lion and toy lamb

Hello boys and girls. [*Hold up the lamb and lion.*] Have you ever heard someone say, "If March comes in like a lamb, it will go out like a lion?" The nature of a lamb is to be meek and mild. A lion's nature is to be loud and fierce. March is usually a windy month. Can we see the wind? [*Wait for a response.*] No, we can't see the wind, but we can see what it does. For example, if you see a flag, you can tell the direction of the wind. You feel your hair blowing. If you fly a kite, the wind keeps it in the air. And sailboats depend on the movement of the wind for the sails to move the boat.

Let me ask you, Can you make the wind blow? And can you make it stop blowing? No, of course not. But the Bible tells us in Mark 4:41 that, "Even the wind and the waves obey him!" This tells us that our God is a mighty God.

PRAYER.   Dear God, guide these boys and girls in a lifetime of service to you. May they understand your mighty power.

SONG.   Lead the congregation in singing "For the Beauty of the Earth" as children return to their seats.

TAKE AWAY.   This week, check the direction of the wind by hanging a flag or windsock in your yard. Which direction is the wind blowing? Make a chart for one week showing whether the wind is from the north, south, east, or west.—Carolyn Tomlin

March 18: Repentance: A U-Turn in Life
TEXT: Acts 3:19
Object: A poster of the letter "U"

This is a capital letter "U." The shape of the letter is round on one end and open on the other. This letter is used to describe a maneuver called a U-turn—when a person is headed one way, like proceeding down this arm of the letter, and then turns completely around to head back the other way. A U-turn illustrates repentance. *Repentance* is a word from the Bible that we hear in church. Repentance is a courageous change of heart that results in a change in action.

Let me tell you a story that describes repentance. Two boys, Cody and Billy, were playing a video game at Billy's house. Billy was called into the other room by his mom and left Cody alone to finish his turn. Because Cody was losing the game, he got mad and threw the hand-held controller down on the floor very hard. Cody heard something crack, and when he picked up the controller to resume play, it wouldn't work. Cody was scared and didn't know what to do. He quickly turned off the video game, and when Billy came back in the room, Cody said, "Billy, I'm tired of playing inside; let's go outside and play baseball." And so they did. Cody never told Billy what happened.

The next day, Billy told Cody his video game had quit working. Billy was upset because the game was brand new. Billy said his dad might take the game back to the store. Cody didn't say anything about what had happened. Cody felt bad about what he had done, but he was afraid Billy wouldn't be his friend if he told the truth. He was also afraid that his parents would be mad at him. Cody felt bad for two more days but finally told his mom what had happened. It was very hard to do but Cody knew he had to tell the truth. His mom didn't get mad at all. His mom called Billy's father, and they arranged to get Billy a new controller. When Cody went to Billy's house the next time, he apologized to Billy and they were friends just like before.

What happened in Cody's life was repentance. It was a courageous change of heart that changed his actions through a U-turn of his actions. Repentance is part of being saved. Listen to this verse. [*Read Acts 3:19.*] When we accept Jesus as our Savior, we repent of all wrong actions. We must make a U-turn from everything we know to be bad. When we do repent we feel relieved the way Billy did when he told the truth and made amends for his wrong action.—Ken Cox

March 25: Make a Joyful Sound
TEXT: Ps. 33:2–3
Object: Musical instrument

Hello boys and girls. There are many ways to praise God through the use of music. One way is to use a musical instrument like the one I'm holding. How many have attended a concert or symphony where all the instruments play together? [*Wait for a response.*] Each individual knows exactly the parts they play. When only one instrument plays, you do not hear the sounds the same way as when all the instruments play together. Another way we praise God is by using our voice to sing. When we attend a church service, part of the worship service is devoted to music. Not everyone has a beautiful voice for singing, but each one of you can worship God through singing. Next time a hymn is announced, find the number in the song book or ask an adult to help you. Soon you will know the songs and blend in with the congregation.

In Psalm 33:2–3 we read, "Praise the Lord with the harp . . . sing to him a new song."

PRAYER.   Dear God, thank you for giving us music to lift our hearts. Help us to praise you by using our voices to sing.

SONG.   Ask the pianist to play "Praise Him, Praise Him" as children return to their seats.

TAKE AWAY.   During this week, learn the words to a new song praising God for his goodness.—Carolyn Tomlin

April 1: Jesus Changes the Passover
TEXT: 1 Cor. 11:25
Object: Picture of Last Supper

This is a reproduction of "The Last Supper," a famous painting by a man named Leonardo da Vinci. Da Vinci finished the original painting on a wall in Milan, Italy, in 1498, just a few years after Columbus discovered America. The famous painting portrays Jesus' creation of what we call the Lord's Supper, or Communion.

Jesus traveled to Jerusalem to participate in a meal called the Passover. During the Passover meal, the special food caused God's people to remember their deliverance from the slavery of Egypt. The book of Exodus is about this liberation. The Passover meal was taken once a year to keep the people from forgetting God's salvation from Egyptian slavery. During the last Passover meal that Jesus observed with his disciples, he forever changed the meaning of the meal. Instead of remembering the Exodus from Egypt, the disciples were to remember Jesus' death on the cross. Through the cross all believers are delivered from the slavery of sin and given eternal life, just as the Israelites were delivered from the slavery of Egypt.

We will be taking the Lord's Supper today. We take the Lord's Supper because Jesus commanded all his followers to take the Lord's Supper so they would not forget what he had done for us. Listen to this verse. [*Read 1 Cor. 11:25.*]

Do you know why Jesus changed the meaning of the supper? Changing from the Passover meal to the Lord's Supper was a huge change. The change was made because everything in the Bible points to Jesus. After Jesus lived with us, died on the cross, and was resurrected, it would have been wrong for a meal to point to anyone or anything except Christ. Everything in the Bible is about Jesus, our Savior. That is why we take the Lord's Supper today.—Ken Cox

April 8: Christ Arose
TEXT: Matt. 28:6
Object: Rock or stone

Hello boys and girls. During the month of April we celebrate Easter. Who can tell me what is special about Easter? [*Wait for a response.*] Is it the new spring clothes you are wearing? Is it the candy you receive on Easter morning? Maybe even some of you were given a baby duck, chicken, or rabbit. No, this is not the reason we celebrate Easter.

In Matthew's account of the death of Jesus, he told his disciples that after he had been crucified on the cross, he would rise again on the third day. It was the custom for a large stone [*hold up a stone or rock*] to be rolled in front of the burial place, usually a cave in a hillside. A seal was placed around the stone to make sure the body would not be taken away. When the women went to the tomb, they found it empty. An angel had rolled the stone away, and the tomb was empty. Jesus had risen from the dead. "He is not here; he has risen, just as he said. Come and see the place where he lay" (Matt. 28:6). Today, we know that Jesus is alive. He is in our hearts, and he hears us when we pray.

PRAYER.   Thank you God for sending your son, Jesus, to die on the cross for our sins. We know that he rose again on the third day, and he lives in our hearts.

SONG.   Ask a soloist to sing "Christ the Lord Is Risen Today" as children return to their seats.

TAKE AWAY.   This week write a prayer thanking God for his Son, Jesus. Return this prayer to your teacher next Sunday. Place it in a book for your class.—Carolyn Tomlin

April 15: New Easter Clothes
TEXT: Col. 3:12
Object: New shirt in wrapper

This is a brand new shirt. It is still in the cellophane wrapper. Soon I will take it out of the package, remove all the pins and cardboard, and put it on. One custom at Easter is to wear new clothing. New clothes are not required, but some folks like to sport new ties, shoes, and dresses on Easter Sunday morning. I did not fully participate in this tradition today, but I am wearing brand new socks.

One reason we wear new clothing on Easter is to symbolize the new life we have in Christ Jesus. When Jesus was raised from the dead, the grave clothes that he was wrapped in were left behind. The old robe of Jesus was taken by the soldiers who crucified him. In some portrayals of the Resurrection appearances of Christ, he is dressed in brilliant white attire. The new clothing on Easter Sunday makes everyone feel special. As we experience the power of the Resurrection through the new life we have in Christ, our appearance is changed, too.

The Bible talks about our attitudes and actions being like clothes. It makes sense. If I'm angry, you can tell how mad I am by the look on my face. If I'm happy, my smile reveals the joy I have inside. Also, acts of kindness clothe us in good, positive feelings. Whenever we do a good deed, the great feeling inside radiates in our appearance to the world. These new clothes are possible because of the new life we have in Jesus through our faith.

Being clothed in compassion and kindness is not to be only on Easter Sunday. We should wear the outfit of gentleness and patience every day. Listen to this verse. [*Read Col. 3:12.*]

On Easter Sunday morning Jesus was wearing clothing appropriate for his new life. We should also put on attitudes of obedience that reveal a new birth has occurred in us.— Ken Cox

April 22: Jesus the Innocent Lamb

TEXT: John 1:29
Object: A lamb (stuffed toy or picture)

This is a "Beanie Babies" stuffed toy. It is a lamb named "Woolly." He is a cute little guy, isn't he? I will use Woolly to help us understand an Old Testament practice that was fulfilled in the life of Jesus Christ. Before Jesus died on the cross to atone for the sins of humanity, God's instructions in the Bible called for his chosen people to sacrifice sheep. They took innocent sheep and put them to death to pay the penalty for the sins of the people. The sheep were sacrificed by the priest under very strict conditions.

Since we are taught to be kind to animals, this practice may seem cruel. We should always be kind to animals. A lot can be learned about people by the way they treat animals. The Bible does command kind treatment of animals. Small donkeys were not to be yoked with larger beasts like an oxen (Deut. 22:10). To do so might injure both animals. Another command is that a lost donkey, even if belonged to an enemy, was to be promptly returned to its owners (Exod. 23:4).

The reason sacrificing a sheep seems cruel is that the little animal is innocent and lovable. The sheep to be sacrificed had to be young and perfect. Sheep never hurt anyone, and the heart of the people would have been touched when they obeyed God's commandment. The Lord's lesson is that only something innocent and perfect could be substituted for the one guilty of sin. A sheep deserved much better treatment. It wasn't fair.

When Jesus died on the cross, he ended the sacrifice of sheep. Sheep are not sacrificed today because there is no longer any Temple or altar for the sacrifice of sheep. God made it so Jesus was the last blood sacrifice ever to be made. Jesus became the fulfillment of the Lamb of God. Listen to this verse. [*Read John 1:29.*] If our hearts are touched by a sheep, we should certainly be touched by the death of Jesus on the cross. Jesus never committed a sin. Jesus was the perfect human; he was innocent in every way.

Jesus became our substitute for the sins we have committed. He died on the cross to pay the penalty for our sins. What we are to do is believe that Jesus saved us. We are also to turn from our sins because sin brings death and destruction to all that is pure and good. The next time you see a sheep, remember Jesus. Jesus is the Lamb of God. He is our Savior.—Ken Cox

April 29: Faith for Living

TEXT: Luke 17:6
Object: Picture of a computer

Hello boys and girls. I'm holding a picture of something many of you have in your homes. Yes, this is a computer. How many of you have used a computer? [*Wait for a response.*] When your grandparents were young, there were no computers. A computer is an amazing piece of equipment. I confess I don't understand how a computer works. But that is not necessary. I know how to use one. And I have faith that it will perform the necessary operations for me to do my work. Maybe you think the Bible is difficult to understand. But we don't have to understand everything the Bible says. As you grow and mature as a Christian, you will want to study God's word and learn more about living a life pleasing to him. We must have faith in living a life for Christ.

Luke 17:6 says, "If you have faith as small as mustard seed, you can say to this mulberry tree, 'Be uprooted and planted in the sea' and it will obey you."

PRAYER.   Dear Heavenly Father, guide us to have faith in the small things of life so we can become all you intended for us.

SONG.   Ask the pianist to play "My Faith Looks Up to Thee" as children return to their seats.

TAKE AWAY.   During the week make a list of items that you do not understand, yet have faith that are present and created by God (for example, the sunrise).—Carolyn Tomlin

May 6: Hanna Devotes Samuel to God

TEXT: 1 Sam. 1:27–28
Object: Picture of mother and son

This is a picture of a mother and her young son. The photograph portrays the love and special connection between a mother and child. You can see the concern in the mom's eyes and smile on the son's face. The picture will help us understand a mother named Hannah.

According to the Bible, Hannah was very unhappy because she had no children. Hannah did what we should always do. She prayed to the Lord for help. One day at the tabernacle Hannah asked that God give her children. A priest by the name of Eli became aware of her troubles and told Hannah that he hoped God would answer her prayer. Hannah promised that if she was given a child, she would devote him to God for his whole life. God answered Hannah's prayer, and she had a son. His name was Samuel. When Samuel was still a toddler, Hannah brought him to the tabernacle, and he learned to serve with Eli, the priest. Listen to these verses. [*Read 1 Sam. 1:27–28.*]

Samuel grew up living at the tabernacle. Hannah visited him often and would bring new robes to wear. God gave Hannah other children, and her life became very happy. Samuel grew up and became a great spiritual leader in Israel. Samuel lived a life of devotion to God.

Parents still devote their children to God today. This doesn't mean that you will live at the church as Samuel did. The devotion of your life to God means that your folks will teach you God's truth about Jesus and bring you to church for worship.

Hannah loved her son just like this mom in the picture. Your parents love you very much, that's why they have devoted you to God. Samuel was a blessing to the nation of Israel. As you spend a life devoted to God, you will bring blessings to God's Kingdom today.—Ken Cox

May 13: Honoring Parents

TEXT: Exod. 20:12

Object: Bible

This morning, I want us to talk about our families. [*Tell the children who makes up your family: possibly yourself, your spouse, and your two children.*] Who is part of your family? [*Let the children take turns responding. Expect a variety of family types. Emphasize that families are all different.*] We have all different types of families, but all families are special and truly gifts from God.

[*Open Bible.*] Exodus 20:12 says, "Honor your father and mother, so that your days may be long in the land that the Lord your God is giving you." This is one of the Ten Commandments given to Moses for God's people to follow. Why do you think God included honoring our fathers and mothers in the Ten Commandments? [*Let the children respond. Tell them there is no right or wrong answer.*]

Honoring our fathers and mothers is a way of showing respect and love to them. God has given us the gift of family. Some of you may have one parent, some two, some aunts or uncles, and some grandparents. Whoever makes up your family, God thought mothers and fathers were important enough to be a part of the ten rules God gave. We should honor, love, and respect those who are our parents. We also need to thank them for what they do for us.[2]—Marcia Thompson

May 20: God Is Forever

TEXT: 1 Pet. 1:24

Objects: Dried flower and fresh flower

Hello boys and girls. Today I want to make a comparison. I'm holding two flowers. One is dried, or dead; the other is fresh and beautiful. Which do you like best? Which would you rather own? The fresh one, of course. The Bible tells us in 1 Peter 1:24, "All men are like grass, and all their glory is like the flowers of the field; the grass withers and the flowers fall, but the word of the Lord stands forever." God is forever. And he will never leave us.

When you're outside, look at the plants God created. You will see some that contain flowers and green leaves. Others have already bloomed and are dying. Everything in life changes except God. He is a constant presence in our life.

PRAYER.   Dear Heavenly Father, thank you for your constant presence in our lives. And thank you for giving us eternal life with you in heaven.

---

[2]Thompson, p. 111.

SONG.   Ask the pianist to play "For the Beauty of the Earth" as children return to their seats.

TAKE AWAY.   Ask your parents to help you place a small plant in a container. Take this gift to a person in your church who is unable to attend services.—Carolyn Tomlin

May 27: Birds Don't Worry
TEXT: Matt. 6:26
Object: Picture of a crow

This is a picture of a crow. Crows are birds that seem to have funny personalities. In comic strips, crows are given big smiles and funny names like Heckyl and Jeckyl. Crows have been observed carrying pecans to the street and placing them where cars would run over and break them. The crows fly back later and enjoy the cracked nuts. Birds are amazing. They are "wildlife" we see every day. Birds have feathers that are lightweight for flight, yet amazingly warm in winter. Some migratory birds fly hundreds, even thousands of miles every year to the same place for the winter. Little hummingbirds fly to South America each year. In spite of these surprising deeds, when we accuse someone of being foolish, we call them "bird brains." Actually, birds appear to be smart because God takes care of them.

Another astounding fact about birds is that they don't worry. Listen to this verse. [*Read Matt. 6:26.*] Jesus spoke this verse so humans could learn a lesson from birds. Most humans worry. Worry is fretting about something that might happen one day. Worry is called "borrowing trouble." You might worry about something that could happen at school. Others may worry about catastrophes in the future. These are concerns about events that could occur someday. The happenings aren't real; they're imagined, and that's what it means to worry.

Jesus said not to worry because God will take care of us because he loves us. God teaches crows how to crack pecans. God teaches hummingbirds how to make it to Guatemala, and God will teach us how to live our lives. The opposite of worry is trust. Trust means to rely upon God for the things we can't do for ourselves. Worrying makes us sad. Trusting makes us joyful.—Ken Cox

June 3: Clean Out Your Briefcase
TEXT: Ps. 26:2
Objects: A briefcase, white and black pages

This is a briefcase. The latches spring open like this. Briefcases are useful when files and other things are transported from place to place. Instead of carrying files, pencils, pens, and calculators in a clumsy stack, the items are organized neatly in a briefcase. Our brains function like a briefcase. Everywhere we go, we carry ideas—good and bad—around in our thoughts. No one can see the particular ideas that we may soon put to use, but they're in our minds, wherever we go.

Let me demonstrate how ideas that shouldn't be in our minds get there. I will place these black pages one at a time into the open briefcase as I name the evil thoughts. One black page can be a curse word we heard someone say. After our minds have recorded the profane remark, we might use it someday. Another black page can be a hurtful remark like, "You're ugly," or "You'll never amount to anything!" Another black page might be a temptation from Satan. Someone might say, "If you want a candy bar, just swipe it and stick it into your pocket. No one will ever know." As I close the briefcase, I am ready to carry those wrong ideas around with me wherever I go. This is one bad briefcase. It's scary to think that our minds function like a briefcase full of bad notions.

Thankfully, Jesus doesn't leave us like that. God is ready to help cleanse our thoughts, and all we have to do is ask for help. Listen to this verse. [*Read Ps. 26:2.*] There are positive thoughts that the Lord puts in our briefcase like these white pages. Let me open the briefcase and add a white page for each good revelation from God. The Lord says, "I love you, just like you are" and, "I made you for a special purpose; you're different for a reason." When we read the Bible other righteous thoughts can be added to our briefcase. In God's word we read Jesus' promise that he would be with us until the end of time. Jesus also said he would return for his children—that he would deliver them from the heartbreaking realities of this world. Christians can have thousands of white pages in the briefcase of their minds.

God does something else. As we walk with him, the Lord takes the harmful, black pages away. He does this by convincing us that the evil ideas aren't true. One-by-one God tears those ideas up through love and truth and throws them away, far from us. [*Demonstrate by removing the black pages.*] That way our briefcase is lighter and our minds are clean. When we love God and read his word, our minds are filled with truth and righteous directions. Let God fill your briefcase with good things that are a pleasure to carry from place to place.—Ken Cox

June 10: The Bible, God's Holy Word
TEXT: Ps. 119:11
Object: Bible

Hello boys and girls. This book, the Bible, is a special part of my life. Did you know this book, written many years ago, continues to be on the best-seller list? Translated into many different languages, this book is God's guide for living. In some countries people are put in prison and prosecuted for owning a Bible. But in our country, everyone can own a Bible and interpret its meaning for themselves.

The Bible is divided into the Old Testament, with thirty-nine books, and the New Testament, with twenty-seven books. I'm grateful to the scholars who translated the Bible from the original Greek and Hebrew. I'm also grateful to those faithful early Christians who continued to spread the good news as they faced danger.

Psalm 119:11 reads, "I have hidden your word in my heart that I might not sin against you."

PRAYER.   Dear Heavenly Father, thank you for giving us the Bible. May we treasure this book and use it throughout our life.

SONG.   Lead children in singing "Holy Bible, Book Divine." Afterward, children return to sit with their family.

TAKE AWAY.   Start this week to memorize the books of the Bible. Begin with the Old Testament and continue with the New Testament. Perhaps you could memorize five books each day. Make a chart and mark your progress.—Carolyn Tomlin

June 17: God's Special Day

TEXT: Lev. 23:3

Object: A birthday card

This is a birthday card. It's not large or fancy. On the outside is a picture of a cake with candles, and inside there is a simple "happy birthday" wish. A birthday is a special day for each of us. Birthdays are celebrated by having cake and, possibly, a party. Most important, friends and family remember that we have turned a year older. If we don't make an effort, the birthday of a friend or family member may come and go without a mention of the special occasion. How would you feel if your birthday was forgotten and nothing was done? Forgetting a special day can cause hurt feelings.

God has a special day. It's called the Sabbath. On the Sabbath day God commands his people to stop their normal work and recreation schedules to worship him. Listen to this verse. [*Read Lev. 23:3.*]

God's special day doesn't come once a year like a birthday; it comes once a week. This once-per-week commandment of God indicates how important the Sabbath is. The benefit of the Sabbath is to God—but also to all who observe the Sabbath.

It is easy to forget the Sabbath day. We have to put forth some effort to observe the Sabbath day and keep it holy. When the Sabbath is forgotten, or treated like any other day, God is offended. God's feelings can be hurt just the way ours can. He has told us that we have six days to work and play, but one day per week is to spend in worshipping him.

When people remember our birthdays, we receive good things. When we remember the Sabbath day, we are blessed. By remembering the Sabbath, we worship God and stay close to his truth and righteousness. These good things of God bring order and meaning to our lives.—Ken Cox

June 24: Let There Be Light

TEXT: Gen. 1:16

Object: Flashlight

Hello boys and girls. I'm holding a flashlight. Now why do we need a flashlight? [*Wait for a response.*] A flashlight gives light when we need it. During the month of June, I'm reminded of catching fireflies as a child and placing them in colored bottles. After dark these tiny insects would make the most beautiful lights. Have you ever caught fireflies? If not, do so this summer. Of course, I always released them to fly away into the night.

When we look up at night and see the stars, I'm reminded of how God created the universe. Genesis 1:16 reads, "God made two great lights—the greater light to govern the day and the lesser light to govern the night. He also made the stars." Without the sun to warm the earth, plants would not grow. And the stars and moon that shine at night have provided a road map for travelers for centuries. Yes, God created light. And he is the Light of the world.

PRAYER.   Dear Father, thank you for creating the sun, the moon, and stars. May we look to you for guidance in everything we do and say.

SONG.   Ask the pianist to play "Send the Light" as children return to their seats.

TAKE AWAY.   During this week, keep a record of when the sun rises and sets each day. How many hours and minutes of daylight will we have?—Carolyn Tomlin

July 1: Celebrate Our Independence
TEXT: Ps. 22:4
Object: American flag

Hello boys and girls. Do you know the American holiday we celebrate in July? [*Wait for a response.*] On July fourth, we celebrate our independence as a free nation. In our country, we enjoy many freedoms. We have the freedom to attend the church of our choice, to vote for any political candidate, to travel to other countries, to choose our own friends—these are just a few. Our forefathers fought for these freedoms. Our men and women in the service of our country still fight today so that we may continue to enjoy the freedoms we cherish. So whenever you see the American flag, think what it represents and the people who have died that we might live in a free nation.

   Listen as I read Psalm 22:4: "In you our fathers put their trust; they trusted and you delivered them."

PRAYER.   Dear Heavenly Father, we thank you for the freedoms you have allowed us to enjoy. We ask that you protect our service men and women who are trying to secure peace in an often hostile world.

SONG.   Ask a soloist to sing one verse of "God of Our Fathers" as the children return to their seats.

TAKE AWAY.   During this week, think about the freedoms you enjoy. Write a prayer thanking God for these freedoms.—Carolyn Tomlin

July 8: Don't Believe Everything You Hear!
TEXT: Deut. 13:3
Object: Picture of an elephant

This is a picture of an elephant. One prominent feature of an elephant is its ears. Some studies indicate that elephants can hear another elephant three miles away. Elephants hear tones in "infrasound." The large ears help them to hear tones two octaves above human hearing and one octave below what humans can hear. The huge ears also help regulate their body temperature. We're not elephants, but we hear more than elephants do because there are so many ways humans communicate. We can listen to CDs, the Internet, television, and radio. There are other speakers and musicians we hear in lectures and concerts. We can listen to recordings from the past and hear others speaking from distant points of the globe.

   With this large capacity to receive information through hearing, we are warned not to believe everything we hear. Moses cautioned the Israelites about listening to false prophets. Prophets are people who profess to be spokesmen for God, bringing divine truth to humans. False prophets claim to pronounce God's truth but are really saying something that is phony. Moses warned that false prophets should not be trusted. Listen to this verse. [*Read Deut. 13.3.*]

How do we know what is true? The ability to distinguish truth and error is called discernment. We become discerning by years of practice. That's why we trust our parents to help us know what is right and wrong. Since parents have been listening longer, they are capable of spotting falsehoods. By listening carefully and seeking after truth, we learn how to be discerning. If we are not careful in listening, dishonest people will mislead us through deception. Deceivers mix truth and error together to make it sound true, but it isn't. Deceivers tell us what we want to hear to take advantage of us. For instance, deceivers will say, "If you take this diet pill, you will lose weight quickly and still eat all you want." God warns us to listen closely and not believe everything we hear. However, we can be sure of one true source of information. We can and should believe everything we read in the Bible because it is God's word.—Ken Cox

July 15: Half Full or Half Empty
TEXT: Col. 2:5
Objects: Glass and pitcher of water

Hello boys and girls. I'm holding an empty glass that I plan to pour water into. [*Pour the glass half full.*] Now, who can tell me something about the glass and water? [*Wait for a response.*] Some of you might say "the glass is half full" and others might say the "glass is half empty." Who is right? Well, both groups are correct. It's all in how you look at things. If we look for positive things, we think it's half full. If we look for negative things, we might say it is half empty. Which would you rather be? A person who sees what is right about life or what is wrong?

Colossians 2:5 tells us, "I . . . delight to see . . . how firm your faith in Christ is."

PRAYER.   Dear Heavenly Father, please help each boy and girl here today to develop a positive attitude toward life. Guide them to see the good in everyone and to place their trust in you.

SONG.   Lead children in singing "Trusting Jesus" before they return to their seats.

TAKE AWAY.   During the week, take a large sheet of paper and draw a line down the middle. On one side draw something that makes you happy. On the other side, draw something that makes you sad. Talk with your parents about your drawing.—Carolyn Tomlin

July 22: Missions
TEXT: Mark 16:15
Objects: Bible, globe

When we talk about missions, we often talk about giving our missions offering. We talk about telling others around the world the good news of Jesus. These are a part of doing missions. Do you ever feel that you're too young to do missions because you don't have much money and can't travel around the world? I brought a globe today. We'll dream about where we'd like to go. First, let's find where we live on the globe. [*Turn the globe and find your location.*]

Where are some places you would like to go if you could? [*Let the children respond. Find the places on the globe.*]

It would be neat to go to any of those places. We could share the good news there. But most of us aren't world travelers, at least not yet. Still, you can follow the teachings of Jesus from Mark 16:15. [*Open Bible.*] And he said to them, "Go into all the world and proclaim the gospel to the whole creation."

Have you ever thought about this? When you share the good news with someone, they may share with another person. That person may share the good news with someone from another place. We never know how far the news we share about Jesus will go. That's why it's important for us to tell others the good news of Jesus right where we are. How far will the good news go?[3]—Marcia Thompson

July 29: No Rocks for Lunch
TEXT: Luke 11:11–13
Objects: Lunch sack, an apple, and a rock

If you watch your mom unload the groceries, some delicious things might catch your eye, like this apple. Then you might request, "Mom give me an apple in my lunch tomorrow." Most moms will respond positively to a request for fruit. You might not have similar luck asking for a Twinkie. Now imagine how you would feel at lunch the next day if you reached into your sack and found, not an apple but this rock. Your feeling might be, "Mom was very confused when she packed my lunch this morning." Another thought might be, "If I try to eat this rock, I'll break out all of my teeth." Now isn't this scenario ridiculous? If you asked your parents for a piece of fruit for lunch, that's what you'd get. Parents love their children and give them good things, not rocks to eat!

Jesus used an example like this when he was teaching about prayer. Listen to these verses. [*Read Luke 11:11–13.*] Jesus wanted us to know that when we ask God for help, the Lord will give us good things. Prayer is a dialogue, a discussion with God. Praying is like talking to your mom when she is unpacking the groceries. Such discussions are good and help us to know and draw close in our love for each other. God will not give us bad things when we pray. The Lord may not always give us the answer we want. Sometimes, we pray for things that God knows will not help us in the long run. Some of the greatest kindnesses the Lord has given to us is a "no" answer to a prayer.

Mom won't give a rock instead of an apple in our lunches, and God won't give us bad things when we pray. Since God loves us, he will always lead us in the right way. He will give us all we need, as we trust and depend upon him.—Ken Cox

August 5: Thanking God for Families
TEXT: 1 Chron. 16:8
Object: Camera

Hello boys and girls. I'm holding a camera that represents something you might do with your family. When our family takes a trip or a vacation, we always make pictures. Later, we have

---

[3]Thompson, p. 109.

photos to remember the good times we shared. God's plan for his people includes mothers, fathers, and children to live together in a home. And spending time together helps to build strong families. Jesus told us to love one another. This means to help your parents and show kindness to your brothers and sisters. Would anyone like to tell us how you show kindness in your home? [*Wait for a response.*] I'm glad that God's plan included families, aren't you? We read in 1 Chronicles 16:8, "Give thanks to the Lord, call on his name."

PRAYER.   Dear God, thank you for giving us a family. May we always treat our family with love and kindness.

SONG.   Ask the pianist to play "God Give Us Christian Homes" as children return to their seats.

TAKE AWAY.   Draw a picture of your family enjoying a special event. Include all members of your family, even your pet. Place your drawing on a wall in your room.—Carolyn Tomlin

August 12: Two Points of View
TEXT: Ps. 119:18
Object: A "two-sided" cutout

I cut this figure of an eagle out of construction paper and glued it on a stick. Can you tell me what color the eagle is? Red? I disagree with you. I'm looking, too, and the eagle is yellow. How can you say it's red? It's clearly yellow. Wait, let me flip it like this. Now what color is the eagle? Yellow? I thought you said it was red? I agree with what you said earlier—the eagle is red.

See what I'm doing? I cut the figure of the eagle out of red and yellow sheets of paper and glued them together. When you look at the side I show you, you see a different color from the one I see. This two-sided eagle demonstrates how differently humans see things. We can look at the same object and have two different views of the same item. These differing perspectives apply to just about everything in life.

Let me give you an example of different opinions. Recently, we had some folks cook seafood gumbo in our fellowship hall. I heard people comment, "What is that awful smell?" When I entered the hall I detected the aroma but thought it smelled delicious. To those who have never developed an appetite for gumbo, the smell was dreadful. I grew up across the street from some Cajuns. I learned to enjoy smelling and eating gumbo. Later that day I followed the odor to the kitchen and had a bowl of gumbo, and it was delicious. I even took some home with me and hid it in the refrigerator so it wouldn't be found and devoured by a family member.

Humans have different opinions about everything. Our opinions are shaped by many factors, including family conditions and where we have lived. Something else is crucial for us to know. God sees things differently than humanity does. He has a different view of many things. We have an earthly perspective; the Lord has a heavenly perspective. When we accept Jesus as our Savior, we begin learning to see things as God does. The Lord does this by opening our eyes to his ways. Listen to this verse. [*Read Ps. 119:18.*] When we learn God's ways and begin to appreciate a divine perspective, we can understand God's wisdom and methods.—Ken Cox

August 19: Trusting Jesus Makes a Difference

TEXT: Gal. 2:20

Objects: Ballpoint pens and paper (one pen that works and one that is out of ink)

Hello boys and girls. I'm holding two ballpoint pens. Now, who can tell me how you use a tool such as this? [*Wait for a response.*] Yes, this is a tool used for writing. Let me see if I can make some marks with this one. Yes, this pen works fine. Next, let us try the other pen. [*Try writing with the pen that is not working.*] Look, nothing happens. I'm trying to write with this pen just like I did the first one, but there are no marks on the paper. What do you suppose is wrong? The second pen is out of ink. Regardless of how much we try, it will never write. Sometimes our lives are like this pen. If we do not have Jesus in our hearts, we will never become what God intended.

Listen as I read Galatians 2:20: "I no longer live, but Christ lives in me."

PRAYER.   Dear God, we pray that each boy and girl here today will know you as personal Savior. Help them to grow and become all that you intended them to be.

SONG.   Lead children in singing "Since Jesus Came into My Heart" as children return to their seats.

TAKE AWAY.   Write a poem thanking Jesus for loving you. Share this poem with a friend.—Carolyn Tomlin

August 26: Obeying God's Commands

TEXT: Exod. 20:1-3

Objects: Coloring book

[*Hold before the children a page from the coloring book that shows exaggerated lines drawn all over the page.*] What do you think about this picture? Yes, it really looks messy, doesn't it? And what about that green dog? Do you think it could be improved? How? Yes, by coloring inside the lines. [*Hold up another picture with drawing within the lines.*] This looks a little better, doesn't it? I suspect most of us began coloring like the first picture. But as we've grown older, our pictures look more like the second.

I'm reminded by this of how some people live their lives. The Bible tells us of Ten Commandments that show us the best way to live—things we should do and things we should not do. There are people who choose not to listen to God's guidelines for living. They just do whatever they want to do—even if it hurts other people. In some ways, they are like very young children who draw outside the lines. They go just any direction with their lives and they think the picture of their lives is beautiful. But when God sees it, it looks like a mess.

Then there are other people who choose to pay attention to the rules for life God has given. They do their best to stay inside the lines. Sure, they will get outside the lines at times but they really try to do what they know God wants them to do. And God is surely pleased.

I wonder which way you will choose to live your lives. Will you live outside the lines [*show the first picture*] or do your best to live within the lines [*show the second picture*]? Let me pray for you and ask God to help: "Father, keep our minds clear. Help us to know your ways by learning from the Bible. Help us to live in ways that will please you. Amen.*"—Lee McGlone

September 2: God's Recipe for Life
TEXT: Rom. 8:28
Object: A recipe book

This is a recipe book. Each recipe lists the ingredients for each dish and gives instructions about combining and cooking the flour, sugar, and so on. The end result of each recipe is a delicious product like this picture of a chocolate cake. Yum!

Our lives are like a recipe. God has a purpose for our lives and knows all the ingredients that are necessary for us to have abundant life while serving him. Each day of our lives, God is putting the recipe of our lives together. We can frustrate God's design for our lives by rebelling against him. Rebellion is refusing to accept God's truth about our world or rejecting his commandments about worship and conduct. When we are following a recipe, we are very careful not to use the wrong ingredients. For instance, if we are baking a chocolate cake, we would not put hamburger or corn into the mixing bowl. Such additions would ruin the recipe. Could you imagine an apple pie baked with onions? Yuck.

Sadly, we live in an evil world where accidents and sicknesses occur in just about everybody's life. When bad things happen to us, God is also unhappy. If we put onions in an apple pie, the dessert would be ruined. We would throw the pie out because nobody would want to eat a piece. However, when something bad happens in our lives, the recipe for our lives is not ruined. Because God is almighty in power, he is able to take unfortunate events and use them in a positive way in our lives. God is never defeated by evil. Listen to this verse. [*Read Rom. 8:28.*]

When we follow the recipe for a three-layer chocolate-fudge cake, we hope that we take a scrumptious delight out of the oven. God has a special purpose for each of our lives. When we cooperate with him through obedience and service, we will discover that he is putting together a wonderful life in spite of bad things that might occur.—Ken Cox

September 9: Learning and Growing
TEXT: Luke 2:52
Objects: Book bag filled with school supplies and a Bible

Hello boys and girls. September is a month when boys and girls return to school. This is an exciting time, as you will meet new people and learn interesting things. Perhaps your parents bought you a new book bag this year. Students place in the bag items they need for school. Let's see what I have in this bag. [*Open bag and take out items.*] I see some crayons, several pencils, a book, a writing tablet, and a Bible. Now, why would a Bible be included in this school bag? [*Ask several children to respond.*] If crayons, pencils, books, and a writing tablet are necessary for learning, don't we also need a Bible? God's word helps guide us and teaches us to follow rules for living a good life.

When Jesus accompanied his parents to the Feast of the Passover, he amazed the teachers by asking questions. We read in Luke 2:52, "And Jesus increased in wisdom and stature, and in favor with God and men." When we study God's word, we learn more about the way he would have us live.

PRAYER.   Dear God, bless each boy and girl as they prepare for a new school year. Thank you for giving us the Bible so that we may know more about you.

SONG.   Ask the pianist to play "Teach Me, O Lord, I Pray" as children return to their seats.

TAKE AWAY.   Select a favorite Bible verse, and write it in bold print on a card. Place this verse in your book bag. Use the verse as a reminder of how God wants you to learn and grow.—Carolyn Tomlin

September 16: The Bible
TEXT: Ps. 119:133
Object: Roadmap

Do you know what this is? Sure, this is a roadmap. When we want to go somewhere, especially if it is somewhere we've not been before, we look at the roadmap and it helps us know where to go. It shows us the roads we need to take that will get us where we are going. If we get lost along the way, then we just look back at the map again and it helps us get back on the right path.

I remember driving late at night on a trip to visit my family. It was raining and I couldn't see the road signs well—and guess what? I missed the turn I needed to take. I thought I had done right, but if I had stayed on that road, there's no telling where we would have ended up. Surely not where we wanted to go. So after driving for a while and finally realizing we were on the wrong road, I took out the roadmap and found the right road that would get us where we needed to be.

In some ways, the Bible is like a roadmap. God has given us the Bible to help us find our way. We face lots of choices in life and sometimes don't know the right way to go. So when we face these choices, we will do well to look to the Bible and find God's directions for us. Even when we think we already know the right way, it is good to listen to the Bible. There may be some things we don't already know. We are promised that if we ask God, God will show us the way to go.

Let me pray for you: "Father, we give thanks for the Bible. Help us everyday to listen and to learn from it. Thanks for not leaving us alone and without a roadmap. Amen."—Lee McGlone

September 23: The Light of the World
TEXT: Matt. 5:16
Object: A "relighting" candle

At one place in the Bible, Jesus said that he was the light to the world. But here he added another word and said that we, his followers, are also light to the world. He also said we are to let our lights shine so other people around us will see our good works and give praise to our heavenly Father.

There's a song I sang when I was a boy, a song you might know. It is called "This Little Light of Mine." Now I am going to light this candle, and Mr. Bob is going to help you sing the words to this song. Here goes: "This little light of mine, I'm gonna let it shine. . . . Hide it under a bushel? No, I'm gonna let it shine. . . . Won't let Satan blow it out, I'm gonna let it shine. . . ." [*As the last verse is sung, blow the candle out each time the word "blow" is sung. Then move the candle about until it relights.*]

Wow! The candle wouldn't blow out! Did you see that? I tried to blow it out, but it kept on shining. You know, Satan will really try to blow your candle out. But if we truly decide to shine for Jesus, Satan can't blow us out. The Bible says, "Greater is he who is in you than he who is in the world." Let me pray for you. "Father, I thank you for these lovely children and for the light they are to us all. I thank you for Jesus who is for us the light of the world. Help us to let his light shine through us. Amen."—Lee McGlone

September 30: A Child of the King
TEXT: Rom. 8:14–17

Sometimes we say that a Christian is a child of God. What does this mean? Does it mean that we don't have our father or mother anymore? Oh, no, it doesn't mean that at all. God has given us our fathers and mothers to take care of us and love us. But we have someone else now who loves us even more and can take care of us even better. That someone is God.

Once there was a great king who was very rich. He had many servants and lived in a beautiful castle made of gold. One day when the king was walking along a street with some of his servants, he saw a little beggar boy who was very poor and had big holes in his clothes. The king found out that the little boy didn't have a mother or father, so the king took him home to live in the palace, and the little boy became the king's son. The king loved his new son and gave him many wonderful presents. When the little boy was old enough, he helped the great king rule part of his kingdom. You and I are like the little boy because we were taken into God's family, and he gives us many wonderful gifts, and someday he will ask us to help him rule.

PRAYER.   Dear Father, how glad we are that you have been willing to let us be children of yours and brothers of our Lord Jesus Christ. We thank you for being so kind to us. We come to you, O God, in Jesus' name.

SONG.   "I'm a Child of the King"—Kenneth Taylor

October 7: Water's Power and Promise
TEXT: Gen. 8:1
Objects: Jar of water, picture of rainbow

This jar contains one of the most powerful liquids on earth. It is not medicine, an explosive, or gasoline. It is water. We take the positive benefits of water for granted. We turn on the tap, and water flows into our homes. God sends rain for crops, lawns, and lakes. In pools, water is fun to splash and swim in.

Water is also a destructive force. The awesome power of floodwaters from a tsunami or a deluge of rainfall can destroy whole cities. A long time ago God used water to judge the earth. The Bible reveals that humans had become very wicked and evil, and they would not stop their evil conduct. God's heart was grieved over the bad actions of humanity, so he caused rain to fall on the earth for forty days. All the inhabitants of the earth were swept away in the flood. Throughout the Bible is the warning that God is against evil. Whenever people fail to heed God's notice of judgment, they must pay the consequences. God always warns people before he judges the earth. Shockingly, many people do not pay attention to the Lord's pronouncements of doom.

At the time of the flood that destroyed the earth, there was one man who listened to God. His name was Noah. Before the flood came, God gave Noah instructions and many years to build an ark. The ark was a big boat, something that Noah had not seen before. Noah listened to the Word of God and constructed the ark for his family and a male and female of every animal on earth. All on the ark were kept safe through the Lord's divine plan of mercy. Listen to this verse. [*Read Gen. 8:1.*]

A beautiful, natural sight is a rainbow. God gave Noah the rainbow as a promise that he would never destroy the earth through water again. The rainbow appeared in the sky after the destructive floodwaters had receded from the earth. Rainbows are caused by water, too. When the sun shines through moisture in the sky, a rainbow appears. So Noah saw the beautiful and destructive products of water.

God took care of Noah during the flood. God will take care of us, too. God saved Noah through the ark. The Lord saves us through our faith in his son, Jesus Christ.—Ken Cox

October 14: God the Creator
TEXT: Ps. 24:1
Object: Colored leaves

Hello boys and girls. The month of October has always been my favorite month. Do you like the fall season? Why? [*Wait for a response.*] For me, it's the beautiful leaves. When I'm outdoors in the fall, I see oak leaves in gold and scarlet, hickory trees in deep yellow, and Bradford pear trees in deep burgundy. Yes, fall is a time when we're reminded of the beauty God created for us to enjoy.

The psalmist wrote in Psalm 24:1, "The earth is the Lord's, and everything in it. The world, and all who live in it." When we see God's handiwork, we see a glimpse of his greatness.

PRAYER.   Dear Heavenly Father, thank you for providing the beauty we see in nature. Thank you for eyes that see his mighty works.

SONG.   Ask a soloist to sing "Fairest Lord Jesus" as children return to their seats.

TAKE AWAY.   Take a walk with your family and collect colored leaves. Press these leaves between layers of newspaper and place inside a heavy book for several days. Use these leaves as a table decoration for family meals.—Carolyn Tomlin

October 21: Clean Hearts
TEXT: Matt. 15:18
Objects: A bar of soap, bowl of water, a towel, and an apple

[*Begin by feverishly washing and drying your hands. Then remove the apple from a lunch bag, shine it on your clothes, and take a bite before the sermon begins.*] Do you always wash your hands before you eat? You do? Well, at least most of the time. We certainly should wash before eating—cleanliness and all that—but Jesus said there was something even more important.

There were some people in Jesus' day who thought it was so important they made it a law—and required that the law be obeyed. Some of those people came one day to ask Jesus why his disciples didn't always wash before eating. I guess they were like us and sometimes just forgot. Jesus turned their question around and said that what came out of a person's mouth, that is, what a person said—the words a person spoke—was really more important than what went into their mouth. Words that come out can often be hateful and hurtful. They can be untrue and damaging to others and ourselves. And words that come out of our mouths really come out of the person that we are. It's important that we have clean hearts—as well as clean hands.

When I was a boy, I often heard the little jingle that goes like this: "Sticks and stones may break my bones," but what? "But words can never hurt me." That's a cute little jingle, but do you know what is wrong with it? It simply is not true. Words hurt us—and often hurt us very deeply. God looks at our hearts. And the heart that speaks hurting words to others never pleases God. Let's be careful about the words we say, and the thoughts we think, because we want to have clean hearts.

"Father, help our words to be pure and helpful. Help us never to speak in ways that hurt others. Help us to have clean hearts. Amen."—Lee McGlone

October 28: God Erases Our Sin
TEXT: Ps. 32:1–2
Objects: Small chalkboard, chalk, and eraser

Hello boys and girls. I'm holding a chalkboard, chalk, and eraser. Would someone come up and make some marks on this chalkboard? Now, I want another person to come up and use the eraser. Can you see what was written after it was erased? [*Wait for a response.*] We might compare the sins in our life to the writing on this chalkboard. But when we accept Christ as our Savior, he forgives our sins. The Bible says he remembers them no more. Of course, when we become Christians, we do not want to repeat those sins. We have become new people.

Psalm 32:1–2 reads, "Blessed is he whose transgressions are forgiven, whose sins are covered. Blessed is the man whose sin the Lord does not count against him and in whose spirit is no deceit."

PRAYER.   Dear Heavenly Father, thank you for forgiving our sins. Help us not to repeat wrongdoings. Help us to know that your love is all-powerful.

SONG.   Ask the pianist to play "Forgiven" as children return to their seats.

TAKE AWAY.   During this week, choose a senior adult from our church and make a visit or telephone this person. Giving of your time is a special gift.—Carolyn Tomlin

November 4: Dividing Up Life's "Pie"
TEXT: Matt. 6:33
Objects: Several drawings of a pie

Here are pictures of a delicious apple pie. The pictures will be helpful in demonstrating how we plan and live our lives. When we have a delicious pie, we have to be very careful how we cut it up for dessert. If we cut the pieces too small, some who prefer a large helping will be disappointed. If we cut the pies unequally, some at the table will feel like we have unfairly deprived them while being too generous with others.

Our lives are often compared to a pie, especially when dividing up our time. Let me demonstrate on this first pie drawing. I'll take this marker and draw a big slice representing the time to be spent in school. Since learning is important, we have to allow plenty of time for education. Next, I'll draw a slice to stand for the time I'll be playing with friends. I'll need to spend some time with family, so I'll draw a slice of time for them. I also need to draw a sizeable portion for practice time. Practicing is necessary for football, piano, soccer, baseball, and other activities. With just those few activities, the pie that symbolizes my time is all gone.

There is a problem with this pie diagram. I've left something out. God has not been given a slice of my life. There is no time left for prayer, Sunday school, or worship. Let me see. I can draw a little bit out of this slice to provide a piece of time for God. No. That's no good. There is not enough time for the Lord; it's like I'm giving the Lord just a tiny sliver of time.

Let's start over. I'll draw in school, play, practice, movies, exercise, and family time. Now let's see where we can squeeze God in. No, it still doesn't work. I feel like the Lord is only getting the leftovers. I know this approach is not right because of what the Bible says. Listen to this verse. [*Read Matt. 6:33.*] The only solution is to give the whole pie to God. We do that by putting God first in our lives. Let me take a whole pie and write "God" across it. There, that's much better. When we do this we ask God to help us in setting goals and allotting time for our various life pursuits. When we put God first, he will never be left out because we count the Lord as the most important part of our life. The Lord knows we must do many things. After we've given the pie to him, he will help us divide it up just right.—Ken Cox

November 11: Who Made Everything?
Text: Gen. 1:1–23

Did you ever make things out of clay or mud? Sometimes it is fun trying to mold clay to look just like real houses or dogs. But did you ever try to make a real dog out of the clay? Of course you could never do that. Only God can make things that are alive. No one, except God, has ever been able to make a living thing.

The Bible tells us that after God made the world, he took the dust from the ground and formed it into a man's body and then breathed into it the breath of life. God alone can give this life.

Two friends named Mr. Jones and Mr. Smith were walking along the beach in the wet sand. Mr. Jones said, "I don't believe that we can ever know for sure whether or not God made the world." Just then they came to a footprint in the sand. "Someone has been walking along here this morning," Mr. Jones said. "Oh?" said Mr. Smith. "How can you be so sure?" "Well, don't be silly," Mr. Jones exclaimed, "here are someone's footprints, so somebody must have been here to make the footprints."

"Just so," said Mr. Smith. "And we can know that the world was made by God because the trees and the flowers and the sunshine and the rain are his footprints to tell us that He has been here."

PRAYER.   Our Father in heaven, we thank you that you made the stars and everything that is good. We thank you for giving us our bodies and our lives. We thank you for letting us come and live with you in heaven always and for Jesus who made this possible—in Jesus' name.

SONG.   "Praise God from Whom All Blessings Flow"—Kenneth Taylor

November 18: A Spirit of Thanksgiving
TEXT: Ps. 95:1–2
Object: Cornucopia

Hello boys and girls. Today I'm holding an object called a cornucopia. We often use this decoration for the Thanksgiving season. Perhaps your family places one on the table for your Thanksgiving meal. This represents the good food that God provides for us to enjoy. Because God has given us so much, we should praise his name. The psalmist wrote in Psalm 95:1 of these feelings: "Come, let us sing for joy to the Lord; let us shout aloud to the Rock of our salvation. Let us come before him with thanksgiving and extol him with music and song." So, during this Thanksgiving season, let us develop a spirit of thanksgiving by praising God with our prayers, music, and song.

PRAYER.   Father, help each boy and girl here today develop a spirit of thanksgiving. Bless each home represented. May they praise and honor your name throughout their life.

SONG.   Ask the pianist to play "Bless This House" as children return to their seats.

TAKE AWAY.   Do you have a cornucopia at home? If not, ask your parents to purchase an inexpensive one. Fill it with nuts, root vegetables (onions, white potatoes, sweet potatoes), apples, and dried fruit. Place on the table for your Thanksgiving meal.—Carolyn Tomlin

November 25: Cheerful Giving
TEXT: 2 Cor. 9:7
Object: Bible

I want to tell you a true story about giving. A children's Sunday school class led a church in a toy drive. The toys were to go to needy children in the area and around the world. The children's Sunday school teacher encouraged them to do odd jobs to earn money. Then they could buy toys to give with their own money. The teacher planned a trip for the class to go shopping and to eat at a restaurant together. The day arrived for the trip, but only one child came to go shopping. This child went with the teacher to buy toys for needy children. He had a wonderful time choosing toys for others. But he couldn't understand why his friends didn't want to go shopping. Why do you think his friends didn't want to go? [*Let the children respond.*] The child's teacher told him that you can't make other people do things they don't want to do.

[*Open Bible.*] Second Corinthians 9:7 says, "Each of you must give as you have made up your mind, not reluctantly or under compulsion, for God loves a cheerful giver." Each of us is to give our money and our time to God willingly. Nobody should make us do it. We should want to do things for others out of our love for God. Each of us has to decide if we will give cheerfully to God. Will you?[4]—Marcia Thompson

December 2: A Star Shines in Bethlehem

TEXT: Matt. 2:1–2
Object: Large cut-out star

Hello boys and girls. The month of December is filled with preparation for Christmas. Our senses delight in hearing carols sung, tasting favorite recipes, smelling the familiar scent of evergreen, and seeing shoppers hurrying to find just the perfect gift. Yes, Christmas is a busy time of the year. But too often, we are so busy with the events of the season we may forget about the real reason we celebrate Christmas. Who can tell me why this holiday is so special? [*Wait for a response.*] Yes, Christmas is the birthday of the baby Jesus. If it weren't for him, there would no Christmas. This year, as you prepare for this day, remember to focus on the King of Kings and Lord of Lords. Think of the star [*hold up star*] that guided the shepherds and Magi from the East to worship him.

    Matthew 2:1–2 reads, "After Jesus was born in Bethlehem in Judea, during the time of King Herod, Magi from the east came to Jerusalem and asked, 'Where is the one who has been born king of the Jews? We saw his star in the east and have come to worship him.'"

PRAYER.   Heavenly Father, we thank you for the greatest gift—the birth of your Son, Jesus.

SONG.   Ask the pianist to play "Silent Night, Holy Night" as you lead the congregation in singing.

TAKE AWAY.   During this week, make a Christmas card showing an event in the birth of Jesus. Give your card to a friend. Ask your parents to read the Christmas story from Luke 1:18–2:14.—Carolyn Tomlin

December 9: The Promise Keeper

TEXT: Luke 1:68
Object: Bible

Have you ever thought about Christmas as the celebration of a promise kept by God? [*Let the children respond.*] Sometimes as we're preparing for Christmas, we forget what it really meant for Jesus to come. If we think back to Old Testament times, God's promise and covenant began with Abraham. Throughout the Old Testament, we have stories of how God's people followed God. Then they would turn away and not follow God. God was always loving and forgiving and never left God's chosen people.

    [*Open Bible.*] In Luke 1:68 Zechariah, the father of John the Baptist, spoke this prophecy: "Blessed be the Lord God of Israel, for he has looked favorably on his people and redeemed

---

[4]Thompson, p. 108.

them." Zechariah knew that God hadn't forgotten God's people. God was going to redeem them, which means to get them back. God sent Jesus to get God's people back.

So we can celebrate God's promise, too, because Jesus is our Savior, the one who brings us to God. What a wonderful promise keeper God is. When we say God keeps God's promise, we're saying that God is faithful. As we prepare for Jesus' birth, let's praise and thank God for keeping God's promise.[5]—Marcia Thompson

December 16: Patient Promise
TEXT: James 5:7–8
Object: Bible

What are some days during the year that are hard to wait for? [*Let the children respond. You may get answers like Christmas, birthdays, the last day of school, and so forth.*] These days are hard to wait for, but they always come. We celebrate Christmas every December 25th. Each of you has a special day when you were born, and you celebrate that day each year. It can be hard to wait for these days. When we want them to happen now, some people may say that we don't have patience.

In our Scripture lesson, James calls for patience. [*Open Bible to James.*] James 5:7–8 says, "Be patient, therefore, beloved, until the coming of the Lord. The farmer waits for the precious crop from the earth, being patient with it until it receives the early and late rains. You also must be patient. Strengthen your hearts, for the coming of the Lord is near." In Bible lands, they had a dry season and a rainy season. The farmer was sure of this pattern and planted the crops at the right time so they could harvest food to eat. James was sure of the Lord's coming. James knew that God was faithful to God's promises.

During this Advent season, as we prepare to celebrate the coming of the baby Jesus in the manger, we can be sure of the promise. The coming of the Lord is near. We are to be patient and ready, for it will happen.[6]—Marcia Thompson

December 23: Call Upon the Name of Jesus
TEXT: John 3:16
Object: Telephone

Hello boys and girls. In my hand is a device that enables us to communicate or talk with others. We can talk, and we can listen. You might say a telephone is like a two-way street. Before you call someone, what do you have to know? [*Wait for a response.*] First, you must know the person's telephone number. If we dial the number correctly, we can talk to the person. Have you ever dialed a number and gotten a busy signal? Or perhaps they were not home, and no one answered. Do we need a phone to talk to God? No. God is always near, and we never get a busy signal.

[5]Thompson, p. 70.
[6]Thompson, p. 8.

The Bible has many stories of how people talked to God. But the best news is that God is always available to listen whenever we call. Aren't you glad that our God loves us and wants to hear our voice?

One of the greatest verses in the Bible is found in John 3:16: "For God so loved the world that he gave his one and only Son, that whoever believes in him shall not perish but have eternal life."

PRAYER.   Thank you God for listening when we call upon your name. Help us feel your presence when we pray.

SONG.   Ask the pianist to play "Jesus Loves Me" as children return to their seats.

TAKE AWAY.   Using a small notebook, write telephone numbers of family, friends, and emergency numbers and give to your parents. This will make finding those frequently dialed numbers easy to locate.—Carolyn Tomlin

December 30: Don't Quit! Persevere!
TEXT: Rev. 2:19
Object: Picture of runners

One virtue of our faith is *perseverance.* That's a big word isn't it? Here is the word spelled out. [*Spell the word out in big letters, possibly on a chalkboard.*] This word simply means, don't give in, don't stop, don't quit. To *persevere* means to keep on living and serving according to our faith, no matter what.

Whenever we decide to walk with Jesus as our Savior, we must learn to persevere. Perseverance is a quality that long-distance runners possess. Here is a picture of two runners. Running is hard work. After running for a while the runners feel like stopping, but the race would be lost if they quit. Marathon runners must have perseverance—a determination to keep on running. Listen to this verse. [*Read Rev. 2:19.*]

There is the need to persevere in witnessing, praying, and supporting the church. But let's look at one particular area of obedience. Jesus asks his disciples to persevere in kindness. The Lord wants us to be loving to members of our church and to those outside the church. This is a challenge because many are unkind. Even in the church some members are harsh and cruel. In the world some folks are very mean. When we live in a hostile world, it is easy to become cruel and angry, too. To be kind in such an atmosphere requires perseverance. We must demonstrate kindness, not only on bright and sunshiny days when everything is going our way but on cloudy days when we have been made fun of and have stubbed our toe. We persist in being kind because we refuse to be inconsiderate.

Just as these runners refuse to quit running, so a Christian refuses to be unkind. Be sure to persevere in your Christian walk. When we persevere we will finish the race that is marked out for us. When we finish, we will enjoy the satisfaction of victory in serving Christ.—Ken Cox

SECTION XI

A LITTLE TREASURY OF ILLUSTRATIONS

ATONEMENT.   The words spoken by Jesus on the cross—"It is finished"—have had many usages:

> A shepherd could have used it as he attended the birthing of sheep. After hours of travail, the moment of birth would arrive. The shepherd could declare, "It is finished."
> The slave went out early in the day to labor in service to his master. He worked through the day to the setting of the sun. Looking back on the day's labor, he could cry, "It is finished."
> The priest would enter the Temple on the Day of Atonement, slay the lamb, and burn its carcass. As the smoke rose to heaven, the priest could cry, "It is finished."
> We complete a degree, build a home, or take a vacation, and there may well arise in our spirit the same declaration.

When Jesus spoke the words, it was a clear proclamation of the fulfillment of his earthly life's task. He did not say, "I am finished," but "It is finished."—Lee McGlone

BIBLE.   One thing that confirms the integrity of the Bible as the Word of God is the fact that, although it makes much of its heroes, it also points out with frankness their failures and shortcomings. A biography written about most of the biblical characters (and about us) would surely have a chapter titled "Warts and All." James, the half-brother of Jesus, said that we are all "of like passion." Such honesty demands respect.—Lee McGlone

BLAME.   Lucy walks up to Charlie Brown one day and says to him, "I want to talk to you, Charlie Brown. As your sister's consulting psychiatrist, I must put the blame for her fears on you."

"On me?" Charlie Brown responds.

"Each generation," Lucy continues, "must be able to blame the previous generation for its problems. It doesn't solve anything. But it makes us all feel better!"

Each wants to blame another for what he or she is. This does not mean that heredity, the environment, or circumstances have nothing to do with who and what we are. They are a significant part. But these factors do not remove our own responsibility for whom we have become.—William Powell Tuck

BOLDNESS.   "My lads," said Napoleon to a regiment, "you must not fear death: when soldiers brave death they drive him into the enemy's ranks." And we, too, when we are bold and unflinching, send panic and confusion into the lines of the enemy. "Be ye steadfast, unmovable." "He will not suffer thy foot to be moved." "The righteous are bold as a lion."—J. H. Jowett

CALLINGS.   *Mr. Holland's Opus* is a movie about a man who sees his "calling in life" to be to use his musical gifts to create a piece of music that would leave his mark on the world. His vocation is to express his passion for music in such a way as to make a contribution to humanity. In order to make a living while writing his piece, he takes a job as band director in a high school. There, his passion—his love, his devotion to music—transforms children, ignites a love of music in many. And by creating that love of music in so many children, he leaves his mark on the world.

Mr. Holland's struggle is to see that he has, indeed, fulfilled his vocation in life, even if he has not accomplished what he thought was his life's work. The heart of God's calling to each of us is not simply to do a particular job. The heart of our call is to be a part of God's working in the world in ways that use our gifts, our talents, our interests, and our abilities, and that bring a service, a hope, a joy, a lift, a benefit to the community.—Rick Brand

CARING.   Pushing down hard with his fists on the table top he heaved himself up to where he was standing. For the first time we saw he wanted one leg. It was gone from the knee joint down. He was hopping sideways to reach for his stick in the corner when he lost his balance. He would have fallen in a heap if Brendan hadn't leapt forward and caught him.

"I'm as crippled as the dark world," Gildas said. "If it comes to that, which one of us isn't, my dear?" Brendan said. Gildas with but one leg. Brendan sure he'd misspent his whole life entirely. Me that had left my wife to follow him and buried our only boy. The truth of what Brendan said stopped all our mouths. We was cripples, all of us. For a moment or two there was no sound but the bees. "To lend each other a hand when we're falling," Brendan said, "perhaps that's the only work that matters in the end."—Frederick Buechner

CHRISTMAS.   A Christmas Day sermon by Phillips Brooks described the reception given that angelic pronouncement by those shepherds. At first, there was a certain dumb, blind movement about everything the herdsmen did. Yet there also was an eager straightforwardness about their behavior. They did not follow a star or go to King Herod, as the Wise Men did. They simply heard a voice from heaven telling them that there was a Savior, and where he was, and so they said, "Let us go there."

Reflecting on their situation, Brooks said, "Always there will be many whose whole experience will be merely this: the hungry, needy, empty, wanting a Savior, they just hear a voice from heaven telling them that the Savior whom they need has come, and they go to him and find him to be all they wanted." That their lives were transformed, we may be assured. That their faith remained strong, we certainly hope. Tragic it would be for this moment to have been forgotten or covered over by the commonplace experiences of life. Those whom a dream had possessed deserved to live forever-after by that marvelous disclosure.—John H. Townsend

CHURCH.   The Broadway play "The Elephant Man" was acclaimed as one of the great dramas of our time. The play is based on the life of John Merrick. He was a terribly deformed young man who lived in London in the late 1800s. His appearance was so grotesque that he was exploited as a freak in traveling sideshows. Early in the drama, he is robbed and abandoned by his manager. Frightened, lonely, confused, and helpless, Merrick is left to wander the streets. One of the most moving, poignant scenes takes place in the Liverpool Street subway station. A crowd, panicked by his appearance, threatens to attack him and drive him away. Fearful that they might actually kill him, the train conductor and a policeman rescue him from the mob's wild assault. They rush him to a nearby room and bar the door. The Elephant Man pathetically cries out for help, even saying the name of Jesus in his plea. But his two rescuers do not understand him. They think he is a deranged imbecile, so they treat him like one.

Finally, a young doctor arrives who can understand him. Gurgling up from deep within Merrick's soul comes a pitiful, guttural, heart-wrenching cry—just two words: "Help me!" The doctor does help John Merrick. He gives him a home in a prestigious London hospital. He treats him, educates him, and introduces him to London society. As a result of his patient, compassionate attention, the Elephant Man is transformed from a pathetic object of pity to an urbane, witty, and respected member of London's aristocracy.

As I read the second chapter of Acts, my mind raced back to that touching scene in "The Elephant Man." When the doctor finally arrived, someone was present who understood the language of need. John Merrick could cry "Help me!" and immediately be helped! Luke suggests that is the way it used to be in the Church—way back in the beginning. When the Holy Spirit came at Pentecost, the Church became "a safe house . . . [for] any of who had need" (2:45b). The lonely, destitute, crippled, frightened, confused, and helpless could cry "Help me!" and could count on being heard and helped!—Gary C. Redding

COMFORT.   A World War II chaplain told of an incident that occurred on Iwo Jima. A young soldier was fatally injured. Under heavy fire, the chaplain made his way to the soldier's side. "Is there anything I can do?" the chaplain asked. The young man replied weakly, "Say green pastures, say green pastures." Suddenly, the chaplain knew what the boy wanted. And so he began, "The Lord is my shepherd, I shall not want. He maketh me to lie down in green pastures, he leadeth me beside the still waters. He restoreth my soul." And the young soldier's fear gave way to peace, and his end was quiet.—Lee McGlone

COMMITMENT.   Everybody has heard of William Booth, the notable founder of the Salvation Army. Someone asked him what he considered the secret of the blessings of God, which had been so abundantly showered upon him. And he made this reply: "A long time ago I made up my mind that God would have all there was of William Booth." Now, William Booth gave himself to the Lord, and in the proportion the Lord gave himself fully to William Booth. We possess all things, as we are possessed of Jesus Christ. To those who are Christ's, "all things are yours."—Perry F. Webb

DEATH.   A pious Scotch minister being asked by a friend during his last illness whether he thought himself dying answered: "Really, friend, I care not whether I am or not; for if I die, I shall be with God; if I live, God shall be with me."—Charles Haddon Spurgeon

DISCIPLESHIP.   One day, as the disciples and their Master were walking down the road, a would-be follower overtook the little band and said to Jesus, "I will follow you wherever you go," as though he were about to embark on the grand tour; he received in return a kind of reality check in these words: "Foxes have holes, and birds have nests, but the Son of Man has no place to lie down and rest."

Jesus said to another man along the way, "Follow me," and received what may have been a quick alibi. The stranger said, "Sir, first let me go back and bury my father," to which Jesus offered the surprising response, "Let the dead bury their own dead. You go and proclaim the Kingdom of God."

Then someone else came along with a qualified offer: "I will follow you, Sir, but first let me go and say goodbye to my family," which evoked a blunt rebuke: "Anyone who starts to plow and then keeps looking back is of no use for the Kingdom of God."

So much for the wannabes who fail to take the radical claims of the gospel seriously. Its sign is the cross—a reminder of his and ours.—George W. Hill

DISCIPLESHIP.   There is a legend that, originally, birds could not fly. They could sing but not fly. God had some work to be done one day and put a load on each bird. At first some thought to complain but instead they obeyed, and as they started off with their burdens, they were turned into wings. And so when their burdens were accepted from God, they were turned into wings so they could fly.

This is just a myth, but it is true that when we willingly take up the work of Christ, we shall discover a new lift of life and soul—a new peace and joy.—Perry F. Webb

DIVERSITY.   Tony Campolo tells a wonderful story about a person who played a tuba in a concert band. The man cut his lip and was not able to play. He had to sit out in the audience for the concert while someone else took his place. He was asked afterwards, "How was the concert?" He said, "It was wonderful. You know, I had forgotten that not everybody plays 'um-pah-pah' all the time."

Not everybody is just like you or me. Not every home is exactly like ours. Not every horizon is the exact one that you see, and yet the horizon of the other person can be God's horizon as well. We are all a part of God's orchestra. We all are necessary in making God's music in this world.—Jim Standiford

ECOLOGY.   Church historian Martin Marty, several years ago, wrote a book with the intriguing title *A Search for a Usable Future.* In that book, Dr. Marty sought to relate what we have learned from the past to our need to ensure a future that will be viable and sustainable. One component of that search for a usable future, wrote Dr. Martin, is Christian involvement in care of the earth. Other important voices have been raised, all insisting that the time is now for husbanding earth's blessings lest tomorrow, disaster overwhelm us.

Adlai Stevenson, in his final speech to the United Nations, gave urgency to this matter by saying,

> We travel together, passengers on a little space ship, dependent upon its vulnerable resources of air and soil; all committed for our safety to its security and peace; preserved from annihilation only by the care, the work, and the love we give our fragile craft.

Caring for creation remains an ongoing—but also a rewarding—task. The reward is found in the enjoyment we derive from all things bright and beautiful, as well as in the satisfaction that our children—and our children's children—will know these blessings, too.—John H. Townsend

FAITH.   From "In Memoriam":

> I falter where I firmly trod,
> And falling with my weight of cares
> Upon the great world's altar stairs
> That slope through darkness up to God,
> I stretch lame hands of faith and grope,
> And gather dust and chaff, and call
> to what I feel is Lord of all,
> And faintly trust the larger hope.—Alfred Lord Tennyson

FAITH.   In Dostoevsky's novel *Crime and Punishment*, Raskolnicov, a young murderer, is driven by conscience to seek out the saintly Sonia and to confess his crime. Earlier, Sonia's mother had died of consumption and her alcoholic father had been killed, leaving Sonia as the sole support for her stepbrothers and sisters. Raskolnicov simply couldn't understand her courage in the face of such horrors. He wondered why she didn't simply give up. So he questioned her, "You pray to God a great deal, Sonia?"

She replied, "What should I be without God?"

"And what does God do for you?" he demanded.

She sat silently. Then overwhelmed with emotion, she answered, "He does everything."—Lee McGlone

FORGIVENESS.   A boy in a school was so abusive to the younger ones that the teacher took the vote of the school whether he should be expelled. All the boys voted to expel him except one, who was scarcely five years old. Yet he knew very well that the bad boy would continue to abuse him. "Why, then, did you vote for him to stay?" said the teacher.

"Because if he is expelled, perhaps he will not learn any more about God, and so he will become still more wicked."

"Do you forgive him, then?" said the teacher.

"Yes," said he, "father and mother forgive me when I do wrong; God forgives me, too, and I must do the same."—Charles Haddon Spurgeon

FUTURE.   More than forty years ago, Dr. Albert Einstein urgently warned us concerning the ominous dawning of a new day in the history of humankind:

> We never relax our efforts to arouse in the people of the world, and especially in their governments, an awareness of the unprecedented disaster which they are absolutely certain to bring on themselves unless there is a fundamental change in their attitudes toward one another as well as their concept of the future.

He concludes, "The unleashed power of the atom has changed everything except our way of thinking."—John Thompson

GOD'S LOVE.   From "The Hound of Heaven":

I fled Him down the nights and down the days;
I fled Him, down the arches of the years;
I fled Him down the labyrinthine ways of my own mind;
And in the midst of tears I hid from Him, and under running laughter.
Up vistaed hopes I sped; and shot, precipitated, adown Titanic glooms of chasmed
fears. . . . Halts by me that footfall: Is my gloom, after all,
Shade of His hand, outstretched caressingly?
"Ah, fondest, blindest, weakest, I am He Whom thou seekest!
Thou dravest love from thee,
Who dravest Me."—Francis Thompson

GOSSIP.   There is an old Jewish story about a woman who came to her rabbi and told him that she had been telling things about her neighbors that were not true—lies! She wanted the rabbi to help her make everything right. He told her to go and pluck a chicken and scatter the feathers all the way from her home to his, then to gather them up again and bring them to him. He promised her that if she did this, he would give her his answer. She agreed and left. The next day she came back and told the rabbi that she had done as he instructed. She had plucked the chicken and scattered the feathers. But she said she could not bring the feathers to him, for the wind had scattered them everywhere.

Then the rabbi said, "Lies are like feathers. Once you have scattered them, it is impossible to pick them all up again. You cannot undo the damage or completely change it. So, from now on, make up your mind to speak only the truth."—John Claypool

GRACE.   In the "Dennis the Menace" cartoon, Dennis and his friend Joey are leaving Mrs. Wilson's house with their hands full of cookies. As you remember, Dennis is not always considerate toward the Wilsons (especially Mr. Wilson). But Joey says, "I wonder what we did to deserve this." Dennis answered, "Look, Joey, Mrs. Wilson gives us cookies not because we're nice, but because she's nice." Paul would say, "Amen."—Lee McGlone

GRACE.   Sometimes I go back to the rural community in Texas where I was born. My father is buried there. The church, which was a thriving country church, has been deserted. On my last visit to the community I saw that the little church was tilting over. The blocks that had supported it had rotted, and the winds were threatening to flatten the little, old church house. Some neighbors had placed three poles on the leaning side to prop it up.

As I viewed those poles against the leaning church, I remembered hearing my father ask God in his prayer, "Lord, prop us up on every weak and leaning side." I did not understand the meaning of that expression when I was a small boy, but well over a half-century after my father's death, I know now what he was saying to God. Decaying blocks, contrary winds, and difficult circumstances beat hard upon us. We must have the support of spiritual props to keep us from falling. Most people today are living a life that is beaten, tilting, and leaning because of cruel circumstances. But thanks be to God, they are propped up by grace, mercy, and the peace of God.—Sandy F. Ray

GRACE.   The sixty-year-old minister who had many stories of his times of great peace with God says this:

Seven years ago I came to the end of my inner resources. So I enrolled in a seminary course on spirituality. There I realized that I had spent my ministry trying to be the servant of the church. I turned the church over to God, it is his church, he will take care of it. Now I am trying to go discover what it means for me to be the servant of Jesus Christ and to use the gifts and the joys and power I have to his glory.

Therefore, being justified by faith, let us have peace with God through our Lord Jesus Christ. At the cross of Jesus is the place, and now and each day is the time for us to find our peace.—Rick Brand

GRACE.   You probably all know the legend of the rider who crossed the frozen Lake of Constance by night without knowing it. When he reached the opposite shore and was told whence he came, he broke down, horrified. This is the human situation when the sky opens and the earth is bright, when we may hear: *By grace you have been saved!* In such a moment, we are like that terrified rider. When we hear that word, we involuntarily look back—Do we not?—asking ourselves: Where have I been? Over an abyss, immortal danger! What did I do? The most foolish thing I ever attempted! What happened? I was doomed and miraculously escaped, and now I am safe!

You ask: "Do we really live in such danger?" Yes, we live on the brink of death. But we have been saved. Look at our Savior and at our salvation! Look at Jesus Christ on the cross— accused, sentenced, and punished instead of us! Do you know for whose sake he is hanging there? For *our* sake.—Karl Barth

HOME.   After R. A. Torrey had become a widely known evangelist, he made the following statement:

I grew up in a godly home, but I was ungodly. . . . And I went away from home an unsaved man. But I went away with my mother's words ringing in my ears, "Reuben, when the way is dark, son, call upon God, call upon God." I wandered far, farther than I ever dreamed that I could wander. Then one night in a hotel room I planned to commit suicide. As I made all the preparations, there came flashing to my mind the words of my darling mother. "Reuben, when the hour is dark, call upon God, call upon God." Then in the depths of despair in my hotel room, I knelt by my bed and called upon God. And instead of taking my own life, I gave my life to the Lord Jesus.

No child will forever get away from the influence of a Christian mother or a Christian father. Never!—Perry F. Webb

HOME.   As a rule, the children of godly parents are godly. When this is not the case, there is a reason. I have carefully observed and detected the absence of family prayer, gross inconsistency, harshness, indulgence, or neglect of admonition. If trained in God's ways, they do not depart from them.—Charles Haddon Spurgeon

HOME.   The poet Robert Frost in his poem, "The Death of a Hired Man," said, "Home is the place that when you have to go there, they have to take you in." But Jesus says so much more. Jesus says home is the place where there is space for you. There is a room for you. Now maybe it is not a physical room all your own, but there is spiritual and emotional space for you in home, and you will be received and welcomed.—Jim Standiford

HOPE.   A pastor was confronted with a member's concerns about God's presence in hard times. He said to her, "You need not worry too much."

The member questioned, "How do you know?"

"Because," the pastor declared, "I've read the end of the book—that's where the answers are."—Gardner Taylor

HOPE.   On the night of December 9, 1914, the great Thomas Alva Edison Industries of West Orange, New Jersey, was virtually destroyed by fire. Thomas Edison lost $2 million that night, and much of his life's work went up in flames. He was insured, but only for $230,000 because the buildings had been made of concrete—at that time thought to be fireproof. Thomas Edison's son, who was twenty-four at the time, found his sixty-seven-year-old father that night standing near the fire, his face ruddy in the glow, his white hair blown by the December winds. "My heart ached for him," Charles Edison said. "He was no longer a young man—and everything was going up in flames."

Something beautiful happened the next morning. While walking about the charred embers of his hopes and dreams, Thomas Edison said to his wife and son, "There is great value in disaster. All our mistakes are burned up. Thank God we can start anew." Three weeks after the fire, Thomas Alva Edison delivered to the world the first phonograph. Edison accepted his lot that night. But he knew that his sixty-seven years were not all loss because he could build again and go on from there.—Thomas M. Conley

IDENTITY.   A man visiting a strange city left his hotel room to go to dinner. On the way he saw a sign in a window that said, "Chinese Laundry." He made a mental note of its location. The next morning he stopped by the shop where he had seen the sign. He laid his laundry on the counter and said, "I'm traveling and a visitor to your city. Could you have my laundry done by 5:00 this afternoon? Nothing special, just light starch in the shirts and package it." The man behind the counter look startled and replied, "What is it that you want?" "I want you to do my laundry. I saw your sign last night and I need these clothes done by 5:00 today. Can you do it?" Then the clerk replied with a smile, "Sir, you don't understand. We're not a laundry. We're a sign shop." The same lack of clarity often attends our lives of faith when we don't know who we are.—Raymond Bailey

IDENTITY.   Arthur Miller's play "Death of a Salesman" speaks volumes to the plight of the modern American male. Perhaps most of us can see something of ourselves in the play's tragic character, Willy Loman. Just before the final curtain, a sad commentary is given on Willy Loman's life. At his graveside the son, Biff, says, "He never knew who he was." Earlier, Willy Loman had said much the same thing: "I still feel—kind of temporary about myself."—Lee McGlone

IMAGE OF GOD.   Visions of Christ:

> The vision of Christ that thou dost see
> Is my vision's greatest enemy:
> Thine has a great hook nose like thine,
> Mine has a snub nose like to mine . . .
> Both read the Bible day and night,
> But thou read'st black where I read white.—William Blake

LEGACY.   Lives of great men all remind us that we can make our lives sublime, and departing, leave behind us footprints on the sands of time. Footprints, that perhaps another, sailing o'er life's solemn main. A forlorn and shipwrecked brother, a seeing shall take heart again.—Longfellow

LIFE'S JOURNEY.   G. Campbell Morgan was one of the great preachers of his generation in England. As a young seminary student he fell in love with a young woman, but he was afraid to propose marriage. He spoke to her about his vision of the future. He was convinced that God had not only called him to the ministry but called him to say some radical and offensive things to the Church of his day. He anticipated that there would be suffering for him and his family, and he did not want to put her through such suffering. He believed that it would only be five or six years of opposition, and then he would be established, and if she would wait for him he would propose marriage to her. But she showed she had more faith even than Dr. Morgan, when she said, "If I can't climb the mountain with you, I'd be ashamed to meet you at the top."

The way of coming to the top of the mountain determines the view you see. It is true of so much of life. We keep working hard to give our children more than we had, and we fail to give them what we were given, which was the journey of experiences that enable us to appreciate what we accomplished.—Rick Brand

MEMORY.   Deuteronomy is a series of sermons Moses preached as God's people prepared to cross the Jordan River and possess the Promised Land. Each sermon rehearses the history that brought them there. Over and over again Moses told the people, "Use your memory. It's a resource for great living." In a day when anything that happened more than twenty-five years ago is suspect, here are words we need to hear. Memory is God's gift to us.—Lee McGlone

MISSION SUPPORT.   In 1792, at the home of Widow Wallis, a group of Christians gathered to discuss the challenge of Christ to go into the world with the gospel. Fresh in their mind was the sermon William Carey had preached at the Nottinghamshire Baptist Association, when he asked, "Attempt great things for God and expect great things from God." In the home of Widow Wallis, the first society for the work of foreign missions was formed, and the modern mission movement was begun. William Carey offered himself as a missionary. "I will go down into the well," he said, "if you will hold the ropes."—Brian L. Harbour

MYSTERY OF GOD.   From "Flower in the Crannied Wall":

Flower in the crannied wall,
I pluck you out of the crannies,
I hold you here, root and all, in my hand,
Little flower—but if I could understand
What you are, root and all, and all in all,
I should know what God and man is.—Alfred Lord Tennyson

PRAYER.   In *The Power of Prayers Today,* George Buttrick tells of the picture drawn by one of his granddaughters of their lake cottage: "a strange crisscross of lines smudged with many a small fingerprint." Noting that it was not possible to recognize the cottage from the picture, Dr. Buttrick reminds us that he did not need the picture, but he did wish it.

Our prayers to God are like that. God does not need our prayers—smudged and stained though they are—but God does want them.—Robert U. Ferguson

RESPONSIBILITY.   Harvey Cox, a theologian at Harvard University, has written a book titled *On Not Leaving It to the Snake.* His discussion begins with Adam and Eve, who would not take responsibility for their own sins. They blamed the snake. Down through the centuries, individuals have constantly blamed other "snakes" for their problems by refusing to take on responsibility for their own sense of sinfulness today. We always believe that someone or something else has caused our problems. The fault always lies elsewhere.—William Powell Tuck

SERMON ON THE MOUNT.   James W. Moore has written a little book called *Can You Remember to Forget?* He reports that James Tucker Fisher, a pioneer in psychiatry and doctor in psychosomatic medicine for fifty years, said,

> I dreamed of writing a handbook that would give a new and enlightened recipe for living a sane and meaningful life—a handbook that would be simple, practical, easy to understand and easy to follow. It would tell people how to live . . . what thoughts and attitudes and philosophies to cultivate and what pitfalls to avoid, in seeking mental health. . . . And then quite by accident, I discovered that such a work had already been completed: the Sermon on the Mount.

Dr. Fisher said, "I believe this to be true: if you were to take the sum total of all the authoritative articles ever written by the most qualified of psychologists and psychiatrists on the subject of mental hygiene . . . you would have an awkward and incomplete summation of the Sermon on the Mount. And that summary would suffer in comparison with the Sermon on the Mount."—Rick Brand

SIN.   I recall one of the first times in my conscious life when I knew I had done something that I really should not have done. I knew what I was doing. I knew I was doing it against my parents' desires. Most of all, I had an aching feeling that I didn't think even God wanted me to do it, but I did it anyway. I do not deny the reality of sin because I know that I am a sinner. I have worked, counseled, and talked with too many other people not to know that we are all sinners. "If we claim to be sinless, we are self-deceived and strangers to the truth" (1 John 1:8). In this small Epistle, John tells us that if we pretend we have no sin or if we attempt to deny our sin, then we make God a liar. God has spoken about the reality of sin within our world. It is here. We cannot pretend to be innocent. When we sin, we sin against ourselves, others, and, ultimately, God.—William Powell Tuck

SIN.   Karl Menninger, who is not a practicing theologian but a psychiatrist, has written a book titled *Whatever Became of Sin?* In that book, he focuses on the reality of sin in the behavior of people. Although he is well aware of the factors that constitute and influence a person's background, he calls for an awareness of personal responsibility in moral values. We can't always blame circumstances and others for our present state. Our sense of guilt, anxious mind, loss of direction, and confusion of thought are rooted in our need for the recognition of sin. He reminds us that sometimes the fault with our present state is a result of the sin within us.—William Powell Tuck

SUFFERING.   Elie Wiesel, assigned to a concentration camp during World War II, tells of watching a ten-year-old boy being hanged by the Nazi solders. The prisoners were forced to watch as the boy lingered in a slow and agonizing death. One of the prisoners raised the query: "Where is God?" No one responded. After the boy's struggle ended, the man asked again, "Where is God?" Again, there was only silence. Finally, when it was clear the boy was dead, the man asked again, "Where is God?" A fellow prisoner replied, "God is there. Hanging on the gallows."—Lee McGlone

SURE FOUNDATION.   On Cape Cod, there is a small parking lot. One end trails off an inclined road, up along the sand dunes, cresting with a magnificent view of the beach and the surf beyond. The road passes within ten feet of a house that once nestled behind the dunes, out of the wind, sheltered and secure. Now the sands have shifted and blown and drifted, and each year the owners must dig considerably to be able to look out of their windows. If you sight along the roof line of the cottage, a certain wavering and drooping is in evidence, witness to the settling below, as the foundation wallows deeper into the unsteady sand. One thinks the house could be claimed by the sand at any moment; nothing seems sure.

Listen to my words and act upon them, Jesus advises, and the structure we build to hold the essence of life will be erected, not on sand but on the bedrock of God's love. Against such a foundation the floods and winds of life will not prevail.—Robert H. Christenson

TRANSFORMATION.   Lady Macbeth was a woman of great force of character. She is the most commanding figure in the entire tragedy. She moves to her purpose with enormous energy, with passionate vehemence, with intense and concentrated decision. She moves to her ends like a rolling stream of lava, and ruin and desolation fill her ways.

Now, when the Lord Jesus Christ, the Sovereign of the Kingdom, comes to men and women like this, and his offer of friendship and redemption is accepted, what happens? He does not destroy their force. *He transforms it.* The energy used in the Kingdom of Darkness would be now enlisted in the Kingdom of Light.—J. H. Jowett

TRUST.   Christianity is not a message which has to be believed, but an experience of faith that becomes a message.—Edward Schillebeecks

UNIQUENESS.   A water-bearer in India had two large pots. Each hung on opposite ends of a pole that he carried across his neck. One of the pots had a crack in it, while the other was perfect. The latter always delivered a full potion of water at the end of the long walk from the stream to the master's house.

The cracked pot arrived only half-full. Every day for a full two years, the water-bearer delivered only one-and-a half pots of water. The perfect pot was proud of its accomplishments, because it fulfilled magnificently the purpose for which it had been made. But the poor cracked pot was ashamed of its imperfection, miserable that it was able to accomplish only half of what it had been made to do. After the second year of what if perceived to be a bitter failure, the unhappy pot spoke to the water-bearer one day by the stream. "I am ashamed of myself, and I want to apologize to you," the pot said.

"Why?" asked the bearer. "What are you ashamed of?"

"I have been able, for these past two years, to deliver only half my load, because this crack in my side causes water to leak out all the way back to your master's house. Because of my flaws, you have to do all this work and you don't get full value from your efforts," the pot said.

The water-bearer felt sorry for the old cracked pot, and in his compassion he said, "As I return to the master's house, I want you to notice the beautiful flowers along the path." Indeed, as they went up the hill, the cracked pot took notice of the beautiful wildflowers on the side of the path, bright in the sun's glow, and the sight cheered it up a bit. But at the end of the trail, it still felt bad that it had leaked out half its load, and so again it apologized to the bearer for his failure.

The bearer said to the pot, "Did you notice that there were flowers only on your side of the path, not on the other pot's side? That is because I have always known about your flaw, and I have taken advantage of it. I planted flower seeds on your side of the path, and every day, as we have walked back from the stream, you have watered them. For two years I have been able to pick these beautiful flowers to decorate my master's table. Without you being just the way you are, he would not have had this beauty to grace his house."—Author unknown

WORLDVIEW.   Social activist Walter Rauschenbush, an American Baptist minister who lived in the earlier half of the twentieth century, developed an interesting family activity. He placed a bulletin board near the entrance to the dining room of his home. There, his children were encouraged to place clippings or pictures that they felt were of special significance. At the dinner table, the children then talked about what they chose and why they thought it to be important. Over the years, that bulletin board became a window looking out on the whole world. The Rauschenbush children, who grew up with that bulletin-board activity, chose in their maturity a lifework of service, a lifework looking out on the whole world. Their hearts (as Edna St. Vincent Millay said) pushed "the sea and land farther away on every hand." That is what Bethlehem is all about.—John H. Townsend

CONTRIBUTORS AND ACKNOWLEDGMENTS

CONTRIBUTORS

Brand, Rick. Pastor, First Presbyterian Church, Henderson, North Carolina

Cox, Ken. Pastor, First Baptist Church, New Boston, Texas

Crawford, James. Pastor Emeritus, The Old South Church in Boston, Boston, Massachusetts

Dever, John. Professor of church and society, Southern Baptist Theological Seminary, Louisville, Kentucky

Dipboye, Larry. Former pastor, First Baptist Church, Oak Ridge, Tennessee

Ferguson, Robert U., Jr. Pastor, Emerywood Baptist Church, High Point, North Carolina

Fields, Henry. Pastor, First Baptist Church, Toccoa Falls, Georgia

Gladstone, John. Pastor Emeritus, Yorkminster Park Baptist Church, Toronto, Canada

Hammer, Randy. Pastor, First Congregational Church, Albany, New York

Harbour, Brian. Pastor, First Baptist Church, Richardson, Texas

Hartman, Tracy. Assistant professor of practical theology, Baptist Theological Seminary of Richmond, Richmond, Virginia

Hiigel, John. Assistant professor of biblical studies, University of Sioux Falls, Sioux Falls, South Dakota

Hollon, D. Leslie. Pastor, St. Matthews Baptist Church, Louisville, Kentucky

Huffman, John. Retired Baptist minister, Louisville, Kentucky

Hull, William E. Research professor, Samford University, Birmingham, Alabama

Lovette, Roger. Pastor, Baptist Church of the Covenant, Birmingham, Alabama

Pope, Greg. Pastor, Crescent Hill Baptist Church, Louisville, Kentucky

Redding, Gary. Pastor, First Baptist Church, North Augusta, Georgia

Richardson, Paul. Professor of music, School of Performing Arts, Samford University, Birmingham, Alabama

Standiford, Jim. Senior pastor, First United Methodist Church, San Diego, California

Stratman, Gary. Pastor, First and Calvary Presbyterian Church, Springfield, Missouri

Thompson, John. Minister of pastoral care, Venice Presbyterian Church, Venice, Florida

Thompson, Marcia. Author of children's material, Sioux Falls, South Dakota

Tomlin, Carolyn. Writer specializing in church curriculum materials, Jackson, Mississippi

Townsend, John. Pastor Emeritus, First Baptist Church, Los Angeles, California

Trotter, Mark. Retired pastor, First United Methodist Church, San Diego, California

Tuck, William P. Former professor of preaching, Southern Baptist Theological Seminary, Louisville, Kentucky, and retired Baptist pastor, Lumberton, North Carolina

Turner, William L. Retired pastor, South Main Baptist Church, Houston, Texas

Twyman, Louis. Administrator, Broadway Baptist Church, Louisville, Kentucky

Vinson, Richard. Dean, Baptist Theological Seminary of Richmond, Richmond, Virginia

Vogel, Robert. Professor of Christian preaching, Southern Baptist Theological Seminary, Louisville, Kentucky

Vowan, Lawrence. Retired Baptist pastor, Cabot, Arkansas

Wheeler, David. Pastor, First Baptist Church, Los Angeles, California

ACKNOWLEDGMENTS

Sermons and Homiletic and Worship Aids

    Excerpt from *The Answer to Broken Homes,* by Billy Graham, copyright 1953 by Billy Graham, used by permission, all rights reserved.

Children's Sermons

    Sermons by Marcia Taylor Thompson from *Help! I'm Leading a Children's Sermon.* Reprinted by permission of Smyth & Helwys Publishing, Inc.

    Devotionals by Kenneth Taylor from *Devotions for the Children's Hour.* Moody Publishers, copyright 1998 by Kenneth Taylor.

A Little Treasury of Illustrations

    Excerpt by George W. Hill from a sermon entitled, "The Cross: Symbol of Our Faith," which appeared in *First Baptist NEWS,* April 5, 1999. Reprinted by permission.

INDEX OF CONTRIBUTORS

SERMON TITLE INDEX

Children's sermons are marked as (cs); sermon suggestions as (ss).

325

SCRIPTURAL INDEX

329

INDEX OF PRAYERS

INDEX OF MATERIALS
USEFUL AS CHILDREN'S STORIES AND
SERMONS NOT INCLUDED IN SECTION X

INDEX OF MATERIALS USEFUL
FOR SMALL GROUPS

TOPICAL INDEX

HOW TO USE THE CD-ROM

SYSTEM REQUIREMENTS

PC with Microsoft Windows 98SE or later
Mac with Apple OS version 8.6 or later

USING THE CD WITH WINDOWS

To view the items located on the CD, follow these steps:

1. Insert the CD into your computer's CD-ROM drive.
2. A window appears with the following options:

   eBook: Allows you to view the electronic version of the book in PDF format.
   Adobe Reader: Allows you to install Adobe Reader software to view PDF files.
   Editors: Displays a page with information about the Editor(s).
   Contact Us: Displays a page with information on contacting the publisher or author.
   Help: Displays a page with information on using the CD.
   Exit: Closes the interface window.

If you do not have autorun enabled, or if the autorun window does not appear, follow these steps to access the CD:

1. Click Start - > Run.
2. In the dialog box that appears, type d:\start.exe, where d is the letter of your CD-ROM drive. This brings up the autorun window described in the preceding set of steps.
3. Choose the desired option from the menu. (See Step 2 in the preceding list for a description of these options.)

USING THE CD WITH A MAC

1. Insert the CD into your computer's CD-ROM drive.
2. The CD-ROM icon appears on your desktop; double-click the icon.
3. Double-click the Start icon.
4. A window appears with the following options:

   eBook: Allows you to view the electronic version of the book in PDF format.
   Adobe Reader: Allows you to install Adobe Reader software to view PDF files.
   Editors: Displays a page with information about the Editor(s).
   Contact Us: Displays a page with information on contacting the publisher or author.
   Help: Displays a page with information on using the CD.
   Exit: Closes the interface window.

TO DOWNLOAD DOCUMENTS

The eBook on this disk is in Adobe PDF format. To download the eBook, first open it. For Windows users, under the File pull-down menu, choose Save As, and save the document to your hard drive. You can also click on your CD drive in Windows Explorer and select the eBook to copy to your hard drive.

IN CASE OF TROUBLE

If you experience difficulty using the CD-ROM, please follow these steps:

1. Make sure your hardware and systems configurations conform to the systems requirements noted under "System Requirements" above.
2. Review the installation procedure for your type of hardware and operating system. It is possible to reinstall the software if necessary.

To speak with someone in Product Technical Support, call 800–762–2974 or 317–572–3994 M–F 8:30 a.m.—5:00 p.m. EST. You can also get support and contact Product Technical Support at http://support.wiley.com.

Before calling or writing, please have the following information available:
   Type of computer and operating system
   Any error messages displayed
   Complete description of the problem.

It is best if you are sitting at your computer when making the call.